ICON1~~~~

John Grindrod is the author of *Concretopia: A Journey Around the Rebuilding of Postwar Britain* (2013) and *Outskirts: Living Life on the Edge of the Green Belt* (2017). He has written for publications including the *Sunday Times*, the *Guardian*, the *Financial Times*, the *Big Issue* and *The Modernist*. He has given talks at the V&A, the RA, the Southbank Centre, the RIBA, the Museum of London, Tate Liverpool, the Boring Conference and universities around the UK and Europe. @Grindrod.

Further praise for *Iconicon*:

'A love letter to contemporary buildings and a fantastic account of recent British history, rich in humour.' NINA STIBBE

'A brilliant, encyclopaedic, funny and often cutting dissection of the kaleidoscopic mess of buildings and places that the British created during most of our lifetimes. A sympathetic survey of the architectural remnants from the no such thing as society era.' DANNY DORLING

'In this eloquent, witty, passionate tour of Britain since the 1980s, John Grindrod provides a superb exposition of the politics and architecture that have shaped a landscape at once both familiar and already strangely historic. In its accounts of the best and worst of recent design, from the marvellous to the mundane to the frankly mean, this is a deeply humane book that does much to explain the world in which we live.' JOHN BOUGHTON

'Few writers on architecture can do what Grindrod does: he astutely observes the landscapes we all live in, weaves them into his own life, researches them with the doggedness of a true geek, talks to those that know them better than anyone – the ones who live in those landscapes – and recounts their stories with wit, passion and a shot of anger, directed with perfect aim at those in power.' TOM DYCKHOFF

'John Grindrod's follow-up to *Concretopia* is, if anything, even better. Again, he has spoken to everyone from council tenants to Right to Buyers to bankers to architects to politicians, and again, his observations are humane and acute. Here, he gives the post-Thatcher era as much benefit of the doubt as he can muster, but as the book goes on it builds into a justified anger, and ends with some very hard-won hope.'
OWEN HATHERLEY

by the same author

Concretopia: A Journey Around the Rebuilding of Postwar Britain
Outskirts: Living Life on the Edge of the Green Belt

John Grindrod

ICONICON

A Journey Around the Landmark Buildings
of Contemporary Britain

faber

First published in 2022
by Faber & Faber Limited
Bloomsbury House
74–77 Great Russell Street
London WC1B 3DA
This paperback edition first published in 2023

Typeset by Faber & Faber Limited
Printed and bound by CPI Group (UK) Ltd, Croydon, CR0 4YY

A CIP record for this book
is available from the British Library

ISBN 978–0–571–34814–5

MIX
Paper | Supporting
responsible forestry
FSC
www.fsc.org FSC® C171272

Printed and bound in the UK on FSC paper in line with our continuing
commitment to ethical business practices, sustainability and the environment.
For further information see faber.co.uk/environmental-policy

10 9 8 7 6 5 4 3 2 1

For my friends

Contents

PART 2: For Tomorrow – 1997–2010

PART 3: Little Dark Age – 2010–2020

High on the urban motorway, among wastelands, urban dereliction and the darkened hulks of Industrial Revolution warehouses,
rolled the gleaming white Triumph saloon. Beneath cranes and
high-rise towers it ran, as wild jazz guitar and screaming brass
urged it onward.

> This is a film for people.
> About the city they live in.
> And how the city is changing for the people.

This could have been the hollowed-out ruin of 1970s New
York or London, a glimpse of the wide collars and violence of
The French Connection and *The Sweeney* to come. But the city
was Glasgow, the year 1971 and this was, somewhat confusingly,
the opening sequence of a film called *Glasgow 1980*.

If visions of the future from the past are your thing, then
Glasgow 1980 is the film for you. Commissioned by the city corporation, this half-hour rush of grainy celluloid holds a glimpse
of what planners and politicians thought possible in the decade
ahead. Director Oscar Marzaroli was better known as a gritty
street photographer, the Diane Arbus of Glasgow. He'd been
recording the city's dramatic post-war turmoil in silver gelatin
prints since the early 1960s, capturing with bleak realism the
people, the sites, the change. And so *Glasgow 1980* has none of
the cheery gloss of contemporaneous promotional efforts made
to sell new towns or petrochemical industries. Instead, here is
the disturbing sight of a city eating itself.

Like the bankruptcy of New York, or the collapse in population of London (down two million since 1939, partly thanks to
the building of new towns and the demolition of old housing),   1

Glasgow's story in the era was one of industrial decline, social decay and disruptive renewal. When the narrator speaks of *difficult but necessary change*, his words could be prefiguring Norman Tebbit's *onyerbike* Tory party conference speech of 1981. This was society, before there was no such thing as it. The eighties as foreseen in Marzaroli's film is a world of streamlined progress, computerisation, new motorways and modern housing. As a child, 1980 felt – and still feels to me – an impossibly futuristic year. After all of that corduroy, concrete and chaos, it would be silver, sleek and sophisticated.

Yet when 1980 did eventually come around, it wasn't really like that at all. Another documentary photographer, Raymond Depardon, helped illustrate the reality of Glasgow in a photo-essay for the *Sunday Times Magazine*. Much as Marzaroli's photos had caught kids playing in the filthy and dilapidated tenement yards of the 1960s, Depardon's find small girls pushing dolls in prams over waste ground and rubble, drunks sitting in a burned-out lot beside a flat-roofed pub, mothers wheeling infants past high-rise blocks, and, to complete the circle, homeless people pushing their belongings in prams. Marzaroli's photos feel unsentimental but Depardon's are deliberately provocative, objectifying rather than empathising with their subjects, presenting the city as an alien world for others to gawp at, a *Star Wars* cantina for the urban romantic.

Glasgow Central, then Britain's smallest constituency, faced a by-election in June 1980. Labour candidate Bob McTaggart broke with his party's narrative of the recent past, acknowledging that the council's standard housing policy – to raze whole districts under comprehensive development powers – had been unpopular with many. Instead of the less invasive strategy of rolling repairs to the existing fabric, these well-intentioned but radical interventions caused widespread displacement.

Long-term tenants either remained in crumbling council homes as their local amenities dwindled or were pushed out to new towns or huge new estates on the periphery of the city. Some simply became homeless. McTaggart wanted his prospective new administration to change tack, to renovate existing tenements rather than constantly wiping the slate clean. With a homeless population of a thousand in this small constituency and a network of nine hostels to look after them, the continued demolition of Victorian tenements seemed a bleak symbol of failure. Meanwhile, Labour party workers in the election campaign were finding it tough to track down prospective voters in new, radically remodelled districts. 'We go out canvassing or leafleting to this street or that and suddenly find it's been knocked down,' one party worker told the *Guardian*. 'It's just impossible to trace all our supporters.'[1] A resurgent SNP were snapping at their heels in this Labour stronghold, foreshadowing a reckoning to follow many years later.

Life had changed considerably for the film crew of *Glasgow 1980* by the time that decade rolled around. Director Oscar Marzaroli's reputation rose so high that a series of coffee table books were produced celebrating his work, images so famous they would spill over onto record covers. Meanwhile, Bill Forsyth, *Glasgow 1980*'s editor, was directing a pioneering indie romcom in the Glasgow overspill new town of Cumbernauld. He and the young cast of *Gregory's Girl* had no idea it would set them on a path to becoming Scottish national treasures.

The post-war period from 1945 to 1979 had seen many changes to Britain, as much to correct the problems thrown up by the Industrial Revolution as from the Blitz. Chief among these changes was the creation of the welfare state, ushering in huge improvements to the way we lived. The NHS, new schools and council   3 housing all helped aim for a more equal society, with millions soon able to benefit from modern hospital treatment, a less hierarchical education system and the joys of indoor toilets and mod cons in the home. It came from a relatively stable period of politics, born from wartime co-operation. Both Conservative and Labour parties engaged in a bidding war to promise ever greater numbers of homes built, whether council or private. To ease overcrowding and modernise the way we lived, 28 new towns were built between 1946 and 1976. Slum clearance programmes changed the face of our big cities. Britain imported designs for slender high-rise towers from Sweden, rough concrete brutalist slabs from France, slick shopping malls from the US and rational motorway planning from Germany. *Glasgow 1980* showed the incongruity of the results, with the Queen Mother standing bravely in the centre of a ten-lane urban motorway snipping a ribbon on the city's vast new Kingston Bridge, dressed as usual in the manner of a Beatrix Potter hedgehog. None of this went smoothly. There were increasing protests against major town planning schemes. A brand new high-rise block in East London called Ronan Point partially collapsed in 1968, caused in part by contractors cutting corners to hit targets. And the oil shocks of the early 1970s killed off many major new schemes. An elderly generation of modernists handed over their grand visions to a rebellious cohort who sought to dismiss those epic schemes in favour of something lighter on its feet, less monumental, more playful, less civic – and more privately financed. A sequel to *Glasgow 1980* was scrapped in 1977 after Marzaroli had shot several reels of film. *Glasgow's Progress* was dropped because there seemed to be no end to the upheaval.

I can sympathise with that. In attempting to write about the places we built in Britain from 1980 to 2020, a line from Alan

4   Bennett's play about the 1980s, *The History Boys*, kept coming

to mind: that history is *one fucking thing after another*. The Right to Buy. Riots. Docklands. Barratt estates. Business parks. Housing Associations. National Lottery-funded museums. The Manchester bomb. The Dome. Devolution. Private Finance Initiatives. Eco-homes. *Location, Location, Location*. The Olympics. Buy-to-leave. Grenfell. Pop-ups. New council housing. Climate crisis. Covid lockdown. And 'Iconic' towers – all of those attention-seeking new landmarks. On and on it goes, the horrors and delights, the triumphs and failures, an exhausting parade of ideas, solutions, achievements and consequences.

Thinking about the way we live now keeps bringing me back to China Miéville's 2009 sci-fi detective novel *The City & the City*. In the novel, two culturally distinct cities – Besźel and Ul Qoma – exist entwined in the same geographical location. Residents of the two cities must learn to unsee the other, the cars, pedestrians, street furniture and buildings of a culture often separated only by the width of a street, the thickness of a wall. Variations on *The City & the City* haunt the Britain we have built since 1980 – beyond the sectarian parallels of Belfast or Glasgow to places like London's Docklands or Cardiff Bay, enclaves for the rich built beside and entwined into old working-class settlements. Our versions of Besźel and Ul Qoma exist in stealthier ways too: in the gated estates hidden from main roads behind older housing, or in the gentrified suburbs, where an incessant invasion of house pimpers extended homes upwards and outwards, and sometimes downwards too. Council estates have been demolished and smaller, more expensive private flats have risen in their place – such as the Heygate in Elephant and Castle making way for the expensive computer-modelled anonymity of what is now called Elephant Park. We train ourselves to unsee what was lost. The resulting disruption is described by estate agents as creating a vibrant urban mix, but how well do these old and new communities integrate? Is the vibrancy merely the vibration of submerged feelings of entitlement and resentment? Our City & the City is still evolving, from the planned and zoned settlements favoured by the modernists to the piecemeal fragments, spectaculars and edge cities built since 1980. And in its icons, of course.

At some point in the age of constructed reality TV and social media, the meaning of the word icon shifted and shrank. Things, people, moments were *iconic* simply because they represented nothing more than themselves with a kind of dumb confidence. *Iconic* has come to mean the coolest version of itself. It's the word for feel-good – or feel-anything – architecture, the easy come, easy go landscape of a CGI blockbuster to be destroyed by aliens, Iron Man or the weather. Disaster architecture for our rolling John Wyndham apocalypse. But the icons of the era aren't always the things that developers want us to take to our hearts – their extravagantly modelled towers, High Tech statements and deconstructed landmarks. For all the money in the world, they don't get to choose what becomes *iconic*. Sure, the Gherkin might represent London, Future Systems' blobby Selfridges the city of Birmingham, the Angel of the North a whole region. But surely our more everyday, prosaic places are *icons* too? Estates of pseudo-Georgian houses with uPVC windows, campuses of fibreglass sheds and surface car parks, town centre office blocks cum micro-flats – icons of taste, technology, power, poverty. Icons the lot of them. And so *Iconicon* is a lexicon of these modern icons, symbols of the ways we have lived, of dreams second-guessed by developers, architects, planners – people who never looked back to the places they created to see if they were right, but who moved on to the next project, fighting an ongoing battle against the universal truism that things fall 6   apart. This is the world that Pevsner guides forgot, beneath the radar of orthodox, canonical consideration. It's the Britain we have actually built since 1980 – chaotic, awkward, clashing and busy, a mixture of outlandish gestures, astonishing creativity, drab conformity and petty meanness, sometimes all at once.

In *Glasgow 1980*, people were being sold a version of the dream they had long been promised: better homes for all, better healthcare and schools. Now, in the age of the icon, we don't build what we need, we build for dreams: for a random lottery win or the lifestyle of a Premiership footballer; 'forever homes'; gleaming towers; gated communities. As our basic rights are ever more under attack, the aspirations of today are peculiar fantasies indeed. Smart homes. Self-driving cars. Adding value. Second homes. The avatars of success. Forget that homelessness, poverty and genuine hardship stalk the land in ever increasing numbers. Our hopes are written beneath the foil of a scratch card, a diversion to blur out the reality of the world we live in.

Iconicon is a journey around the City & the City we have created in Britain since 1980. Wimpey homes. Millennium monuments. Riverside flats. Wind farms. Spectacular skyscrapers. City-centre apartments. Out-of-town malls. Perhaps more so than any other cultural artefacts, the buildings designed in our lifetimes encapsulate how we as a culture imagined we one day might live. And yet their built reality is often a reminder of how those dreams may have fallen short, or come to represent something very different from their original intentions. To fully understand what has happened, we need not only to revisit these plans with the benefit of hindsight, knowing how the world has turned out, but also to allow voices from the time to explain the original visions of these icons of our age. What did the future look like to us back in the eighties, nineties or noughties, and how does that measure up to where we are now? The upheavals and events of the last ten years have a tendency to make the foresightedness of previous decades look timid and misguided. And certainly there has been a current of wilful ignorance around environmental and housing crises in the way that we have built this modern world. But there are also powerful visions here that have helped shape the way we live in more positive ways, and this is an attempt to tell that story too, currents sometimes lost under a welter of Twitter accounts, lobbyists and reactive voices assuring us that everything is shit. These icons of our age, be they modest or monumental, present us with a living history of Britain, complex – and sometimes all too facile – reminders of the political, financial and social forces at play that have shaped our modern landscape. So, are you ready to go time travelling with me? If so, park up the DeLorean, I have a much more appropriate vehicle in mind. See Richard Rogers's Lloyd's Building over there? Well, join me in one of those futuristic toilet pods that cover its gleaming surface – you'll understand later – and let's take a trip in this High Tech time capsule. Back to the year when I was ten, when the Rubik's cube, Post-it notes and Pac-Man were released, the Corkscrew rollercoaster opened at Alton Towers, the Austin Metro went on sale and we all dressed like David Bowie in the 'Ashes to Ashes' video.* Welcome to 1980.

* Probably.

'On the day I went to view it, it was pissing with rain.' Gaby
Charing had a way with an anecdote. Perhaps it was her richly
modulated voice. 'And I thought, this is good. I've got to be able
to bear living here when it's pissing with rain.' White-haired,
redoubtable and bohemian, Gaby was taking me back in time to
1978 and a council flat on the Isle of Dogs, an area of Docklands
in East London. For that first viewing she hadn't been given the
door number, she recalled, in case she might squat it. 'But that
Sunday morning when we drove down, it was just *wonderful*.'

Gaby was going to be moving into Galleon House, a glass-
balconied sixties block facing Island Gardens, just across the
Thames from Greenwich. At that time, the Isle of Dogs – that
bollock-shaped bulge in the Thames, as Gaby described it
– was as different as could be from its historic, globally celebrated neighbour. 'I got the flat because the whole of the Isle of
Dogs qualified as hard to let,' she explained. 'I'd been living in
flatshares and I'd had enough of it. And I didn't have enough
money to buy. Someone told me about the hard-to-let scheme,
and I just imagined what it would feel like if you were a very
poor person who had always been living in ghastly private rented accommodation. You would think you'd have died and gone
to heaven being given a place like that. It was light, it had high
ceilings, and it was *wonderful*! It was absolute *heaven*.'

Gaby and her partner, Liz Day, had met on the island some-
time after Liz moved there in 1979. Working in a bail hostel, Liz
was living with her then partner on the ground floor of another sixties block, Alice Shepherd House. 'The ground-floor flats
were particularly hard-to-let ones,' explained Liz. 'There was
a guy who lived next door who I think had a long-term mental 11

health problem, and next door to him there was a young woman who I think had probably been in care. Next door to her there was a young man who was a drug user, and then there was a young man who had been in Barnardo's.' She turned to Gaby. 'Did you know Bobby?' she asked. 'He lived on the top floor, was covered in tattoos.'

'Noooo,' said Gaby slowly.

'He was a drug dealer,' she said brightly.

'Riiiight.'

'He was very nice. We got invited to his son's baptism at the Catholic church.' A lot of her neighbours had been there many years. 'There was a family where there were three sons and they were all fairly wild. And I remember the social worker had come round to visit them, and they held him over the balcony by his feet till he agreed to pay for shoes for the kids. It was that sort of place. It was a bit like the Wild West in some ways.'

Architect Mike Davies remembered being taken there by his father in the early 1950s. 'The old docks, the Royal Docks were closed for two reasons,' he told me with the certainty of someone used to dispensing them. 'It was closed because of the advent of containerisation. And the advent of containerisation was because dockers always broke some of the cargo, so a small percentage of the cargo was always gone. And so security was an issue. And that's why they had the great high walls around. There were two and a half thousand acres of London which were not London. They were in another country. We could never go there.' But Mike could. His dad, a geographer, was fascinated by the docks and knew the coppers on the gate. Father and son would visit on a Sunday morning. 'He used to go *copra, bananas, palm oil, Ellerman Lines, Blue Funnel, Cunard*. He knew all the ships, because he was an economic geographer. I loved it. My father loved it, it was fantastic. Little did we know that I'd end up working there.' Davies, alongside Richard Rogers, would help master-plan the regeneration of the Royal Docks after the ships had gone.

By 1980, London's docks were a strange and haunted place – after their industrial heyday, which Mike Davies had seen, and before the Filofaxes, BMWs and bankers moved in; before the rebranding as Docklands, even. Few navigated the Thames by boat, but if you did you'd see a grim post-industrial landscape here, miles of rusting and crumbling relics, abandoned wharves, warehouses with the windows put through. Eight and a half miles of exhausted docks lay strung out along the Thames, the machinery silent, the work gone. Yet still 40,000 people lived here, 38,000 of whom were council tenants, most in estates built between the twenties and the seventies. The docks had been in decline for decades, and now many of its working-class inhabitants were unemployed, and some desperate to leave. In 1978, the year that Gaby was moving into her heavenly hard-to-let flat, Surrey Docks – one of the last remaining working docks in London – closed, its work moving upriver to Tilbury. The Port of London Authority released a bleak statement to the press. 'There are large numbers of people who draw pay from the PLA, but for whom there is no work, and there never will be again.'[1]

There seemed little urgency to save the docks from terminal decay. Plans came and went like the tide. Take the Greater London Council's 1973 effort, five competing schemes squabbling over the ashes. Most pushed for private houses and flats. Office centres and industrial units would be small-scale affairs. The banks of the Thames would be greened with thousands of trees and shrubs. Many transport systems were promised: urban motorways, an automated mini-tram network, and the Fleet Line – London's new underground route – snaking beneath the old docks. It might even become the terminus for a cross-channel tunnel, as Britain edged its way into the European Economic Community. All of the ideas were predicated on the watery docks being filled in, rather than made a feature of, as in the rebuilding of Antwerp, say, or Vancouver. Swamped in a succession of 1970s political and financial crises, many of these ideas leaked away. Some flotsam remained. The Fleet Line would become the Jubilee, reaching Docklands in the late 1990s. Those automated mini-trams became the Docklands Light Railway. Timid office centres made way for the hyper-development of Canary Wharf. A colossal rise in private development would sweep aside thoughts of welfare-state-era council housing. That vast Thames-side park? Forget it.

Perhaps the most tantalising vision of the future of Docklands comes in the 1979 film *The Long Good Friday*, starring Bob Hoskins as a gangster with an idea of turning London's derelict docks into the site of a future Olympics with the help of some dodgy US finance. 'The London that *The Long Good Friday* depicts has disappeared,' wrote architectural critic Tom Dyckhoff in 2017. 'It could just as easily be the London of *Gaslight* or *Sherlock Holmes*.'[2] Back in 1971, councillor Ted Johns saw what was actually coming, as he watched a tiny development of eleven private town houses being built on the banks of the Isle of Dogs. 'The frightening thing is that this is just the start of what is bound to happen in the future,' said Johns. 'The riverside is gradually being taken away from the East End and this must be realized before it's too late.'[3]

Meanwhile, it was a stretch of the Thames riverside in central London that had roused the interest of a junior environment minister in Edward Heath's government in the early 1970s. 'I was appalled by what was happening on the south bank of the Thames. I still am appalled,' said Michael, now Lord Heseltine, who I interviewed in his shiny steel and glass office in Victoria.

'You see one of the great waterscapes of the world which is architecturally awful. It was self-evident in 1972 how awful it was.' As he spoke, I quietly kicked my Southbank Centre tote bag under my chair. Perhaps he'd seen it as I'd come in, and was being deliberately provocative – I wouldn't put it past him. Given how that collection of buildings – the National Theatre, Hayward Gallery and Festival Hall – are probably my favourites in London, symbols of post-war hope and reconstruction, I was resigned that, as with so much of our interview, we would have to agree to disagree. 'And so I instructed officials to prepare a Development Corporation to take over the planning of the south bank.' Development corporations had been used to create the new towns built after the Second World War, from Stevenage in 1946 to Milton Keynes in the late sixties. As it turned out, a reshuffle meant he never got the chance to intervene on the south bank as he became Minister of Aerospace in 1972, responsible for Heath's beloved airport scheme for Maplin Sands in Essex. Despite his best efforts, it would remain unbuilt. 'To get to Maplin Sands you flew by helicopter across London,' said Heseltine. 'And so I saw this incredible dereliction. And I saw more of it in the mid-seventies so by the election my whole focus had changed from architectural vandalism on the south bank to physical regeneration on a scale unbelievable.' Heath's government lost power in 1974 and Heseltine became shadow environment secretary. He told me that those images of Docklands from the air remained with him.

Not discernible from those helicopter rides were the people living in this post-industrial landscape. The white working-class majority were barely visible to the wider world, the district's significant Bangladeshi population and diverse waves of immigrants even less so. The story of Docklands is one of racial and class tension, of poverty and gentrification. It would be the poor

Bangladeshis rather than the subsequent waves of rich yuppies and middle-class incomers who would bear the brunt of anti-pathy from some of the dockers. Back in 1968 a number of locals had come out in support of Enoch Powell when he was sacked from the shadow cabinet following his racist 'rivers of blood' speech, marching to the Palace of Westminster brandishing placards with slogans such as *Back Britain, not Black Britain* and *We want Enoch Powell!* These attitudes persisted into the eighties. One Bengali woman told sociologist Janet Foster: 'I did hear rumours that the Isle of Dogs [was] very racist and Ben-galis wouldn't live on the island 'cos of the racial attacks. So I was having second thoughts, but you know, there's nothing you could do, you had to take the accommodation they offered you. Or you was out on the streets.'[4] Today you can walk about in parts of Docklands – the 1960s Samuda Estate on the Isle of Dogs, for example, with its low-rise blocks and high-rise slabs – and see parts of the old pre-gentrification Docklands still sur-viving in the shadow of the towers.

When the bigger changes of the 1980s came, and the middle classes began to move into new private housing, it had an impact across Docklands. Gaby Charing told me that 'one of the people that we knew and saw quite a lot of through the community centre was the Catholic priest, Jim. And he said his entire congregation had changed and it had been taken over by the middle classes. He wasn't very happy about it at all, because he felt that local people who had been members of that church for years were just being sidelined.' A *Times* editorial in December 1987 offered a solution to this awkward class divide. 'As for young Cockneys in the East End tower blocks overlooking Docklands, the message to them should be clear. Don't resent your yuppie neighbours; join them.' A new tide was coming to the docks.

Right to Buy and Other Transformations

'When they suggested Wythenshawe we said no thanks,' Peter Logan told me. That was back in the late 1960s, when he and wife Peggy and two young kids had just moved from Northern Ireland. They opted for a council flat closer to central Manchester, but by 1971 they were hoping to move somewhere bigger. Again they were offered a house in Wythenshawe, one of Europe's largest council estates. This time they took it. 'You get lost in Wythenshawe very easy,' said Peter. 'I mean there were 100,000 people living here when we moved. That's a big estate.' These days, the Logans still live in the same house on a street on the edge of the park, part of a classic 1960s estate of huge slab blocks and towers, low-rise maisonettes and terraces of modest pale-brick houses. Estates all over the country share this vaguely modernist aesthetic, from an era sandwiched between their more loosely planned garden-city forebears and the complicated cul-de-sacs that came after. 'Our living room looks straight onto Wythenshawe Park,' said Peter. 'You could pay a lot of money and you couldn't buy the site, you know?' By the late 1980s some of their neighbours had taken up the Right to Buy – the government's scheme for council tenants to buy their homes – and so they began to look at it seriously themselves. 'We paid rent on the house for years and years and years,' he explained. 'When we looked at it, we were actually paying more in rent than we would have been paying in mortgage.' Because of the generous discount from the Right to Buy, they discovered they wouldn't even need a deposit. 'We got it and it's ours, and it's a lovely house. It's only two bedroom, but there's only me and Peggy here now, so . . .'

What sort of things did they do to the place after they bought it? 'We put a small extension on the back of it,' said Peter. 'We extended the living room by about four metres by three.' Of the terrace of six houses, three were bought and three have remained social housing (no longer run by the council but by Wythenshawe Community Housing Group). According to Peter, those who bought have watched WCHG put 'new bathrooms, new doors and all that jazz' into the homes they manage. 'We've never qualified for anything, even free boilers, because we both had reasonably good jobs and both had pensions. Anything that's been done to the house we did it. We've never had insulation or anything done.' Although on the flipside, he wasn't sure they could have afforded to stay living here if they'd remained renting. 'If you were a retired person now and you had a reasonable income you'd pay top whack for rent now. Rent on this house now would be an arm and a leg.'

'The day I arrived in the ministry I had lunch with my permanent secretary,' recalled Michael Heseltine, 'and I gave him an envelope on which was a list of ten things and one of them would have been the Right to Buy.' It was perhaps the most emblematic policy of the first Thatcher administration, but it wasn't new. Examples of similar programmes stretched back to the 1920s, and many of the post-war new towns had seen some of their rental homes sold off as they attempted to pull in ever greater numbers of upwardly mobile residents. In the 1960s the Conservative-controlled Greater London Council had encouraged flogging council houses to their occupiers and the 1970 Conservative General Election manifesto contained the promise to 'encourage local authorities to sell council houses to those of their tenants who wish to buy them'.[1] Peter Shore, the Labour environment secretary of the late 1970s, had also tried to continue Heath's push, though Labour councils keen on retaining their housing stock were seen as the sticking point for any future attempt. By November 1978, Heseltine was claiming that Right

18

to Buy would 'bring about the greatest social revolution of our time'. With each new council home costing the taxpayer £1,200 a year,* explained Heseltine, 'it is we who will give council and new town tenants the legal Right to Buy their homes at generous discounts. It is we who will set them free.'[2] Residents of more than three years' standing thinking of buying their council homes would receive a 33 per cent discount on the market price of their home, rising to 50 per cent for longer-term tenants. By 1984 the minimum tenancy was dropped to two years and the top discount raised to 60 per cent. Flats, which were proving harder to sell, were going for a whopping 70 per cent discount. Right to Buy would go on to be worth £40 billion to the government in the first forty years.

In the Commons in May 1979, Margaret Thatcher explained that the policy 'will give to more of our people that freedom and mobility and that prospect of handing on to their children and grandchildren which owner-occupation provides'.[3] A golden sunset bathing millions of home owners in some form of hereditary advantage. The big issue that made Right to Buy so controversial was a moratorium on council-house building. 'I secured an agreement at the time in the very early eighties that two-thirds of the proceeds of the sales would go to rebuilding new social housing,' Heseltine told me. 'That lasted as long as I was secretary of state. When I went to defence, the money was' – he paused carefully – '*removed* by the Treasury and incorporated in a wider pot.' The first Thatcher administration famously

---

* Between 1992 and 2017, the number of people renting from private landlords doubled. In time, Heseltine's cost saving would be dwarfed by the amount paid in housing benefit to private landlords. By 2014 the government was directly subsidising commercial investors through housing benefit to the tune of £9.3 billion, compared to £9.4 billion given to housing associations and £6.1 billion to councils.

made huge cuts to government budgets: three-quarters came from housing. The very nature of the Right to Buy struck at the heart of the post-war settlement – where council housing had sat alongside universal healthcare, the welfare state and comprehensive education. Once this double whammy hit – selling off council housing and refusing to build replacements – dreams of making society more equal through the places we lived were over.

The first public inquiry into Right to Buy came in Dundee in February 1981. Sixty demonstrators crowded into the chamber and sat on the floor with banners. Leader of the protest was George Galloway, who told the inquiry that 'these people will have to be dragged out kicking and screaming'.[4] Worried that his much trumpeted legislation might be challenged in court, Heseltine had sent officials to the Bar to 'find the most expert and renowned housing silk, instruct him as though he was instructed by a communist controlled local authority with infinite money to break this legislation. And he did.' The same lawyer had then made the bill watertight. The Dundee protest and many like it were swept aside.

By September 1984, 700,000 homes had been sold off, 11.5 per cent of the total council homes available for sale. And while some local authorities were vehemently opposed, others were desperate to divest themselves of this municipal burden. Under the corrupt leadership of Shirley Porter, Westminster City Council disposed of 10,000 council homes between 1986 and 1994 in a bid to make the borough more attractive to affluent residents by washing their hands of the poor and disadvantaged. In some areas of the UK, hard-to-let flats and houses on underfunded estates soon became the only council homes available. In this way, Right to Buy didn't benefit all council estates through the supposed 'trickle-down' effect of private owners bringing the area up. Instead, new owners sold and moved on, and impoverished ghettos began to emerge in areas left behind by the collapse in traditional industry and escalating unemployment rates. Still the sales went on, and by 1997 an astonishing 1.8 million council homes had been sold across the country, a quarter of the entire stock. The arrival of buy-to-let landlords pouncing on ex-local authority housing as it came up for sale from its first wave of right-to-buyers would change the face of former council estates more than those optimistic initial buyers would have imagined.

I grew up on a council estate in Croydon and can remember the offer to buy the house coming from Croydon Council, or rather, our baffled reaction to it. Why on earth would you *buy* a house? The council, for all its flaws, looked after us. The house was pretty solid, they came and painted the doors and windows every few years, and more than that, replaced them and adapted the house for my mum, a wheelchair user, with a more accessible kitchen and downstairs loo. Besides which, the only person we knew who owned a house was my mum's older brother Reg, who lived in a massive ranch-style bungalow in Hampshire after making a packet from decorating the Mars chocolate factory. I remember the acres of shagpile rug space in his opulent 1970s living room, the garden so big it had a wood at the end, and the ornamental fishpond with carp in it, into which I was once chased by his Great Dane, Bryn. But we weren't like Reg. My dad was a car mechanic, frequently unemployed and in poor health, my mum was brilliantly clever but at that time battling with depression and disability. Reg had made it; we knew our place. And so we all reacted with the sort of high emotion typical of my family. We shrugged. Not for us, thank you. Over the years I've wondered if this was a bad decision, but with two chronically ill parents the council house suited us fine; it meant that a lot of the worries that might have plagued them as home owners – responsibility for faulty drains or rewiring, say – were taken care of. We were a happy municipal family. And so it seemed funny all these years later meeting Heseltine, Mr Right to Buy, the man who made us an offer we could not refuse, knowing that we had. Our decision to snub one of the defining phenomena of 1980s Britain hadn't been particularly political, principled or driven by a financial motive. It was more instinctive than that. We felt lucky to live in a nice council house, with all the services we might have needed nearby, and there was a sense that owning a house would bring nothing but expensive heartache. All these years later I can't help thinking that given the way the world has gone, owning a home no longer feels like the security blanket it might once have seemed. The millions who took up the offer have quite varying experiences of it.

Family politics played a major role in the Right to Buy. Take Janice Richardson, who bought her parents' council house in Rotherham for them. 'I don't know why me dad came up with it but he wanted someone in the family to buy the house,' said Janice, 'because they couldn't afford to but they'd like someone in the family to have it. And me dad just approached all the family to see if anybody was interested, and only me and my ex-husband were.' The house was in East Dene, Rotherham's first council estate, built in the 1920s. Streets of small red-brick terraces and pebble-dashed semis display a variety of modifications, be they extensions, loft conversions or ersatz bay windows. There's no trees or grass verges in the street, which gives it a more industrial air than a garden suburb of the same vintage, but it still has a reassuring suburban feel to it. 'So we purchased it,' explained Janice, 'and I think me dad were pleased, made him happy someone was going to have it.'

Janice and Ernie, her then husband, were only able to afford it because he had recently been made redundant from Northern Foods and had received a decent payout. The recipients of this act of generosity were Eric and Iris Oates, Sheffield steelworker and cleaner respectively. Helen Angell, Janice's niece, recalled how surprisingly right wing Eric had been for a steelworker, and how he had supported Margaret Thatcher, which presumably piqued his interest in Right to Buy in the first place. Janice paid for new windows, but otherwise the house was already like new, as the council had just refurbished it, with a modern kitchen, bathroom and central heating. 'I were surprised how cheap it was!' said Janice. 'It was bought for £13,000. It's ridiculous in't it? It sold for £90,000.' This was in 2019, when Iris died. She certainly had no regrets about buying it for them. 'It was a win-win really. Mum and Dad didn't pay any rent or anything then, they lived there for nothing. And that made their life a lot more comfortable. And then we knew one day me and Ernie we would sell it. They willed it to us you see, and one day it was like a pension for us.'

Another family with a complicated Right to Buy story was Simon Lee, who wrote to me with remembrances of his family moving from a tied flat to a council house in Totley, Sheffield, in 1981. 'Central heating, hot water whenever we needed it, a bedroom for each of us, and TWO indoor toilets. And a telephone. We hadn't the money to get one installed at our previous home. This was an amazing change in our circumstances. However, the cost of the rent was far higher than that of the flat and it included other fees. Once we moved here we never had another family holiday. We had no spare money.' 'Here' was near the boundary of the Peak District National Park, a council estate of plain blond-brick homes built in the early 1970s. 'My parents always voted Labour and did not approve,' recalled Simon of the Right to Buy. This moral dilemma was what the government had been banking on, destabilising the post-war settlement that had once promised municipal housing for all.

Simon and his sister were still living with their parents by the mid-nineties. It was then that his sister suggested buying the house for their parents. 'My dad was opposed. As I wasn't working' – Simon had recently been made redundant – 'I allowed my mum to have the casting vote. Although both my parents were Labour supporters who both worked for the co-operative movement, my mum felt buying the house would give us security and enable them to leave something to the kids.' Mortgage repayments would be less than the council rent. 'We were worried about taking on debt. We usually paid cash, up-front, for everything. My parents never had credit cards.' But they took the plunge and bought the house. Simon's parents passed away a decade later, and he has lived in their ex-council house ever since. 'Of the twenty-one houses on our road, I think only four others have the same people living there now as did when we moved here in 1981. Several people got good prices for the houses they sold and have bought a home in a different area of Sheffield. That probably would not have been possible before Right to Buy put them on the property ladder.'

'Seen from the air on a sunny day Granby ward could still be mistaken for one of the more prosperous parts of Paris,' wrote a researcher for Shelter in a 1972 report on Liverpool 8, a working-class suburb of the inner city.[5] By the late twentieth century, Liverpool was no longer the major Empire port it had once been, home for Commonwealth imports, berth of great liners, wealthy financial centre for shipping magnates. Monuments of its Empire past still dominated the waterfront: the neo-baroque Edwardian splendour of the Mersey Docks and Harbour Board; the Royal Liver Building with its huge bronze birds staring out over the 24 water; and the Italianate Cunard building. But it was places like

Granby, a Victorian suburb of Liverpool 8 close to the city centre, that had been most affected by these changing fortunes. 'In this district there are people who for years have lived with frustration, fighting against odds far too big for them to cope with,' local resident Mrs Fitzgerald told researchers of *Another Chance for Cities: Shelter Neighbourhood Action Project*. These were people 'doing all in their power to keep this the kind of district we remember it to be, not snobbish, but clean and pleasant to live in'.[6]

It was here that the eleven houses of Ducie Street contained an astonishing sixty-three families, with just fourteen bathrooms between them. There had been demolitions in the area but a few of the old streets remained because the city council was aware that knocking too many homes down would create a homelessness crisis they couldn't cope with. Shelter's project resulted in a transformation for Granby. There were fewer families sharing facilities, and houses had new roofs and bathrooms. Trees were planted, new street furniture installed, pedestrianisation trialled. But the report's conclusion went far beyond some tame action points. 'To neglect the urban problem is to extend an open invitation to social conflict,' they declared.[7] They predicted a flashpoint in the near future would destroy these communities. 'When the combined effects of race and poverty erupt in anarchic violence it may be already "too late",' they wrote. Racist violence in 1972 led to black residents in Myrtle Gardens having the windows of their houses put in after arguments about the allocation of new council homes, which led to retaliatory action over the next few nights. 'In the end,' wrote the researchers, 'it requires very little to spark off a spontaneous reaction.'[8]

Nine years later, in July 1981, Liverpool 8 was the epicentre of what became known locally as the uprisings. These followed the arrest of Leroy Cooper, a black youth who was taken in for allegedly assaulting police officers. In fact, Cooper had been caught up in a confrontation between police, who were trying to arrest an unknown figure on a motorbike, and a crowd of angry bystanders. Police struck one of them with a baton, after which stones began to be thrown. Anger grew over the evening, and by the next day a more concerted response came from the locals. First they blocked the broad expanse of Upper Parliament Street with burned-out cars. Petrol bombs were made. 'I became increasingly involved, night after night,' said one of the rioters, Jimi Jagne, when interviewed by journalist Andy Beckett for his book on the era, *Promised You a Miracle*.[9] A quiet youth who'd been assaulted by the police some months before, Jagne had become fascinated by reports of the Brixton riots three months earlier, and the writings of Malcolm X. 'For us, they were the first major breakthrough,' said Jagne. 'We stepped forward and said, "We're here and this is how we feel."'[10] It followed other flashpoints around the country, including St Paul's, Bristol, in April 1980, a riot that occurred after a raid on an illegal club. Brixton in London, St Paul's in Bristol and Liverpool 8 each faced issues the Shelter report had warned of a decade before: poverty and high unemployment (in Liverpool 8, unemployment in those days of recession was running at 40 per cent, but for young black people it was even worse, as high as 70) combined with a culture of aggressive, bullying, racist policing. For people being ignored and demonised, a show of protest had become inevitable. And it manifested itself in a violent reaction not just to the forces that were controlling or mistreating them, but also to a sense of place that seemed to represent the abandonment they felt. More than seventy buildings were torched in Liverpool.

Three months before the uprisings, Tate & Lyle – one of the city's most prosperous Empire-era businesses – had closed its doors with the loss of 1,600 jobs. A sense of desperation gripped Liverpool. In the immediate wake of the riots, Heseltine called

26

for a £100 million cash injection to the city to help stabilise the situation. £15 million was allocated. 'I cannot help feeling that the option of managed decline is one that we should not forget altogether,' wrote the Chancellor, Geoffrey Howe. 'We must not expend all our limited resources in trying to make water flow uphill.' Sensing how explosive this idea was, Howe wrote that 'this is not a term for use, even privately'.[11] When I spoke to Heseltine, he was determined to show that Howe's comments were not the whole story. Peter Shore, his Labour predecessor as environment minister, had forged a partnership with Liverpool to help them face their acute housing problems. When Heseltine took over in 1979, he agreed to carry on partnering with the city. Hoping to polish up his planning act before he unleashed it on London Docklands, he told his staff to 'find the second worst site in the country and give me order-making powers to designate', he told me. 'Where's the second worst? Liverpool. So Liverpool got its development corporation in 79, it got its Garden Festival in 79. So from 79 I had a closer relationship with Liverpool than anywhere else, actually. Development corporation, partnerships, Garden Festival, and the working together. Oh, and I listed the Albert Dock. Totemic.' When the riots happened, he felt a personal responsibility to do something, he told me. 'I said to Margaret, *Look, we can just say it's law and order and back the police and we have got to do that, but I want to walk the streets.* And that is when the enormity of the problems became apparent. My philosophical approach – individualism, competition, partnership – were all there before 81. But *my God*, the need for it and the intensity and the opportunities of it in those three weeks walking the streets.' The incongruity remains fascinating. Ronnie Hughes, who had been working for a housing association in the city at the time, said of Hezza, 'In Liverpool we always say about him that he wasn't bad for a Tory. He's an arrogant tosser but he stuck to the place in a way and he did some good things, to our total derision.'

Upper Parliament Street, the initial site of the Liverpool uprisings, is now an anonymous urban expressway flanked by some forlorn bits of development. This busy multi-lane highway cuts across the path from Liverpool 8 to the city centre. It forms a forbidding boundary for the people that live here. In front of the road's handsome, ornate Victorian town houses, rioters had once overturned a police van, petrol bombs had been thrown, and standing battles fought. Demolitions have long since removed the blackened, fire-damaged buildings, where now anonymous nineties blocks stand. The Rialto, a dashing 1920s former cinema and ballroom, was one of the high-profile places torched. Now a dinky, insubstantial postmodernist version of it stands on the site, more key fob than building. These repairs to the urban fabric are gestures: the area doesn't feel knitted together, instead it unravels, the hopes of the original pattern pulled, holey and straggling. The varied building styles could have made for a splendid cross-generational urban party but instead it exudes the awkwardness of patients socially distanced in a waiting room. It feels as deliberately insipid as possible, the ultimate passion-killing environment, a bloodless riot-free zone.

'I walked around, it was only the next street, and saw the damage and everything, and just felt really sad,' said Ronnie of his post-riot explorations. 'Sad for Liverpool and sad that it had had to happen. But I did think it had to happen. And I could see why.' A few streets back, Lodge Lane, the secondary target of the rioters, has taken longer to recover, but these days is more likely to appear on a foodie podcast as a haven for world cuisine than on the news pages. In some parts, the riots were tidied away as soon as they could be. In Granby, the district investigated by Shelter a decade before, the effects were more lasting, and devastating. The rehabilitation of the area in the 1970s meant all the houses had been occupied, and conditions improved. But immediately after the riots it became a no-go area; residents were blamed, moved out and moved on, leaving boarded-up houses behind as if cursed. A whole ward of haunted houses. A few plucky souls remained, waiting it out until things might begin to slowly improve.

On 4 August 1981, Heseltine took one of his biggest risks yet. In a typically theatrical flourish, he invited some of the richest business leaders in Britain on a coach tour around Merseyside, in an attempt to sell these run-down places as areas of opportunity. Heseltine sat at the front of the coach with a slender microphone, part tour guide, part Tonight-Matthew-I'm-going-to-be-Tony-Hadley, while behind sat rows of suited grey men peering out of the windows with expressions of bemusement and consternation.

'I was on one of those buses,' said Ronnie Hughes, to my surprise. 'It wasn't Heseltine on my bus, it was Patrick Jenkin, the "nice guy" in the first Thatcher government.' Jenkin was then Secretary of State for Health. 'We took him around. We were actually showing him the nice things we had done. We were quite proud. We were showing him good stuff. And he turned round and said, *this is awful, isn't it!*' Ronnie laughed and did a double take. '*Is it?*'

The business leaders had been briefed not to promise Heseltine any money. 'They were frightened these guys would be seduced into giving millions, billions! Anyway, we went round, these extremely smart, very well-heeled gentlemen – they were all gentlemen, interesting – and we got out of the buses and walked the most desolate, derelict parts of Liverpool and they talked to the tenants and all of that. And then one or two of them said, *I was born in this city*. And an interesting bond emerged.' Before they returned to London, Heseltine took them for tea at the Adelphi, the vast crumbling hotel by Lime Street station. 'They all sat in rows like you're sitting,' he said, pointing at me, 'like this', and he mimed hunching over defensively – which I hadn't realised I'd been doing – 'and I said *marvellous of you all to come, most engaging wonderful visit – I don't want any money.* They all shot upright!' Instead, he asked them each to second a bright young employee to come and work with his team for a year, to look into how to get private companies to invest in large cities.

His newly minted Merseyside Development Corporation's first task was to tackle the derelict docks. A 250-acre section at Dingle – the old Mersey Foundry and a former municipal tip, Dingle Tank Farm – was chosen as the site for the Liverpool International Garden Festival. Before anything could be done, vast amounts of methane had to be pumped from the industrial waste, as the site wasn't just unappealing, it was hugely dangerous. A competition was held in 1982 to design a centrepiece, the Festival Hall, which was won by engineering giants Arup. A few years later and it might have been termed an icon, because that was its purpose, to represent the new spirit of the city, to become its logo. Arup had only twelve months to build it, hence the relative simplicity of the structure: the Festival Hall was a High Tech greenhouse whose lightweight tubular frame was clad in aluminium and ribbed polycarbonate sheeting. Thirteen different countries were represented in exhibits on the site, and a quarter of a million trees were planted. There was a nature trail, a sculpture zoo and – of course – a Beatles maze. The festival was opened by the Queen and Prince Philip on 2 May 1984.

Local reaction was split between curiosity, hilarity and anger. Terence Fields, Labour MP and enthusiastic member of Militant, was never going to be a fan. 'What does it mean if you are unemployed? What does it mean if you are living in a hovel in an area of Liverpool that is not one of the council's housing priority areas?'[12] Ronnie Hughes had initially been unconvinced by the gardens too. 'By then I lived in a house that was only just over the fence from the Garden Festival,' he said. 'I only went once. It was nowhere near ready as a garden because they were just like bedding plants that had been stuck into the soil. Eventually it turned into a real secret garden over the years as they couldn't find any uses for it and it grew of its own accord. What eventually tempted me over the fence to take a look at the thing was partly its popularity – most people seemed to like the look of the thing – and partly just the fascination of seeing anything new that had clearly had a lot of public money and establishment will put into it. But I could never get over the fact that just up that hill was our beloved Liverpool 8 where none of this money was getting to, none of these jobs as far as I can see was getting to.'

The Festival Hall was to be turned into a regional sports centre after the show, but this never happened. Instead, the neglected ruin stood there for years, surrounded by debris – the rusting remains of garden attractions and bits of infrastructure long since grown over – like some starliner crashed in an urban woodland.

Liverpool Garden Festival in full swing. © foundin_a_attic

A few years back, I climbed into the derelict gardens and explored it. Those oh-so-eighties postmodern features – tubular archways, primary coloured metalwork and fibreglass – were rusting or stained but still standing, as was the neat little Chinese Pagoda and Japanese Garden. It was like being on a film set – a *Planet of the Apes* reboot, perhaps – exploring the remains of fun gone by, with only the occasional dog walker breaking the spell. It was one of Britain's most magnificent modern ruins, until in 2011 it was partially renovated. Some of the features, most notably the Yellow Submarine, had been moved out to John Lennon Airport. I went back again in the summer of 2019 and the once wild landscaping was now being carefully looked after by volunteers. Those flimsy, rusting gates had been replaced by strong wooden ones surrounded by crates of rock, also used liberally throughout the garden to shore up some of the more dramatic features. I got talking to an elderly man who, unprompted, told me how much he loved it then and now, and how awful it had been to see engineers arrive on site that summer taking readings of the methane levels beneath the soil to see if it was suitable for building on. So far the trees are winning, suspended over their toxic bubble of landfill and gas.

Further along the Mersey, towards the centre of the city, stood Albert Dock, an impressive series of warehouses on the waterside designed by Jesse Hartley and Philip Hardwick and opened in 1846. The buildings had stood derelict since the 1950s, and the development corporation had plans to completely refurbish the whole site, in partnership with property management company Arrowcroft. The regenerated Albert Dock opened in May 1988, with many of the warehouses converted to luxury flats. On the ground floor level there were spaces for shops, a TV studio for Granada's *This Morning*, hosted by Judy Finnigan and Richard Madeley, and an art gallery, Tate Liverpool, whose warehouse space was converted by James Stirling. Environment minister Patrick Jenkin had been keen to broker the deal for Tate to move in, prompting the deputy leader of the council, Derek Hatton, to remark that 'it's a pity Mr Jenkin didn't show the same interest in the thousands of Tate & Lyle workers who lost their jobs there last year as he is showing in the Tate art gallery'.[13]

Liverpool became an experiment in privatisation. At the 1960s Cantril Farm estate on the edge of the city, public–private partnership was trialled, between Tory government, Labour council and a group of private developers. Abbey National building society and Barclays Bank bought the estate, a place Heseltine described to me as 'a real, real slum', and Hezza placed a man he described as 'one of my heroes' – tough-nut developer Tom Baron – in charge of the redevelopment.* 'The troublemakers left and no one asked too many questions,' said Heseltine. What sort of solution is that, I wondered. What happened to them, those former council residents deemed too undesirable for housing?

Then in inner-city Toxteth in May 1982, less than a year after the riots, housebuilders Barratt stepped in to buy and renovate Myrtle Gardens, 300 interwar flats. 'When we heard they were about to be demolished we pleaded with Liverpool Council to stop,' said owner Lawrie Barratt. The deal he reached was 'we buy them for £1,000 a unit, completely refurbish them and then offer them at a far lower cost than people would normally have to pay for two-bedroom flats'.[14] They'd bought the estate for £25,000 and then put each flat on the market for between

---

* Cantril Farm was named 'one of the worst estates in Europe' in a 2016 ITV show about actor Craig Charles's early life there, after which the *Liverpool Echo* on 11 September 2016 was full of residents defending it. 'I've lived here for 46 years and never had anyone sell drugs outside my house,' said resident Lisa O'Connor. 'We all know it's not perfect but I know many good people.'

£20,000 and £25,000. It became a gated community called Minster Court, complete with security guard in a lodge. The resulting edifice was known as 'the compound'. There was no doubt that the security features had worked: by 1987 the once notorious estate had faced just six break-ins in three years. 'What sold the place to me was the security,' said Joyce Hardacre, who relocated with her husband, Tom, to be near his job in the docks. He was made redundant shortly after their move. 'You can even leave your car unlocked in here. Just over the fence we can hear the cars being pinched. But once you are inside you are as safe as houses.'[15] Their upwardly mobile neighbours included academics, graphic designers, an air steward, and the area manager for Glaxo. Though the gulf between what support they could expect in a private gated community when compared to council housing came as a shock to some. At parking disputes or problems with the interiors of the flats, Barratt shrugged their shoulders. Sort it out yourselves. Welcome to private life.

In an era of increasing public protest and private ownership, security became a priority for many. Geographer Alice Coleman, then head of the Land Use Research Unit at King's College London, was the figurehead for this movement. She was a disciple of US urbanist Oscar Newman, whose 1972 book *Defensible Space* argued that areas of municipal ownership created crime, and that residents would only be safe if allowed to exercise some inbuilt territorial instinct to defend their space from behind doors, gates and bars. Newman cuts a rather visionary preacher figure, while Coleman has more than a touch of Mary Whitehouse about her, not least a shared penchant for dispensing moralising wisdom and a disgust at the dirty realities of modern life. 'Nobody could have been brought up in greater poverty than me and I can tell you that poverty per se does not have that effect. My family was extremely ethical, honest, hard-working and so on,' she told film-maker Tom Cordell for his documentary *Utopia London*. 'If you've got people who are properly brought up, they survive.'[16]

In Elizabeth Wilson's critique of Coleman's work in her book *The Sphinx in the City*, she writes that 'the reverse side of this belief is that there can be no public or social responsibilities or obligations. The ideology of "defensible space" legitimates a paranoid attitude to "strangers" and "aliens" and easily fits into racist paradigms of who "intruders" are.'[17] A surprising early adherent to Coleman's teachings was Liverpool's Militant council, who created an Urban Regeneration Strategy in 1984 in which they identified seventeen deprived areas, replacing 'unsatisfactory' flats and maisonettes with houses and bungalows in cul-de-sacs. They had demolished 7,500 flats by 1987, converted others and built new houses totalling 9,000. Unfortunately, unlike the flats they had replaced, many of these remained unlet because they were simply too small for the families they were intended for.

More and more security became a private issue that affected the public sphere. Police officers returning from a research trip to the US in 1982 to look at the latest in crime prevention strategies recommended creating a voluntary organisation to monitor and report crime. This network of community action would coalesce into the Neighbourhood Watch movement. The first place to trial what was then called the Home Watch scheme was the village of Mollington in Cheshire, 300 homes where a wave of burglaries had left the residents restive. Throughout the 1980s and 90s the scheme grew, with orange stickers on windows and signs on poles announcing the prying eyes of nosy neighbours to any burglar or disruptive influence. I remember we had one on our living-room window when I was growing up. We had no idea who the local co-ordinator was, and had no interest in poking our noses into our neighbours' affairs. Rather it was placed there as a magic talisman, a supernatural warning, like a shrunken head or wicker figurine. The neighbourhood might be watching, but we weren't.

As academic Chris Moores explains in his fascinating essay on Neighbourhood Watch and Thatcherism, just five years after that first group was created there were 42,000 schemes across the country covering 2.5 million houses.[18] In 1989, Margaret Thatcher spoke to her local Neighbourhood Watch group in Finchley. She admired their work on crime prevention, shifting the emphasis from costly nanny state to a freelanced nanny public. 'Much of the work must come from citizens themselves,' she told them. 'There comes a point when the government can't do anything more.'[19] And it formed an irresistible template. As Moores notes, 'An entire sub-genre of "self-help" community watchdog organisations including Vehicle Watch, Taxi Watch, Pub Watch, Boat Watch, Shop Watch, Caravan Watch and even Sheep Watch were all created during the 1980s and early 1990s.'[20] Much of the success of Neighbourhood Watch rested on neighbours protecting 'people like us' and there was plenty of research to suggest that these organisations were overly white and middle-class. In the Metropolitan Police's first stab at publicity material for the scheme, they produced a leaflet in which the only black person shown was mugging an elderly white woman.

Heseltine recalled 'people were queueing up to buy! By the 1983 election we were meeting people out when we were canvassing who had bought their council housing. And we had a pretty good idea of the gains they had made: they got a big discount because property prices were rising, so they had made very substantial sums of money from the process.' I wondered how he felt about it now, given how divisive the policy has been. 'I believed in the policy and still do,' he said. 'I have much regret that the cash was diverted from social housing, but equally I was very pleased that we had created the private rented sector which has been crucial to many millions of people.'

This revolution is thrown into stark relief by the 1986 English House Condition Survey, which gives a good idea of the state of the buildings we were living in as the Thatcher miracle was supposedly leading to a national housing boom. A million homes were described as unfit for human habitation, three-quarters of which were still inhabited. In the worst condition were houses built before 1919. Most tellingly, almost two and a half million privately owned houses were in bad condition, dwarfing the half million council houses in a similar state. Of 8,000 council estates, a quarter were described as run-down. The worst housing was to be found in the urban areas of London, the North West, Yorkshire and Humberside. And the residents of the worst properties tended to be from ethnic minorities, single parents, those living on their own, on low incomes and tenants of private landlords. The simple fix of private good, public bad seemed not to be addressing the right problems.

Meanwhile, doing up ex-council houses became a kind of mania. As a teenager in the mid-1980s, I had watched with fascination as a form of warfare broke out on our street. You could tell which council houses in New Addington had been sold through Right to Buy. These were the pebble-dashed ones, bringing a slightly seaside suburban touch to the streets of red-brick semis. Look at our home improvements, they were eager to say. We've climbed a ladder and you've been left behind. But then the council fought back. Borough workmen began making their way around the estate, going from house to house fundamentally altering the homes of the remaining council tenants. They were replacing all the single-glazed aluminium-framed Crittall windows in the houses with uPVC ones. The originals were beautiful but left the place cold and damp: the doctor told my dad that they were the primary cause of his bronchitis. These replacements made a huge difference, even though their much thicker plastic frames blocked out a significant amount of light. Pretty soon, a walk around New Addington would reveal those houses bought but not improved – those with Crittall windows still intact – as if the council was keen to demonstrate the value of municipal ownership through plastic double glazing. Double glazing had been pioneered in the US in the 1920s but it was the arrival of uPVC from West Germany in the 1970s that would dramatically change many of our homes. In 1976, less than 10 per cent of UK homes had double glazing; by 2007, 83 per cent of homes had it installed. PVC – polyvinyl chloride – was one of those wartime inventions, designed as a bendy and stretchy alternative to rubber. uPVC is a refinement of that process, the 'u' for unplasticised, meaning it was rigid rather than bendy.

A 1980 advert for Astraseal Windows extolling the revolutionary properties of uPVC frames was accompanied by a picture of tall Georgiabethan fake-leaded tilt and turn windows on a bungalow down the road from us in South Croydon. The same year, an ad for Reed Windows of Timperley claimed that 'Reeds's slim, solid white frames blend beautifully with British homes – unlike some bulky Continental types'. And how else to prove that than 'Georgian-effect leaded lights available upon request'.[21] By the end of the decade, the ubiquity of uPVC windows replacing those on both council and private housing meant that for some they had become a menace. Heritage campaigner Gavin Stamp wrote of a visit to Douglas on the Isle of Man that 'almost worse than the demolition of the buildings that give Douglas its character is the systematic mutilation of the historic buildings that remain. Nowhere else in Britain have I seen so many of the dreadful plastic windows and "Kentucky

38

Fried Georgian" front doors that succeed, through the ignorant self-indulgence of gullible owners, in transforming handsome Georgian buildings into hideous travesties.'[22] They weren't much better on our 1950s council houses either.

'There's quite a lot of people have said they shouldn't have sold the council houses because it left people nowhere to live,' Wythenshawe right-to-buyer Peter Logan told me. 'A lot of the people who bought the council houses couldn't have afforded to buy a house!' The Logans had lived there for seventeen years before they bought it. 'We'd have well paid for it in that time. If they hadn't sold the council houses the people living in them *then* would be living in them *now*.' In the end, it was Peter and Peggy who had bought who were still living there today. 'They couldn't have afforded to go to the market and buy one. You've never heard of any company building houses cheap. They say the lower end of the market, but the lower end of the market is quite expensive. You ask any young couple now who are trying to save up for a deposit for a mortgage. It's not easy.'

Janice Richardson was rather more conflicted about the council house she'd bought in Rotherham. 'Because they've done this Right to Buy, people can't get a house. There's no stock now because it's all been bought up. I know we did it, but now I wonder if they wish they'd never done it because there's no council houses. Not as many would have been bought if it wasn't for the fact that they were so cheap. But they were just ridiculously cheap.' One of the big changes caused by the Right to Buy was the emergence of a whole new wave of private landlords buying up ex-local authority houses. 'I know there's a couple of those houses what's been bought,' said Janice, 'and now whoever's bought them are renting them out. And so they're coming and going.' It was something right-to-buyer Simon Lee mentioned too, how the arrival of private landlords has begun to change

the character of his Sheffield neighbourhood. 'The initial tenant bought the house and it was then sold by the family to a
property developer who rents it out. The current tenant says
living here is the only way he could get his kids into the local
schools.' Competition for school places, for local amenities once
run by the state, for the ownership of the homes we live in are
all part of the revolution brought in by Margaret Thatcher's
government in 1979. Today, the mosaic of changes to the way
we live, each a seemingly isolated development, awkwardly
interconnects across our lives. And the Right to Buy remains
a pivotal moment, when the state began to sell off its assets to
private individuals, and a whole chain of consequences was set
in motion for decades to come.

Andrew Wadsworth had big ambitions. Back in 1978, aged twenty-three, the young Mancunian took his girlfriend for a walk along East London's largely derelict riverscape in search of the perfect warehouse for conversion into a New-York-style loft apartment. They didn't have to walk very far. Just 200 yards from Tower Bridge, they struck gold. An old Victorian grain store, water tower and mill: New Concordia Wharf. 'It was absolutely empty except for one floor given to storing redundant sixties computers. But it looked terrific,' said Andrew. 'It was love at first sight.'[1] He had a sympathetic bank manager too: an East End ex-pat, misty-eyed at the thought of this young entrepreneur saving an old Docklands warehouse. Following the oil crisis of the 1970s, property suddenly looked to be a safer investment, and so investors like Andrew were increasingly drawn towards projects like New Concordia Wharf. By the time his conversion was finished it contained sixty flats, along with workshops, offices and a restaurant. Wadsworth was exactly the kind of private enterprise pioneer that Reg Ward's London Docklands Development Corporation was set on encouraging. And so pretty soon his venture, Jacobs Island Company, set to work on another, yet more magnificent set piece.

The Circle is a treat, a little bit of knock-off Gaudí in the heart of Southwark. It's a short hop from the southern end of Tower Bridge down the scrubbed-up Industrial Revolution canyon of Curlew Street – imagine seeing a curlew here! – emerging beside the second of Wadsworth's Docklands landmarks. At first, the Circle seems oddly square – a pair of matching eight-storey buildings facing each other along much of the narrow length of Queen Elizabeth Street, on the site of what had once been the

The owlish silhouette of the Circle. © CGP Grey

Courage Brewery stables. It's immense: 302 flats, with shops, offices and a health club. And unlike its many close neighbours, it's not a conversion but an extraordinary group of postmodern faux-warehouses in yellow stock brick, with balconies balancing on dark-stained pine logs and bulky steel trusses. Victorianate windows and golden balconies peep out across the street and between buildings, arrayed in striking diagonal rows. Above me the roofline undulates, echoing some of the more decorative warehouse parapets. But these details are just an aside. Suddenly the opposing facades have pulled back into two deep semicircles, creating a whirl of open space in this long narrow street. Two curved walls with steeply diagonal rooflines are glazed from floor to sky in shiny tiles of a shocking cobalt blue. Tucked away as it is, it still creates one of the most arresting and unlikely modern outdoor spaces in London.

It launched in October 1987 as London's financial markets were crashing around it. A helicopter winched in the final flourish of this elaborate set piece: a large bronze statue – Jacob, the Circle Dray Horse by Shirley Pace – to set off the scheme. Jacob because this land had once been Jacob's Island, the seedy setting for Bill Sikes's death in *Oliver Twist*. It was also the name of Andrew Wadsworth's company. Today, Jacob stands there quite serene, a sturdy reminder of the site's heritage, a cute detail the architects must have whooped over when some wag suggested it. When it was grade II listed in 2018, architect Piers Gough – the G in architects CZWG – recalled that 'it was an exciting time to work with young entrepreneurial clients celebrating an overtly witty and theatrical response to the surrounding creative city'. Theatrical I can deal with. It's the 'w' word from a 1980s architectural giant – summoning up images of wanging on in a West End wine bar – that remains off-putting. Even so, I have a soft spot for the Circle. Don't ruin it, Piers. 'Colourful postmodernism reacted to the dreariness of debased modernism,' he explained, 'with a rich fusion of historic and modern architectural devices inspired by the found context as much as the imagined future.'[2] And certainly here, jammed into the tight historic streets around Shad Thames, it fits right in with the expensively converted warehouses. If these were the kind of blue dreams people were going to have in Docklands then the head of the development corporation, Reg Ward, was going to be delighted.

That bright February morning I'd walked from the new London Bridge station, a kind of trussed whale flip-flopping by the Thames, through the excruciatingly named More London, a Very Serious looking series of wedge-shaped grey-black offices   43 and chain stores. They funnelled me towards Norman Foster's dinky City Hall, a tight Brussels sprout of a building nestling beside Tower Bridge, very much the full Christmas dinner with all the trimmings. But it was what lay immediately beyond the bridge that interested me, where that modern bling gave way to the shady canyon of Shad Thames, a set of warehouses tarted up in the late 1980s. I recalled being taken here on a date nearly twenty years ago. The man, who I'd met on an early hook-up site, had been strangely eager to show off this Industrial Revolution street: the fixed-up walkways that ran between the warehouses; the gentrified buildings, now flats and cafés and gift shops. He presented Shad Thames with a cheery *Ta-da*, like he'd laid it on especially for my benefit. Did I recognise it, he asked. *Oh no*, I thought. *I know where this is going.* He'd brought me here because it was the location of a 1984 *Doctor Who* story, 'Resurrection of the Daleks'. At that moment, years before the show had been successfully rebooted, I had put away such childish things, and had adopted interests in more grown-up pursuits, like *Buffy the Vampire Slayer*. To compound my sense of mortification, my date began to theatrically describe the opening scenes to passers-by: the abandoned warehouses stained black with a century of industrial grime, the ramshackle wrought-iron walkways hung across the street, where once barrels had been swiftly offloaded from ships in the dock. Between 1984 and my awkward date these tall, empty Thames-side structures had filled up, become expensive real estate. The hatches through which hapless daleks were thrown were now Juliet balconies and picture windows, the soot-stained brickwork jet-washed to a cheery yellow, the dilapidated walkways renovated as characterful balconies for pot plants and loungers. On another day I might have been up for a bit of time travel, but right then all I wanted to do was get home and change my profile on that hook-up site.

Another of CZWG's outrageous designs for Docklands was the Cascades, built by developers Kentish Homes, whose 171 flats sold immediately when they went on the market in 1986. The Cascades is one of the most famous landmarks of new Docklands, a take-no-prisoners statement on the shoreline of the Isle of Dogs, a bold triangle and early contender for 'icon' status. It's one of London's most notable postmodern landmarks. And yet . . . As a building there is something transitional about it. The ramped form takes its shape from a nearby coal conveyor. The concrete balconies on the lower floors are curiously brutalist, fellow travellers of Portsmouth's long lost Tricorn Centre. The filigree metal balustrades on the upper storeys recall the jaunty Festival of Britain style of the early 1950s. Modernist architects fetishised the design of cruise liners, and there are so many of those motifs on display here, from the portholes and funnels to the location on the dockside of the Thames. The steep angle suggests ocean liner struck by iceberg, the queasy outline of a stricken ship's prow sticking out of the water, waiting for rescue. In all of this *Poseidon Adventure* excitement, it's clear that the Cascades is all about blockbusting fun and showing off. I just wonder if it might be showing off more than anyone intended: displaying debts to what were at the time the hated 1970s, the failed 1960s, the forgotten 1950s when it was fashionable to instead be referencing neoclassicism and the Empire. Even its three tall funnel chimneys sprouting from the ground – so achingly Pompidou Centre – are merely backing singers in the overall song here. The Cascades is architectural sampling, produced in the era of Paul Hardcastle. It is '19' in concrete, fibreglass and stock brick, telling the story of the *Titanic* rather than the Vietnam War. N-n-n-n-nineteen twelve.

*

It was Heseltine who in 1981 founded the London Docklands Development Corporation, the body who would transform this stretch of the city. It had been a struggle, thanks to Chancellor Geoffrey Howe and Thatcher's mentor Keith Joseph. 'Geoffrey's objections were for money – the Treasury always objects – Keith Joseph's more interestingly were intervention,' Heseltine told me. It was only the unexpected backing of Margaret Thatcher that saved them. Heseltine put a friend, property developer Nigel Broackes, in charge of the LDDC, with ex-Labour housing minister Bob Mellish as his deputy. 'I put the local Labour borough leaders on the development corporation but made sure that they were in a minority so that the private sector had the ability to stop it becoming another local government department. So it was a balance, reflecting the government's priorities, the local interest, party balance.' Reg Ward, the chief executive, was under no illusions about the limits of his role. 'Explicitly we were to have no responsibility for, no direct involvement in, social housing, community development, community support, health, education, training, etc.,' he told sociologist Janet Foster. 'We were not to be involved in major transport or infrastructure developments.'[3] The post-war new town development corporations had been community builders. These new ones were happy to deal in isolation. Criticisms of these corporations included a lack of local accountability, the public funding of private projects, and potential clashes with local regeneration or planning strategies.

Docklands felt from the off like the will of the government made concrete. And nothing in the changing landscape of 1980s Britain screamed dynamic monetarist revolution like Enterprise Zones, a government wheeze to encourage building and business by discarding as many rules as possible, be they land tax or planning controls. Enterprise Zones offered businesses small islands of low-regulation buccaneering, allowing them to queue-jump like a BMW driver ignoring all the rules of the road. Okay, so they would be less successful at creating new jobs than expected – and even then, of the part-time, low-wage and low-skilled variety. And they were expensive, too, with government subsidies working out at £30,000 per job created. But Docklands was going to adopt many of these market-driven experiments. Everything was designed to make money.

An early experiment was from John Laing and the London Industrial Association (not a band) who created Skylines (not an album), now known as London Docklands Professional Park (not a park). It's a cute village of domestic-style offices designed by Maxwell Hutchinson. The initial forty self-contained studio-style workspaces were completed in January 1986. It was later named worst building of the year by *Private Eye* magazine. Walking around these tiddly units today, there's a cottage industry scale that seems out of place beside the huge towers nearby, those later monuments to Michael Douglas's mirrored sunglasses. These low-rise buildings are gloriously wonky in brown brick, with exposed red frames and exaggerated monopitch roofs created by the jazzy triangles of double-height windows. The name suggests these angular rooflines were an homage to the dense streets of working-class homes of East London, the sort being cleared further east as the development corporation moved in. The scale of it feels oddly subversive in the midst of all that coked-up ambition, though perhaps that was more to do with the modest ambitions of the first wave of Docklands redevelopment. The first residents in this business village were comfortingly old-fashioned: a book publisher, a building surveyor, and – incongruously – a landscape gardener. It's still busy, with a Turkish barber, nail salon and the London Floatation Centre. In some parts of Docklands, you struggle for signs of life. Here, people can be glimpsed through the smoked glass, networking in the car park, or queueing at a coffee van parked in the corner. So attractive and successful is it that obviously there's a plan to knock it down. I can't help hoping Skylines can continue to stick it to 'the man'. It's a Tom Hanks/ Meg Ryan romcom waiting to happen. *You've Got Faxes*, perhaps.

It was located near one of the most derelict of all the sites in eighties Docklands: a backwater called Canary Wharf. In 1985 the video for Mick Jagger and David Bowie's Live Aid single 'Dancing in the Street' was filmed in an empty warehouse there as the dynamic duo dad-danced and high-kicked their way through the night, Bowie in a mac, Jagger in dayglo trousers. There wasn't much dancing in the street at Canary Wharf in those days. Few people lived or worked there, and the one or two streets that remained were often closed for demolition work. One of the only signs of life was a 1950s rum and banana warehouse, which had been transformed by architect Terry Farrell into a grey-walled, smoked glass and steel television studio complex in 1983. This was Limehouse Studios (which, as former local Gaby Charing pointed out to me, 'shows the total lack of respect to locals, as it was nowhere near Limehouse'). When Channel 4 was launched in 1982, its programmes would be made by a new wave of independent production companies, many of whom were based here, making everything from *Treasure Hunt* to *Whose Line is it Anyway?*

Farrell was also drafted in to rework the derelict framework of Tobacco Dock, a brick-built Georgian warehouse, into what was hoped to become a rival to Covent Garden. It opened in 1989. Yet within five years the experiment had failed and the whole place returned to silence, with just the odd corporate hire to keep it from dereliction. Beside that sit the ghostly remains of another lost enterprise: Fortress Wapping. In January 1986 this became Rupert Murdoch's top secret and highly computerised new printing plant for News International, publishers of the *Sun*,

Skylines, still working the angles. © Phineas Harper

News of the World, *The Times* and *The Sunday Times*. Murdoch had signed the deal to move from Fleet Street before the LDDC was set up. An industrial dispute lasting fifty-four weeks was triggered by 6,000 printworkers whose roles had been taken by computers in the new works. The police helped put down the strikers in a series of violent operations, and with the full backing of the government, fresh from their ruthless breaking of the mine-workers' strikes. There's news footage of the police charging the trade unionists, and accounts of the printworkers caught up in the dispute trying to save their jobs, records of a time both

49

frightening and heartbreaking. You might think a trace of that charged situation might still crackle around the streets here, but as I walked about it felt dully inert. By 1988 most of Fleet Street had moved to Docklands and adopted the technology Murdoch had championed, including the *Guardian* and Richard Desmond, erstwhile pornographer turned newspaper magnate. Murdoch's printworks has recently been pulled down, and builders strolled to and from the vast building site, all of that ire and history lost to the restless Docklands tides.

Back in 1981, and a week into Reg Ward's new job he had a life-changing meal with his fellow Docklands bigwigs at the new NatWest Tower, then Britain's tallest building. 'They held the lunch in one of the dining rooms pointing east and so for the first time one saw one's manor.' The sight of those eight and a half miles might have humbled some. Reg was elated. 'I was totally taken aback and I could not help saying "But where's the bloody problem?" It was the most magnificent waterscape you could ever have hoped to see and yet it was seen as a problem.'[4] He quickly moved their office away from the City to the centre of the action, Norman Foster's High Tech former headquarters for the Fred Olsen shipping line, which had been completed in 1970 and were by then standing empty. The serene glazed walls gave a dramatic, panoramic view of the former industrial site, and its super-modern stylings helped point the way to the future rather than the past. Ward's romantic vision meant that much of Docklands built in the 1980s was less a strategic venture than a fantasia conjured from passing fancies. Old men and young pretenders feeling the time was right for dancing in the street.

Postmodernism Parties Like It's 1989

I once demolished a postmodern masterpiece. Marco Polo House was a late-eighties office complex designed loosely in the style of an ancient temple, tucked away beside the ruin of Battersea Power Station. Its facade was a particularly clanging classical reference. Verticals of glossy grey and white cladding – an expensive yet extraordinarily cheap-looking material called Neoparium – stood proud of curtains of black glass, giving the impression of pillars before a shadowed colonnade. The roof's triangular pediment had a circular detail cut into it, similar to the 'Chippendale' motif on Philip Johnson and John Burgee's ostentatious 1984 AT&T building in New York. If that skyscraper had caused a sensation for its crowning anti-modernist detail, Marco Polo House went one cheeky bants further – architect Ian Pollard claimed the hole was simply there as a riff on his building's name, to resemble a Polo mint.

Marco Polo House was home to cutting-edge media companies of the age: satellite broadcaster BSB; the *Observer* newspaper; shopping channel QVC. Compared to the futuristic concrete modernism of my home town of Croydon, this riot of crystalline cartoon classicism broke my head every time I saw it from the train to Victoria. In my first year at Bournemouth Polytechnic in 1990, I created a computer animation inspired by the building and its seemingly computer-rendered walls. In 'Whoops Acropolis' (I know, right?), a suitably postmodern red ball dropped onto the roof and completely demolished the building. Beside all the proto-Pixar works my fellow students were exhibiting, it passed deservedly unremarked. These synthetic buildings had started out as structures of exquisite perfection, their shiny walls and bold Rubik's styling not built to withstand the treacherous realities of the weather or changes in fashion. Unlike its illustrious classical forebears, the poor thing didn't get the chance to make a handsome ruin. Luckily for us, Marco Polo House and much of Docklands from this era has been preserved in the BBC techno-thriller series *Bugs*, a glorious time capsule from the mid-nineties filmed almost exclusively in High Tech and postmodern locations.

It can be hard to respect buildings that have grown up in your lifetime. Memory of the world before makes them feel ephemeral, malleable, inconsequential. And postmodernism's gleeful embrace of those three qualities has not helped its longevity one bit. We are in the early days of considering postmodern buildings as heritage. In 2018 a number of them were listed, including CZWG's China Wharf flats in Docklands, and John Outram's impossibly colourful Judge Business School in Cambridge. But many of the most extraordinary manifestations of this wilful style have either disappeared or are already altered beyond repair.

Back in the late 1970s when a brave few in Britain were experimenting with postmodernist architecture, they found themselves urged on by an influential young cheerleader. Charles Jencks was born in Baltimore, and moved to London in his mid-twenties. He'd studied for his PhD at University College London, where he'd been a pupil of brutalist champion Reyner Banham. Afterwards, he became desperately keen to bury the legacy of Banham's modernist heroes. When the vast 1950s Pruitt-Igoe estate in St. Louis, Missouri, was demolished in 1972, Jencks called it the moment modern architecture died. Bye bye Miss Utopian Pie. He saw his 1977 book *The Language of Post-Modern Architecture* as reading the last rites to a 'moribund modernism which was trying to die', while celebrating a new style
52   that 'broke the taboos which had hemmed in so many designers

trained in the puritan mode of self-denial'.[1] No matter that post-modernism was already being dismissed by critics as 'populist, pseudo-historical, consumer kitsch, pastiche or *Petit Bourgeois*'.[2] In the US, exponents such as Denise Scott Brown and Robert Venturi were shaking up the world of modernist puritanism with their fascination with bad taste and historical juxtapositions. Rebelling against the perceived seriousness of the modern movement, their architecture and outlook felt fun and fresh.

In 1981, Jencks confidently listed *the* six British postmodernists of note: John Outram, whose most famous building would turn out to be a pumping station on the Isle of Dogs; Edward Jones and Jeremy Dixon, who'd set up practice together and designed an unbuilt glass pyramid that was to have been Northampton's County Hall; Piers Gough of CZWG, soon to be architect of several Docklands landmarks; James Gowan, James Stirling's much-underappreciated former partner; and already the most successful of all, Terry Farrell. It seems a strange partial list now, but probably gives some idea how small (and male) Britain's pomo architecture scene was at the time. Jencks contrasted them with a group he called the late modernists – yet more men – such as Michael Hopkins, Norman Foster and Richard Rogers, who were producing forward-looking architecture that would come to be known as High Tech, structures such as the Lloyd's building in London or the Sainsbury Centre art gallery in Norwich. Piers Gough wasn't interested in these new puritans. 'The mistake seems to be to have the same theories all the time,' he said. 'Consistency is a dull bolt-hole.' Instead, he hoped 'the public would enjoy our eclectic zest for building. Because at the bottom, that is what all this back-to-the-past business is about: being liked again, or it damn well should be.'[3] So there we have it, postmodern architecture as Sally Field's Oscar speech.

Postmodernism is synthetic, sometimes sold as authentic, a mash-up of what we have had before, a dressing-up box of pop stylings. This is not necessarily a bad thing; an appreciation of artifice has brought us many great things, not least from Davids Bowie and Hockney. If brutalism's romantic landscape of puddles, rain staining and high-walk edginess was soundtracked by the earnest, doomy post-punk of the Human League or Joy Division, postmodernism had a cheerier accompaniment – Michael Nyman's neo-baroque experiments, perhaps, or air-punching mullet-sporting synth-rock, buildings bright as a keytar, florid as a soft rock solo. *American Psycho* in fibreglass, a landscape fit for Walkmans, ghetto blasters and skateboards. In the UK, much postmodern architecture seemed a style influenced as much by Neville Brody's graphic design for *The Face* and Duran Duran album covers as it was by architectural precedents. A jaunty offshoot of 1950s diner graphics and dressmaking fabrics, as well as the gleaming excesses of 1970s Italian industrial design.

The variations on this pomo dream were manifold. One route went back to the follies of a Capability Brown fantasia: hermitages, pagodas and rustic cottages reimagined for decorative effect, or references taken as much from the geometric topiary of neoclassical country houses as the architecture. Another was seduced by the sleek painted fuselage and porthole windows of the Boeing 747 – garish graphics and all – just as the early modernists had been by the pristine ocean liner. There was a colossal version of postmodernism that revelled in shades of marble and granite last lionised in the Edwardian era: those sickly pinks and greys that would create buildings redolent of the colours of an endoscopy. The Las Vegas school crafted pyramids in red steel and mirror glass, uPVC crystal palaces, fibreglass colosseums; a riot of jolly Early Learning Centre primaries to counteract all that heavy grey brutalism. In Milton Keynes, one of the most extravagantly postmodern towns in the UK, the local centres are decorated with graphic devices of the sort more usually found on 1980s toasters and bread bins.

'Postmodernism is a term redolent of the promise of freedom,' wrote Margaret Thatcher's pet urbanist Alice Coleman in 1986, in a typically Monty Python-esque-sounding essay *Whither Post-Modern Housing*.[4] Her self-consciously fusty writing style accompanied splenetic thoughts on the prevailing architecture of the day. For her, postmodernism 'betokens the fall of the most pretentious and autocratic architectural ideology the world has ever known: the functionalist Modern Movement'. Not that this meant she was in love with this new style either. She saw within it three directions. There was what she called 'new gimmickry' – High Tech architecture using lots of untested new concepts, and so therefore BAD. Then there was 'revivalism', which she might have liked, except they were to her mind championing the wrong sort of revival – 'all assiduously avoid the most highly evolved pre-modern style – the interwar semi'. A third sort, 'community architecture', won her praise. These were architects working with local communities, as in Lea View, Hackney. There, she'd seen 'the disappearance of litter, graffiti, vandalism, and excrement, and a complete cessation of crime'. As her influence rose, she became another nail in modernism's coffin.

Charles Jencks was determined to live the postmodern dream. He and wife Maggie Keswick Jencks hired Terry Farrell, one of many architects to work on their 'thematic house' – a conversion of a Victorian London terraced home into a postmodern extravaganza. The clients had already worked out what they wanted, and Farrell was brought in to realise it. The result was published in *Architectural Design* in 1984. It was quite the theatrical number. There were exuberant additions to the Victorian facade while inside Michael Graves, Piers Gough, Eduardo Paolozzi and others fashioned extraordinary decoration: busts raised on pillars, spiral stairways, stout marble columns in the kitchen, and endless circular and semicircular motifs. Now named the Cosmic House it has been Grade 1 listed and opened as a museum. Jencks was an exacting client, and Farrell's team produced over a thousand drawings. When I interviewed him, Farrell was not entirely convinced by the finished product, and told me: 'I deviated from Charles Jencks because I thought it was all about fashion and I thought there's much more important things – that postmodernism was all about rediscovery of history, of context, public participation, whose taste is it, the everyday.' No one could accuse Jencks's house of being everyday.

It wasn't just architects who were making an impact on our environment with grandiose artistic statements. One of the most daring of all pomo stunts was achieved in a quiet suburb of Oxford. To commemorate the forty-first anniversary of the bombing of Nagasaki, Bill Heine of 2 New High Street, Headington inserted a 7.6-metre fibreglass shark in the roof of his house, as if it had fallen from the heavens onto this suburban street. The surrealist artwork, *Untitled 1986*, by John Buckley, caused local uproar and tabloid delight. Prosaically, Heine hadn't been given planning permission for such an action, and the council decided it was unsafe. But finally, a ruling by the government in 1992 allowed the shark to stay, a permanent memorial that never fails to shock, in what is now one of Britain's most eccentric Airbnbs.

'I was always labelled a Thatcher person,' Terry Farrell explained to me, 'because I wasn't espousing left-wing top down.' When I went to see him, Farrell was about to move out of his celebrated apartment, a converted Spitfire factory near Edgware Road.

56

Instantly recognisable with his shock of white hair and clear-framed specs, he met me at the door, all smiles. Now well into his eighties, Farrell's voice was a little husky, but he was still extremely perky and great company. His home was filled with plywood models of his most famous buildings, while carp swam in antique Chinese bowls and colourful wooden aircraft hung from the rafters. Though he is famously confident and can-do, I was surprised how vexed he was by the obstacles that had fallen in his path along the way. He had spent his earlier career designing housing and rebelling against what he felt to be a council-led desire to stifle individuality. He'd grown up a working-class boy in a council house in Newcastle and had struggled the rest of his life against the effortless superiority of his more privileged Oxbridge peers. 'That fear was always with me that I was over-reaching,' he told me.

Although he'd qualified in the sixties and had formed a partnership with Nicholas Grimshaw ('who was very much one of *them*'), it wasn't until he went it alone in 1979 that he felt he'd made it. Reacting against his clubbable rivals, Farrell told me he took inspiration not from the elitist but the commonplace. 'I found art deco absolutely fascinating because it was universal and it was appealing to everybody, not just a few.' This interest began to flood into his work. 'I was teaching in 79 in the AA [Architectural Association] and I did a project called Learning from Chigwell, which was about what people did with their houses at the lower rungs of the ladder. What plastic lions and pediments they did in their front garden. And what they did in their back garden was sheds and greenhouses and so on.' By 1980 he was bringing these interests to bear on Oakwood, an estate of timber-framed houses in Warrington. 'I made it fun,' he said. 'I did sunburst inserts in the front doors which were none of them the same.' He also did a study predicting what would happen to them within thirty years, the new doors and cladding, the extensions and styling. 'It was a social snob thing but it was also self-expression. Pride in ownership. I was fascinated by expressions of personal taste.'

After splitting with Grimshaw, one of Farrell's first big solo projects featured perhaps his most dramatic postmodern take on art deco. TV-am was a company created to make breakfast television, an innovation in early 1980s Britain where there were only four TV channels, all of which closed down overnight, save for the odd Open University broadcast. Farrell fully embraced the fluffy absurdity of the product – I told him that the TV-am studios reminded me less of, say, BBC Television Centre, and more of a golden-age Hollywood studio. He lit up. 'Well, I was interested in Hollywood of course and Hollywood was a great uplifter of people.' When it opened in 1983, a banker confronted Farrell, complaining how expensive the building had been. Farrell retorted that it had actually been phenomenally cheap. 'And then he thought for a while. And then he said, *yes, your sin is that you made it look expensive.* And I thought that was interesting. Because at that time there was Lloyd's of London, which was all "techno-bits".' There was almost a Victor Meldrew delight as he chewed on these two damnable words. 'External bathrooms and escalators. And it cost four times as much as our building, or more than that, but you registered all the bits were "techno-bits", that it seemingly had an earnestly utilitarian origin. Whereas I had done the non-puritanical thing.' He leant towards me and said with great gravity, 'I had lashed together and fruited up a whole concoction.'

He makes it sound like he found the designs in a fifties minibar and, looking at the result, that may have been so. The front,

Terry Farrell at home, with TV-am egg.

back and insides were all designed to have different personalities, depending on their context. 'I was surrounded by modern architecture that was consistent,' said Farrell, 'and that was seen as a virtue, that the front, the back and sides and the interiors were all the same.' And as far as ornament-as-crime goes, Farrell grinned, guilty as charged. 'I've got one of the eggs there,' he said. I turned round, and by the stairs in his flat stood, on a pedestal, an egg in an eggcup the size of a grizzly bear. How on earth had I missed that? But in Farrell's colourful, exuberant, *Alice in Wonderland* flat it looked quite at home, a giant yellow egg sitting there, looking both regal and utterly absurd.

'I was on holiday in Venice towards the end of the project and I suddenly realised all the skyline of Venice had silhouettes of things on them, so I said the back wall should have eggcups!' And so, in the last weeks of the build phase, his team got to work fashioning these dozen outrageous fibreglass Humpty-Dumptys. 'We did them all in absolutely iconic eggcups and painted the eggs bright yellow. But Peter Jay and Wiltshires [the construction company] refused to pay for the eggs, they thought that was frivolous. So I paid from my own pocket for the eggs, £1,200, £100 per egg, got them made under the arches. Wiltshires put the fixing bolts in and my office staff put the eggs in and bolted them up!' So enamoured was Farrell that when Saatchi's hyper-expensive ad campaign for the channel flopped, and his eggs began to appear on screen instead, he felt he had won a great 1980s prize: architecture as branding. An icon! 'The eggs gradually took over,' he said delightedly. 'It was called Eggcup House. They gave out trophies, little eggcups. They had a big eggcup they opened for raffles. So the eggcups had a real presence. Advertising gold.' Eleven of them remain on the roof. The twelfth – now sitting in his lounge – had been up for sale at Christies. 'I got my secretary to bid for it,' said Terry. 'I told her £2,500 was the limit.

She kept on and on, and she paid £5,500.' Not quite the nest egg he had imagined.

Who owns the space above your head? It's an extraordinary philosophical question. The Land Registry might help with the ground beneath our feet, though often that is a chase through endless shell companies and derivatives, and the world of super-basements is making even that a baffling exercise. But working out who owns the sky is more complex still. Speculators call this 'air rights' – an issue that unsurprisingly evolved in the vertical cities of the US. It's a new way to make money, to sell the unused space above a building, perhaps to a neighbouring developer. The first place this happened in the UK was above Charing Cross station on the north bank of the Thames. The front of the station is an elaborately decorated French renaissance-style hotel opened in 1865, now run by 'Europe's largest four-star hotel brand' Amba. It had suffered the usual run of indignities over the years: the original station roof collapsed in 1905 and the hotel and platforms were heavily bombed in the Second World War. There have also been numerous unrealised plans to relocate the station (perhaps even to the south bank of the Thames), and to build a double-decker road/rail bridge. By the time developers Greycoat were looking to build above the station in the mid-eighties, it was looking pretty shabby.

Terry Farrell won the commission. It was to be a huge job, stitching together various disconnected elements of the city's urban fabric. A walkway in the air, connecting Hungerford foot-bridge with the station concourse. Creating a second entrance to the station platforms. Converting the vaults below into shops and a theatre space. Landscaping neighbouring Villiers Street and the edge of Embankment Gardens. Farrell even recalled changing the direction of the one-way traffic too. And above the platforms floated the money that drove the whole project, in the form of a massive office complex for financial services firm Coopers & Lybrand.

Farrell and his team of fifteen had also been working up plans for a second – even bigger – air rights scheme, Alban Gate, across a dual carriageway in the City of London. Sudden expansion was on the cards. 'I had committed myself to 150 staff and I was in temporary housing, and we were all moving into here . . .' said Farrell, gesturing around the old Spitfire factory. At that moment, both Charing Cross and Alban Gate looked like they might not happen. 'When I was asked to compete for the MI6 site by Regalian I said yes, because I thought that could take up the slack. And then we won that, and then the other two came back!' Suddenly Farrell had three massive London projects on the go simultaneously, projects that would define his reputation in Britain to this day. At TV-am he introduced postmodern complexity to what could have been a simple shed. By contrast, at Embankment Place it was the sheer complexity of the site that helped drive those postmodern flourishes. 'It was unbelievably complicated,' recalled Farrell. A strict price cap meant they were constantly scaling back from initial designs. Even so, 'we deliberately had complexity in mind. It was multilayered. We designed all the Villiers Street buildings in different bricks.' Entrances varied from polished marble to granite. 'We deliberately did things varied. I was very conscious of the small scale and the medium scale, and the big scale from the river. Which was very different from City Hall by Fosters,' he said, referring to the High Tech home to London's mayor beside Tower Bridge, 'which once you've seen it it's complete. It's like a candle,' he said, picking one up from his table and turning it round in his hand. 'It's a complete functional object, and I was opposed to that and I still am. I think complexity and multilayered and extending the boundaries of the project to include pavement and streets . . .' He drifted off, as if the complexity he'd conjured up had suddenly leapt from his hands and was now swirling around the room and out into the universe through the skylight above.

Embankment Place is quite definitely a postmodern building, taking decorative motifs from the history of the site – 1930s wirelesses and moderne ocean liners – yet it's also home to a significant number of High Tech design features. Seen from across the river, the cat's cradle suspension technique that floats this massive building above a pre-existing railway station becomes clear. Just as in a Michael Hopkins structure, say, there's an echo of Victorian engineering, a Brunel element to the design, and appropriately so, as Isambard had built a long since replaced railway bridge here in the mid-1800s. Yet rather than the trademark spindly High Tech crochet of Hopkins, the diagonal buttresses flying inwards at the top of Embankment Place have the feeling of heaving the building into the air, the seemingly chunky masonry a stubborn tug of war team full-out. Instead of High Tech cold steel, we see jauntily striped stone cladding and arched windows. As you walk down Villiers Street, the private–public space created in Embankment Place makes it the friendliest of good neighbours, allowing you to promenade under the colonnade of pillars on a rainy day, or browse in the cafés and shops beneath the old railway arches. And some of it is quite literally Heaven: the 1980s gay mega-club, that mecca for dance music enthusiasts, hi-NRG obsessives and hen nights, sits subversively beneath the ground under this railway terminus and its financial services hub. Opened long before Farrell arrived with his complexity fetish, Heaven is a reminder that redevelopment doesn't always have to scrub away all traces of lives vividly lived. But maybe the arrival of air rights

Embankment Place looming over London Charing Cross station. © Matt Buck

means that they are forced further underground than ever. The current owner of Farrell's air rights building is the Sultan of Brunei, who introduced stoning to death in his country for adulterers and men who had sex with men. The presence of Heaven beneath the building feels more subversive than ever.

It wasn't the only one of Farrell's imperial-phase schemes haunted by the ghosts of gay London. Another venerable venue, the Royal Vauxhall Tavern, would find itself neighbour to the last of Farrell's 1980s mega-schemes. This was to be an office complex built for the government next to Vauxhall Bridge. Vauxhall is a strange, transitional place, once home to London's notorious pleasure gardens, and never far from delicious sin since. It was a place where several different sorts of London collided. The affluence of Pimlico; the bacchanalia of Vauxhall; the industrial decline of Wandsworth; with a Thames view all the way up to the Houses of Parliament. In 1982, when Farrell's association began on the site, a giant brutalist cold-storage unit stood on the south-western side of the bridge, with a wasteland of car parking and industrial sheds leading all the way down to Battersea Power Station. To the south-east was a neglected gap site, beside the fearsome one-way system and a series of Beatles-era riverside offices.

Farrell had been encouraged to enter a design competition for the site by the president of the RIBA. He wasn't keen on architectural competitions, he told me, but in this instance he'd been informed that no one else had entered. 'I said, *that sounds like my kind of competition*!' The developer wanted to build flats on the site, but Lambeth, the local council, weren't keen 'because the housing was all for sale and they realised it brought the wrong kind of voters in', according to Farrell. In the end, the bottom fell out of the residential market and the plan was scrapped. It was then that a government holding company moved in and bought the site instead. The architects were unaware it was on behalf of the British secret service. Just two of his team were vetted and allowed to attend client meetings, where the job was explained to them as if in code. Designing offices for such a picky undeclared client was not easy. The functions of the spaces remained top secret. There was much focus on a single central room in the building, a circus that all others needed access to. The designers kept giving this impor-tant room fantastic views, and their clients kept telling them not to, until finally they admitted what it was for. 'They said, *we'll come clean about that room*,' recalled Farrell. '*It's the shredding room*.' He chuckled away at the memory. With the final twist worthy of a le Carré, it was only when it was finished that Farrell discovered his mysterious client had been MI6. 'In fact it was a news item on CNN,' he said. 'I was in Tokyo and I was flicking around screens in the middle of the night because

I couldn't sleep. And I suddenly saw a picture of the building! And it said, because the KGB was open to the public now the government had decided that they'd own up to MI6 to be in this building.' He mimed surprise. 'And I thought all along it was for the Department of the Environment.'

If Embankment Place is a fully inflated balloon above Charing Cross station, the MI6 building is a sharply featured ziggurat. The resulting flamboyant ostentation recalls the video for Queen's 'Radio Ga Ga' – itself a colourised, postmodern take on Fritz Lang's *Metropolis*. From Vauxhall Bridge you can imagine crowds of Queen fans clapping in sync before it, Mercury prowling on the pinnacle, Brian May's hair rampant on the ramparts. If MI6 had wanted to remain invisible, Terry Farrell was not the architect to have chosen. There is a camp theatricality to these offices, a swagger that doesn't just belie its use as the home of the secret service but laughs deliriously in its face. It's the Gotham of Jack Nicholson's Joker. Like Embankment Place, there are art deco radiogram elements to the form, but here the vertical green elements that make up the central section look like a bundle of circuit boards. And as with all of Farrell's postmodern London buildings, MI6 displays a grand optimism, unafraid to make a colourful and extravagant statement. Also, it's been blown up three times in James Bond films, which is pretty cool by any standards. For many years I used to go clubbing at the Vauxhall Tavern. Most nights I would take a break, to walk along the riverside at 1 or 2 a.m., beside the mysterious bulk of this curious spy HQ. Something about its proudly deviant form and purpose seemed just right for Vauxhall, with its secrets and pleasure gardens.

One of the most famous Terry Farrell buildings in Britain isn't even by him. Quarry House in Leeds looks for all the world like the demented offspring of Embankment Place and MI6. But in fact it was designed by the Building Design Partnership, an endlessly adaptable, faceless architecture company who a generation before had created another sensational one-off: the brutalist landmark of Preston bus station. As at Preston, they had succeeded in nailing the predominant style of the day to maximum effect. Quarry House is insane. A vast drum of a building, it sits on a hill on the eastern edge of the town centre by the inner ring road. Fireworks could go off above it every night, Rapunzels could let down their hair from the top turrets, and princesses could be dodgily kissed awake in the car park, and still it couldn't look any more of a cartoon fairy-tale palace. From the ring road it is an apparition, looming above a landscape of traffic lights and low sheds. It feels entirely out of place, a florid postmodern gesture suited for the waterfront or a more central setting, but sitting here by the ring road it's *The Wizard of Oz* in reverse, the palace transported to Kansas.

'The city tried to do iconic structures along this road,' artist Clifford Stead told me. He'd lived in Leeds for most of his life and was thinking of the first wave of modernist landmarks, structures like John Poulson's International Pool, or the impressive *Yorkshire Post* building. Laconic and wiry, Clifford was full of stories of the neglected corners of the city, a place he'd been exploring and watching change since the inner ring road was constructed in the early 1970s. 'At the end was the ultimate: Quarry Hill.' This was a huge, enclosed council estate, built in the interwar period, the first of its kind in Britain, decades before modernist structures like Park Hill in Sheffield or London's Barbican sprang up. From the back of his dad's car, young Clifford used to admire the 'big concrete cliff' as they sped around the ring road. 'Gradually over time there were less and less lights on. You go past at night and it was a blaze of lights and curtains. About 900 flats in there. It got to a point I can remember,' – he paused for dramatic effect – '*one light* in *one block*, and all the rest was in darkness. At the back they were trying to knock it down – and it took about six years. And bit by bit it disappeared.'

The site stood empty for over a decade, the painful demolition seemingly to have been for nothing: Leeds doing its classic Leeds thing of demolishing the sort of modernist social housing other northern cities were championing and building instead fast roads and corporate structures. What eventually went up in its place was Quarry House, headquarters of the NHS and the Department of Social Security (now the Department for Work and Pensions). It immediately became known as the Kremlin. Clifford dug about in his bag and produced a book of gritty photographs and hyper-real paintings he'd made over the years of Leeds city centre. 'I always put that in my work,' he said, pointing to the Kremlin rendered in psychedelic shades of scarlet and cobalt. 'It's got a Ceauşescu sort of look to it. There's *something* about it.' He'd watched it go up on the long-neglected gap site at Quarry Hill with a mixture of horror and amazement. 'As the thing started to grow everyone was like *what the hell is that*. It was like something that would go up in the Soviet Union. And when this thing went on the top, this massive sort of crown thing, it really did turn heads.' This was all during the 1991 recession at the start of John Major's government, when building everywhere else had stopped. 'In the midst of all that this thing was going up in Leeds. And what was interesting was it was like a carbon copy of Quarry Hill flats in terms of scale, even the shape.'

People's assumption that the Kremlin was designed by Terry Farrell isn't just down to the stylistic similarity to his work. Farrell's company had master-planned the area for the council

The Kremlin – on the site of the pioneering Quarry Hill flats. © Paul Brow

in the late 1980s, before any reconstruction work had begun. 'I can't say that was hugely successful,' was all he had to say on the matter when I asked. Its lasting achievement seems to have been the creation of a straight route from city centre to Quarry Hill, a grand pedestrian boulevard with, it was hoped, equally grand buildings and a park constructed alongside. The Kremlin stood at the apex of this path, surrounded by a forest of complicated cowled lamp posts, like a group of nuns banished from a giant medieval convent. But there's something curious about the Kremlin's positioning on the site. It sits back to front. The impressive colonnaded porch, the extravagant spire, the grand entrance all face the ring road, and so the path to the city centre on the other side leads up to the considerably less dramatic – though still bonkers – back elevation instead. Why? Well, perhaps it wasn't built for the people of Leeds. 'The DSS building was all about coming into Leeds,' was Clifford's theory. 'It's a massive statement.'

69

As you walk down Terry Farrell's boulevard towards the city, on your left you slowly approach what appears to be an Asda, all carelessly pitched rooflines and timid cream brick. But it isn't an Asda. It's one of Britain's finest artistic institutions, the West Yorkshire Playhouse, now Leeds Playhouse, a theatre with a global reputation. Instead of the dramatic vigour you might have expected such a building to project, the 1990 version was the weakest, milkiest cup of tea you'd ever had to drink.* And its misfortune was to sit below the crazed absinthe-dream of the Kremlin, whose deranged potency swept all before it. Here, any defence that it might have attempted – that it was being con-textual, that it was what the postmodernism of the time or the city expected – was entirely undermined by its contemporaneous neighbour. 'West Yorkshire Playhouse looked like it could be an old people's day centre,' said Clifford. He remembered reading an interview with the architects, Ian and Marjorie Appleton, discussing their careful use of brick and pattern, how it would be a landmark for the city. 'And when we saw it I thought, *my God*. How can you get excited about *that*?!' He laughed. 'Imagine if Sydney Opera House had been built in Leeds in the 1980s. I mean, what would we have had? The bridge and water behind, and just this one-storey block in cream brick with a slate roof.'

Two thousand two hundred government staff were to be moved into Quarry House, the new headquarters for the NHS executive and the Benefits Agency, built by construction giant Norwest Holst, who described their project as a 'traditional building with strong civic presence'.[5] But on completion the Kremlin found itself the target of unwanted media attention, and dubbed 'the House of Fun'. The *Daily Mail* stuck the knife in

* A refurbishment in 2019 has seen the addition of a neon sculpture to the facade and a new entrance facing the city centre, giving the whole edifice some much needed oomph.

to the 'luxurious edifice' where 'the mandarins have been provided with atriums, statues and courtyard gardens where water displays provide a "refreshing early-morning mist" giving way to "cascading afternoon streams". In one department they tread on a hand-woven carpet which cost £14,000, while admiring the exotic paintings on the walls.'[6] They disapprovingly listed the swimming pool, bar, gymnasium, sports hall and hairdressing salon as among the perks for this cushy government building. A wave of criticism across the media led Mike Sparham of the National Union of Civil and Public Servants to write to the *Independent* to correct some of the myths that were doing the rounds. 'Families were uprooted, partners had to give up jobs, children had their education disrupted,' he wrote. When they did move into the building they found it still being constructed around them, Norwest Holst's work unfinished.

'It is galling then to find everyone bracketed in the category of "civil servants living a life of luxury". Working conditions in Quarry House are already cramped, and an internal wall collapsed twice while staff were working near by. False fire alarms are a weekly, indeed sometimes daily, occurrence. The water supply is regularly turned off. Facilities in the building are also not the perks they are made out to be. There is a sports complex with many excellent features but staff have to pay the market rate to use them. There is a shuttle service from the station, but it is not just for senior management; rather it was put on because of pressure from the unions after staff had been assaulted in the area around the building.'[7]

Pretty soon, it was this new narrative that had stuck. Three years after these initial skirmishes, the National Audit Office released a highly critical report on Quarry House. There was 9 per cent less space than had been specified, meaning that the

71

roof of the building had to be converted into offices, and both departments were still having to rent rooms elsewhere. And the space that they did have had been so poorly allotted that no allowance had been made for what you might have thought were essentials, such as equipment or corridors. Quarry House had been designed to dance on the grave of boring old post-war functionalism. But sometimes a bit of attention to function doesn't come amiss. Meanwhile, the West Yorkshire Playhouse might have been a total failure as a landmark for the city, but the award-winning productions inside suggested that it was just what the performers needed.

Back in 1981, Irena Bauman had newly qualified as an architect and had returned home to Leeds to work. As we sat in the buzzy office of her architecture practice in a striking new build in a quiet suburban Leeds street, she remembered back when the city centre was '*unbelievable* still. There was only one café, I remember. It was closed after 5:30, the city centre was empty. Then on Sundays it was completely empty because the shops were closed. And it was still black! Because the effort to clean up the soot only started in the mid-eighties. You would not recognise it. People don't remember how it was. The town hall was covered in soot.' She had taken a job as a junior architect working on one of Leeds's many shopping malls, the St Johns Centre. 'It wasn't my cup of tea,' she said. '*At all.* The language was strange, the concern about footage. Everything was numbers. And also I really thought we didn't need another shopping centre.'

In many ways, the fortunes of Leeds in the last forty years feel like a microcosm of England over the period. By which I mean, if you were to follow the stories of Sheffield, say, or Liverpool, you might think that English history since 1980 was a tale of constant turbulent left-wing political revolution, of struggle against right-wing oppressors. But instead, stodgy centrist dad Leeds, with its almost imperceptible swaying between Labour and Tory, seems to more encapsulate the overriding mood of the times, where voters rejected Michael Foot's leftism, say, or Michael Howard's authoritarianism. Instead of the rebel spirit of many northern cities, there is an isolationist exceptionalism to Leeds in its refusal to work with neighbours Bradford, Wakefield or Huddersfield, to insist that it always knows best. And here, waves of service sector jobs – financial, retail, food and drink – have saved the city time and again, even as the gap between rich and poor has widened.

On a train swooshing round the leisurely curve from Headingley into the valley, I could see the result of all this blustering stodge: New Leeds spread out before me, a cluster of fibreglass frontages, medium-rise flats, offices and hotels with bird-wing roofs and facades in terracotta, silver-grey, Wedgwood blue and Horlicks drab. Crumbling red-brick walls defend the cracked concrete of the buddleia belt. These are the remains of David Peace's Red Riding, the dreams and schemes of councillors and businessmen from another time, who razed Victorian factories for post-war structures that have been razed in their turn. In New Leeds, bloated lumps of mega development abut one another, a forest of cheap repetition and jaunty promise. It reminds me of Docklands, endlessly reaching. Irena Bauman had a couple of sayings that summed up architecture in Leeds. One was '*it's blocks and plots*. That all we've done is develop blocks and plots, we didn't have any strategy to tie it all together.' The second is that '*Leeds always takes the last seat on the bus*. So we always start doing what everyone else is finishing doing. And it's really true!' She pointed to recent examples, the arena, built after the 2008 crash, along with a rash of new shopping centres, just as contracting high-street shopping was becoming the trend.

Unlike in many northern cities, the powerful in prosperous Leeds embraced the Thatcher revolution, saw an opportunity to jump on board and make a killing. But this required an about-face. The trappings of competitive municipal modernism to which it had paid lip service were out. And in their place came Victorian Values, something Leeds could wholeheartedly embrace. As an Industrial Revolution city whose heyday was in the nineteenth century, Leeds had been only superficially invested in the post-war modernist project. This return to the values of its distant heyday suited the council and the Civic Trust. Here was renewal of the mill-owners' dreams, the warehouses singing once again, this time with the song of the yuppie, the 1980s version of the Victorian empire builder and industrial magnate. The rich could live where the poor had toiled. And Leeds needed visible symbols of this confident renewal, to shout told-you-so from sturdy balconies, red-brick turrets and extravagantly pitched rooftops.

This Victorian fantasia found reality in a curious offshoot of postmodernism: the Leeds Look. Brian Walker, chairman of the city's development council, denied such a thing existed, but a walk around the city centre disproves that. The first Leeds Look building was a mid-rise office block, Westgate Point, standing at a junction as you enter and leave the centre by one of its many thundering multi-lane highways. Designed in 1987 by David Lyons & Associates, the impulse for a landmark feels right, but something about it has gone horribly wrong. Everything about Westgate Point is ill fitting, like trying to squeeze into a favourite suit two years after giving up the gym. Middle-age spread has affected the silhouette of this lumbering chunk. A tiny pitched roof sits meanly on top of a fat tower, like a paper hat on a bouncer. Titchy windows punctuate its 74 vast midriff like the buttons popping off a waistcoat. Clifford

Stead wasn't impressed. 'We were told we were getting this incredible building. Saw these artists' impressions. It was a cut and paste bit of everything. You name it, chuck it in.' As a late-eighties building boom took hold in the city, more and more Leeds Look buildings began to appear. 'I'd get so upset. When a crane appears abroad it's usually something interesting or quite nice. But here you knew what was coming. You knew as soon as the bulldozers came in it looked like a Barratt house. Eight-storey Barratt house with a slate roof. It would be a case of the little slivers of brick might be cream or they might be blue.' The Leeds Look, and the associated pitched-roof brick buildings that began to spring up around the country in the late eighties and early nineties, symbolised a different side of the Tory boom. If the bright, sometimes shocking postmodernism of Farrell or Quarry House was akin to Thatcher herself, the disruptive force in an electric-blue suit, the Leeds Look was pure John Major. It was the timid bureaucrat pushed centre stage, uncomfortably underdressed for the occasion and with little stagecraft to pull it off.

Nowhere is the Leeds Look exemplified more than across the road from Westgate Point, at the Magistrates Court. You assume it's supposed to be riffing on English vernacular architecture – red-brick cottages, mills and town houses – but there's a distinct whiff of Mitteleuropa here. A Bavarian castle – well, perhaps small hall – made from cheerful red and yellow brick, every facade stacked with awkward additions, cuckoo clock turrets and romantic balconies tacked on at random in case you might for a moment get bored. But like someone trying too hard to be fun on a date, boring is exactly what it is. Because it's exhausting. This chaos of unnecessary additions and fuss creates an ignorable vortex as blank as any system-built facade. Try to follow the sense of those windows, the projections and pitched roofs, the balconies   75

The apotheosis of the Leeds Look – the Magistrates Court. © Michael Taylor

and recesses, and the whole place morphs into an Escher painting before your eyes. Perhaps Leeds Magistrates Court doesn't
really exist. Every effort has been made to make it so. The interior is gleaming white marble. 'You go through the door and
you enter what they really would have liked to have had on the
outside but were too scared,' said Clifford. He remains baffled
by the Leeds Look to this day. 'Lots of the architects didn't like
what they were building. They were building because they were
prescribed a look. They didn't have a choice.'

'I've always been lumbered in London with postmodernism,'
Terry Farrell grumbled as our conversation was drawing to
a close. 'Simon Jenkins said, *but Terry, you've had your turn*.
But I thought, in Newcastle in Hull in Manchester, they don't

think that, but in London they did – and they do.' Because of all those big eighties landmarks, I wondered? After all, in that era it's hard to think of an architect who had a more spectacular effect on the fabric of central London, before the march of those High Tech icons. 'I think they're all handsome buildings. It's not become conservative. It's a funny thing, conservatism. You could look at all the things I did in the eighties as conservative. But they were progressive then. They were tongue in cheek, they were fun. And they still are.'

The vogue for postmodernism was short-lived, and the backlash, when it came, was vicious. 'It all went quiet in 1991,' recalled Farrell. He remembered an evening at the Architecture Club, one of the exclusive and mysterious members' clubs of which barely anyone is aware. 'I faced such hostility from my fellow architects. I remember one question was *what do you think of Walt Disney*. And I thought, that was a very loaded question. And so I said I admired Walt Disney, and the drawing in of the hissing sounds . . . Disney was their touchstone of what was wrong with the world.' And Disney was what they thought Farrell was creating, with his stone-clad castles and fairy-tale embellishments. Yet, it seems to me, they were pointing their fingers to the wrong sorts of movie precedents. Because in his eighties work it's the evocation of the golden age of cinema that he strove for, whether the Busby Berkeley razzle dazzle of Eggcup House or the Fritz Lang potency of MI6 and Embankment House. To the denizens of the Architecture Club, however, postmodernism was seen as a kind of emotive cartoon architecture, too eager to please, too trashy. 'I knew the tide was turning. I remember saying to Maggie' – his wife – '*I think I should look at overseas. It's getting so unpopular here, and apart from anything else there's a recession.* And then the phone rang and it was somebody in Hong Kong.' And within a   77

year he had three major projects there, none of them in his recognisably postmodern London style. He, like the architecture
that followed, was starting all over again.

Town planner David Lock spoke to me with the kind of authority and calm that suggested he knew where all the bodies were buried. Back in 1981 he was working for Terence Conran's urban planning company, designing a regeneration scheme at Greenland Dock in Southwark. He described how Coopers & Lybrand had put little asterisks on a map to denote 'star sites' – parts of Docklands they considered had the highest potential for development. And Greenland Dock was one of these stars. Despite these enticing money-making asterisks, the reality was a population living almost entirely in council housing. 'What we found out was they weren't all poor people,' said David. 'Some of them were very successful business people in their own way. The trouble with that area had been if you'd made it and you wanted to progress you had to move away because there was nowhere to progress into. So part of our concept was to provide the next step or two for the local people who were on a rising fortune ladder. You could stay local but improve their circumstances and living conditions. But we also wanted to attract international investors.'

Getting the place built was tricky, given how slowly the LDDC was moving, so Peter Hadley, the director of the Surrey Docks area, suggested they try something that had been done in Milton Keynes to speed things up: they set up the Greenland Dock Development Company. It meant they could be funded by private investors rather than the government's development corporation. And so they borrowed £18.6 million of private money, on the understanding they would have to hit some strict repayment dates. It was incredibly risky, because it depended on the idea that the market wouldn't slow down, or worse, crash. 'The corporation was severely reprimanded for this technique,' said David, 'and they were instructed to never do it again, because of course they lost control.' But they were lucky: the gamble paid off, and Greenland Dock made £38 million in the boom before the bust. 'We had the first housing development that was done there, by Daniel Homes,' recalled David. 'That was then a huge exposé on the TV because it turned out the houses were so small that they'd made seven-eighth scale furniture for the show house, so that people thought that they could get a wardrobe and chest of drawers and a bed in and all that and so they couldn't.' This sharp practice wasn't limited to Docklands, of course. It would be a scam that developers – and their unfortunate buyers – would be caught out on time and again.

'The reaction of most groups in Docklands is not whether the developments are public or private but whether local people will be able to afford the homes and will have first chance to buy them,' LDDC chief Reg Ward told the *Observer* in 1981. 'We intend to see that they can buy them. People on council housing lists will be given first opportunity.'[1] As part of the Tories' strategy for remodelling Britain, it wasn't just Right to Buy that was tempting council tenants to consider buying rather than renting. New houses and flats were being built by private developers with the express aim of drawing these residents into owning their own home. At first, in hard-to-let Docklands, this was tricky – the developers didn't want to build the new homes, the council tenants didn't want to buy. Yet very soon all that had changed: the housebuilders were cashing in on a Docklands miracle, and buyers would stop at nothing to have their way.

One of the first things the LDDC did was to choose an area as a test bed for their private housing policy. They selected Beckton at the eastern end of the docks. 'We aim to build at least 10,000 homes eventually,' explained Ward in 1981. 'Our initial

600 houses will be on the ground this winter and we hope to accelerate very quickly that figure.'[2] He made it sound effortless. In reality, it was only through a drastic simplification of the planning process – and the promise that they could take all the profit without the LDDC clawing any money back – that the hesitant housebuilders were convinced to take the risk on Beckton. After this initial speed bump had been overcome, housing minister John Stanley was thrilled by the subsequent speed of the operation, and what that meant for his government's wider plans for home ownership. 'The private building industry is coming through in an enormous way,' he said, glossing over the desperate tactics of the LDDC. 'Clearly there is an opportunity to bring a very large increase in owner occupation.'[3] When Michael Heseltine opened the first phase of the Beckton scheme in February 1982, protesters booed and barracked him. 'We cannot even afford to pay our rents, let alone £19,000 for a one bedroom flat here,' said Lillian Hopes, secretary of the Newham Council tenants' federation. 'I think it's disgraceful that Mr Heseltine has the cheek to show his face in Newham, especially to open these rabbit hutches.' Hezza's day went from bad to worse when he was pelted in the face with eggs in Southall. He blamed 'the wild forces of the left'.[4]

To keep Reg Ward's original promise, local residents had been given first option to buy these new homes. They were offered them at discounts of anywhere up to a third off. The emergence of a housing boom in Docklands drew bigger fish, and not a few sharks. Property speculators could taste blood. Very soon they overwhelmed the LDDC's ability to police their own scheme. Developers had to check the buyers against the electoral roll, see their council rent books and cross-check with rival sales teams across Docklands to try to stop themselves being scammed. Such was the scramble for cut-price homes in this promising boom town that there was even a growing black market in rent books, like some Ealing Comedy with Alec Guinness and Alastair Sim swindling working-class residents out of their new homes. And, of course, rich profiteers found a way. Entire blocks of flats were sold not to local residents but to single buyers at knock-down prices. Speculators didn't mind breaking a few rules when they could make an instant £20,000 profit per flat by selling them on. Bob Colenutt of the Docklands Consultative Committee was scathing about the record of the LDDC when it came to looking after the existing population. 'Instead of balance, regeneration has created division,' he said. 'Massive amounts of public funds have subsidized the speculators. It is immoral, period.'[5]

There were rich pickings for the developers who'd moved in on the area. Beside the ever-present hoardings of Ideal Homes, Barratt, Wimpey, Wates, Costain and Laing came some for companies on their last legs – Comben and Broseley Estates – as well as newcomers such as Regalian Homes. The main problem these builders found were not age-old issues of land shortage, planning permission or lack of buyers. It was finding and keeping skilled labour. 'Before the tiresome business of completing a site hoves in view, the building workers are off to the next job,' journalist John Brennan recorded. 'It is an understandable way of ensuring continuity of employment from their point of view, but it is also an exasperating aspect of Docklands' development that has persuaded various builders to advertise for teams of builders from the north of England to help rebuild London's East End.'[6] This in some ways mirrors how police from the south had been bussed northwards to help put down the miners' strike two years earlier. The resulting deprivation this caused there, compared to the booming affluence these northern builders created in the south, was a bleak exchange indeed.

Show homes at a Wimpey development on the Isle of Dogs, built in 1987.
© Robert Clayton

The most expensive places you could buy in Docklands weren't new builds but converted warehouses beside the river. Gun Wharf, a listed former tea and spice warehouse next to Wapping station, became Barratt's flagship: seventy-three flats, from small studios to extravagant penthouses with views to Tower Bridge, roof terraces, garden rooms and his-and-hers whirlpool baths. I took a walk round the area in 2019 and sat in a nearby pub overlooking the river while two old men at the next table effed and jeffed about joggers, posh coffee and the old days, a reminder of how many different Docklands still exist, cheek by jowl, entirely discrete. The white working-class Docklands of the ages; the poor Bangladeshi Docklands of the 1970s and 80s; the manicured Docklands of the rich incomers.

In the mid-1920s the London County Council built low-rise blocks in Wapping to replace notoriously insanitary slums that had once stood there. Now they share the same streets with the converted warehouses. Although the development corporation aimed to transfer the locals from these LCC blocks into the new houses and flats they were building, many remained behind, alongside new waves of immigrants to the area. It was in these blocks and the 1960s slabs nearby that many of them had weathered the changes. The brick of the old warehouses had long since been scrubbed clean, their functions changed utterly. And now, despite their original chains, ironwork rails and planking, it is not the Victorian structures that hold the history of the area. It is the twentieth-century buildings, the interwar and post-war flats, that continue to house the spirit and memory of place. Rather than being the destroyer of worlds and the tabula rasa of nightmarish dystopian visions, here modernity has acted not as disruptor but as conservationist. Meanwhile, the 1980s and 90s flats and houses in Docklands don't revive the original spirit of place, no matter the application of faux-Victorian decoration or notions of philanthropy. They are the workers' cottages of compliance officers and actuaries. A new city has not replaced the older, poorer one, but exists like a theatrical curtain before it, pushing to the front, wrapping and rebranding the streets and waterside. These Docklands exist simultaneously, two cities inextricably interwoven and yet entirely separate.

3: The Chatsworth, the Queensborough, the York

A Warm Welcome from the Housebuilders

Professor Deborah Sugg Ryan was showing me a photograph on her phone. It was from the late 1970s, the golden tinge giving the image a nostalgic, familiar tone. 'So you can see it's like a close,' she explained. 'The executive homes were in the top corner, and I think there were four. You were quite posh if you lived in one of those – although we weren't posh at all!' The eminent house history expert from the BBC's *A House Through Time* was showing me one of modern Britain's most significant domestic institutions: the Barratt home. Deborah was twelve in 1977, when they moved into the modern Barratt house in Hedge End, a village rapidly turning into a sprawling suburb. 'The kitchen was at the front, and in some ways not dissimilar to their previous (former) corporation house in Stevenage,' which was where they had just moved from. 'And my parents had inherited this taste for things quite modern from my maternal grandparents. We had an Ercol pine dining room suite – a bit rustic. My dad had upholstered the chairs in turquoise vinyl. And I think we had an orange feature wall, and white built-in units all down one wall. Avocado bathroom suite, because we bought that house from new so we chose everything. It was that very late-seventies version of modern. My parents had made it.' We kept going back to the photo. 'There were groups of the executive homes – they're the semis, and then the detached executive homes. We were detached! *Proper* executive. Four bedrooms – although the fourth bedroom was min-*ute*. We had a fish tank in the hall.'

Her parents had met on an RAF base and in the early days of the 1970s her father became an electrical engineer for IBM. House moves followed throughout the decade: to the Cotswolds;

Deborah Sugg Ryan with her sister outside their Barratt home in 1979.
© Deborah Sugg Ryan

to the groovy new town of Stevenage; and then to what she called 'the Barratt dream home' near Southampton. 'And they caught that early-seventies mad inflationary boom. They trebled their money! No one had ever owned a home in my dad's family, and in my mum's family really interestingly my grandmother's sister bought a house and all the family chipped in. So it was a really big deal becoming home owners.' With all of this moving about, it was easy to see where a young Deborah would have got her fascination with house history from. 'I just don't think that kind of social mobility would happen now,' she said. 'I think it was a moment when it could happen.' The rapid rise of Deborah Sugg Ryan's family through the 1970s tells us a lot, not just about class, changing lifestyles and social mobility, but also about the prehistory of the Barratt homes before their 1980s and 90s heyday.

The company had begun in the mid-1950s, when a young Newcastle accountant, Lawrie Barratt, realised it would halve the cost of buying a house if he built it himself. And so he dug the foundations and fixed the concrete, like one of those ill-advised folk on *Grand Designs* who decide they are going to project manage while working a full-time job. By 1979 Barratt had become the UK's number one housebuilder, knocking out 10,000 homes a year for the first time. Their annual report for 1980 reads like the provisional wing of the Tory party: 'Around 80% of British families would like to own their own homes. Only 56% actually do so. Potentially Britain needs 200,000 new private houses every year. But for the last decade this demand has never been met. The need is still there and Barratt are doing more than any other company in the country to meet it, currently building and selling over 11,000 houses a year – 11% of all new private houses in the nation.'[1] A 1980 ad for Barratt from the *Observer* tells the home buyer what they might expect. 'Barratt, Britain's major house-builder, offers the largest choice of top-value houses, bungalows and flats, from £11,000 to £100,000. You can buy Barratt for as little as £16 per week. Barratt have over 350 developments throughout Britain and every Barratt home comes complete with a mortgage.'[2] The mortgage would be no more than two and a half times the applicant's annual salary, 'with some societies making an allowance for a wife's earnings'. It was a point picked up by Deborah Sugg Ryan. 'Once we had the equal pay act and women could be signatories on mortgages that's when prices start going up, and the norm starts to be two salaries not one.' The increase in home buying became inextricably linked to the rise of women's employment, a form of interdependence that would have the unplanned effect of encouraging women's independence too.

Lawrie Barratt had a helipad installed in the grounds of his home, enabling him to visit two building sites a day to check on progress and generally shit everyone up. Actor Patrick Allen   87 stood in for him in a series of television commercials, jumping down from a white helicopter to make thunderously feel-good statements about the ease and simplicity of it all. At one point they had a promotional parachute troop: a photograph shows a team of five, including a couple of men with Magnum PI taches and a woman in an avocado boiler suit. As their marketing got more pervasive, there was a branded bus (you could even buy a Corgi toy of it) and sponsored racing cars. Barratt's speciality became a type of house designed to tempt first-time buyers onto the property ladder – the starter home. 'When Barratt came on the scene with their marketing techniques, Wimpey just said that's a complete waste of money,' said David Penton, director of Barratt's old rival.[3] 'I'm always amazed at the way Lawrie Barratt has persuaded the rest of us that we are in a marketing business rather than a building business,' said Tom Baron, founder of another, Whelmar Homes. 'He alone convinced the industry that it had to be market-orientated.'[4] Barratt sold the idea that a new home could be cheap, exciting, easy and fun, not an enormous burden but a fashion accessory for an aspirational lifestyle. Then there were people like Moira and Trevor – interviewed for *Signs of the Times*, a BBC series on taste from 1992 – who bought a show house and kept all of the furniture and fittings, and spent their entire time marvelling at the good taste in china busts of Mozart and dried flowers they had inherited.

Peter and Jill Elliott bought their first house on the Goldsworth Park Estate in Woking, built by New Ideal Homes, one of Barratt's biggest competitors. 'I'm not sure they had got the phrase "starter home" in 1981,' Peter said. 'But it was obviously designed for people like us. The people to the right got married half an hour after us.' Kindly, cheery and white-bearded, Peter had the photo albums out as we talked. How had he and Jill ended up there? 'The main reason we bought it was because we couldn't get a mortgage for anything else. 1980–81 mortgages were in short supply. There was some sort of government scheme where if you saved up regularly for a year, say, they would double your savings, so we started doing that. Went to the Halifax, and they said *Oh no, there's a waiting list*. And we had looked at a couple of houses in the older bits of Woking, and one of the agents said *They're building all these houses on Goldsworth Park. And new houses come with mortgages, go and have a look at that.* And I remember we were not keen on something that was effectively a cardboard box, but realism was such . . .'

From the pictures he was right, it was barely more than a box, quite the contrast to Deborah's executive Barratt home. To keep prices down, Ideal didn't provide fripperies such as heating, and so the day after their honeymoon they moved in and had radiators installed – the only real choice as the house didn't have a chimney. There was an avocado bathroom suite, which, unlike Deborah, they hadn't chosen. 'We didn't have any choice at all. You didn't get anything. I think we got a plant, a begonia. No carpets, no heating, no curtains, no baton across the windows to put the curtain rail into.' The reality was made harder to grasp thanks to some sneaky tricks by the developer. 'We went and looked at the show house,' said Peter. 'It was the same design, except it was a mirror image. And we later realised that they had put in, shall we say, smaller than average furniture. I remember doing an awful lot of fiddling about with graph paper and cut-out furniture to work out how we could fit things into the rooms. I'm not sure at what stage it dawned on us that the show house was a bit optimistic . . .'

A 1982 document Ideal Homes produced for local authorities – 'Working in Partnership' – is a startling insight into the thinking of housebuilders of the day. 'We can help authorities to increase home ownership in their areas by enabling them to   89 offer homes for sale at no financial risk to the authority,' went the blurb. 'These could be lower cost or general purpose houses, homes especially designed for the disabled or elderly persons bungalows or flats.' They were selling their services based on what the government was pushing for. Their homes 'could be offered to nominated purchasers thereby relieving the burden on council housing and putting tenants and other families on the home ownership ladder'.[5] It had initially been exciting for Peter and Jill waiting for the house to be finished. 'We used to go around more or less every Sunday,' said Peter, 'just to see if they had got any further with it, and towards the end with our noses against the glass to see if anything had happened inside. In the end we couldn't see any progress so we ended up effectively badgering the sales office and said *We're getting married next week, can we get the keys*!' Ideal were planning to build 4,500 homes for the estate. 'It grew from the edges in,' he recalled. 'There were a few roads that had already been set out without buildings on them, just so you could get about on the park. I remember going for a walk one weekend and thinking, there used to be fields here.' There were few social facilities on the estate, and in this rapidly growing commuter town there wasn't much to do in the centre either. 'It used to be that Woking was good for trains to London – if you wanted to stand – supermarkets and car parks,' said Peter wryly. Local band The Jam's splenetic 1982 single 'Town Called Malice' is thought to be a portrait of Woking. Jill and Peter lived there until 1985, before moving away to St Albans. 'We didn't really feel we had put down much in the way of roots.' The first wave of starter-home buyers heading off for their next adventure.

Before Barratt, buyers generally had to find a solicitor, a mortgage and to buy all of the white goods for their new homes. In Woking, Jill and Peter had help with the first part, but still moved into a bare box. Barratt was different. 'We translated all that into virtually one-stop shopping,' explained Lawrie Barratt in 1997. 'We took account of everything and put it into a single financial outgoing. We looked at what people earned, worked out a multiple of three times their income – or three and a half times of whatever [back in 1980 it was two and a half times] – and from that we could work out what people could afford to buy. Then we worked backwards to how many square feet of house we could afford to build. We wrapped the whole thing up into a package and that gave people a certainty about what their house was going to cost them.'[6] Housing no longer a human right but a product like any other. Economies of scale – building the same few house designs over and over – allowed housebuilders like Barratt to make a killing, while the dazzled buyers were left with a huge mortgage and a snagging list as long as your arm.

The influence of architects on mass housing diminished throughout the 1980s, thanks to the developer-builder and their in-house teams of marketing-led designers. By 1988 it was estimated that fewer than five in every hundred homes had been designed by an architect, a dramatic fall from the municipal estates and new towns of the post-war period, where the great architects of the day had cut their teeth with varying degrees of success. Roger Humber, chair of the Home Builders Federation – an organisation funded by developers – was breezily unbothered. 'It is impossible to calculate how many architects had a hand in the design of a house, and it doesn't really matter,' he told the *Daily Telegraph* in 1988. 'What matters is the amount of research that goes into the product. He who draws up the plan is not working in a vacuum; he has to get feedback from the builder on what he can construct for the money, comments from the sales people on what the consumer wants, study what the opposition is doing and find out what the local authority will allow. Few architects have the skills on their own to meet the needs of the modern housing market; they simply are part of a team dealing with such diverse things as estate layout, landscaping and building materials.'[7] Those eighties buzzwords – consumer, product, market – feel so small and superficial when set against those community-sized ones from the grand plans of the post-war era – overspill, neighbourhood, zone.

The familiar housebuilder estates of the 1980s and 90s are recognisably different from their municipal forefathers. They rejected their major influences. Back then, post-war planners had been terrified of the effect of the car, and so pedestrianised zones with car parking set away from the homes became all the rage, based on a go-ahead 1930s town in New Jersey called Radburn. Then there was Le Corbusier's much admired 'city in the park', siting blocks of modernist towers in large green multifunctional plots. Another big influence had been the garden city movement, which aimed to combine the best of the town with the best of the country. Between the 1940s and 1960s a series of new towns born out of this movement were planned and built across Britain, from Craigavon to Peterborough, Irvine to Crawley. By the conservation-minded 1970s there was a backlash against these machine-age ideas, the international connotations of modernism rejected in favour of a more home-grown heritage style, and by the 1980s the welfare-state-era communalism of municipal estates and new towns was being turned over to privacy and private ownership. Perhaps the most famous manifestation of this was to be found in a new-build estate in Merseyside: Brookside Close. Launched on 2 November 1982, the first night of new TV station Channel 4, *Brookside* was a soap opera set in a cul-de-sac of houses built as part of a bigger estate by Broseley Homes. Created by Phil Redmond of *Grange Hill* fame, *Brookside* started slowly, the houses becoming occupied over time rather than all at once, to reflect the lonely nature of moving to a new build. It began as a slice-of-life drama meant to reflect the reality of those new estates that the media had completely ignored. But over the years the soap became more daringly controversial and eventually pretty unbelievable, before coming to a messy end in 2003 with a lynching. Carroll Properties bought the thirteen derelict shells at auction in 2013, and to turn them into actual homes had to have basic utilities like gas connected to the close.

The developers of these estates took inspiration from an influential book produced in the heartland of what would become Thatcher's Britain: Essex. *A Design Guide for Residential Areas* – known more commonly as the *Essex Design Guide* – was produced by the county's planners in 1973. It aimed to steer private developers to ditch any lingering modernist pretensions, which the guide accused of creating places that were 'depressingly characterless and "subtopian" . . . ignorant of the local vernacular tradition'.[8] Instead, they wanted housebuilders to embrace 'the unique building character of the county and to re-establish local identity'. Homes proposed in the guide should 'generally employ external materials which are sympathetic in colour and texture to the vernacular range of Essex materials' to fit within the picturesque qualities of an existing area.[9] Accompanying photos showed these to be aged brick of red, creamy gault and yellow stock, alongside houses clad with white render or black-and-white boarding, with Welsh slate or clay tile roofs. Their rules suggested returning to pitched roofs and away from flat ones, with architectural detailing and the size and placement of windows to match those of nearby buildings. Essex planners wanted to see 'architectural detailing being used to reinforce the character required by the design and its location'.[10] On the surface they shared the municipal housebuilders' commitment to

93

building homes to the standards of Parker Morris, whose 1962 government report *Homes for Today and Tomorrow* focused on creating decent liveable space in new local authority houses. Yet the *Essex Design Guide* was written not for council-house builders, but for private developers building houses for sale. And so they anticipated houses would be smaller than those that Parker Morris standards would allow, with room to extend as necessary.

In 1976, three years after the *Essex Design Guide* was published, the ambitious New Town project was abandoned with the last and biggest, Milton Keynes, just off the drawing board. Gone were ideas of building satellite towns and freeing up space in cities. The guide captures that moment of change, suggesting there were just two sorts of areas to be built: either rural – placing buildings in a landscape – or urban – requiring landscaping within a built-up area. A third possibility – suburbia – was entirely absent. Developers were encouraged to build the maximum number of homes possible on a site by building upwards, over garages, and losing the familiar sprawling grass verges and green spaces used to divide homes from the street – and each other – since the turn of the twentieth century. The *Essex Design Guide* called these tightly clustered picturesque plans an 'informal arcadia'.[11] 'The whole question of design is wrongly being regarded as a matter of opinion, or taste,' went the guide. 'Only an architect proficient in Urban Design can provide the subtle degree of refinement which can turn the principles into places that delight the eye.'[12] And never afraid to employ the caps lock, the guide criticised buildings that were 'too loosely grouped or of insufficient height to enclose space. THIS IS THE FIRST AND MOST IMPORTANT REASON FOR THE VISUAL FAILURE OF RECENT HOUSING DEVELOPMENT,' they shouted.[13] Instead, 'IN THE URBAN SITUATION INDIVIDUAL BUILDINGS SHOULD BE DESIGNED

94

TO FORM ARCHITECTURALLY COHESIVE GROUPS TO GIVE ADEQUATE VISUAL INTEREST AND A UNIQUE IDENTITY TO EACH PARTICULAR SPACE.'[14] How harmonious.

There was also a desire for more privacy than modern estates afforded. Out went those large modernist windows, so easy to stare into. In came cunningly sited back gardens that were not overlooked. 'Seclusion is vital to arcadia, and designing for privacy will also reduce to a minimum the "public zone" which will virtually become the area of the roads and footpaths,' went the report.[15] The roads remaining would be short curving streets leading to enclosed spaces. Farewell mid-century ideals with straight rows of houses separated by asphalt and garage blocks. Douglas Jennings-Smith, Essex's county planner, concluded that the book would show 'a practical way how, without increasing overall costs, developers will be able to give house owners better value for their money'.[16] These were private estates for private people.

The first garden city had been leafy Letchworth, the first postwar new town streamlined Stevenage. The *Essex Design Guide*'s prodigy was the small and indigestibly named town of South Woodham Ferrers, by 2019 housing approximately half that of Letchworth and a fifth of Stevenage's population. Here the developers' take on postmodern runs riot, if by riot you mean eating a biscuit while wearing a small hat. At South Woodham Ferrers there's a fine balance between grabbing your attention while desperately hoping not to challenge or offend. And in that effort they have created somewhere as relentlessly perky, brisk and blank as a daytime TV studio or the Oxo family's lifestyle. South Woodham Ferrers and the *Essex Design Guide* that inspired it is the concentrated squash that would be diluted to a weak lemon drink by housebuilders across the UK in the decades that followed.

What the authors of the *Essex Design Guide* might have wished for – subtle architect-designed homes of local flavour – is not necessarily what they got. And instead of rejecting suburbia, it became the very model of a whole new wave of it. House-builders took the basic details of the guide – the cul-de-sacs, the heritage-inspired pitched-roofed houses – and offered a corporate version, much as a supermarket might offer produce nominally labelled 'farmers' market'. As architects were sidelined from the business of designing these houses, they began to cause a fuss. 'Houses are increasingly a commodity to be traded,' said Maxwell Hutchinson, president of the RIBA, in 1990. 'Judgments on their appearance, efficiency and comfort are secondary to their potential second-hand value. We are not proud to own good design in this country.'[17] Developers, so good at making all the right noises, made all the right noises. 'The RIBA have felt, and they have been right, that the quality of design is not good enough,' blarneyed Roger Wilson, chief architect at Wimpey. 'We discussed who was to blame and how to prevent it.'[18] The increasing conservatism of developer houses was put down to a need to rush blandly uncontroversial design through planning. Even the speed of their construction was alarming. As The Housemartins sang on 'Build', their poignant 1987 single about these new estates, the speed of work makes you sick.

Roger Wilson of Wimpey Homes spoke to Penny Guest of the *Independent* in 1990 to talk through the issues that led to developer housing ending up as it had. He put much of it down to the research done by his sales and marketing departments, which decided what sorts of houses from Wimpey's stock designs might sell in a particular area, from starter homes to luxury estates. The arrival of CAD – computer aided design – had been as transformational for housebuilders as it was for architects, and had no doubt taken the lessons of the *Essex Design Guide* even further from their roots. At Wimpey, house designs could be saved to disc and sent to their eleven regional offices, where a bit of fiddling could be done to, say, choose appropriate materials. Or not. 'We are merely servants of the company,' Wilson said, a veritable Uriah Heep. 'We must produce that which they say they need. We tailor the job to suit the finances available, houses produced on a restricted budget at a price that people can afford. Unlike private practice, we never meet the client. You must realise that they are only a number to us, we rely heavily on what our marketing department tells us people want.'[19] Which is 'we can't be bothered' as a corporate slogan. And looking ahead to the 1990s, what people were telling those marketing departments was changing fast. Lifestyle 2000, a research project by Crest Homes in 1989, predicted that 'studies, dens and family rooms' would replace the 'old kitchen, lounge and diner concept'.[20] Open plan was becoming the modern householder's dream.

As home ownership began to increase once more in the late 1990s, so did claims of shoddy workmanship. Complaints to the National House Building Council rose from 889 cases in 1989 to 4,732 cases in 1998, with the biggest number levelled against major players Barratt, Laing, McAlpine, Persimmon and Westbury. New-home horror stories have been a mainstay of local and national newspapers for decades. Take the tale of Val and Richard Hockey, who paid £300,000 in the mid-nineties for a new house in Wingrave, Buckinghamshire, put up by a small developer. They told *The Times* that 'the stairs were not attached to the house, water came through the kitchen ceiling from the shower, and the chimney caught fire'.[21] On top of that, the developer went bust, at which point the Hockeys discovered the entire structure of their house was unsound. Damage was estimated to cost £60,000–100,000 to put right. They were offered £1,000 for remedial work.

These days you can find terrible tales of new builds on rival Facebook groups such as the Barratt Homes Victims Group, Taylor Wimpey – Unhappy Customers and DO NOT BUY a Persimmon Home. In June 2019, one of the largest, concerning Persimmon, with some 14,000 members, found themselves victim to a particularly dystopian twist. By then Britain's most profitable housebuilders, Persimmon hadn't achieved that position easily, and weren't about to relinquish it thanks to some naysayers on social media. Members awoke to discover that Persimmon had been granted administration rights to the group, had changed the name to Persimmon Homes and Customer Services, and had blocked them from commenting in their own group. Who needs Russian troll farms when Persimmon's marketing department is around?

It wasn't just houses that all these developers were building, of course. I chatted with Leigh Bird, who moved into a one-person flat in Hull, a design strongly influenced by those of market leaders Barratt and Wimpey. She'd been living in a rented flat above a greengrocer's ('vile' was her word for it) and then shared with a mate for a while, until that friend got hitched. 'I thought right, I'm gonna buy,' said Leigh. 'I had a decent job, so I moved home for about eight months, even a year, to save up for a deposit.' This was in 1988, when the property market was booming in places that hadn't been monstered by high unemployment. 'Hull was going through a little renaissance at the time,' she remembered. 'Some of the areas were being redeveloped so lots of lovely apartments and flats were popping up.' And so she started looking, and saw one she thought she could afford in an advert in the *Hull Daily Mail*. 'It was relatively cheap compared with the lifestyley places in town. It was pretty basic and it was affordable, which meant I still had quite a bit of disposable income.

98 I was single and I worked a lot, but when I played I liked to

play. So having disposable income was great!' Her parents had been the only members of their respective families to own their own homes and they encouraged Leigh to make the leap. 'I was being quite bullish about it with my parents in terms of *this is me, I want to do this*. And really it was shit, frankly! I saw an advert in the paper and the whole buying process was done with I think one site visit where they were being constructed and I don't think I saw a flat with the finish inside it or anything. And it was done with telephone calls with Pauline in the office – I'm sure she was called Pauline – and information posted out to me. I don't remember a glossy brochure but I remember photocopied architect's drawings and plans and side elevations and that kind of thing and that was about the face of it.'

It was built by Hogarth Construction, a local family-owned company, rather than a large developer, though the homes they were building were as fashionably bland as any by the larger firms. 'I remember a friend of a friend, called Jacko, he was a builder, and he'd actually worked on the flat,' Leigh told me. 'I found out when I put a deposit down. He went, *that's a mistake, you don't want to be buying that place. I helped build it, it's shit!* So we had one of those conversations! This is gross, but then I'm a Hull girl so there you go: he said, *someone's probably taken a shit under your floor*, that kind of thing . . . He said, *don't jump up and down over the door joists cos they won't be that safe*. I just had the view that I've done it now, I've bought it, you're just telling me scare stories Jacko. Off you go.'

Leigh's flat was built in the no-frills housebuilder style of the day: red brick, dark brown wooden window frames, pitched roof. The raciest detail was a single course of bricks upended all the way round at chest height, like a thin strip of ribbon stretched around a large cardboard box. 'It was all a bit low rent really compared to how things are these days with lovely shiny show houses and that kind of thing,' said Leigh. Inside, it was as plain as out. 'I think I got a choice of carpet colour but I think it was the most basic skanky carpet that you can have, there's no pile and no underlay under it, and there was chipboard floor underneath. Where it had not been nailed down properly you got a ridge in it where they joined up chipboard. The kitchen was all a bit pap. And I got a choice of bathroom colour. It was quite small but I'm a bit of a slattern so it was great because I didn't have much to clean.' It might not have been groundbreaking design, but Leigh remembers the residents got along and looked out for one another, with the exception of her downstairs neighbours, 'a succession of shaggers, basically. I could always hear them having sex in the bedroom below me, which was *marvellous*.' Leigh could sound pretty harsh on the old flat, but she did appreciate what she'd had. 'I'm glad I had it, as a young person I felt good about myself I guess, because I felt responsible and independent and I could do what I wanted to it.' As a young single woman buying her own place in the late 1980s, she was part of a whole wave of people living their lives in new ways, outside of traditional nuclear families.

Developers jumped on the trend for single-person flats in the early eighties. Barratt showcased their version, Studio Solos, at the Ideal Home Exhibition in 1981. Aimed at ambitious twenty-to twenty-five-year-olds, it's as if Soft Cell's anthem 'Bedsitter' of the same year – a bittersweet tale of young people living a lifestyle of night-time clubbing and daytime regret and anticipation – was stitched into the very fabric of the flats. Barratt advertised their Studio Solos as 'Britain's first fully furnished, fully fitted, fully decorated mortgageable one-person home'.[22] For the money you'd get a fitted kitchen, with a washing machine, tumble dryer, cooker, fridge, kitchen furniture, as well as a pull-down bed, dining table fixed to the wall, chairs, curtains and carpets.

After one day of national advertising in 1981, an astonishing 25,000 people called or wrote to the company expressing interest. Wimpey followed close behind with their version, the Super Single, and suddenly the young person micro-flat had become a phenomenon. Never one to miss a trick, Barratt followed up with a version designed for young couples, called the Studio 2. They initially built 500 of these flats around the country and all of them were sold within a week. By February 1982, a block of Wimpey Super Singles faced a block of Barratt Studio Solos across the street in Beckton, the first part of London Docklands to be redeveloped. These days, that would be a dating show format.

A year after launching their Studio Solos, Barratt brought another innovation to the Ideal Home Exhibition, this time at the other end of the domestic spectrum. To mark Information Technology Year 1982 (of course it was), they demonstrated a home office designed for their executive houses. Here, business people could beat the Reggie Perrin hell of commuting by staying home and working in their jim-jams, an experience that would become all too familiar to many of us thirty-eight years later. It featured, in the words of a report of the day, 'a microcomputer, word processor, facsimile transmitter (for sending and receiving copies of documents by phone), and a Prestel Unit. This last to be used to book hotel rooms and hire cars and for shopping by phone as well as calling up pages of business information.'[23] Basically, the full beige *Tron*.

Combining new technology with heritage-influenced designs, these developers' homes were a philosophical conundrum. There is more than a little of the TV-in-wooden-doored-cabinet or half-timbered Morris Traveller to these houses. The homes might have adopted pastiche historical motifs, but in Barratt's case their rise had embraced the latest prefabrication techniques. By the early eighties, more than 40 per cent of Barratt's homes were built using pre-assembled timber frames. It took an episode of Granada's investigative programme *World in Action* in June 1983 to shake the developer. On site, the reporters claimed, the timber frame was poorly clad and became susceptible to damp. Shares in the once unstoppable company took a beating. 'To say we are bitter is the understatement of the year,' said Bob James, Barratt's finance director. 'Spitting blood would be a better way of describing our feelings.'[24] A second *World in Action* programme showing how the people who had bought Barratt starter homes were losing money did them no favours either. And so Barratt made a change. Timber frames were dropped, and while first-time buyers accounted for 45 per cent of their business in 1986, within a decade that figure had fallen by 70 per cent.

Work on the sites, with the repetitive designs and construction techniques, could be monotonous. Lynne Strutt, who has worked for over thirty years in housing, started out in 1982 cleaning newly built Wimpey homes. She kept a diary, which gives a fascinating – and sometimes appalling – glimpse into site life for a woman in the era of *Auf Wiedersehen, Pet*.

Tuesday August 3rd 1982

I was shown what to do by a girl my age called Karen (who was hoping the man who came for the interview yesterday wouldn't get the job as she didn't think she could tell a man what to do! He however, is thinking of suing for sex discrimination!) We scrubbed floors in one house which was supposed to be handed over last Friday. We had to hang around waiting for plumbers and joiners to finish. It's a very sexist atmosphere. The men whistle and make comments from afar – they're ok to talk to. It was very boring and time went slowly.

Entries over the next few days concentrate on the grimness of the task: on Wednesday, 'another dusty filthy day at work'. And by the Friday, 'I feel like I'm already suffering from inhaling too much dust into my lungs. I'm wondering about giving up this job on health grounds. If I suffer from bronchial trouble in the future I shall sue Wimpey for not providing me with a mask.' A month later and her contract was up. Her final entry a typical instalment: 'Suffered a bit of sexual harassment – whilst looking down a drain one bloke grabbed me from behind and pretended to push me in.'

In 1985, as land values crept up, Barratt launched their 'Premier Collection' – larger detached houses with up to six bedrooms, often in gated communities. There were fifty of these vaguely heritage styles available, featuring fake half-timbering, arts-and-crafty tile hanging or classical columns, on display at four show 'villages' in Bracknell, Birmingham, Glasgow and Manchester. Gone was any vestige of those *Essex Design Guide* principles of local materials and character. Barrattland was where a mix and match of historical styles met value engineering, a Frankenbethan mishmash of Victorian conservatories tacked on to half-timbered houses, with Georgian front doors and pediments. They came with a pick-and-mix of details pilfered from old pattern books – sundials, weather vanes, hipped gables – anything a bit posh and not too tricky to mass produce.

In the eighties, my mum bought a large ornament for our front room that reminds me of these conflicting styles: a hollow alabaster-style statuette of a classical lady standing on a large ornate cylindrical base of gold plastic, with matching fancy circular roof above her. Clear wires ran from roof to base, surrounding the figure, and when you switched it on (reader, it was electric powered) it lit up and oil droplets ran down the 103 wires, creating the effect of slow-moving rain. She knew it was ridiculous, and named it The Tat Lamp because it was a camp load of old tat. That didn't mean we didn't enjoy it. So it was with the endless heritage-style affectations tacked on to executive Barratt homes. It was ostentatious bad taste nonsense, but sometimes enjoyably, absurdly so. As fake rusticated as any number of ornamental tankards shaped as country cottages and windmills. A Monty Python animation of Empire-era grotesque rendered in brick and stone.

In his riotous illustrated book *Pseudo-Georgian London*, artist Pablo Bronstein expands on his love of the most successful and most stripped back of all of these developer styles. 'My interest lies in the haphazard, cheap, desperate architecture of the everyday,' he says.[25] The attractiveness of pseudo-Georgian for developers over other pastiche historical styles was its flexibility, with no need of extravagant bay windows or sprawling suburban layout that you might expect in neo-Victorian or Tudorbethan. 'What the Georgian model permits the pseudo-Georgian developer is to construct in small units which allude to single family occupancy,' writes Bronstein. 'Stylistically content with a flat façade and a simple front door, the pseudo-Georgian can squeeze into any available space.'[26]

Katrina Navickas's family moved into an executive home in Rochdale in 1988, a house with brand new leaded windows and half timbering, as well as a garage. Built by Alfred McAlpine, the north-eastern subsidiary of lumbering construction giant Sir Robert McAlpine, their house type was called the Juniper II. Katrina's dad still lives there and had dug out the paperwork that came with it, and so we sat on her mid-century sofa in South London staring at a booklet whose contents evoked the 1980s more strongly than a waft of Obsession, Shake n' Vac and Body Shop dewberry soap: it was a list of McAlpine house types.

The Beechwood.

The Chatsworth.

The Fensham.

The Farnham.

The Gloucester.

The Hamilton.

The Juniper.

The Kenilworth.

The Ludlow.

The Montrose.

The Queensborough.

The York.

Katrina and I read them aloud and afterwards sat there in awed silence, as if this incantation might conjure a very particular form of the eighties back to life, the spirit of shoulder pads, big hair and bat-winged jumpers emerging through dry ice. It reminded me strongly of the new builds satirised in a number of novels. In David Lodge's *Nice Work* from 1988, Marjorie Wilcox is besotted with the en-suite in her new house, so much so that her husband reflects that if a perfume called *En-Suite* was launched she would wear it. In Fay Weldon's 1983 novel *The Life and Loves of a She-Devil*, Ruth lives in a brand new house in a suburb called Eden Grove, which the soon to be she-devil announces is initially clean of resonance. In an equally fantastical tale of haunted suburban women, Hilary Mantel's 2005   105 novel *Beyond Black* follows a medium, Alison, pursued by spirit guides into a new house on a new estate. All three novels are funny and savage, while Weldon and Mantel's are also casually supernatural, showing how these clean new domestic settings are soon polluted by their owners' ghosts and dark magic. Nothing remains new for long.

The brochure for Katrina's dad's house was a thing of exquisite social engineering. 'These don't feel northern,' she said, staring at the houses. 'It looks like Surrey.' Which, funnily enough, was where Sir Robert McAlpine's head office was based. Equally, it could have been Essex. In the brochure, two women with Lady Di hair and boxy check dresses stared out, sirens luring us back to the future. *Come inside*, they seemed to be saying. *We can make you southern too*. In 1988 Barratt supersized their executive premier formula, launching the California Collection, a selection of US ranch-style houses called things like the Pasadena. For the occasion, the Stars and Stripes was raised over the show estate in Milton Keynes, reflecting the fashionable conspicuous consumption of people aspiring to an upscale American lifestyle. The size of houses tells us something about the spread of social mobility. Rebecca Tunstall of the University of York has carried out some fascinating research into this and shown that those who owned the most space in 1981 were the people who ended up with the biggest growth of space a decade later. They were either buying yet bigger homes or extending what they already had. In the 1970s the best-off 10 per cent of households lived in three times the space of the worst-off tenth of the population. By 2001 that figure had increased 3.7 times.[27] Of course, extending your home was anathema to Lawrie Barratt. He called it 'a waste of money. When it's too small, it's time to call it a day and move on.'[28]

As time wore on, two VIP residents would come to embody Barratt's premier dream. 'Thatchers buy premier collection retirement home,' ran a *Guardian* headline, somewhat over-optimistically, in August 1985. Margaret and Denis Thatcher had bought a Barratt new build in Hambledon Place, beside Dulwich Park in South London. Seamus Milne, the reporter, pointed out that the Prime Minister had knighted her friend Lawrie Barratt in 1982, and that Barratt had given £10,000 to the Tory party in 1984. With its red-brick facade, classical pediments and rusticated quoins, the faux-Georgian frippery looked like the set of *To the Manor Born*, though its stunted proportions, neighbours a stone's throw away and the busy suburban road at the bottom of the drive were a constant reminder that this was no crumbling country pile. Even so, it's a massive house, especially for two. 'The couple swept in after police with sniffer dogs had scoured the entire area,' ran the report. 'They looked round two houses and were "very impressed" according to Mr David Pretty, managing director of Barratt Central London.'[29] One of the attractions seemed to be the security of this new build in its gated surroundings: there was even a panic button to activate floodlights in the garden. But the dream did not last. It was not the swift drive through the suburban streets of South London to Downing Street they had been promised. The Thatchers put their Hambledon Place home up for sale in June 1991, a year after Margaret had been ousted as Prime Minister: they had only spent six nights there in six years. The lucky new buyers of their Dulwich house could be reassured that all of Margaret's hand-picked furnishings would remain, including Italian floor tiles, German kitchen equipment and the ubiquitous heavy chintz both Barratt and Thatcher so boldly embodied.

From the days of the *Essex Design Guide* and South Woodham Ferrers through to the thousands of developers' houses built on fields on the edge of towns across Britain, on land formerly owned by the Ministry of Defence, the Water 107

Board or British Rail, most of these estates are still standing in one form or another. They might be slightly out of scale, getting smaller as the cars in the drive have got bigger, and they might have issues with lack of light through tiny windows, the smallest room sizes in Europe and a complete lack of storage space, but the pattern-book housing of the big developers is still being built around our towns today. If success is measured purely as a transaction, and then only catalogued by the winners, the shareholders and the lucky ones who bought and sold at the right time, then success they have been. Some of the resulting homes are curious follies and delightful eccentricities, while others are monstrously oversized in tiny plots, or shrunken Wendy houses unfit for purpose.

Recessions were the nemeses of private housebuilders like Barratt and Taylor Wimpey, and booms tended to turn quickly to bust. After the recession of 1980–81, the number of private houses built per year grew from 115,000 in 1981 to 200,000 seven years later. With that, average house prices rose around 12 per cent each year between 1983 and 1987, before jumping an astonishing 30 per cent in late 1988, thanks in large part to the ending of double mortgage interest tax relief. By the middle of the following year they had crashed, and recession lasted for the next decade. The number of houses built per year fell 30 per cent between 1988 and 1992, and the mortgage rate peaked at 15.4 per cent in March 1990. In the 1970s recessions, it was the housebuilders who went bust; in the 1990s, banks stepped in to help building companies – and instead it was home owners who shouldered the debt. Thousands of people found their expensive new build worth less than they had bought it for – the trap of negative equity – and thousands of homes were repossessed.

Repossession was the flipside to that Barratt marketing formula
that made private home ownership seem achievable for all in a

way that it never had before, all of that security giving way to insecurity.

Two years after moving into the Barratt dream home, Deborah Sugg Ryan's parents split up, her dad running off with his nineteen-year-old secretary (eventually buying another Barratt home on a mock-Georgian executive estate 'where all the IBM executives lived'). Her mother took the kids to another, smaller new house nearby. 'She, in a fit of snobbery, didn't want to live on the estate any more, but the father of a school friend was a builder and had built a small development of two-bedroom terraced houses.' For them, the love affair with Barratt was over.

Carla Picardi moved to London from New York City in 1985. She remembered a culture war that played out at innumerable dinner parties she attended. 'They'd say, *so what are you doing in London?* And I'd say, *I'm working on the concept of Canary Wharf.* And, as if I said I molested children, people would snap. I don't think I could have gotten a worse reaction . . .' She trailed off. Carla was one of the original team members on the development of Canary Wharf, and later Associate Director of Design and Construction. 'At that point people would start yelling at me. *You Americans think you can get people to move there, you have no idea what London is like, people are not going to the East End, who do you think you are?* It was a hated project and the people involved were considered villains. We were continually told it could not be done! If we had bought into that concept, we would never have built Canary Wharf.'

The war was going on long before Picardi arrived in London, and wasn't confined to Canary Wharf. 'They are stark raving mad to think I am going to let property men rip off London by putting up Centre Points and £180,000 penthouses all over the docks,' said Bob Mellish, combative Labour MP for Bermondsey when the soul of the development corporation was still to play for.[1] Back in the 1980s, London was still haunted by the Centre Point scandal. A concrete office tower completed in 1966, it had not been occupied for ten years because its Machiavellian developer, Harry Hyams, wanted to squeeze the maximum possible rents out of the eventual tenants. This was the climate into which property developer Peter Palumbo sought in 1963 to build what would have been pioneering modernist architect 110 Ludwig Mies van der Rohe's only tower in Britain, at Mansion

House in the City of London. It was a project that would be dragged down by inertia, savaged by Prince Charles, attacked by heritage campaigners and ridiculed in the press. Twenty-two years later, this lost scheme of the modernist age, now quite out of step with a new reality, would be finally pronounced dead.

In 1985, the same year that Mies's tower was finally defeated, a trio of new Docklands buildings were approved at Canary Wharf, each three times the height of that unbuilt landmark. In stark contrast to the widely publicised dreams of Mies, no one seemed to have a clue what these buildings would be like. With Chancellor Nigel Lawson ripping up the rules of financial regulation, there was no time to think about mere form. Aesthetics, like lunch, was for wimps. Rather, where would the fibre-optic cabling go, the satellite dishes and microwave transmitters? These buildings needed to accommodate huge trading floors, with storeys tall enough to house all the cabling above and below that was beginning to make modern banking run smoothly. City property agent Peter Oswald explained: 'The need is for watertight, multi-storey, clear-spanning, regular shaped factories capable of multi-occupation,' he said. 'Most important of all they need speed of design and construction and maximum internal flexibility.'[2] These breezy demands would trigger a war between the Mies-killing London establishment in the City and the new flexible private finance entrepreneurs of Docklands.

Architectural critic Martin Pawley observed dispassionately that 'in the new demanding world of global finance, buildings are like technical instruments like computers, cars and video screens. The sense of bewilderment and outrage that the Canary Wharf project has generated is future shock – and London will have to come to terms with it if it really wants to keep its place in world banking.'[3] Realisation of this would, like the resulting buildings, cast a long shadow. Panic gripped the Royal Fine Art Commission, who supposedly had final say over the impact on the London skyline of buildings like these, but who suddenly found themselves entirely bypassed. They turned to Kenneth Baker, then minister at the Department of the Environment, but as one of this new breed of pinstriped free marketeers he wasn't much fussed about launching a public inquiry into this money-making wheeze. Modernist architect Stephen Gardiner called the scheme emerging at Canary Wharf the 'biggest architectural disaster ever to threaten London'.[4] Pushed through so fast, it had the feeling of a well-organised coup.

Nigel Lawson's 1986 Big Bang – the deregulation of London's financial markets – created a boom in the sector and increased demand for modern office space. Carla Picardi painted a vivid picture of the earliest days of Canary Wharf. Then twenty-nine years old, single and ready for an international challenge, she left her job as a vice president and director at Citibank and moved to London. 'Then I heard about these guys at the 47 Park Street Hotel who were working on this crazy idea that was ruffling feathers, creating *Manhattan on the Thames* and calling the project Canary Wharf.' She picked up the phone and said '*Hi, my name is Carla Picardi. You don't know me but I think you need me because I know what the US corporate client wants. And they said, Great! Come on in! We need all the help we can get!*' She was the eighth person to join the team and the only woman at that point. The group was led by Kentucky real estate entrepreneur G. Ware Travelstead and Long Island banker Michael von Clemm, who had hit the big time by financing the Roux brothers' London restaurants in the 1960s. It had been Von Clemm's visit to the abandoned warehouses of Canary Wharf in the early 1980s, in search of a place for a
112   food processing plant for his restaurants, that had triggered his

interest in the site. What he saw was a much bigger opportunity, a landscape that reminded him of the regenerated warehouse flats and offices of post-industrial Boston. Canary Wharf might just be the perfect base for financial services companies who were looking for a home in Thatcher and Reagan's brave new world, companies like Credit Suisse and Morgan Stanley. Ware and Michael von Clemm went down to look at those wharf buildings said Carla recalling the story of that famous visit. 'Michael von Clemm said, *Where the hell are people going to get lunch? Where are they going to eat? How are they going to get to work?* That was supposedly when they looked at each other and said *Let's create Manhattan on the Thames*. Ware Travelstead was a big booming guy. If you knew Ware, every other word was the f . . . word. There's a lot of things you could say about Ware. He could be a charmer and a real son-of-a-bitch. On the other hand, it took that kind of personality to create and sell the concept of Canary Wharf.'

The gulf between the Brits in the LDDC and the North Americans out to build Canary Wharf was wide. The LDDC had certainly not envisaged a project of the scale and density of what was being planned. 'We needed their support to get things off the ground as well,' said Picardi. 'Although Canary Wharf eventually became the paradigm of what the LDDC understood they needed to *demand* from every other developer, in the early 1980s there were several incompatible buildings created! There were numerous discussions between our team and the LDDC about the quality we envisaged on Canary Wharf and its supporting infrastructure, in conjunction with the inconsistency of their permitting someone to design a little shed here and there, or simply renovate an old wharf building. These small solutions would defeat the whole purpose of the big vision.' The Isle of Dogs Enterprise Zone didn't know what was about to hit it. 113

Terry Farrell's warehouse conversion, Limehouse Studios, was immediately earmarked for demolition to make way for Canary Wharf. 'If you're going to appoint Terry Farrell, think outside of the box . . . and *that* was the point. At that time it was difficult for anyone to imagine that there could be *amazing* buildings on the Isle of Dogs. It wasn't until Canary Wharf with their Design Guidelines, Master Plan and Master Building Agreement demonstrated the requirement for a *critical mass* that the LDDC truly thought about the enormous potential to make the East End of London like the West End, with parks, formal squares, gardens and tree-lined streets!'

Terry Farrell well remembered the absurdity of it all when they had been building Limehouse Studios just five years before. 'The LDDC had refused to sign off the lease because we had built the rooftop housing for the plant a metre too tall,' he told me. 'I had a real problem on my hands, because they needed the lease to get the finance. And then it all went quiet.' The next thing he knew, Ware Travelstead was poking about the site. 'And he then turned round and said *I want to build the tallest building on this site* . . . Far from it being a metre too high, it was the tallest building in Europe!' All the thinking got big, and fast. One of the major issues for any developer thinking of creating something as large as Canary Wharf was around infrastructure promised by the LDDC, chiefly the Docklands Light Railway. Initially, the light railway only ran between Tower Bridge and the Isle of Dogs, which meant it connected to neither the heart of the City of London nor Canary Wharf. A private member's bill was hurriedly rushed through parliament to extend the line to Bank and across the Isle of Dogs, and to increase its capacity. 'It had to be a ten-minute ride from Bank to Canary Wharf because every potential tenant said, *more than ten minutes and 114 we are not going,*' recalled Carla.

The driverless trains of the DLR remain little time capsules of 1980s design. Travelling on the DLR in 2019, there was still a sense of excitement. It still feels slightly temporary; the fibreglass bulkheads and enamelled fittings have none of the sturdiness of, say, a train carriage or Tube train. Instead, the DLR's mobile modules feel light as bubble cars, with the chipped and dulled patina of aged kitchen utensils. Before they came along, transport was generally a bit of a nightmare here. 'You take a taxi down there,' recalled Carla, 'and the driver would say, *I don't want to go there*, and you had to beg them! *I'll pay you double on the meter, please don't leave me!* We had no way to get back, there were no taxis on the Isle of Dogs, no one would come to get you.' For London cabbies, it was literally off the map: the docks did not form part of the Knowledge.

Just as all this exciting building work was getting going, the fluttering effects of chaos theory began to swirl around Canary Wharf. On Friday 16 October 1987, a hurricane hit southern England. Among many of the unexpected consequences of this unlikely event was that trading on the UK stock market was paused that day. It would have unexpected consequences in an already febrile global economy. By the time the stock market opened on the following Monday, the hurricane – combined with various other destabilising world events – had begun an economic crash. Hong Kong's stock market fell by 45.5 per cent, and the other major players followed suit throughout the day. This was Black Monday. For those big finance companies for whom Canary Wharf was designed, this looked like a catastrophe. More localised turbulence hit the project on the ground too. Carla Picardi recalled going to a special dinner in the painted hall at the Royal Naval College with the planners from Greenwich – over the Thames from the Isle of Dogs. They had climbed the hill in Greenwich Park before dinner to 115 stand on the Greenwich Meridian Line and admire the view that was about to be altered forever. 'They looked at us with pleading eyes that said, *how can you do this*! I said when Inigo Jones created the Queen's House I'm sure people stood up here and were very concerned about that building ruining the view across to the Isle of Dogs from here,' she explained. 'And a hundred years later when Christopher Wren did the Royal Naval College people were outraged that his building would flank the Queen's House. And I do hope that 200 years from now people will stand here and be upset because some other building will ruin the view of Canary Wharf. That's life! And we can't be frozen in time. London has been frozen in time for too long.'

Not all progressives agreed. Richard Rogers, then becoming one of Britain's most successful architects, had strong words to say about the Docklands that was being created. 'Many of the buildings, be they modern or post-modern, reflect only too well the victory of money and short-term ideals over vision,' he said. 'We have to face that behind *all* architecture there are economic and political constraints – but behind *them* should be questions of ethics.'[5] These were sentiments shared by former wharf-side worker and local councillor Ted Johns. Known locally as 'President Ted', he had spent years campaigning against the commercialisation of Docklands. Challenging these huge corporate developments was no easy task. He told the *Guardian*, 'we were in the impossible position of coming home from work, having our tea and then chasing off to a meeting with people who had worked on their proposals for perhaps two years.'[6] Community activism could feel hopeless, and Ted did bleak very well. 'We are at the bottom of a well,' he said. 'Big developers are pissing on us from the top, and it is become a flood. But what they do not realize is that we will float to the top.'[7] Optimism had never sounded so unappealing.

Opposition manifested itself in many forms. In July 1986, Travelstead organised a symbolic launch for Canary Wharf on site. He invited 200 bankers from across the world, along with Robin Leigh-Pemberton, chairman of the Bank of England, who was to turn the first sod of earth. Protests had already begun in earnest. Two months prior, local opposition activists had marched to Canary Wharf with an empty coffin and held a mock funeral to mourn the death of their community. But on the day of Travelstead's grand launch, an even more spectacular demonstration was planned. A lorry filled with a herd of sheep and three beehives had been driven into a shed on site the night before. During the event, as the bankers sat by the marquee, a group of protesters on cranes above the site unveiled banners emblazoned with the slogan *Kill the Canary. Save the Island*. Sheep and bees were quickly driven to the marquee. The sheep were shooed towards the seated bankers, creating chaos. 'All of a

Protests against Canary Wharf, 1986. © Mike Seaborne

sudden there's all these sheep going through the chairs,' recalled Peter Wade, who had masterminded the protest, 'and about half a dozen sheep flew over to the podium 'cos they saw all the flowers and start eating all the flowers . . . and Leigh-Pemberton started laughing, he couldn't stop hisself.'[8] Not to be outdone, the beekeeper placed a hive on the spot where the ground was to be dug, and then promptly kicked it over. 'All these hundreds of thousands of bees just went out,' said Wade, 'and me included were stung.'[9] It sounds more like the finale of a *Police Academy* film than a political protest. 'The Americans couldn't understand it at all, they were horrified,' recalled Reg Ward.[10]

'You can imagine all of these angry East Enders,' said Carla, 'and you can understand it! The land values there were so depressed. Nobody wanted to go to the East End. We came in, we negotiated with every ma and pa business . . . almost all of them got *ten times* the value of their land! Now, let's face it, if you have something that's worth £25,000 and you get £250,000 in 1985–6, that's a lot of money. Afterwards many people said *oh, my land was worth much more and they screwed me*. But think about it, without Canary Wharf happening, would their land have been worth that much more? *No!*'

Residents weren't only up in arms about the financial implications. Many were having a tough time just existing in the midst of all this construction work. Back in the mid-eighties Liz Day had been a resident in a sixties block called Alice Shepherd House, facing an old Thames-side pumping station that was being rebuilt. 'I was quite good friends with a couple of the guys from the pumping station because one of them built a fence for me,' said Liz, 'just came over and built it once. And there was a time when someone dropped a can of black gloss paint out of the top of the thing and that landed on the roof of my car, and they came over and cleaned the car with me.

So we knew guys in the pumping station quite well in a way.'
What they were building was not going to be any bog-standard
piece of engineering. Postmodern architect John Outram had
designed the building as an extraordinary decorative Egypti-
anate structure. 'I have to say that I remember being showed
the plans for it by Ted Johns, and everyone was just laughing at
it!' said Liz. 'Because of the look of it.'

Even when you know what to expect, walking around the
Isle of Dogs Pumping Station is a shock. Here was a building
that could have just been a blank shed, but instead it's a bold

Stargate postmodernism courtesy of John Outram. © Jason Sayer

bit of Egyptian art deco. A huge turbine – the Eye of Horus as jet engine – sits at the centre of the gable, observing all. Colourful pillars styled as cogs and sprockets stand on either side of this all-seeing eye, a steampunk Hoover Building. Outram called it 'a temple for summer storms'.[11] The barn roof is held up with further chunky, graphic sprockets along the facade. Placed beside the raw concrete of Alice Shepherd House and the churning river, this colourful intervention is a jaw-dropper. It is the sci-fi Egyptian of *The Mummy* or *Stargate*, of aliens-built-the-pyramids conspiracy theories, of the all-seeing Freemasons eye. I could well imagine residents laughing at it back in the early eighties. But I'm also sure that months of deep pile-driving later there were few laughs to be had. 'Things fell off the walls, you know?' said Liz. 'It was extraordinarily noisy, so you couldn't have the windows open. It was a very hot summer. It was just awful. All these insects came out of the building, apparently they're called brick beetles.' My God, I thought, it really was *The Mummy*. 'It was the pile-driving and the shaking of the building, so you had them all over the place. So it was very difficult.'

For all of Liz's mild manner, she finally snapped during the building works for the pumping station. And that's when she got creative. A hoarding had gone up, and they had been given permission to decorate it. 'And so what I did was design the poster, you see,' she said, and she passed me a scroll from the ancient 1980s. I unrolled the bold image, a circular design, red on white, a parody of the LDDC's aspirational graphics, with the words *Let's distress and destroy the community* written across them. 'And so we copied it and we just plastered it all the way along the hoarding.' She described a party atmosphere as residents pasted up these posters all over the LDDC's hoard-120 ings. Midway through they received a visit from the police. 'We explained that we had permission to put these up,' said Liz. And so, remarkably, they were left alone to finish their highly visible street protest.

Liz and her neighbours were not the only residents to show their disapproval of all that was happening. In the 1980s, graffiti, such as the six-foot-high lettering spelling out *LDDC are bloody thieves* on a riverside hoarding in Rotherhithe, could be found all over Docklands. Residents had put up with intense disturbance from vast construction sites, an influx of rich new neighbours snapping up flats in the fancy warehouse conversions along the waterfront, and now there was the looming threat of redevelopment of Canary Wharf on a scale no one could quite envisage. But then something no one had foreseen happened. Buccaneering sweary Ware Travelstead went bust. Time ticked on for his partners to sign the paperwork for the Master Building Agreement with government for the enormous commitment to undertake Canary Wharf. 'Morgan Stanley and Credit Suisse realised, *we're investment banks*,' recalled Carla Picardi. '*We are not developers! We don't want to sign an agreement like this. We need office buildings!*' The whole thing looked as if it was on the verge of unravelling.

What happened next is, according to Michael Heseltine, not widely known. 'This is where Margaret becomes critical in the story – revealingly indicative of the real Thatcher rather than the theoretical Thatcher,' he said. 'Far from just sort of non-intervening, she picked up the phone to Paul Reichmann, who was the boss of Olympia & York, a huge Canadian company developing some huge New York facility, and the conversation was quite simple. *Mr Reichmann, this is the British Prime Minister. You are the only man in the world with the money and the vision to exploit the opportunities that we have here in London.* Paul said, *Oh Prime Minister, I'm very flattered.* What else could he say? And he turned to six of his senior executives one by one and in private and said *I've had this Prime Minister on the phone, she's got some idea. I want you to go to London, don't tell anybody, just case the joint. Tell me what you think.* Five of them came back and said *Paul, don't touch it.* One of them came back and said *Paul, I think it's worth a visit.* Paul made the visit on a Friday and he signed the documents on the Monday. And that,' Heseltine said with his trademark challenging stare, 'was the non-interventionalist Thatcher.' On 17 July 1987, Olympia & York took control of Canary Wharf. And once again it became a ghost town.

4: The Prince and the Paupers

Fantasy vs Reality in the 1980s and 90s

In Stephen King's 1986 novel *It*, the children of a small town are terrorised by a shape-shifting fear, which takes on whatever form would frighten each of them the most. Most memorably It manifests as Pennywise, a sinister clown hiding in the drains. To architects and planners working in Britain through much of the 1980s and 90s It would have had a different face. It would have taken the form of Prince Charles. He became the newspaper columnist's fear of siding with progressive ideas; the planners' fear of local backlash; the architect's fear of being a hate figure, or worse, of not being a hate figure; the conservationist's fear of change; the progressive's fear of backsliding. 'I do not expect everyone to agree with my opinions,' said Charles in his book *A Vision of Britain*, published in 1989.[1] But he did expect to be heard: to have public speeches on architecture reported in the national press; to make a BBC TV documentary, a book and an exhibition at the Victoria and Albert Museum; to create a school of architecture; to launch a magazine; even to build a small suburb in Dorset. It didn't matter if you agreed or disagreed, for a couple of decades his opinions on architecture were the ones you always heard first and loudest.

Charles wasn't always the go-to aristo for opinions about our built environment. For decades, Prince Philip was your standard royal for opening high-tech labs and daringly engineered bridges. He had a genuine enthusiasm for them, and acted as a tastemaker in the heady post-war days of major construction projects and innovative architecture. His eldest son, who trod the line between young fogey and ascetic crank, was rather less enthusiastic. But it was at a 1984 gala dinner at Hampton Court to celebrate the 150th anniversary of the RIBA that he finally broke free of his duties as an agreeable handshaker and nodder. He was there to give an award to Charles Correa, who'd spent his life working on low-cost housing in India. Instead, he ditched his pre-prepared speech and read one he'd penned away from the constraints of protocol. 'For far too long, it seems to me, some planners and architects have consistently ignored the feelings and wishes of ordinary people in this country,' he told the packed assembly of planners and architects, as well as the media.

'Perhaps when you think about it, it is hardly surprising as architects tend to have been trained to design buildings from scratch, to tear down and rebuild. . . . Instead of designing an extension to the elegant façade of the National Gallery, which complements it and continues the concept of columns and domes, it looks as if we may be presented with a kind of vast municipal fire station, complete with the sort of tower that contains a siren. I would understand better this type of high-tech approach if you demolished the whole of Trafalgar Square and started again with a single architect responsible for the entire layout. But what is proposed is like a monstrous carbuncle on the face of a much-loved friend. . . . Why cannot we have those curves and arches that express feeling in design? What is wrong with them? Why is everything straight, unbending, only at right angles and functional?'[2]

His speech drew gasps from the audience, the very people he was rubbishing. An RIBA spokesman told the *Daily Telegraph* 'it was an extremely interesting speech which is bound to be discussed in the profession'.[3] No shit. 'I was a bit surprised when Prince Charles started because we were there to honour a very distinguished Indian architect,' said RIBA president Michael Manser crossly.[4] Newspaper editors, loving a public scrap, pounced on this most entertaining of prejudices and commissioned endless reports and features. Later, Charles said he was 'interested and heartened to see the overwhelming degree of editorial support throughout the media for many of the views I expressed,' playing the wide-eyed ingénue for all he was worth.[5] A furious Peter Ahrends, whose complex High Tech design for the National Gallery extension was the 'monstrous carbuncle' of Charles's speech, said 'his comments about modern architecture in general show his reactionary position'.[6] Later, Charles would claim mildly that his comment was 'meant merely as a personal observation'.[7] He would contradict himself in the same publication. 'I would just like to emphasise that my particular interest in architecture and the environment is not a result of my trying to find something to fill my day.'[8] Not comfortable with playing the amateur, Charles would go on to churn out endless florid criticism of the post-war welfare state world, a place that just didn't match up to his idea of British life and landscape. His target was 'the sheer unadulterated ugliness and mediocrity of public and commercial buildings, and of housing estates, not to mention the dreariness and heartlessness of so much urban planning'.[9] Timothy Cantell, vice chairman of campaigning organisation Save Britain's Heritage, was thrilled by his RIBA speech. 'Millions of people feel that too much of the old has been needlessly destroyed,' he said, 'and too much of the new is needlessly tasteless,' he continued, tastelessly. The prince found himself deluged with mail, almost entirely in agreement with his views. Charles hadn't confined himself to offending Peter Ahrends. There was Mies van der Rohe's long-proposed Mansion House tower: 'a tragedy if the character and skyline of our capital city were to be further ruined by yet another glass stump better suited to downtown Chicago than the City of London.'[10] Peter Palumbo, the developer, was clear Charles's intervention torpedoed his long-held scheme. 'I think he was the one who was responsible, really, for the defeat of Mies's project.'[11]

By complete coincidence, three months after the speech the minister of the environment, Patrick Jenkin, turned down Peter Ahrends's design for the National Gallery extension. Of Charles's comments, he said 'it would have been quite wrong to have taken any account of them', as if talking to camera in *House of Cards*.[12] And so a competition was rapidly held to replace Ahrends's modernism with something that the prince wouldn't be horrid about. It was an interesting moment for Charles's intervention, because the architecture scene of the day thought it was already addressing the issues he'd raised, with postmodernism over-indexing on an abundance of historical references and High Tech summoning the ghost of Victorian engineering. Ahrends's design had beaten a version by Richard Rogers, which had suggested ways of linking Trafalgar Square with nearby Leicester Square through some cunning back street pedestrianisation and offered a viewing tower too. To clear things up, the National Gallery carried out some helpful polling that suggested Rogers's version was both the most and least popular entry.

The saga of Prince Charles and the National Gallery extension reminds me of Alfred Hitchcock's exploration of obsessive love, *Vertigo*. For one, there's the art gallery at the centre of it, and an infatuation with a historical reference – in the case of *Vertigo*, a nineteenth-century painting of tragic Carlotta Valdes. Then there's the scene where James Stewart's obsessive character orders a flustered personal shopper to bring in another rail of skirt suits in an effort to dress Kim Novak as she had once looked when he first met her at the gallery; in London, six new shortlisted schemes were hurriedly wheeled out in an attempt to satisfy the haunted prince. They included a curiously restrained

126

number from pomo pranksters CZWG, sober classicism from US firm I.M. Pei with the air of an expensive double-breasted suit, Jeremy Dixon's angular skirt, and easily the most daringly postmodernist of the lot, a frock to shock from James Stirling, more Grace Jones than Kim Novak.

Stirling's design would be dismissed, but elements of its chevroned exuberance would reoccur in a rare late project he would get off the ground: No.1 Poultry, the building that would succeed on the site where Mies van der Rohe's venture had failed. The architecture of Stirling's No.1 Poultry is a strutting rooster indeed. Where Mies's tower was to be calm and businesslike, Stirling's city landmark preens and crows. It's such a marvellously complex beast that every angle reminds me of something else. From the front it's a deconstructed art deco submarine. You stand facing the prow and it seems to be coming for you, a monumental gastropod, antennae up, squeezing the house on its back through the streets of the City. The argument against Mies's tower had been all about disrupting the historic context, which makes it ironic that it was replaced by a building that seemed to scream *I AM the context* while elbowing its way down the street. It's hard to imagine Charles liked it any more than the previous version (he called it a 1930s wireless set, and later Stirling would defensively remark in response that '1930s wireless sets are really rather beautiful objects'), though I'm sure the prince appreciated it was shorter than Mies's design, at least.[13]

The first thirty or so times I saw No.1 Poultry, I was a little terrified by it. It felt less architecture, more a Lewis Carroll dream landscape, a nonsensical wedge of cheesecake chopped through, cheery pop-modernist on one facade, sober stone close up, outrageous pyjama stripes when you stood back, with so many odd projections and details that it's tricky to comprehend. I also find it hard not to love it for all the same reasons. And 127

Inside the belly of James Stirling's beast. © Tony Higsett

it's on the inside that it starts to make sense. It's all drums and triangles, courtyards and internal windows, places you can spy from, hide in, cut through and call across. This is not the simple boldness of an 'icon' – it's too complex and snook-cocking for that, too inward-looking and blank in places, too fiddly and unreplicable in others. You can sketch the Shard or the Gherkin with a couple of lines. No.1 Poultry, like the best dreams, defies coherent recollection. And while Stirling may have lost the competition for the National Gallery, he was responsible for a successful addition to Tate Britain at Pimlico. The Clore Gallery wraps around one side and connects beneath the existing structure. There is a glamour to this extension, and the structure peeps through to the old buildings at strange unlikely points, just as in No.1 Poultry, and reveals it in a way that his favourite drawing type – the worm's-eye axiometric – does. Stirling's favoured architectural sketches were taken from beneath a

128 building, so you could see the spaces underground hidden in

more traditional drawings. At the Clore Gallery, he seemed to be creating a building to be enjoyed upside down too.

Meanwhile, back at the National Gallery, the competition winners who got to dress Kim Novak for the prince were the world's original postmodernists, an American duo who had inspired and pushed on the movement since the mid-1960s. It's worth remembering that Robert Venturi and Denise Scott Brown were no safe choice either. Their work was as provocative as it came, championing complexity, historicism and 'bad taste' in the face of functional modernism. In this instance, they found exactly the right kind of provocation to face down the right kind of 'It'. 'They were out to choose the architect and not the design,' explained Venturi of the selection process. 'The designs were part of it of course', but the gallery were more interested in 'our background, our interests, our philosophies'.[14] The panel lapped up their love of Vanbrugh, Lutyens and Soane, and of how the British excelled at compromise (wow, remember that version of Britain?). 'The British are so good at accepting rules and then modifying them,' said Venturi. 'The French and the Italians would never compromise like that.' Denise Scott Brown described their work as 'both cerebral and sensuous . . . It's how we look at problems.'[15] And their winning design was indeed an opulent creation, pulling references and scale from William Wilkins's 1838 neoclassical facade, and then allowing those details to fade away as the building progresses, like a memory or a well-used bar of soap. It encapsulates precisely their love of compromise and modifications, and was therefore not purist enough for their peers nor traditional enough for the conservationists. As a result, Venturi and Scott Brown's only UK building has been generally overlooked by the architecture establishment of all hues. It's not a masterpiece but it's a better building than the hammy old crock it's attached to.

Meanwhile, Charles's influence in architectural circles continued to grow. On 28 October 1988, the BBC screened *A Vision of Britain*, a seventy-five-minute *Omnibus* documentary. An accompanying book was published the following year, alongside an exhibition at the V&A. *Architectural Design* magazine published transcripts of it, recording royal favourite Quinlan Terry insisting that 'classical' architecture 'can – and must – replace modernism. I don't believe that modernism is art or architecture at all. . . . unlike a modernist house my houses do not set out to break new ground. One must avoid originality and not be ashamed to copy – yes, copy if you can – the details from older houses.' Terry's determinedly retro Richmond Riverside scheme in West London was 'designed not for the architectural critics but for the people who work there and the public too . . . I hope it looks English and provincial.'[16] He got that right. If the National Gallery extension is *Vertigo*, this is *Mary Poppins Returns* – an attempt to mimic every element of something that has gone before, but with bright new technology. Like the low-flying Jumbos and Airbuses rattling its windows, what might have once seemed an immense and extravagant absurdity now feels a little too ordinary. The facade pretends this is an agglomeration of different eighteenth- and nineteenth-century buildings, but for a real blast of English provincialism it needed some mock-post-war infill, too: a small brutalist Barclays Bank or a glass-panelled former shoe shop. But that, of course, would distract from The Project. 'This kind of design is all too often ridiculed as "pastiche",' wrote Charles in *A Vision of Britain*. 'People use the word disparagingly. They mean "fake" or a direct copy, something utterly unimaginative. But there's nothing "fake" about building in an established tradition, or in trying to revive one.'[17] Ironically enough for the man throwing around insults, he was upset by 'wearisome references to

"Disneyland"' that accompanied his efforts to build these neo-classical edifices, as if disagreement with his royal common sense was beyond imagining.[18] This was a world where image was everything. But beyond those high-flown debates, a more pressing issue was taking over the streets of the towns and cities of Britain.

'Let our children grow tall and some taller than others if they have the ability in them to do so,' Margaret Thatcher had told the Institute of SocioEconomic Studies in 1975, while Leader of the Opposition. 'Because we must develop a society in which each citizen can develop their full potential.'[19] Behind that remark lay the thought that some people's full potential would be correspondingly small indeed, and that these people would – and should – be left behind. As the 1980s moved on, the reality of this philosophy would come clearer in human terms.

In November 1985, researchers at Leeds University showed that since 1970 homelessness in London had risen a staggering 700 per cent. This might partially have been due to a difference in the way homelessness had been recorded, but to walk around the city it felt very true. Homelessness was becoming a spectre that would continue to haunt Britain down the decades. By the mid-eighties, two factors were creating this new wave. In affluent areas like the south-east of England, house prices were booming, pushing them out of reach of people on normal salaries. Meanwhile, the supply of rental property had begun to dwindle. As this squeeze continued, by 1987 a record 112,500 families in England found themselves homeless, up 10 per cent from the previous year, with a 20 per cent rise in families placed in temporary accommodation. This meant that some 25,000 families were now living in bed and breakfasts, hostels and mobile homes: more than double the number just three years before. The crisis was compounded by the fact that local authorities were only statutorily required to find housing for homeless people defined as priority cases: pregnant women, people with disabilities or mental illness, the elderly and disaster victims. Housing charity Shelter reported that 'the main reason why the use of temporary accommodation rose so rapidly was the increasing shortage of council homes for rent',[20] for which the National Audit Office named the biggest culprit as the Right to Buy. Between 1978 and 1989 the number of council homes fell from 5.12 million to 4.17 million, and municipal and housing association building programmes collapsed, from building 104,000 homes in 1978 to just 22,000 in 1989.[21]

Speaking in 1989, Bryan Symons, director of homeless advice centre Alone in London, summed up the government's view as being that 'the vast majority of young people can and should stay at home. It's all part of the ideology of the family . . . If you can define people as alcoholics, or drug addicts, or mentally ill, then the problem stems from them, it's not a problem that has been created because we don't have enough housing. But once you start talking about homelessness in itself, it starts becoming a social rather than an individual problem, and the Government doesn't like that.'[22] Such was the conscious denial that a confidential briefing pack was given to Tory MPs from Conservative Central Office in 1988. 'Government's approach is designed to divide homelessness into a number of discrete issues,' it went, 'with a reasonable tale to tell on each, and to avoid treating it in general terms as a large amorphous issue which could only be approached by the injection of unrealistically large amounts of public money.'[23] And when they did talk about it, their rhetoric was harsh. Environment secretary Nicholas Ridley said in 1987 that homeless people were 'jumping the queue' to get a home, while Thatcher picked on 'young single girls who deliberately become pregnant in order to jump a housing queue and get welfare payments'.[24] The poorest and most vulnerable painted as the most powerful, cynical threat to social order.

In September 1988, new legislation meant that if a young person left school and was neither employed nor on a Youth Training Scheme, they would not be eligible for any welfare payment from the government. Centrepoint, a charity working with London's young homeless, published a report the same year called *No Way Home,* which estimated that there were now at least 50,000 young homeless people in London. A thousand of them could be found in hostels, another 1,800 in bed and breakfasts; 900 had found short-term housing, and another 2,000 lived in squats. That left 45,000 sleeping on the floor at friends' houses, with the remainder found living on the streets.

Campaigning journalist Michelle Beauchamp produced a book in 1989 called *On the Streets*, uncovering the lives of young people sleeping rough in London. The portrait painted by Beauchamp and the young people she interviews is heartbreaking, an all too vivid vision of city life, one many of us recognise but encounter only in the most fleeting way. The young men and women spoke of being propositioned for sex while begging; of the inevitability of alcoholism and drugs; of lacking ID after being thrown out of their homes; kids with no national insurance number or birth certificate to show, and so no access to Youth Opportunity Schemes and the attendant benefits; of young men who didn't stay in hostels because they were bug infested and because they got interfered with by older men; of those hassled by the police for sleeping rough in parks; of the ones resorting to shoplifting because otherwise there would be no way of feeding or clothing themselves; of the young homeless who tried to hold down jobs while on the street, keeping as low profile as possible at work; the perilous pregnancies and doomed romances;   133 the rent boys and coppers, squats and shelters. Russ, one of the young homeless people followed by Beauchamp, knew exactly why he'd ended up where he was. 'If I had a family I know for a fact that I wouldn't be in this boat now,' he said. 'I know for a fact I wouldn't. It's only 'cause I was put in children's homes, abused, kicked around as if I were a bit of shit, that I'm where I am now.'[25] Meanwhile, Dane, another young homeless man, had a clear idea of the priorities that were keeping him there. 'The Government would rather put people on the streets than actually help them,' he said. 'It's like they're saying now, right, anybody between 16 to 21 who's been unemployed for more than six months or so, try this Youth Opportunity Scheme, right. . . . Most people ain't gonna go for it anyway, 'cause they can't pay their rent, or pays their bills or whatever.'[26]

As the 1980s drew to a close, the lasting effects of Right to Buy were widely discussed. Home ownership across Britain had risen from 52 to 68 per cent in the decade to 1989, a statistic and a legacy seized on time and again as an example of how Britain had improved. And yet twice as many people were officially homeless than in 1979. As the pool of council housing stock dried up, the deputy housing chief of Doncaster Council said that 'we are left with the poorest queueing longer for the worst houses, with 5,000 families and 9,000 elderly people facing waits of up to five years'.[27] Then there was Margaret Thatcher's home town of Grantham, a classic example of changes in the private property market. A fast train service had been introduced in 1986, making it just fifty-seven minutes from King's Cross, turning the Lincolnshire settlement into a dormitory town 123 miles from London. Houses that had recently cost £40,000 now commanded £225,000 as commuter boltholes, causing no end of resentment to local people no longer able to afford to stay in
134 their own town.

Starter homes, that other success story, were proving not to be the safe investment promised, as first-time buyers struggled to keep up dauntingly high mortgage repayments. I remember the unease generated by those constant news stories of record property highs due to the interest rate lows of 1987–88. It was the time when Barratt made a record pre-tax profit of £61.5 million. Queues were forming twenty-four hours before new phases of estates were released for sale as people strove to join the Thatcher home-owning project. It seemed that it would never end. But then, suddenly, it did. The housing market began to fall in 1988 and by the following autumn it had collapsed, pulling the whole economy with it like an acutely ill diner dragging the tablecloth and crockery down with them. When interest rates doubled, it soon became clear that building societies had encouraged many thousands of people to borrow beyond their means. Repossessions became the frightening reality for many, the people who'd been sold the home-owning dream seeing it taken away from them. The building societies blamed divorce, poor household management and unemployment, anything other than interest rates or their lending policies.

The Bristol branch of Shelter recorded their first mortgage-related suicide in November 1988. 'Mortgage interest rates are like a time bomb waiting to go off,' said Jenny Smith, a caseworker there, warning of a coming wave of repossessions that would dwarf the recorded figures. Tricia McLaughlin of the Building Societies Association accused Shelter of scaremongering. 'It is highly unlikely that there will be tens of thousands of repossessions when only 9,770 homes were repossessed by building societies in the first six months of this year,' she told *The Times*.[28] But the figures climbed just as Shelter had predicted: 15,810 repossessions in 1989, 43,890 in 1990 and 75,540 in 1991. Mortgage arrears were worst in areas that saw the highest rise

in unemployment in the late 1980s – not the famously impoverished north but the supposedly wealthy south-east of England.
Jimmy Black, spokesman for the Citizens Advice Bureau, said
'we are seeing more and more cases of repossessions, and it is
often part of a wider pattern of debts, particularly for council
house buyers who may have done improvements and added the
cost to their mortgages. A 13.75 per cent increase has stretched
them way beyond their means, and we are expecting a surge in
homelessness that will manifest itself in the next two months.'[29]
House prices fell by 10 per cent in 1990, and two million people
ended up in negative equity, with houses worth less than what
they had paid for them.

The homelessness crisis had an echo across the Atlantic,
where the 'trickle-down' of Reaganomics had similarly left
many without hope or a safety net. Visiting New York at the start
of the 1990s, Gordon Roddick, co-founder of The Body Shop,
bought a copy of the newly launched *Street News*, a magazine
sold by homeless vendors to help them get back on their feet. So
impressed was he by this social enterprise that on 10 September
1991 his company financed the launch of a British version, *The
Big Issue*, edited by his pugnacious friend John Bird. *Big Issue*
vendors – be they homeless, in temporary accommodation or
vulnerably marginalised – got to keep four-fifths of the 50p cover
price. The government under John Major tried to get a grip on
the crisis. The Rough Sleepers Initiative, founded in 1991, aimed
to get those sleeping on the streets into temporary accommodation, but progress was slow and underfunded. The alternative
approach was to make life even harder for rough sleepers. At
Waterloo in London, where a cardboard city had grown up in
the underpasses beneath a roundabout, the drastic solution was
to clear the homeless and build a cinema on the site, to erase
136 the memory of the place. A short walk away, at the increasingly

busy Lincoln's Inn Fields, a historic square that formed the centre of the legal profession, homeless people were discouraged from sleeping there by temporary barriers erected in 1992. When the last rough sleeper was ejected the following year, charming mock-Victorian wrought-iron fences were erected to lock them out permanently. It never eradicated a problem that has not gone away. To this day, despite the fences, Lincoln's Inn remains a gathering point for London's rough sleepers, with a soup kitchen visiting in the evenings.

The rise in house prices and slump in buying eventually bounced back on the big developers. A sudden flood of repossessed homes on the market eclipsed anything they could provide: 'House buyers seek out repossessed bargains' reported *The Times* in 1990, with the sort of misplaced glee matched only by the presenters of *Homes Under the Hammer*.[30] In 1991, those eighties dreamboats Barratt made a sudden £100,000 loss. It was such a shock that their sixty-three-year-old founder was brought out of retirement to save them, like a particularly grouchy ex-superhero from *Watchmen*. Alongside all the problems affecting the housing market as a whole, Barratt had been dragged down by their unhealthy habit of land banking – collecting undeveloped sites they now no longer urgently needed, and whose cost had spiralled. As demand dried up, Barratt completions sunk to below 5,000 homes that same year, less than half that from a decade before. And all the while, those at the bottom of the chain – homeless people – found themselves literally shut out from the mainstream of society.

With his charitable organisation, the Prince's Trust, Charles had been raising money since the late 1970s for schemes supporting young people who were in poverty or homeless, to provide training and try to get them in employment. But in his   137

1989 book *A Vision of Britain*, Charles had written ten principles he'd like to see followed in architecture, while paying little attention to the purpose of the resulting buildings. It was an odd disconnect. Buildings should blend into the landscape, he said. A hierarchy of buildings should give you an idea of their relative importance. They should be of human scale. They should be harmonious with the surrounding buildings. They should provide enclosed spaces, such as courtyards. Local materials should be used. Decoration should be applied. Art should be part of every public building. Signage and lighting should be elegant. And any new plans should involve the local community from the outset. These, it turned out, weren't abstract ambitions, but ones he hoped to follow in the creation of his own new town, to discover 'how to build in our countryside without spoiling it'.[31]

Since 1983, Charles had been planning a privately financed settlement: Poundbury, a suburb attached to the Dorset town of Dorchester, built on land owned by the Duchy of Cornwall. Christopher Martin, the BBC producer of *A Vision of Britain*, said that Poundbury 'should not be another corner of England given over to charmless sprawl with the superstore as its principal focus'. The town's planner, Luxembourgian Léon Krier, had started his career as a Corbusian modernist working for James Stirling, before reacting against twentieth-century planning and design. 'A city can only be reconstructed in the form of streets, squares and urban quarters,' he wrote. 'The streets and squares must present familiar character.'[32] For *A Vision of Britain* he conjured up beautiful illustrations of the town, though they feel oddly neutered. But then there was a lot riding on them. On the one hand, Krier was designing the classical forums and baths demanded of him. On the other, he was dealing with the prince's other obsession, community architecture – tough when there was no community yet to speak of. 'The voice of the people, so disastrously shut out from an actual say in the shaping of their own environment elsewhere, would certainly be heard in Dorchester,' claimed Christopher Martin. And so a five-day charrette – an intense US-style public workshop – was organised by urban designers Hunt Thompson Associates to canvass opinion. In his white suit, hat, silk scarf and dark glasses, Léon Krier wandered the proceedings on those hot days looking 'like a figure from German Expressionist cinema'.[33]

Charles told the cross-party Environment, Transport and Regional Affairs Committee in 1990 that planners had wanted Poundbury zoned just as the post-war new towns had been, but that he was determined to mix together the shops, housing, leisure facilities and workplaces, 'in the face of the attitudes of professionals whose Sixties mind-set was a major obstacle to improvement'.[34] In many ways he was regurgitating the arguments of US campaigning journalist Jane Jacobs, whose 1961 book *The Death and Life of Great American Cities* had been used as a stick to beat architects and planners for decades. Her plea was for the street life of traditionally bustling areas to be replicated in what she saw as bleak and empty modernist plazas and zoned housing projects. While much of what she was arguing for was humane and reasonable, her thesis would be used by politicians, developers and private landlords to justify pushing poor people from potentially fashionable areas as they gentrified cities across the world. In London, this process was recorded in Jonathan Raban's 1974 book *Soft City*. Writing decades later, Raban recalled 'the pioneer knockers-through who gentrified Islington, the vegan squatters of Notting Hill' who transformed those suburbs of the city.[35] It's a process still happening, with suburbs like Catford and Croydon being embraced by middle-class incomers who can't afford the skyrocketing prices of those once poor districts Brixton and north Peckham. 139

By embracing this philosophy so wholly, Charles may have helped erase the possibilities of his Trust alumni being able to stay in the areas they hailed from.

Chris Gough grew up in Dorchester a couple of streets away from where the prince's new suburb was to be erected, and so, three decades later, he took me around Poundbury to explore the delights. We walked through an estate of red-brick council semis, and in the distance it looked as though we were approaching the old town. But then that's the trick of Poundbury: on a cursory glance it could seem to be the existing centre around which this mid-century council estate had grown. But when you get there, there's no hiding its true origins: one of the first things you see on crossing the boundary bollards is a small electricity substation about the size of a garden shed, designed in a neoclassical style. Four pillars hold up a stone roof, while on the side the wooden doors warn of danger of death. The whole edifice was surrounded by temporary aluminium crash barriers – very much Poundbury's calling card, as I would soon discover – like spilt milk in Tesco, or a sinkhole.

You don't get much of a warm-up between council and royal. The first house I saw had a fake window-tax bricked-up aperture facing the old estate. Beyond that we strolled down a facsimile small-town lane, winding along with faux-Georgian cottages of all hues and cosy dwellings of sponge-cake brick and shortbread lintels. A friend likened it to the village in *Shrek*, so pristine and CGI is it. These lanes are bizarre, but they are also perfectly *fine*. An experiment in whimsy executed with a certain degree of charm. I might have a yen for mid-century municipal modernism, but not to the extent that I want everyone to think similarly, and everywhere to look the same. These buildings are well kept, apart from the odd flaking protruding window or the ugly bleed-through of brick on white render. A short way down and we encounter our first square, not, as I might have imagined, occupied by a market or some posh loos and benches, but by cars. Every square we come to is crammed with great bulbous 4x4s, and every house has at least one parked outside. After a while, what seems more noticeable here are the cars rather than the buildings. Here is the upshot of Krier's dogmatic assertion that we should only build in the form of streets, squares and urban quarters. The streets and squares are clogged with parked cars, and by refusing to acknowledge there is a problem the urban quarter is entirely dominated by them. This adjunct to the historic Dorset town of Dorchester isn't over-served with alternative transport options either – we saw one bus all day – and the residents here are, I suspect, not of the bus-going persuasion.

Danger! High voltage archi-prank.

Indeed, there is nothing about Poundbury that suggests the residents spend any of their waking time in the estate. It is largely deserted on this weekday, and I'm assured by numerous frowning locals that the streets and squares are similarly deserted on weekends too. Out-of-town has stolen a march on new-old town.

After all of this faithful reproduction, one of the most curious surprises is how quickly we encounter buildings that are pure John Major pomo: the thin yellow brick timidity of Melrose Court, whose many eager gables and turrets cannot summon any sort of recognisable historic style beyond 1990s Leeds Look. It overlooks a vast lumpy area of open land, with houses peeping over it from all sides, apart from the end, where a graveyard dating back to 2001 sits. This large green, with its playground and mown areas, is a curio in all of this trad mania. It's not a village green, it's pure municipal modernism, and reminds me of New Addington – the housing estate in Croydon where I grew up – more than it does any of the small historic towns and villages Poundbury is so eager to copy.

We stop for lunch in a pub inevitably called the Duchess of Cambridge, on the corner of the suburb's most extraordinary feature, Queen Mother Square. Given that Poundbury is not a town – it's a small suburb of Dorchester – Queen Mother Square is a glimpse at the egos behind this project. Rather than Dorset vernacular, it evokes St Petersburg, hilariously outsize pomp for such a titchy development. A walloping mansion block contains a Little Waitrose, another has Viennese trompe l'oeil pillars painted on its yellow walls. This all smacks of bad parenting, the prince giving in to decades of snivelling demands from unreasonable egos, and so ruining his own vision of Britain in the process. We walk past a second-hand wedding dress shop, 142 just crying out to be a metaphor for the whole estate. Too easy, lads, too easy. Later, we pass by Poundbury Wealth Management – not exactly a branch of Cash 4 Gold. There's not much in the way of affordable housing, nowhere for those council-house dwellers next door to gain a foothold.

On the outskirts, new roads are laid and more buildings are going up. A couple of Victorian workhouses and Industrial Revolution warehouses are nearing completion. Behind scaffolding, a new manor house shows its breeze-block frontage. We pass a small faux-Georgian square, where the powder-coloured doors are pristine. These homes have yet to be occupied, they are box fresh. An estate agent stands in the middle, being videoed for some promotional content. It has the allure of the historical TV drama, where no one has black teeth or dies in poverty aged twenty-four. As we walk round, Chris, who has been airing his disgruntlement at the sheer audacity of the place to have dared exist on his doorstep, is being quietly seduced. *It's lovely and quiet, John*, he says, as we pass some builders having a rest by a new curiosity shop. *It's so clean*, he says, acknowledging that this might be because we are looking at brand new unoccupied houses. *I might have a look at house prices when I get home.* Because it is alluring. It has a sense of place to it, even if that place is a dizzy glitterball of sundry other places, a Spotify playlist of light classical. It's easy to imagine that life is a jolly high-budget romcom here. But we see so few people, other than the odd high-vis in a hurry, that it seems this spectacular suburb is simply a posh dormitory.

As for the prince's insistence that they ignore zoning and instead mix up housing, industry and shopping all over the place, it means that there are lots of lonely shops dotted about, ignoring what makes for a destination. Chris's stepmother tells me that you can't send kids out to buy a loaf of bread, because the bakers is beside a massive industrial unit with huge lorries 143 roaring in and out each day – or was, until Dorset Cereals deserted the town for Poole. In the rush of nostalgia that has made the primary decisions here, there is a denial about the way that people live now, and what they might expect from a town. These streets and lanes and snickets were made for people like Chris and me, tourists to meander and coo in delight or confusion at some extravagant brickwork or an excellently executed hipped gable, or collapse in a fit of the giggles at its campy excess. Instead, there was little evidence that anyone did anything more than jump in their car as soon as they left their front doors. Perhaps an acknowledgement that actual planners might know what they were doing, a little humility, might have worked wonders here. Because among the trashy bombast there are some beautifully designed nonsenses that I'm sure are wonderful to live in. But if the town falls down on the most basic of levels to keep people within it when they are out of their houses, then it has failed as somewhere to live.

Not immune to the realities of the market, Poundbury found itself hobbled by the collapse of the housing market in 1991, and struggled throughout the decade to recover, perhaps showing that Charles's campaign had less to do with timeless truisms of common sense and more the vagaries of fast fashion. In 1996 there was a purge of trustees at his architectural institute, and a switch away from philosophical pursuits to the practical. By 1998 it was in serious trouble, with some of the courses failing so badly that people were being paid to attend them. As the New Labour era dawned, it would be the superstars of High Tech – Richard Rogers, Norman Foster, Michael Hopkins and Nicholas Grimshaw – who were seen working hand in hand with the new government. The prince's crusade felt tethered to another era.

When Charles's magazine *Perspectives on Architecture* closed
144   after just four years, its final editor, Giles Worsley, thought the

prince and the modernists were by then speaking the same language on sustainability and use of traditional materials. But he was bracingly honest about the result of all that talk of humane architecture. 'The Prince's response to buildings is determined ultimately by their appearance,' he wrote. 'He has been forced into the hands of a narrow architectural clique which is doomed to remain largely irrelevant . . . The story of the Prince's involvement in architecture is a sad tale.'[36] These buildings evoked a past beyond Thatcher's middle-class Victorian Values, pillaging the Empire styles of Georgian terrace and Industrial Revolution warehouse. This was seeing the past through rose-tinted spectacles, the splendour without the poverty, the Empire without slavery, an antiseptic version of the past. This was not classicism, it was denialism. And when faced with the realities of the day, it was entirely superficial and aimed upwards at coddling a clique rather than solving the kind of problems the Prince's Trust had so admirably been attending to all those years. Aesthetics trumping ethics.

Back in 1989, journalist Michelle Beauchamp followed a small group of teens trying to sleep in a community garden behind Shaftesbury Avenue, and climbed over the high fence with them. As they settled down, one of them recalled that a police officer had told them he would be round to evict them at 3 a.m. Jason, one of the group, was justifiably raging. 'Why do they come to the park at three in the morning?' he said. 'Why, what were you doing wrong? I mean, you're only sleeping, there's no fucking elsewhere to sleep. They can't nick you for sleeping rough, there's no harm in that. If you ain't got nowhere to go, you gotta sleep, haven't ya?'[37] The very basics of life, denied young people who were completely beyond the system. The Prince's Trust, a worthy and very successful charity, might have been trying to help the youthful poor, but Charles's campaign

145

about architecture seemed to come from a different place, and with no reference to the urgent problems that surrounded all of that abstract debate of style and hierarchy. Ultimately, his fight was with modernist architects disrupting the order of the universe, rather than the ills or wants of the age, which, however flawed, was what had preoccupied the now despised planners and architects of the previous age. It was 'the denial of God's place in the scheme of things and substitution of man's infallibility' that riled him.[38] But for many in a selfish, disconnected age, neither God nor fallible man or woman was coming to help.

You might have thought that a Docklands architect like Matthew Halland would be excited by the possibilities presented by this vast project, but instead he seemed weighed down by the cares of history. All around he saw decay amid the resurrection as his team attempted to create a corner of a new city for a new century. Halland is the conflicted protagonist of Penelope Lively's 1991 psychogeographic novel *City of the Mind*. Although the character is fiction, his struggles reflected the baggage many of us were carrying when it came to envisaging something so new in this old city. And for Lively, writing at the moment the first phase of Canary Wharf was due to open, the construction of Docklands was a neat way of linking London's long past to its tall present. Alert as Matthew was to his place in history, the real builders of this new city within a city might have found those meandering thoughts rather baffling. Because they weren't in the business of continuity, of history, of London, even. They were creating a zone of globalisation, a place as abstracted from the old streets and docks as the complex financial transactions it would house. The Docklands that was growing up would have more in common with the business districts of Hong Kong, Manhattan, Shanghai or Frankfurt than Penelope Lively's eternal city.

Much as Docklands sought to free itself from the confines of history, so the tentacles kept reaching out and tethering it again to human experience. 'I came in in early '89 partly because two of the project executives for Olympia & York died in the Lockerbie crash,' explained project executive Sara Fox. Sara would end up working across the massive Canary Wharf building scheme alongside Carla Picardi as what she termed 'ministers without portfolio', deployed to do the jobs that didn't fall into the remit of their fellow executives ('Let's just say that if finesse, subtlety and diplomacy were required it was Carla, and if the door needed to be kicked in it was me'). The intersection of two of the biggest stories of the 1980s – the bombing of Pan Am flight 103 and the rising of Docklands – made my stomach lurch. Perhaps it shouldn't have surprised me, so frequently were the staff of Olympia & York flying back and forth between the US and UK at that moment in time. But then perhaps I had become seduced by the myths of new Docklands, and grown used to disconnecting Canary Wharf from history. After all, you can imagine a scale model of it built entirely from stacks of Francis Fukuyama's fatefully naïve 1992 tome *The End of History and the Last Man*.

Sara Fox and Carla Picardi weren't the only Americans I spoke to about the construction of Canary Wharf. There was architectural historian Catherine Flinn too, who began her working life in 1987, answering an ad for a large US architectural firm who were expanding into London. This was SOM – Skidmore Owings and Merrill – one of the great survivors of the mid-century modernist boom. They had won two huge contracts: to master-plan Canary Wharf and to design the new buildings at Broadgate, another of those fashionable air rights schemes at Liverpool Street station. Although Catherine had trained as a landscape architect, what clinched it was not her hard-won qualifications, but her ability to use a feared and fundamental piece of 1980s kit – a word processor. 'I don't remember that there were any women architects,' she told me. 'There certainly weren't any women engineers.'

It was an extraordinary moment to be joining SOM. 'There was a shit-ton of money around,' she recalled. 'There was so much money in development. SOM had a lot of work and they had to keep staffing up.' Some of those newbies were Brits, who tended to get offered the lower-ranking jobs. But for the most part they shipped over experienced workers from their Chicago office – mainly young single men. 'I ended up dating one of them. Not a good idea . . .' She hurried on. 'And they didn't know anybody. So we used to go and socialise all the time.' She described the big hair, the shoulder pads, the full *Working Girl* eighties dream. 'These guys got brought over and put into really posh beautiful flats. And the expense accounts they gave them were *mind-blowing*! Their living expenses were covered and then they had an expense account. So I just used to get to go everywhere by taxi with my friends, get taken out for dinner all the time because they were all on expenses and they just had the money to burn!'

It wasn't just the social aspect that was eye-popping. I loved the portrait she painted of SOM's corporate culture too, puffed-up with pointless brand guidelines carried out with the zeal of a military operation. It wasn't the first time along the way that Docklands had reminded me of the 1983 Monty Python short film *The Crimson Permanent Assurance*, where an office block breaks away to fight on the high seas. Terry Gilliam's comedy brings together Docklands' past and future in a single absurd image. 'Everything was controlled about the appearance,' she explained. 'I had to dress properly, I had to wear heels, I was not allowed to use a pen that didn't have a black, silver, grey or white casing. Everything on the desk had to be of a certain kind of colour. Appearance was so controlled. I was not allowed to leave stuff on my desk that I was working on, it had to always be clean.' As far as Canary Wharf went, Catherine recalled the sense of anxiety that surrounded the project. 'I remember everyone was really edgy about it.' This was partly because, although they were master-planning the whole area, this giant architectural practice was finding it hard to get hired to design any of 149 the actual buildings. Eventually, like Penelope Lively's protagonist, Catherine began to see a disconnect between what was being designed and built, and the history of the place itself. 'The thing that I remember most about Canary Wharf was that to me it looked like someone had said, *okay, let's take all of this dock area that's derelict and demolish everything and put something completely new there*. So as far as I was concerned they were doing what you would do in the States on a massive piece of agricultural land. It felt to me that it was being treated as if it was a blank slate.'

The constant back and forth across the Atlantic made this entire project possible. Models of East London's derelict waterfront reborn sat in the busy New Haven offices of architects César Pelli and Associates. Pelli's team had won the contract to design the tallest of the proposed towers at Docklands, One Canada Square. At 235 metres, this was going to be Britain's tallest, with three storeys of retail space around it at the base, and, if the developers got their way, a station for the extended Docklands Light Railway beneath. London had seen a number of high-rise towers spring up in the post-war period, the last being Richard Seifert's NatWest Tower, opened in 1981. This US-designed landmark would be something quite different. 'The tower is an element that comes not from old London but from the requirement of modern business practices,' explained Argentinian-born Pelli.[1] He approached the design with some stone-cold certainties. 'It was clear to me that such a tall structure had to be a skyscraper and not just a high-rise,' he told *Architectural Design* magazine.[2] This was a dig at the blunt modernist towers of Mies and Seifert that dominated the post-war period. 'The Chrysler and Empire State buildings are skyscrapers, while the Seagram building and National Westminster Tower are not.' Not only 150 that, according to Pelli a true skyscraper was 'a building which recognises that, by virtue of its height, it has acquired civic responsibilities'. Not civic responsibilities as post-war architects and planners might have understood them, where civic buildings generally embodied values of public service or the welfare state. By the mid-eighties, civic responsibility represented nothing so public-spirited. For Pelli, it was about creating 'a human presence in the sky' – an interface between gods and people.[3] Yet despite all of this heady Olympian thinking, his landmark would be 'a straightforward form for a straightforward problem'. Bish bash bosh, as Zeus would no doubt say. His heavenly tower would be completely clad in stainless steel, supposedly to reflect the industrial past of the area, with the lower buildings clad in a more traditional stone. There it would stand, immune to context, history and culture. The masters of the universe were here now, it seemed to say. And they needed ever bigger buildings for their towering ambitions. With its gleaming bulk and impossibly broad shoulder pads, One Canada Square would stand like the oversized white suit of Talking Heads' frontman David Byrne, an exaggerated tic almost satirising itself – if Pelli's architecture was capable of such self-awareness. Watching it being built in the early 1990s, it really felt like something extraordinary, so tall it would have a light blinking on the roof to alert passing pilots. It had a very un-London swagger and cool to it.

It was on the ground that the trivial details of history and context sometimes failed to mesh with the grand ambitions of the developers and architects. The roads beneath Canary Wharf were a classic example. Sara Fox pointed to the indirect road lighting that had been created by placing lights between carefully angled louvres on the walls of the tunnel leading to the car park. Designed out of the Chicago office of SOM, one tiny problem had occurred. 'They put them so they're facing the wrong way,' she explained. 'Most of them had never been to 151 the UK and didn't have a clue that you drove on the left.' And so, helpfully, the supposedly concealed lighting instead dazzled the subterranean driver. To the Americans working on Canary Wharf, it was clear that to achieve the shiny globalised business district that would finally emerge, it was unlikely to be a British firm that would pioneer that new way of working. 'Essentially Olympia & York were recreating New York in London,' said Sara. 'And there was no precedent for that in the British market.' I recalled walking around the first phase when it was just finished. The landscape of towers and shiny plazas didn't feel like Britain – but then it didn't feel like *anywhere* – the walkways spookily quiet, with dock after dock deserted, the water and windows still and dark. 'And that was part of the reason it was so difficult to let,' said Sara. 'Because it *was* an alien environment. And also at the time transport links were just horrendous. It would take ages to get in and out of Canary Wharf in the old days. Which was part of the reason that O&Y bought a boat. Because it would pick people up at Westminster Pier or Embankment and just – *zzz*!' It was not only people who were brought in by boat. The materials needed to build Canary Wharf – steel, concrete, glass – were brought up the Thames by barge too. The river reclaiming its central role to the district, even if only temporarily. One last hurrah for the Thames docks.

One of the great thrills of urban walking is the excitement of never really knowing what you might see around the next corner, even if it's an area that you know well. Things change so quickly, and memory holds on to redundant detail or sheds pertinent ones so that even your daily commute can be a revelation if you're paying attention or have had too much coffee. But to make a comfortable walk possible, a few amenities are required. What results from all of this privatisation and rebuilding is a landscape that lacks the basics of civic life. Heaven help you if you have a weak bladder or are in need of a sit-down. This lack of generosity feels like a fundamental flaw. In the decades since the regeneration began, Docklands has been taken by councils all over the country as an example of what can be done if you sell off the land and infrastructure and defund social projects in favour of private intervention. Yet if you compare the landscape of the post-war new towns – with their public art, local centres and community organisations – their 1980s children all start to feel terribly mean. Here, it's not just lunch that is for wimps, it is any bodily function. Other than sex, that is. Docklands is, after all, a clumsy landscape of sex. The braggadocio of the towers, the inviting dark waters of the docks, positives and negatives everywhere.

The Isle of Dogs has a riverside path. To walk it is to encounter just how much of the riverside no longer belongs to us, just as Ted Johns had so powerfully warned back in 1971. The frequent and sometimes extensive detours inland due to blocked-off stretches are depressing and frustrating, not just for the walking experience, but for what it says about what has happened to Docklands since the 1970s. Four decades of private flats have pushed themselves to crowd the banks, like a crush of flag-waving royalists to a temporary barrier on The Mall. Great stretches of the Thames Path have been fenced off by many of these unworthy private developments, where tiny groups of residents have grabbed an arbitrary bit of riverside walk to themselves. These are often not even bespoke landscapes, but simply areas where the walkway and the street furniture continue behind steel gates, where the enclosure has been hastily improvised. Behind them sit the homes that were here before, rows of Victorian workers' cottages scrubbed cleaner than when they were built, or low-rise former council blocks, with the somehow inevitable scene of people moving a mattress along a balcony. There are blocks mimicking   153 old warehouses, complete with pretend cranes and chutes over-hanging the roofline; others with balconies detailed in red steel or glass facades trussed in a High Tech style; this one has vintage automobile curves, the next balconies as wagon wheels, like some misguided upcycling project.

What still surprises are the remaining patches of waste ground. Surely they should have all gone by now? But no, here brown-field sites are not always quickly reclaimed, the marshy ground or industrial spoil unsuitable for building on. Until, that is, some-one does. The yellow arms of JCBs plunge again and again into the earth, while the Thames makes a satisfying thick splooshing sound on the river wall. Amid the thousand faux-warehouse flats of Millwall, a conversion of actual warehouses appears. Burrells Wharf is a series of Industrial Revolution structures, including a former iron works. Its late-eighties makeover intro-duced some chintzed details, some jauntily painted ironwork and more cottage garden flowers than an episode of *Midsomer Murders*, while a few of the buildings retain a hint of their more serious history. Black-brick warehouses overlook the remains of the hulls of old sailing ships, now engineered into the ground, perhaps to commemorate the launching of Isambard Kingdom Brunel's SS *Great Eastern* in 1858. A few hundred yards away, a couple of security guards flick cigarette butts from the balcony of an old council block beside Island Gardens, sharing a fuck-my-life conversation while staring out at the steroidal development in Greenwich on the opposite bank. Workers have looked out at the Thames here for hundreds of years, watching their lives drift with the flow of the tide, yearning for escape. Now Dock-lands itself is the escape, the fantastical structures and promise of wealth drawing people from across the globe.

The displacement of a generation of post-war British architects felt complete at Canary Wharf. The closest any of the grandees got was the practice set up by Frederick Gibberd, architect planner of Harlow new town and Liverpool Metropolitan Cathedral. His firm acted essentially as glorified snagging on the UK side of One Canada Square, which was being constructed thousands of miles from its architect César Pelli. Even the builders weren't trusted. 'A lot of people forget this,' recalled Sara, 'but Olympia & York had to throw the British contractors off of One Canada Square and replace them with Lehrer McGovern because they were so far behind schedule.' The construction workers had been on strike, which in the Thatcher-Reagan eighties was a provocation too far for their corporate clients. 'We had to do literally a dawn raid. We went in at six o clock in the morning. We changed all the locks. We cleared all the desks. Disconnected all the phones. And when they showed up to come to work we said *no*. We had it all worked out legally, we had the severance documents that made it all legit.' This kind of hardball North American tactic was just one of the things that helped separate Canary Wharf from its unionised post-war forebears.

Walking around the overstuffed landscape of Canary Wharf today, the first wave buildings are easy to spot. It's not just their familiarity, those buildings you glimpse from the corner of your eye from so many distant parts of London. They feel a little bulkier than the more modern designs, these pumped-up remains of a late-eighties future with the pre-digital feel of a big budget Schwarzenegger film, *Total Recall*, perhaps, or *Terminator*. And, just like those movies, Docklands is experiencing remakes too. The garish old pomo and shiny towers of that initial boom are rapidly being upstaged by scores of more nimble imitations. Cheaper productions, thrown up with the help of CGI, without any of the expensive problems that plagued those early innovators. The late twentieth-century monuments are slowly being surrounded by a forest of new towers. Even One Canada Square, 155 so recently the tallest building in Europe, doesn't feel so tower-ing. It's been overtaken in height by the Shard, and surrounded so tightly on all sides by newer builds that it feels diminished, hassled even. Back in the nineties, a day out in Docklands was a bleak affair, in which you'd find yourself adrift in a cold, hard landscape of bankers, pubs, towers and water, both bottled and canalised. As I amble along, juvenile plane trees scatter brown leaves on the block-paved walkways. I weave around the deter-mined paths of mothers – or are they nannies? – with prams, and high-vised-up workmen, sous chefs having a crafty fag out the back and service staff exchanging low-key gossip at the start of a shift. Life is going on here. I still can't quite adjust to how busy it has become. There are people behind glass climbing steps to the DLR or cashing up in Costa Coffee. Legions of workers fill each of these huge buildings. It may be relatively quiet on the ground, outside of rush hour or the lunchtime scrum. But it no longer feels like a ghost town. Cheeping coots and bobbing gulls bring constant life to these once barren watery plazas. They remind us that the cool reflective surfaces of Docklands are not always glass or steel. Cleaned up and dredged, these pools are filled with life-giving water.

Olympia & York moved into the twenty-ninth and thirti-eth floors of One Canada Square in 1991. But they were one of very few takers for these ambitious new offices, which had been commissioned in a boom but were opening in a bust. 'It was all exciting times,' said Sara. 'And then it went into administration.' Canary Wharf had been largely funded through the selling of bonds in the US. But when the property market began to tank at the start of the 1990s, suddenly the bonds were worth more than the property they had paid for. A consortium of banks held the debt, and now some got nervous and decided to call in what 156 they were owed. Combined with that, Olympia & York owed

£40 million towards the extension of the Jubilee Line to Canary Wharf and beyond. In 1992 funding dried up and, like Ware Travelstead before them, Olympia & York and their unfinished corporate experiment at Canary Wharf lurched into bankruptcy. 'That was all pretty traumatic,' recalled Sara. 'It was a very, very small group of people who made it through to the other end of the administration process. It was wholesale slaughter. I basically didn't work for two years by choice, I was burned out.' It seemed an appropriate dog-eat-dog end for Olympia & York, who'd taken on the scheme from another bankrupt firm, played hardball with the LDDC, contractors and workers on site, before falling foul to even greater forces than it could control. The following year, John Major would put up government funding to allow the extension of the Jubilee Line to go ahead anyway, and eventually, against the odds, Olympia & York would come back from the dead to take control of Canary Wharf as they had intended. But walking around the mostly empty hulks of Canary Wharf in the early 1990s, burned out was how they appeared. And across the city, other major projects were snuffed out too: Richard Rogers's proposal to cover the Southbank Centre with a glass 'wave'; Norman Foster's master plan for King's Cross goods yard; several plans for the rebuilding of Paternoster Square beside St Paul's; any number of proposals for Battersea Power Station. As the *Architects' Journal* put it, 'The Party's Over'.[4]

5: Out-of-towners

The Rise of Tescobethan Sheds and Business Parks

In the late 1990s I worked in a business park in Brentford, West London. Capital Court, Capital Interchange Way was the refined address of Waterstone's head office back in the days when they still had an apostrophe. The name Capital Court left no room for ambiguity about its reason for existence; maybe our neighbours were called Fixed Cost House and Liability Towers. Like most business parks, we were off a bypass, well away from such frivolous amenities as cafés and shops. For lunch, the sandwich woman arrived on a bike with a wicker hamper of mildly exotic sandwiches, or you could go to the Express Tavern, a pub seemingly conjured from some decades-old British New Wave novel, where you could have some crisps on a plate. The office itself was an early-nineties bit of ranch-style pomo hokum, clad with smoky-grey windows and dark brown brick beneath a steep slate pitched roof. Inside were endless glossy beech-wood laminated fire doors, and carpets made of the sort of drab grey jazz pattern you find on the car seats of a 1995 Nissan Micra. You'd see sales directors from the big publishers having a last-ditch fag in the surface car park before a big presentation, hyped up on coffee and a commute playing Tina Turner's 'The Best' on a loop, before flicking cigarette butts into the corporate planting and buzzing for reception. Business parks are an environment away from the reality of houses and kids and consequences, and so you can see how the bullshit bingo of action points, blue sky thinking and out-of-the-box management speak has flourished in them since the 1980s. I wonder what it had been like to be part of a pioneering generation discovering for themselves the joys and pitfalls of these
158 strange out-of-town environments.

'We introduced one of the first word processors, believe it or not!' I met Laura Wilkins in the Costa Coffee concession in Bath Debenhams. Laura had worked for one of the largest US computer companies of the early 1980s, DEC, later part of Hewlett Packard. 'At that time Bristol was quite a hotbed of small IT companies,' she told me. 'The company positioned itself as a competitor to IBM. So they were soaking up young talent.' So, in her late twenties, in 1983, Laura went for an interview as a software engineer at DEC's offices in Fishponds, a suburb to the north-east of Bristol. This low-rise 1960s block had been built for the spool-to-spool era of computer technology, whereas the company was now on the verge of a very exciting breakthrough into the personal computing age. In 1982 DEC were the second tenants to move into a brave new experiment called Aztec West, a few miles north-west of their previous Fishponds offices, and so Laura became one of the first people in Britain to work in an out-of-town business park.

They feel a very late twentieth-century phenomenon, but business parks had ancestors. There had been trading estates like the one at Slough, a former army repair works where in the mid-1920s a group of art deco factory units was erected. Then there were science parks, which by the 1970s had begun to spring up across the US for universities to capitalise on their locations and reputations. In Britain, these two ideas collided in a new type of industrial estate, pioneered at Aztec West in 1980. It was built just beyond the boundaries of Bristol, where the M4 and M5 met in Gloucestershire, funded by the pensions of the electricity industry, essentially to create a US-style science park model without the adjoining university campus. A number of teams worked on the original 1980 design: Farrell Grimshaw and Partners were master planners; Bruce Gilbreth Architects were responsible for co-ordinating what was actually built; and 159 landscape architects Brian Clouston and Partners were responsible for the extravagant park itself, in what became the largest private landscape project in Britain since the eighteenth century. Arlington Securities, the property wing of British Aerospace, bought Aztec West in May 1987. At that time 43 acres had been developed, and it was raking in over £1.6 million in rent a year.

Much as I love a sci-fi utopia, the roaring traffic and green fields of Gloucestershire didn't prepare me for the strange *Gattaca* landscape of Aztec West. The essential out-of-town-ness means that many of us have never been into our local business park. For a non-driver and non-local like me, visiting Aztec West wasn't straightforward (hello double-decker bus on a motorway), and as a pedestrian business parks make little sense. You are a moving bollard, part of a hedge that has freed itself, trainee roadkill. This one is supermassive, with a calm, Silicon Valley campus feel. Beautifully maintained banks of evergreenery hide the surface car parks that surround the blank business structures. Thick shrubs act as fortifications between each unit, the space divided up by smug laurels and spiky dog roses. The tyres of passing cars spit and purr over the brick-style paving. All the modern styles are here. Flouncy pomo and steely High Tech. Value fibreglass sheds for the cheapskate, and for Laurence Llewelyn-Bowen there's a faux-medieval pagoda-barn. Want a red one that thinks it's Toyah? Check. A big silver over-engineered job? Coming right up. Pitched-roof agglomerations abound. There's a spa hotel styled like a ranch from *Dallas*, where you might expect the therapies to be taming wild stallions or shooting your boss, but are more likely steam rooms and pedicures.

DEC's offices at 500 Park Avenue were a High Tech affair. A startling blue building with red accents, there was no attempt here to blend into the green landscaping being planted all around. This long, low, two-storey shed had the services – stairs, ducts, machinery – visible on the outside. So striking was the architecture and landscaping that these early buildings at Aztec West became a sought-after location for car advertisements and the like, realising the futuristic dreams of ad execs. Inside, DEC's building was equally High Tech, a vast open space with studded rubberised flooring throughout and very few fixed offices. They had embraced a new product by top-of-the-range office furniture designers Herman Miller, a moveable office wall system called V-Wall, to form partitions in the hangar-like space. Laura recalled the configurations changing over time as the office became busier, bearing out the designers' hunches about how it might need to adapt in future. It's not common to hear people talk so enthusiastically about a workplace, but Laura was very sure of her feelings on it. 'There was a certain pride in working there and enjoying the building,' she said. 'It worked, the building worked, it was warm, it was comfortable, it was flexible.' Despite all of that flexibility, it wasn't the work itself but the demographics of the workforce that would run ahead of the patrician designers. 'I think what they didn't get right was there were never enough loos,' said Laura, 'particularly ladies' loos. There were plenty of women working there – all parts of the building, engineering as well.

'The speed of the development at that time was staggering,' Laura told me, thinking back to those heady early-eighties days of computing. 'I got quite into it. We had a computer called the DECmate, which was the first stand-alone word processor, so the software and the hardware all together. Like a computerised typewriter.' Later, I looked it up. The DECmate was a classic oatmeal-coloured box containing a green vector display screen, with a keyboard twice the width of the small portable-TV-sized monitor. Because of the cutting-edge work, DEC employed a lot

A fiesta of Ford Fiestas outside the DEC offices, late 1980s. © Mark Wilkinson

of relatively young people. Laura met her husband there; her brother worked there too. 'Socially it was a great place to work,' said Laura. 'My job was basically to go into companies, look at the processes they were using at the time and advise them how they could computerise.' These days she is keenly aware of how, over the years, the introduction of computers has affected the livelihoods of many people. I thought of those 6,000 printers striking in Docklands when Rupert Murdoch introduced the computerisation that lost them all their jobs. But back then it felt as if their work was entirely positive. 'It wasn't about getting rid of people so much,' she said, 'it was about making things faster and more efficient. The impact on employment came along much later.'

I encouraged Laura to describe her desk. 'It had a computer screen. It was called a VT100.' I looked this one up too. It was a late-seventies model, a beige box with screen set over to the left and small keyboard attached, almost identical to the one on the cover of Kraftwerk's *Computer World*. 'And of course we 162 smoked in those days so we had an ashtray on the desk as well.

My colleague and I, we used to pass the fags over the desk. Or you used to stand by the coffee machine and have a cigarette. The air conditioning must have worked quite well because I can't remember it being shrouded in smog.' They also had a form of instant messaging on their green screens from the day she started, which was almost unheard of for the time and must have revolutionised her working life, I thought. 'To be honest,' she said, 'we used phones.' And what phones! DEC were early adopters of mobiles. 'I just thought it was a bit ridiculous. You used to have to make a case to have a car kit' – one of those giant brick-like mobile phones and even larger batteries – 'so you could use it in the car.' Full eighties power dressing? 'Oh yes. I had some lovely suits.' She laughed. 'People took a lot of pride in how they looked.' They also had a restaurant in the office, 'which is again something you don't see a lot these days, is it?' she said. 'I just thought I was so lucky to work in such a lovely place!' These days, Aztec West Village Centre contains shops, restaurants, bars, banks and a medical centre. There's a swanky hotel and a Starbucks, vast green landscaping and endless sur-face car parks around big box offices. But back when DEC moved in there was none of that, just a shed in some fields by a roundabout. Though soon it got a postmodern trim trail designed in 1984 by Iannis Zachariades of Bruce Gilbreth Architects. It's all bright primary colours and bold angular shapes, so using it is like swinging through the title sequence of a 1980s quiz show.

By 1987, an amendment to the planning act by Nicholas Ridley loosened the definition of what could be built in 'science parks' like Aztec West, and they became home to any corporation looking to build cheap new premises on greenfield sites. And so joining the tech companies were financial services, ad agencies, housebuilders and estate agents. At Aztec West, even Oscar-win-ning animators Aardman would eventually set up their studios, 163 in a landscape every bit as flexible as Morph. Critic Martin Pawley was less than impressed at the mission creep at Aztec West, writing in the *Guardian* that 'all the later buildings at Aztec, and notably those by Docklands pranksters Campbell Zogolovitch Wilkinson and Gough, with their stripey brickwork and knife-edge perspective crescent facades, are plainly out-of-town offices of no more use to "science" than the Tower of London'.[1] CZWG's 200 Aztec West, a Battenberg cake chopped into curves and triangles and playfully rearranged, is a game of symmetries and differences. Slender wings jut out, and there are theatrical cut-throughs. They must have created some of the most awkward internal spaces for business to busy itself in. That in itself seems somehow astonishing, a petulant gesture in a place whose entire point was as a greenfield site where you could rationally build exactly what you needed with no wastage. Despite the needless rococo flourishes of some of the architecture, the resulting environment was being described by investors as a 'total business landscape'. Pawley had a far-sighted hunch about the eventual fate of these new business parks. 'At Aztec and Stockley, the "new towns" of offices may in the end prove no more rational than the dead High Streets full of banks, building societies and double yellow lines that our older towns and cities are turning into.'[2]

On 3 December 1989 Margaret Thatcher attended the summit at which Mikhail Gorbachev and George H.W. Bush declared an end of the Cold War. Twelve days later she was opening the Aztec Centre, a mini-mall at the heart of the business park with cafés and a Martin McColl. Thirty years later I sat for a cup of tea at the park's Starbucks, situated in the stone farmhouse that is all that remains of the farm that stood here before Aztec West. It shares the building with a pub, The Black Sheep, to which Thatcher had improvised a visit all those years ago, powering over the green landscaping pursued by journalists and camera crews. 'It was a really pleasant surprise,' said young head chef Mike Riordan.[3] On the same day, she had opened another building by the owners of Aztec West, the British Aerospace Technical Centre at Filton in Bristol. At the time, there had been an engineering strike at Airbus. 'I have no sympathy for strikers,' she said, to the surprise of no one.[4] Her visit had been kept secret to the last minute for fear of protesters, but fifty brave souls still made it and heckled from a distance.

Outside the Starbucks in 2019 there are bowls of water for the dogs of walkers who ramble over the park. Around chunky wooden benches sit groups of Aztec Westerners in business shirtsleeves, business slacks and business skirts, as they come together to celebrate smashing those Q4 budgets, a colleague's birthday, a new arrival, an unexpected bonus. Initially it looks as if everyone is conforming, but of course they aren't, and some sleeves are of tattoos rather than polycotton, and some clothing is of the deconstructed variety, dungarees or lumberjack shirts. Once, these garments would have caused a stir at a suited-and-booted business park, but the world has changed. Yet informality still sits uncomfortably here, a place that has the feel of one of those pubs with bouncers who eject you for wearing trainers.

Business parks were not the only out-of-town developments of the time that would change the way our towns functioned and our lives were lived. Following a successful experiment at Brent Cross in North London in the mid-1970s, out-of-town shopping began to emerge as a challenge to our historic town centres. Brent Cross was the first large covered mall away from a town centre, and set a trend followed next in the Midlands at Merry Hill, opened in 1986, built on the site of the old Round Oak steelworks. That same year, an even bigger venture, the MetroCentre in Dunston, Gateshead, opened its doors. The developer, Ashington coal miner's son John Hall, had been inspired by US malls he'd visited, as well as the success of Brent Cross, though his baby would grow up to be twice that size at a cool 2 million square feet. It started out as some unpromising land he'd bought in the early 1980s, a former tip owned by British Coal, situated between slag heaps and the local power station. It was another of those Geoffrey Howe-backed Enterprise Zones, though it took years of schmoozing to persuade imperious ice maidens Marks and Spencer to build their first out-of-town shop here, after which the other chains began to come on board. When the MetroCentre opened in 1986, it was an impressive half-mile-long structure in dark red brick topped with a series of glass pyramids. Inside were different themed zones in the manner of the Crystal Maze. 'Today we are seeing fundamental changes in society,' Hall told *The Times* in 1987. 'People are buying different goods from those they used to and they are buying them in a different way. They do it now by motor car and the city centre does not cater for the motor car. There isn't the space.'[5] His new shopping monolith would solve these problems and more. 'The MetroCentre is not just about shopping. It is about how people spend their leisure time. What I have tried to do is bring the outdoors indoors, to create the sort of atmosphere you get in a square in a town in Portugal. If you go into Eldon Square shopping centre [in New-castle] there is hardly anywhere to sit down. Where here you can sit in the garden, you can stroll, you can have something to eat – I see food as part of leisure – and later this year we will be opening a spectacular entertainment centre for all the family.'

I spoke to James Perry, an architect who grew up in Mid-dlesbrough and remembered his family driving an hour to visit the MetroCentre back in the 1980s. 'It had fake villages inside in some sort of courtyard. There were lots of people in fancy dress and there was lots of entertainment. I've still got quite a haunted memory of the Birdie Song, sat watching from some sort of balcony of all these children doing synchronised dancing. That's one of my key childhood haunting memories.' Perry recalled the findings of a study on the MetroCentre by Australian academic Kim Dovey. 'It's essentially designed to trap you,' he explained. 'It's almost like this disorientating experience where you have no understanding of where you are, how you got there, how you leave. It was probably intrinsic in the design of the MetroCentre to draw you into different areas and before you know it it's six o'clock and all the shops are shutting.' Never one to undersell his achievements, Hall claimed that henceforth 'city centre retailing will never be the same again'. Within six months of opening, his epic gamble was beginning to pay off. The MetroCentre was pulling in a disproportionate number of affluent ABC1s compared with the surrounding city centres, each spending on average a healthy £44 per visit.

Around London, the new orbital motorway, the M25, was the perfect enabler for a ring of out-of-town shopping centres. By 1986 plans were on the way for Sundon Springs in Bedfordshire, Waterdale Park in Hertfordshire, Lakeside in Essex, Bluewater, Leybourne Grange, Hewitts Park and the Runnymede Centre in Kent, and Elmbridge Mall in Hampshire. When challenged about the effects of all this out-of-town shopping on town centres, the minister in charge, nicotine-stained Nicholas Ridley, offered a classic faux-humble statement. 'It is a bigger force than I,' he said. 'It is a mistake to say I must stop it or that it can be stopped. Examples from all over the world show that it can't. It can be accelerated by traffic congestion.' And besides, he said, if development were proposed on 'some old sidings on the edge of an industrial town it would be very hard to find any reason against it. It is a good use of land to put a derelict site back into proper use.'[6] We have ended up with a mere sixteen of these huge covered 167 out-of-town malls, such as the cruise-liner themed Trafford Centre outside Manchester and the ever expanding Cribbs Causeway near Bristol. Instead, most out-of-town shopping in Britain has been at a rather more humble end of the spectrum: retail parks.

The retail park of my youth was Purley Way in Croydon, sprawling over the site of the old Croydon airport, power station and factory units, a place where products including Tizer had once been manufactured. Industry had grown up beside the A23 trunk road, which had opened in 1925, but by the eighties the airport and power station were long gone. Instead, my folks used to cruise on down to Queensway Furniture Store, the first of the big new retail sheds, which opened there in 1980. The bendy white laminated chipboard furniture in my bedroom came from MFI, the flatpack furniture giant who arrived in 1981. All the big box retailers moved in over time: Payless DIY in 1983, Do It All in 1986, and Ikea on the old power station site in 1992. Purley Way was a place where retailers piloted their stores too: the first Sainsbury's Homebase in 1981, the first PC World in 1991. What a crucible. Because central Croydon had such a vast and dramatic concrete shopping centre, I remember being confused by my parents' obsession with these scrappy sheds sitting awkwardly by an urban motorway. In contrast to this semi-derelict post-industrial land, the futuristic 1970s town centre felt like *a place*, even if that place was the overcrowded metropolis of a dystopian futuristic world glimpsed on some low-budget teatime TV sci-fi. The fibreglass sheds of Purley Way, with their endless surface car parking, felt barely a place at all, a scribble in the margins, the superstores giving off an air of abandonment before they even opened. They were the enablers of a kind of super-sized consumerism, DIY kits to build DIY stores, flatpack shops for flatpack furniture, industrial sized premises for 168 industrial sized products. This wasn't no-frills, it was actively anti-frills. Forklift trucks and wooden pallets, massive packs in massive stacks, barrows instead of baskets. It was in some ways a throwback to the pre-supermarket days of pick-your-own, where a trip out of town might be to a local farm to gather punnets of strawberries or rummage through outbuildings and perhaps fall on a rusty nail.

Some retailers had been championing this kind of shed-based shopping experience for decades. The first out-of-town supermarket in Britain opened in 1964 in the small village of West Bridgford outside Nottingham. It was started up by GEM, an American operator, who essentially ran it as a series of franchised stores within. It didn't catch on, and the shop was failing before a Leeds-based company founded by Associated Dairies and Asquith the butchers took it over, renamed it Asda and turned its fortunes around with an emphasis on discounting and patting their back pockets.

One rather more notorious out-of-town retailer began in the early 1960s near Liskeard in Cornwall, and has slowly grown into a small chain of department stores in the south-west. Trago Mills was founded by Mike Robertson, and was transformed from its small shed-style beginnings when in 1978 he hired Cornish architect Charles Hunt to redesign the sites. You might claim the results are postmodern, but instead they feel like the sort of thing a re-enactment society with an unexpectedly massive legacy might want to throw up for rough 'n' tumble role play.

I visited Trago's Liskeard branch in 2018 with my partner's family. We drove in off the main road and dodged the rare breed chickens running loose in the car park. There in the leafy countryside sits a mock Bavarian-style castle, Lilliput Lane scaled up to human size. There is half timbering and rough plasterwork, turrets, witch's-hat outbuildings, and gargoyles, one of which is an alien. It sounds fun; it wasn't. Through the automatic doors, 169 you are confronted with the crushing reality – the interior is an endlessly drab hotchpotch of Portakabin-style oblongs plonked together as if to maximise the number of awkward changes of level and randomly constructed walls. The selection of products on offer remind me of Alexei Sayle saying if the Walkman had been invented in Britain it would have come in a massive teak box with the headphones from a Lancaster bomber. Trago Mills is not so much out of town as out of time; the dark ages, to be precise. The walls are plastered with countless gloating notices about shoplifting, written in a tone somewhere between Lord Haw-Haw and a particularly worrying s/m contact ad. This fantasia, it seems to be saying, is an island outside of the law, where only its own hang 'em and flog 'em rules apply. For all of the suggestions that when you enter Trago Mills you are encountering the real Britain stifled for so long under EU rules, a place with a respect for our great history, the building instead reveals a worrying thought that real history is a cheap trick. In the eighties, Mike Robertson placed ads in the local press calling for gay men to be castrated, and his son, Bruce, has continued the tradition, with Muslim-baiting ads and endless propaganda for Brexit in store and advertising. Service has been replaced by security. The cash desks feel more like a Cold War checkpoint. Receipts are checked on the way out. It's a fantasy railing against perceived inequalities, a haven of white heterosexual Anglo-Saxon dominance because we don't have many of those. While we were there, we got stuck in a lift for ages. It was the only good bit.

A challenge for food retailers in the late sixties was that only 47 per cent of people in Britain had fridges, and deep freezers were a rarity. Even so, there were thirty-three Asdas in the north by 1970, the year Tesco announced they would follow their lead out of town. So successful was this strategy that in 1984 their deputy chair, Ian MacLaurin, announced: 'I cannot see Tesco ever again developing a shop in the high street.'⁷ Supermarket chains started to expand into out-of-town sites, and each developed a unique look. In classic sitcom *Never the Twain* style, competitive neighbours Tesco and Sainsbury adopted opposing philosophies with gusto, be it one-size-swamps-all hokey pitched-roof barn-style Tescobethan or super-modern Sainsbury pretending new stores were bespoke High Tech installations derived from Norman Foster's Sainsbury Centre art gallery. Over-varnished craft centres turned out to be Morrisons and knock-off Palladian villas Safeway. Asda, who had formulated the big box supermarket before anyone else, stuck with anonymous fibreglass airships and blank red-brick facades, a style best described as Asdustrial. In 1987, after all of this rush to the outskirts that they'd helped create, Tesco commissioned a report into the state of the high streets they had abandoned. US-style out-of-town retail parks were changing Britain, they gasped. 'Such developments could well lead to a serious rundown of the traditional high streets, many of which are already in a precarious state,' wrote the report's author Dr Ross Davies, director of the Oxford Institute of Retail Management and the useful idiot of the day.⁸

The big boxes continued to multiply, with the amount of large retail warehouses of the likes of Toys "R" Us and PC World rising across the UK from barely any in 1985 to nearly 6 million square feet in 1988. Yet, as if to prove that nothing stayed the same, in June 1992 the first of a new breed of urban micro supermarkets opened. Tesco Metro arrived in Covent Garden, precipitating a rush for supermarket chains to colonise once more the inner cities they had so recently abandoned. There was also a rearguard defence action being fought against their European competitors Netto, Aldi and Lidl. Major-era environment minister John Selwyn Gummer worked with Asda, Sainsbury's and Tesco on an extraordinary law that would make it much harder to build new   171 out-of-town supermarkets. The drawbridge was being pulled up. It wasn't only space these big chains colonised, but time as well. Christmas 1990 saw a number of supermarkets and DIY stores flouting the Sunday trading ban and opening to the public, with little consequence other than profit. The same happened the following two Christmases, until Sunday trading was legalised in 1993. Whatever the big supermarkets wanted, they got.

It was visiting this kind of 1990s out-of-town infrastructure that helped sustain me through the UK's first coronavirus lockdown in the spring of 2020. I spent those months in Milton Keynes at my partner's house. We took our daily exercise walk through a nearby business park to a network of lakes designed to balance the city's water table. Late afternoon visits revealed rabbits and heron and mistle thrush and moorhen living a rustle and hop away from pomo sheds, home to Interpower, SAI Global, Envisics, Riskex – modern businesses that might do just anything. This was not on the outskirts, mind, it was near the centre of this new town, whose Los Angeles aspirations meant edgelands and centre have a similar feeling, thanks to everything being spaced out by high-speed grid roads. But on the actual edge of the city near the M1, just off a roundabout adorned with a steel sculpture of local Olympian Greg Rutherford leaping high above the traffic, sits one of the most remarkable infrastructure landscapes I've seen.

Magna Park was master-planned by Chetwoods, architects of many a colourful corporate shed, as an environmentally friendly business park, or as environmentally friendly as a lorry-based business park beside the M1 can be. Here, the vast warehouses for John Lewis, Waitrose, River Island and Amazon have been painted in a scheme of horizontal bands, dark blue at the base fading to white at the top, which means something peculiar happens as you glimpse them: the enormous long oblongs seem to dissolve into the sky. You can still see them – my God, they're enormous – but like dazzle ship camouflage they interrupt the ability of the eye to properly process what it is seeing. We drove up to a car park – a generous five spots, usually occupied by off-duty cab drivers – and walked down a small path to a decent-sized lake, densely planted all around with a mixture of deciduous and evergreen trees, a great stretch of grassy tundra off to one side, no doubt awaiting the arrival of more giant sheds from space. And there were those warehouses themselves, startlingly clean and absurdly hard-lined against the trees, like an abandoned layer in Photoshop accidentally switched on.

In the centre of all this activity sits the lake itself – a fragment of Broughton Brook linear park – busy with ducklings and cygnets and dragonflies. We walked around, found a bench, cracked open the soft drinks and a crossword. The friends who'd told us about it wandered by and we had The Socially Distanced Chat we've all grown used to. Beccy assured us we would see deer, Phill spotted a fox on the far bank sunning itself in a glade. There are hares in the vicinity, apparently, and a badger sett, not that we'd see evidence of either. A while later we thought we saw a deer in the distance, in the long grass, but can't be sure. Maybe we'd just hyped ourselves up, perhaps it's another hidden layer in Photoshop peeking through. But on our way back to the car, there, on the path ahead, stood the tall form of a Chinese water deer, a strange, fanged creature like the world's least threatening vampire, who stared at us for a long moment, and then was gone. Seconds later, the fox was there too. Above them a huge sign for John Lewis. They do everything, you know.

Mid-afternoon at Aztec West I sat down by another artificial lake, where a lone goose bobbed about nearby. The silent park was animated by the cries of secondary-school kids cutting   173 through the park. They threw stones at the fish, wrestled on the grass verge, moaned about life. A lone boy approached the lone goose, and there was a momentary connection. After the kids had streamed through came the dog walkers. The free-flowing landscape here is the opposite of Capability Brown. Rather than opening up to successive impressive vistas and picturesque scenes, the landscape of Aztec West is one of denial, as if to say there are no features here. As I walked back to the start of my journey I passed a middle-aged couple having one of those classic affair arguments in the car park of a budget hotel. *What?* shouted the man as she walked off, *what have I said now?* Aztec West was built for the lifestyle of *Dynasty* or *Howards' Way*, an endlessly flexible landscape of 1980s high-end soap opera theatrics, and I was happy to see it being used that way.

One of its great advantages, at least for a while, had been embracing its out-of-townness. Laura would drive from her central Bristol flat against the traffic, doing her make-up on the way, and be at work in fifteen minutes. Nowadays, with so much business moved out there, those roads are some of the most notoriously snarled up in the country. Over time, Aztec West grew up around DEC, without any of them really noticing. The surface car parking became slowly overcrowded, with people parking on the green verges and spoiling the utopian landscaping. By 1992 there were eighty companies at Aztec West, the landscaping had matured, and over 4,000 people worked there. By 1995 there were plans for over 800 business parks, including semi-urban sites on the former Cowley and Longbridge car plants in Oxford and Birmingham.

Back at DEC, events had begun to overhaul the computer company. As the battle between the big players in the world of personal computing began to heat up in the late eighties, DEC 174 found themselves lagging behind, and by the early nineties some

Business park meets Capability Brown.

poor management decisions left them struggling. 'I don't know if we got too big, but when it started to fail it failed very, very quickly,' recalled Laura. Redundancies started, and eventually she and her team, one of the most successful parts of the whole enterprise, were let go too. As befitted a tech company of the day, it happened over email. 'We were probably one of the first!' said Laura, ever the frontierswoman. 'It was, *I think we've just been made redundant!* We phoned our boss at the time and he said, *yes, I think I have as well.*' The leaders of computer workplace rationalisation living and dying by the sword. Later, their state-of-the-art offices were demolished too, after just thirty years. Rumours swept the network of old DEC employees, who kept in touch via Facebook groups and occasional meet-ups. Were they sad when they heard about that? 'Oh yeah! Everyone was devastated. Word went round that they were knocking the building down, they were like, *ohhh*!' A collective wistful sigh from the tech pioneers of Aztec West, the green screen cursor finally blinking out on their digital adventure.

Docklands: Ghosts

If you can find your way to the water's edge at Wapping, peeping out from between the Victorian brick depots you can see along the river towards Canary Wharf. On this cold January day in 2019 the steel and glass towers were partially obscured by a blue wintry haze, the precise geometries smudged to a broad illuminated gesture. By chance, at around the time I was admiring the crystalline complex at a distance, a man inside was falling to his death. Thirty-two-year-old Osazuwa Otote had broken free from his carer and jumped from the top of an escalator at Canary Wharf Underground station. He died instantly. Public distress is rarely glimpsed in the carefully controlled atmosphere of Canary Wharf. This tragedy happened in the open, in the public–private space at the heart of this new city, in the midst of a financial district starting another cold new year. In this frigid landscape of chilled sophistication, it seemed almost incomprehensible that someone could have met such a violent end. The wheel here grinds slow. The tapestry of complex human feelings and unknowable anxieties felt by Otote was not what the mechanistic world that is Canary Wharf was built to represent. But that did not stop suffering or tragedy occurring here. Indeed, the next day another man, Richard Gent – a father and a quantity surveyor two decades Otote's senior – stopped a few minutes' walk from where the other man had jumped and sent a final text. Then he climbed over the guard rail of Canary Wharf's Cabot Place shopping centre and jumped. The landscape of Docklands is purposefully impersonal and hard-edged. But that is not to say it is a place that does not experience high emotions. In many ways, given its atmosphere of high-pressure business

dealings and cloned chain cafés and shops, it may provoke them more profoundly from us. What has been created here is a landscape of high stakes, winners and losers, life or death. And it has replaced another, the hard world of dock work every bit as unforgiving and intense.

By 1987, the transformations that the LDDC had set out to effect were becoming more and more tangible on the streets of Docklands. Most of the Victorian warehouses not pulled down had been converted into luxury apartments. Small houses and extravagant flats were being built along the old watersides. New businesses were being established in the area too. It was claimed the LDDC had attracted £9 of private money for every £1 of public money spent. This was Heseltine's dream made real, the very model of urban redevelopment in a new private-spirited age. Hopes were pinned on a vaguely defined and unproven concept, the trickle-down effect. Surely being surrounded by all of this new wealth would transform the existing population? Yet during the 1980s there was little evidence of that. By 1987 unemployment in Docklands was as high as 22 per cent. Homelessness had increased in the area 120 per cent since 1981. And while by July 1987 the LDDC could point to 7,897 jobs having been created on their watch, 5,059 of them were at incoming firms who'd imported existing staff into the area. Meanwhile, some 3,355 jobs had been quietly lost at existing companies.[1]

To this day, anywhere on the Isle of Dogs you are never far from the noise of construction. The boom of piles being forced deep into the earth. The chug of JCBs and earth-movers. The tap and bang of scaffolding or construction tools. The scream of angle grinders or electric screwdrivers. The ruthless remodelling process continues, the whole island and its history swarmed over by developers and private finance. Hard labour still goes on here, but now it's builders rather than dockers. How these wharves and docks would once have teemed with workers of a different 177 sort. How quiet they are today, how domesticated. It's not just a loss of the past here, it's the loss of a realistic idea of the future too. What is fuelling all of this activity? And post-Brexit, will it last? It depends, it seems to me, not just on trade but on another form of supremacism – of language or culture that has accepted this is the rightful capital of global finance. But now our real feelings about all of that globalisation have been revealed, where does that leave Docklands? It's all too easy to imagine it as a ghost town, the DLR driverless trains cruising from nowhere to nowhere, the towers boarded up or empty. Or offices turned to residential use, like a giant Croydon, the booming South London town of 1970s financial services that Docklands usurped. Meanwhile, those luxury riverside flats become the new hard-to-let ones, falling down through lack of funds and maintenance. The dreams that created the new Docklands can be as subject to whim and fashion as the dock work that came before. And it could be a bleak place once more without the abstract financial transactions that have – perhaps temporarily – passed through here.

'Just two weeks ago some Italian friends whose daughter is working in London sent me a picture,' Carla Picardi told me. 'They said, *look where we are!* And there they were standing on Greenwich meridian time, with the Queen's House and the Royal Naval College and Canary Wharf in the background, and I thought *life is so amazing!* They said they had to *wait* to get their picture taken there on that spot – even on a rainy day!' It's a different world from the one the do-gooders and schmoozers of the LDDC might have recognised. And it's certainly different from the one the working-class residents could have predicted. Is it a better world? I'm not sure. If you can afford it.

PART 2:

For Tomorrow

1997–2010

'We got our big architectural break in 1996 or so.' Irena Bauman studied in Liverpool in the eighties and together with Maurice Lyons formed a buzzy young practice in Leeds. 'One of our schemes got published and got lots of awards – a promenade in Bridlington. Which was a very, very big project for us.' They regenerated the existing fabric of the promenade and created all sorts of new attractions, from chalets, cafés and shops to public toilets, showers and a paddling pool. They also worked with artists Bruce McLean and Mel Gooding to create a new seaside landmark fit for the Britpop age. 'We felt that we'd arrived on the scene and were very pleased with ourselves,' she said. It was wonderfully reviewed at the time, with Jeremy Melvyn in the *Independent* calling it 'a triumph for inventive architects and an enlightened council'.[1] 'And then we went back,' said Bauman, 'because usually you go back to projects to see how it was doing, about two or three years later – and it was *absolutely savaged*. Vandalism and weather. No matter how much we studied the subject – marine environments, and big numbers of people visiting, we didn't get it right. Things were rusting much quicker, sand was getting into locks of the chalets, that kind of thing.' A chasm had opened up between the expectations of the architects and those maintaining it on a daily basis. 'So the maintenance guys just wanted to paint it all,' she recalled. 'The scheme was all white – marine white – but they started to paint it with burgundy red because it hides rust better.' In some ways it had also become a victim of its own success, and wasn't robust enough to stand up to the sheer number of people using it every day. 'We thought we designed for vandalism, for the marine environment. We thought that everyone was behind the vision, that because   181 it was a very well-known project everyone was going to look after it.' The reality changed the way Bauman has approached architecture ever since. 'We go back to every project now and get feedback, and work with local people to get the brief right in the first place.'

In some ways, Bridlington's prom, which opened in 1997, was a pilot fish ahead of a whale. It had been part funded by the local council, with cash from the European Regional Development Fund, the government and a cool £1 million from the National Lottery. So much cash was being generated by this almost accidental money-spinner that the Millennium Commission was set up in 1993 to try to find projects to give it to. Commissioners included astronomer Heather Couper, TV presenter Floella Benjamin, journalist Simon Jenkins and – there's no easy way of saying this – Michael Heseltine. 'I don't remember being involved in any discussions about it until one day he [John Major] called me in and said I want to make you a millennium commissioner,' Heseltine told me as he polished his spectacles. 'I said that's very nice. And then we discovered the enormity of the money, which – if I remember correctly – we had two billion to spend in the six years.'

And spend it they did. Many of the icons created are so famous it's almost impossible to remember a Britain without them: the Dome, the Eden Project, Tate Modern, the Lowry. Cardiff was home to the ingeniously named Millennium Stadium, the first of these buildings to be completed, and the equally imaginatively titled Millennium Centre, which was one of the last. The majority would be new museums and attractions with an emphasis on family, accessibility and that goal of goals, lifelong learning. And so we were encouraged to geek out by exploring space (Leicester), marine life (Hull), geology (Edinburgh), industry (Rotherham) or, you know, just good old *science* (Glasgow).

These were monuments designed to create a country of enquiring minds. Because ideas of 'the millennium' gave off a futuristic resonance, these projects were united through a suitably sleek steel and glass sheen of High Tech design. The historic playfulness of postmodernism was out and the prevailing culture was expressed instead through the earnest thrills of precision engineering and computer age tech. These would become the spectacular icons of our dial-up modem and flip-phone era, the final exuberant flourish of optimism in technology in that 'don't be evil' moment before the reality of social media and smart tech began to embed itself into our lives in ever more mundane, domestic and invasive ways.

Critic Jonathan Glancey spoke for many when he declared that architects deserved to be celebrated for their contribution to creating this astonishing variety and scale of new attractions for the millennium, but hoped that afterwards 'maybe architects might get down – market willing – to thinking about housing and urban design, before a country awash with glittering new museums and galleries is swamped by a tide of crass red brick, neo-Georgian fanlight doors and brass-effect coachlamps set between wallet-stripping shopping malls, mind-numbing theme parks and even more car parks'.[2] Was Britain having a crisis in old age? These days it looks like one last spin around the dance floor for our twentieth-century dreams before old certainties were swept away by tech, Brexit and Covid-19. Glancey perfectly caught this transitional moment when timid national insecurity was about to give way to wilder, more extreme forces. Looking at the list of projects, it is hard to overstate quite how remarkable all of this millennium effort was, especially when inspired by something so intangible and so fleeting.

6: Unfinished City

Manchester and Inner-City Regeneration

'Me and my brother had a joke,' said Jack Hale. 'It'll be great when it's finished, this city.' We were sitting in the office of the emphatically lower case manchester modernist society, surrounded by the clutter of mailings to be mailed and archives to be archived. The society had begun as a geeky hobby of Hale and Maureen Ward, joined soon after by Eddy Rhead, and it had since got a bit out of control, celebrating the post-war past of the city in publications, tours and events. But we were talking about two eras of Manchester's history that fell outside the society's orbit: the city's grand nineteenth- and early twentieth-century industrial buildings, and their conversions into warehouse flats in the 1990s.

The eighties had been a difficult time for de-industrialised Northern English cities, but by the following decade Manchester had begun to regain some of its swagger, and ever since it has been a place of constant reinvention. Jack had been one of the first residents to move into India House, an ornate former textile warehouse on Whitworth Street, a canyon of grand warehouse blocks near the city centre. Built in 1906, India House's huge windows and mouldings fit in well with the elaborate late Victorian and Edwardian splendour to be seen along the street. The gothic brick frontage doesn't prepare you for the view from the rear ('Queen Anne round the front, Mary-Ann round the back', as Eddy put it). Here, a wipe-clean wall of white ceramic tiles looks to be part of another building from a different era altogether: the functional dreams of the Bauhaus rather than the extravagance of turn-of-the-century mercantile glamour.

Back in the 1960s, all of these fancy listed blocks had been compulsorily purchased to make way for an urban motorway.

But like so many of Manchester's grand civic dreams of the era, that scheme never materialised, although they successfully managed to kill a large area of the city centre through decades of planning blight. Ironically, it was exactly that blight that saved the place. By the late 1980s, developers had begun to home in on the warehouses of Whitworth Street to bring them back to life. 'When I moved in some of the others hadn't been touched yet,' recalled Jack. 'They were tatty and they had trees growing out the roof.' Being one of the first in, he loved exploring the derelict bits of India House before the builders finished the conversion. 'They looked like they should have had private detectives: they had that gilded writing on painted windows, on the ripply glass screens that partitioned the offices. They would have been small little businesses.' This was a haven for struggling concerns and tatty regional offices for local reps, although many of the warehouses had floors that were never let. 'Now you look at them and think, how could that ever have happened?' said Jack. 'Now they've got creative industries in there and whatnot.'

Aged twenty-two in 1990, Jack saw an ad for the flat in the local paper. 'I knew the building, and I thought, *living in town? How continental! And modern.* And living in that fabulous building – sign me up! So I applied with my other brother as homeless people, because technically we were.' They had been kipping at their eldest brother's house. 'So we applied and got in without any hassle at all. They invited us down to have a look and I thought, *oh, yes please!*' India House was a project by Northern Counties Housing Association, who were taking a big risk with this and the nearby Arndale Centre flats. They were encouraged by grants from the Central Manchester Development Corporation, who were trying to knit together the surviving bits of the town centre into a commercially viable pattern. 'It was very generous spatially. We were on the front corner so we had two of those big windows, there's a great big arched gate which, when the gate's closed, creates a perfect circle. So my living-room window was directly at the side of this beautiful arch.' Like all conversions, it was slightly awkward. 'There were no windows in the kitchen or bathroom,' recalled Jack. 'But we were like, *we'll take it thanks*. It was completely empty. Chipboard floor. So being lads and not working fully in a grown-up kinda way, we never really had much. It was a student-y lifestyle. It was mattresses on the floor and a cheap cooker from a second-hand shop. It could have been luxurious if you were that way inclined or had the money, but we were just lads. We never had curtains. The thought of paying for someone to come in and put a curtain rail up . . . ! We wouldn't have done that. Too poor and too immature I guess.'

The first wave of Urban Development Corporations in the early eighties were for the Black Country, Docklands, Merseyside, Tyne and Wear, Teesside and Trafford Park. By 1987, Nicholas Ridley, the then Secretary of State for the Environment, was under pressure to keep the momentum going, and so rushed out a further batch of mini-UDCs, given a paltry £15 million compared to the £160 million each for the first batch. Bristol, Leeds, Manchester and Wolverhampton were the recipients this time, expected to make a massive change with little investment. Even Mrs Thatcher's friend Lawrie Barratt was unimpressed. 'The level of funding needs to be substantially increased if the problem is to be tackled,' he told the press. 'Cutting public spending is all very fine in isolation but you have to look at the problems in the country as a whole and there is no bigger problem than the neglect of our inner cities.'[1]

Manchester had clung on to a legacy of municipal socialism. Would it follow the rebellious example of Liverpool, where the Militant council had been determined to offer a full socialist programme of local amenities and support, and had bankrupted itself as a fuck you to the government's narrow spending limits? Or would it take the approach of neighbouring Salford, which had bent over backwards to work with the private sector? When the docks closed in 1982, Salford City Council bought up the site and together with private investors began to redevelop it, cleaning the polluted water and planning for a bright future of offices, galleries and private flats, named Salford Quays. This unseemly scramble for all investment opportunities going was bluntly successful, though left the city with the hard landscape of desperation.

Back in Manchester, it would be the Labour council's willingness to work with the Tory administration that allowed them to regenerate. Council leader Graham Stringer pledged in the mid-eighties to make no cuts locally, which meant that to push ahead with any regeneration projects he'd have to consider working with the private sector. He'd already been working on a number of regeneration projects when Nicholas Ridley swooped in with his Urban Development Corporation, claiming Stringer's work as his own. It did mean that there was money for developers to transform the empty warehouses of Whitworth Street, and to begin planning for a local tram network, the Metrolink, which would open in 1992 as Britain's first new private railway for half a century.

City Challenge, another urban regeneration fund, was launched in the early 1990s and Hulme in Manchester was selected as a pilot. The Hulme Crescents, a series of cool but poorly constructed deck-access flats completed in 1972, dominated the area. A survey in 1975 revealed that already 96 per cent of residents wanted to leave. Deprivation and poverty were high, flats were squatted, and by 1986, 69 per cent of adult men living there were unemployed. Yet for a while it was also the epicentre of the city's alternative culture, producing a generation of artists and musicians whose work would go on to inspire the expensive regeneration of the whole city. The flats were demolished in 1993. To replace them, the council created the Hulme design guide for architects and developers to follow, with echoes of the *Essex Design Guide* from two decades before. 'The guide gave us all a clear understanding about what worked and what didn't work,' explained Howard Bernstein, the town hall's then Deputy Chief Executive, 'and Hulme was a classic example of telling us things that didn't work. At one level this is simple stuff but at another level it was quite revolutionary.'[2] 'The first housing plan presented by developers was horrible and we said no,' said Richard Leese, long-term leader of the council, 'which was very difficult to say because they had done lots of work with tenants who thought the presented plan was wonderful. So there was a lot of work to be done to justify why we didn't want that form of development. But the point is, we learned all the time.'[3]

'There was no one living in town,' said Jack Hale. 'That was the odd thing.' At the time, the idea of building housing in the city centre was radical. Manchester's population was almost entirely suburban: only a thousand people lived in the city centre, in places like the Arndale Centre flats, or in Granby House, the first warehouse conversion in the city. Granby had been pioneered by Wimpey, fresh from similar projects in Wapping. It was a great place for single young things like Jack, but the appeal of these flats was limited. 'Families with kids didn't move in there,' he remembered. 'It wasn't designed for them – there were no facilities.' But even those young people out for a good time found their lifestyles curtailed by the historic pattern of the city. 'A lot of pubs closed at the weekend,' recalled Jack. 'Their clientele were people who came after work. There was no community of people.'

A venue at the bottom of Jack's street would help the centre of the city attract a younger crowd and kick-start Manchester's famous café culture. The Cornerhouse was an Edwardian department store that had been converted into an arts centre in the late 1980s by architects Fletcher Priest. A further mid-nineties extension by up-and-coming young architect David Chipperfield added a glazed wall, opening up the building, and stripped back the insides to create a fashionable festival of industrial chic. 'The Cornerhouse was cool and hip if you were bohemian,' recalled Jack. 'It would have people in the window in black polo necks smoking Gauloises.' It was a glimmer of what the city might be able to offer a booming youth counterculture. An alternative to the city's plethora of old men's pubs came when Factory Records, that indie music darling and home to Joy Division and New Order, founded a bar, Dry, in 1989. On Canal Street, the first of a series of gay bars, Manto, opened in 1991. 'It was continental,' recalled Jack, 'and you could sit into the window and have a coffee and not a pint.'

Jack's colleague Eddy Rhead recalled how a DJ friend of his who worked at Dry had moved into that first warehouse conversion, India House, in the mid-nineties. 'It was a chicken and egg thing,' said Eddy. 'People like us who started going out in town and working there needed to live in town. It was a no-brainer.' Some venues were allowed to open late because they served food, a typically bizarre rule dreamed up by 'God's Copper' James Anderton, head of the Greater Manchester Police. 'He closed them all down if you didn't serve food, that was the regulations. That's why the Haçienda used to have a café.'

Ah yes, the Haçienda, the most mythologised of all Manchester venues. Another Factory Records venture, the nightclub was opened in 1982 in an early warehouse conversion on Whitworth Street and would be a pioneer of acid house, with memorable 189 performances from everyone from Frank Sidebottom to Madonna. It closed in 1997, with massive losses incurred as its punters turned from buying booze to taking pills, and was entirely demolished. Its replacement – the Haçienda Apartments, completed by Crosby Homes in 2004 – is a brown-brick faux warehouse apartment block with metal railings on the balconies and grey cladding panels on the penthouses. It feels as if all that deviant energy has dissipated, just as it has in hundreds of other pubs, bars, clubs and live venues closed down and converted in towns and cities across Britain in the last two decades. I walked by the canal around the back, following a mural that snakes along the old warehouse at ground level. Here, the new stations of the cross are listed: historic gigs by The Smiths, New Order and Spiritualized. It ends with a triptych of entries cataloguing its closure, rebuilding and the Situationist quote that inspired the whole venture – 'The Haçienda Must Be Built'. Although 'The Haçienda Must Be Demolished' might be more appropriate. The next window along, also part of the Haçienda Apartments, displayed an equally powerful message, printed on A4: *Find our properties on Rightmove*.

The chaotic, rebellious energy of early 1990s 'Madchester' represented by the Haçienda would change for good on 15 June 1996, a sunny Saturday. The Euros were in full swing, with key matches played at Old Trafford. Anti-terrorist officers were on high alert as all-party talks were taking place over the future of Northern Ireland. Outside M&S, on the corner of Cannon Street and Corporation Street, a Ford Cargo van was parked illegally, hazard lights flashing. At 11.17 a.m., following a tip-off, police robots were on their way to carry out a controlled explosion of the van when a 3,300lb bomb went off. A photographer on the scene, Paul Sanders, told the press that 'a police officer ran off to a wall where there were some building workers leaning over and shouted "get back, get back". Then there was an enormous explosion. I was covered in brick, glass and dust.' 'There was a massive big blast and I ended up on the floor knocking my head,' said Sylvia Glen, who had been caught up in another terrorist bomb in the city two years before. 'It was as if everything was in slow motion.'[4]

Just before the explosion, police saw a woman who had missed the mass evacuation start across the Arndale walkway above where the van had been parked. To their relief, as the robot fired at the van to disarm the bomb, she was scared off. Seconds later, the broken frame of the bridge hung in the air, the canopy of M&S was flattened, and nearby low-rise office building Longridge House was wrecked. The 1970s Arndale was also badly hit, as was its block of flats and office tower. 'There was glass and debris all over the place and the alarms were ringing out a cacophony of noise,' said Richard Christmas, MD of P&O Shopping Centres, which owned the Arndale. 'Fashion store dummies had fallen out of shattered shop windows. It was eerie.'[5] This was the busiest part of the city and the police had managed to evacuate some 80,000 people from the area. No one was killed but the bomb still caused more than 200 casualties. The IRA claimed responsibility.

'I knew I had to do *something*,' Michael Heseltine told me. He was at that stage Deputy Prime Minister. 'You just can't sit here and let people bomb your cities. So I set off for Manchester, and I thought *what the hell am I going to say when I get off the train*? And I thought, *go for it. We'll take the team that has done the Hulme estate and put them in charge of the redevelopment of central Manchester. We will go to international world competition.*' By which he meant inviting the most prestigious architecture practices to compete for the project. 'And on that basis I will put some public money to help, but you've got to show what the private sector will do.' Howard Bernstein was also clear on the potential. 'We all knew what we wanted to do,' he said. 'There was a requirement to replan and the catastrophe of the bomb just gave us an opportunity to accelerate that process.'[6] Richard Leese was even more energised. For him, 'the rebuilding process was something like a three year adrenaline rush'.[7] It reminded me of the reaction of the politicians and planners in wartime Coventry, who in the ashes of Blitz destruction celebrated the possibilities offered by this tabula rasa.

The winners of that competition were revealed in November 1996, led by planners EDAW. Their list of required elements was extensive and went far beyond a simple rebuild – this was a chance for a generation of architects and planners to show what they had learned from post-war experiments and eighties interventions. Alison Nimmo, project director at Manchester Millennium Ltd, said that 'the bomb exploded in an area that was not the prettiest part of Manchester so we decided to create opportunity out of adversity'.[8] Their chief aim was to reconnect areas that had been blocked up by the megastructure of the Arndale Centre. They wanted to put pedestrians first, create a constant flow of activity day and night, and create parks, which former industrial city centres like Manchester and Leeds so woefully lacked. A new plaza, Exchange Square, was created on the site of Longridge House, so heavily damaged by the blast. Audaciously, they moved the Old Wellington Inn – a half-timbered pub built in 1552 – 300 metres to create vista and another new plaza, Shambles Square. The task force responsible for the regeneration received £200 million from the European Regional Development Fund and a £20 million National Lottery grant. They replaced the destroyed sky bridge with an exquisite new one designed by Hodder+Partners, whose hyperboloid glass and steel form twists across the street above where the bomb exploded.

In November 1999, the city centre reopened with a parade featuring acrobats and fireworks. The new M&S was launched

The sky bridge at the Arndale. © Catrin Austin

by three-year-old Sam Hughes, who had been injured by flying glass in the old shop. His mum, Lisa, said, 'We thought hard about doing it but decided . . . the store opening was a good, positive thing for Manchester'.[9] There had been a race against time to complete it for commercial reasons too. Away from the heart of the city and its tricky planning restrictions, a vast new shopping mall and cinema complex had opened in 1998: the Trafford Centre. At a quarter of a million square feet, the new city-centre M&S was a monster, and an unfortunate overstretch. Within two years they had leased half of the floor space to Selfridges. A huge new museum – Urbis, by local architect Ian Simpson – rose up too. This wedge of green glass and steel dedicated to exhibitions on urban design opened in 2002. They overestimated interest in such lofty pursuits, and it closed after eight years. These days it's a museum of football. I spoke to Peter Higgins of Land Design Studio, who'd worked on the 193 original exhibition at Urbis. 'Although Urbis was a huge failure for all sorts of reasons, it was really badly conceived as an idea,' he said. 'And the building was dreadful. It was streaming sunlight into these levels. It would have been better off as a Selfridges than a museum. So we were spending all our money trying to block the light out because we were trying to create media installations.' Higgins recalled run-ins with Ian Simpson over the design. 'It's very clumsy and the building clearly isn't fit for purpose.'

But perhaps the most startling symbol of the new city's ambition and swagger wasn't the horizontal sprawl of shopping and leisure in the city centre or its rivals out in Trafford. Viewed side-on, Beetham Tower looks against nature. Manchester's tallest building looms, hoodie up to the elements, skin as thin as a cyclist's waterproof. It revels in its artifice and absurdity. Neither glamorous and pretty nor industrial and tough, Beetham represents a new version of new Manchester. It's a bloke of a building: tall, hunched shoulders, cantilevered pot belly poking out over tight trousers, dressed in laddish greys and blues. Round the front, the only showy aspect of the ground floor is the jutting facade of the Hilton, a rough-clad element to set off the glossy whole. At ground level it's a studied attempt at normcore: nothing to see here, it seems to say. Instead, it meets the ground with the same seeming indifference with which it interrupts the air. You might not notice the tower here at all – well, on a calm day, at least. Despite various baffles and tricks, when completed the wind and its howl grew as famous as the tower itself. *New Scientist* said on windy days it makes a noise like a UFO landing. *Coronation Street*, filmed half a mile away, had to add extra background noise to muffle it.

The developer was Stephen Beetham, then aged twenty-eight. He'd become director of the family property business,

Oastdren Investments, at the age of twenty, after working as a handyman since leaving school. When Stephen was sixteen, he changed his name from Stephen Frost and ran away from his mother and a strict religious cult – the Plymouth Brethren – to be with his dad. 'Once you leave the sect you are cut off and told you will be a failure,' he said, in perhaps the most personally revealing interview ever given by a developer. 'People have told me that's the reason I'm being so successful and maybe that is why I have strived for such high buildings.'[10] Whatever the reason, his output was prodigious. In his early twenties he converted an old polytechnic library in Liverpool into luxury flats and turned Wilberforce House – a 1960s building belonging to Liverpool's city planning department – into what the architects describe as aspirational city-centre apartments, Beetham Plaza. 'Of the banks we approached for the Plaza plan,' he recalled, '85 refused to back us on the basis of the fact that the scheme was in Liverpool.'[11] Once he'd found backers, he also bought the triangular site of the old St Paul's eye hospital, where he built the first Beetham Tower, Liverpool's tallest at thirty storeys. 'When I bought the eye hospital site, I was told I was paying too high a price,' he said. 'Today the site would go for at least ten times what we paid for it. There was little interest in developing city living in Liverpool when we started in the 1990s.' His ambitions quickly moved beyond Merseyside. In Holloway Circus, Birmingham, he started work on what would be that city's tallest tower too, at thirty-nine storeys.

Manchester's Beetham Tower was designed by Urbis architect Ian Simpson and stands forty-seven storeys high. He was at pains to explain that the sort of inner-city high-rise he'd designed was a world away from the council towers of the sixties. For one, this was not in any sense social housing. Antisocial housing, given how unlikely it was that you would ever meet   195

Beetham Tower, an icon of Manchester's regeneration.

your neighbours. 'The big difference now is that the people who live in these buildings are there by choice,' said Simpson. 'Those who lived in the sixties tower blocks were decanted there against their will because of an idealized view of city living.'[12] The likely residents were expected to be either first-time buyers and young professionals or ageing empty nesters retiring to a glamorous city-centre life. Such was the theatre created by Beetham and Simpson that all 198 apartments had sold and Hilton had agreed to occupy the first twenty-three floors before planning permission had even been granted. Simpson had always intended to live in the penthouse, and indeed he does, with its olive grove, his collection of Scandinavian and Italian mid-century furniture and glass, and 200 different seating spaces. He shows us around in an extraordinary 2016 film, the magnificent views, the light, the vast double-height spaces, the immaculate enormity of it all.[13] Yet all I could think about was the time it was haunted by that ominous David Lynch hum.

Wandering round in 2018, I saw Beetham Tower being joined by several other high-rise blocks going up in the centre. There was Axis, half-clad in a kind of jazzy zigzag, giddy as the synths in a Duran Duran single and just as optimistic. Some months later, the finished article would cause a huge fuss in the city: a central panel of the building's facade given over to a colossal digital advertising screen, suddenly less 'The Reflex' and more *Blade Runner*. Behind that crystalline oddity rose a cluster of much taller and more regular towers, the Owen Street project, soon to be renamed Deansgate Square. Two were almost topped out, with two more in the early stages of construction. They had their own impromptu concrete factory in a vacant lot nearby, where mixers transported concrete and flatbed lorries brought in the steel reinforcements. These grey-clad bevelled towers were a mid-century throwback, to   197 the design of Millbank Tower, briefly London's tallest building in 1963. They were going up in a busy landscape of flats and offices built in the last two decades, blocks of red brick and tile, fake warehouses with exposed steel beams and metal balconies. In a stagnant water feature beside one of the apartment buildings, sheets of bubble wrap, plastic bottles, polystyrene burger cartons and cans bobbed about. *You haven't got any money for a cup of coffee have you mate?* asked a guy in a wheelchair. *We live in that doorway there*, he said, pointing round the corner at a newly built alleyway. All of these new homes going up, what chance him being rehoused as a result?

With a new Imperial War Museum, the Lowry art gallery and MediaCity – a massive hub for the BBC and ITV – Salford had gambled and won big. And so Manchester went one bigger, bidding to host the 1996 and 2000 Olympics. Tom Bloxham, co-founder of local development company Urban Splash, identified a turning point for the city as that second Olympic bid. 'There was a huge party in Castlefield and people grasped the idea that Manchester should no longer consider itself in competition with the likes of Barnsley and Stockport. It was now up against Barcelona, Los Angeles and Sydney and its aspirations increased accordingly.'[14] When the city won the right to host the 2002 Commonwealth Games, some of those Olympic dreams were finally realised. Much of the infrastructure was planned for Ancoats, the world's first industrial suburb and famously Friedrich Engels's exemplar of ruinous neglect. By 1998, four-fifths of its aged business premises were empty, and dereliction together with high unemployment had blighted the place. Yet since those sporting bids had been launched, property speculators had begun to buy up chunks of the district. Some were Industrial Revolution-era conservation areas, but there was also

198

a 1970s pocket, the Cardroom Estate, set for complete redevelopment and a rebrand as New Islington.

This was part of a master plan drawn up by Will Alsop for Urban Splash, promising 1,400 homes with amenities including a health centre, park and local shops. With it, the developers offered a whole range of breathy *this is not just a housing estate* aspirations: 'a new primary school that tops league tables'; 'a chic little Italian'; 'a restaurant with three Michelin stars'.[15] Urban Splash was founded in 1993 by two young graduates: Hampshire-born Tom Bloxham, and Jonathan Falkingham, an architect from Bradford. They made a name for themselves refurbishing overlooked urban spaces, from old council blocks to former industrial buildings, converting them into private flats and offices: buildings such as Birmingham's futuristic Rotunda, Sheffield's listed Park Hill flats, the Matchworks in Liverpool and Lister Mills in Bradford. New Islington would see their gentrification philosophy written on a grand scale.

I spoke to Charles Holland, back then architect at a company called FAT – Fashion Architecture Taste – who worked on Islington Square, the first piece of this redevelopment. The plot they had to build on was roughly the size of a football pitch, with the idea that they would be building new housing for the current residents of the Cardroom Estate to move into. 'We did lots of consultation with the residents,' recalled Charles. 'Very intense consultation but very direct. We sat down with them at the beginning and we said we're going to design some houses, how do we design the houses? It was almost like having twenty-odd clients. And you'd sit down with your client and you'd say, what do you want your house to do? Where do you eat dinner at night? Do you want to have an open-plan space? Because it was quite a hot potato and quite a contentious site and the first site that was developed I think there was a sort of view that if 199 we could win the residents' trust and they were on board then everyone else would be happy.'

As well as Urban Splash, the partnership in Ancoats included the council; a regeneration quango called New East Manchester; English Land, whose job was to clean up brownfield sites to put in the infrastructure to enable the development to happen; and a housing association optimistically called Great Places. Partnerships, championed by the Thatcher and Major administrations, were enthusiastically embraced by New Labour and became one of their most emblematic policies. There were Public–Private Partnerships – PPPs – like at New Islington, co-funded by private and public bodies; and, more controversially, Private Finance Initiatives – PFIs – where the public sector bought buildings on credit, with projects funded by the private sector and paid back with massive interest by the public sector over many years. Of those early PFI schemes, by far the largest was the Channel Tunnel rail link.

The lines between public and private were quickly blurred. In December 1996, Robert Osborne, special projects director at construction giant Tarmac, got a secondment to the Department of Health to broker deals for private companies to build and run NHS hospitals. By that time, Tarmac were already the preferred bidder in six PFI hospital schemes. Public infrastructure was being built for the profit of private companies, such as Serco, Amey, Capita and Carillion. In 1997, New Labour secured the go-ahead for their first two PFI hospitals, the Norfolk and Norwich and the Darent Valley in Kent. By 1999, Dr Jean Shaoul of Manchester University had carried out a study of the benefits of fledgling PFI hospital schemes. They were only meant to go ahead if they could demonstrate 'clear benefits to patients, value for money, affordability, saving to health care purchasers and good management', explained Dr Shaoul. 'But an examination of a number of business cases reveals that they fail to satisfy any of these criteria.'[16] In many cases it appeared that their business partners had simply shifted any liability back onto the government.

By 2001, the idea that private companies would be better at saving money than any supposedly profligate government department had begun to unravel. The first wave of PFI hospitals had saved money by delivering 30 per cent fewer hospital beds than had been planned in 1996. In Northern Ireland, the new Balmoral High School, funded under an education PFI, closed after six years due to falling student numbers. The fall had been predicted before it was built, yet the Northern Ireland office was obliged to keep paying off £7.4 million to lease the school from its private partners till 2027. Meanwhile, eight PFI schools built by Balfour Beatty for Knowsley were found in 2015 to have fire safety issues. Developer Stuart Lipton, the government's architecture tsar, was not complimentary. 'The majority of PFI buildings are poorly designed and will fail to meet the changing demands of this and future generations,' he said in 2002. 'The government has embarked on the largest public building programme for a generation – £43 billion worth. There is a danger that in the push to meet delivery targets before the next election design quality will be compromised.'[17] At this point, 250 PFI projects had been completed, with another 275 in the pipeline. What of those first two New Labour PFI hospitals, the Darent Valley and Norfolk and Norwich? In Kent, Carillion, one of the original four consortium members, flogged off their share in 2003 and made a 50 per cent profit. In Norwich, the consortium there refinanced its borrowing, increasing the return for their shareholders from 16 to 60 per cent.

Back in Manchester, the architects at Islington Square were shrugging off the constrictions of its many partners, even if the work that FAT did was very much more exuberant and eccentric   201 than the developers might have wanted. 'I think we won it as a mixture of design and accident,' explained Charles Holland. On the way to Manchester with fellow architects Sam Jacob and Sean Griffiths of FAT to talk through their shortlisted redesign for the Cardroom Estate, they suffered a technical hitch: their laptop broke. 'We had this whole slideshow, all the usual, this is what we've done, this is wonderful etc, and we went into the room and we had no images. So we just talked about our approach and the residents and the other members of the panel really liked us and they selected us to do it, and one of the reasons they selected us was we didn't come in and show them a load of flashy images!' The more intentional bit was that the brief was full of contradictions, and for a trio as contrary as FAT this was a dream commission. 'I look back on it now and think that we weren't trying to resolve all the contradictions. We were possibly trying to let them come out. So you know, they're little houses that want to be a bit bigger. They're individual houses that also want to be a collective thing. We wanted to perhaps not entirely smooth off all the rough edges but allow some of those frictions to inform the architecture.'

With so many partners involved in the project, all the creativity might have been trampled out of the scheme, but it was the residents who turned out to be much braver than the developers. 'The root of it really was a very big difference between taste and aspiration between the existing residents and Urban Splash's idea of what the place would become,' explained Charles. Urban Splash's master plan was a sleek New Labour vision of metropolitan living – long, tall blocks of apartments with ribbon parks in between. 'And the residents were not keen on any of that,' recalled Charles. 'They had what they called traditional housing and they wanted to have that again. So they wanted front doors, they wanted front gardens, they wanted street access, they wanted private space, they wanted a very traditional model of how you live. So the brief that we wrote was very much to square the circle between two very different visions of what to do.' For the partners, who approached their work as much as a group of arty academics as they did as architects, this was the perfect brief, a collision of class, taste and all those problematic notions of gentrification that had followed such schemes since the end of mass council-house building. Holland summed it up thus: 'British housing, different taste, different cultures, working-class Mancunian community with a sort of aspirant middle-class Urban Splash vibe. And all the politics of decanting and changing public housing to private housing.' For all the success of their scheme, it is this last point that hangs over all that has been done in Ancoats and places like it.

Getting stuck into the taste of the residents would prove to be one of the most rewarding parts of the process for FAT. 'The houses had a remarkable amount of DIY changes in them,' recalled Charles. 'People had knocked through walls and made all sorts of new interventions in all sorts of strange styles. There were archways between the living room and dining room, someone had built a fish tank into the wall, someone had built a bar. I remember one of them where everything was entirely pink. I'd never seen a pink oven before.' Years later, Holland and FAT would work on the House for Essex with Grayson Perry, another artist with a keen sense of class, taste and the absurd. With their houses in Islington Square, you can see all of those interests already bubbling over. And that was without the basic issues of functionality for the residents. 'In those days, this was pre-tablet, pre-iPhone, so normally the households had one computer in the house which was used by everybody,' recalled Charles. 'And invariably the computer was in someone's bedroom. So there was some kind of exclusivity over who could use it. So one of the things we designed in the plans was this kind of home office that was on the landing, 203 so the computer could go there and everyone would have access to it. And another one was kids having a bit of autonomy, so the taller houses had a kids' floor. They lived in houses that hadn't really been designed with dining rooms, everyone had a dining table and they were always awkwardly not quite fitting in. So designing a dining area was a really important thing.'

One of FAT's bugbears was the limited source of references used by architects – always harking back to 1930s ocean liners, say, or classical motifs. They were much more interested in bringing imagery and ideas from pop culture and everyday taste into their buildings. As a result, the finished houses are incredibly playful and not a little bit outrageous. The facades are built around a kind of magnified Dutch roofline, their frontage criss-crossed with red, grey and cream brick in the kind of bold patterns you'd find on luxury luggage, say, or Argyle socks. As frozen music goes, it's Bach does eurotrance. Behind that facade lurks another layer, modernist white boxes with roof terraces and large windows. There was loads of press coverage, the *Daily Mirror* calling the result Colournation Street. You might think the boldness of the design might have been the most difficult aspect for the residents, but not so. More challenging were problems caused by the build quality of contractors Richardson Projects, which left gaps in the insulation in the roof, leading to condensation and mould in some of the houses. A year after residents moved in, they told the *Manchester Evening News* that 'the workmanship is appalling. There was black mould growing on my ceiling, and our boilers were faulty' and 'I've had lots of leaks, doors coming off and an upstairs window almost fell in.'[18] Eventually, the roofs were replaced and faulty balconies repaired by the housing management company.

Despite setbacks, there was a feeling of optimism around
204 New Islington. 'For years people have looked down on this

The jigsaw pieces of FAT's New Islington homes. © John Lord

area,' said Nick Johnson, Urban Splash's development director, in 2007. 'Now they're jealous. Good.'[19] A couple of years later, he went on record to say that 'the vision of Manchester council has allowed this area to reinvent itself and has tempted a range of income groups to an area that was ostensibly very working class'.[20] Hasn't it just? A report by Shelter in 2010 revealed that only 13 per cent of Manchester's new housing was affordable, well below the council's stipulation of 20 per cent. Despite pockets of new social housing like that at Islington Square, poor areas like the Cardroom Estate were being bulldozed and replaced with new homes the former council residents could no longer afford. And two decades on, that redevelopment of Ancoats by Will Alsop and Urban Splash is still far from finished. It does contain Will Alsop's first residential project in Britain, the Chips building – in a form that resembled a heap of thick-cut chips – containing 143 flats, a third of which were shared ownership.

There was also a self-build street, filmed for the BBC – because after all, by the 2000s if a house was built in a city without a film crew, was it really built at all? But as for the rest, Manchester is haunted by the ghost of those creative folk from the Hulme Crescents, the most successful of whom are able to buy expensive new pads in estates like New Islington.

By 2009, the Manchester property miracle had temporarily faded. A few glossy towers were still rising, but with far fewer in the pipeline. 'Although it seems thriving in some way because there's buildings going up, it's not a really booming economy,' Jack Hale told me. 'That empty lot on the corner there,' – he pointed out of the window – 'has been empty fifty to sixty years. And when I moved into India House there were a lot more of them. There's still some now.' And although the hipsterfication of the city centre has continued over the years, basic amenities for the growing number of residents hasn't kept pace. 'We were new, and we knew there was no shops and no doctors,' recalled Jack. 'But it's thirty years now. They should have sorted something. The tower blocks are for youngish childless people who probably then move out to the suburbs. There's no schools, no playgrounds. Not once have they tried to put a park or a new garden. Not for thirty years has there been any attempt to make it more liveable. The council boast that in 1989 there were a thousand people living in the city centre and now there's 30,000! Isn't it great. But they've not done anything for them. It's just housing. And now it's just *luxury* housing. It's not become a diverse community,' he said. 'You don't see old people or people with children.' What has been built are symbols of aspiration. Manchester as world city, reaching up into the clouds, untethering itself from its roots and the streets below. Manchester flying.

'*London!*' exclaims a hearty, fresh-faced young man from a city rooftop. 'One of the most lucrative property markets in the whole world!' A young woman with a heavy fringe stands awkwardly beside a small Victorian terraced house. 'Take this house, for example,' she says. 'In the last two years it's doubled in value. It was worth £120,000, now £240,000.' Fresh-faced is on some stairs. 'It's good news if you're selling,' he says, 'but a complete *nightmare* for first-time buyers.' Heavy fringe asks, 'So, how do you get on the property ladder if you've got less money to spend than the average house price?' Hearty boy replies, 'It's our challenge to find someone a home in the city for £100,000. We're professional house hunters . . . It's a race against the clock.' The wobbly camera and constant zooming and chopping could make this film a late-entry Britpop video. *Location, Location, Location* is almost unrecognisable in its first episode, from Phil Spencer and Kirstie Allsopp's perky energy to the frantic pace of the show. In the winter of 2000, these two represented the new rock 'n' roll, in a Channel 4 show that would still be running two decades later.

Nothing quite captures the aspirations of the New Labour period more than three hit TV property programmes launched on Channel 4 around the millennium. *Grand Designs* began in April 1999, *Location, Location, Location* in May 2000 and *Property Ladder* in September 2001. After the success of 1990s home makeover shows like *Changing Rooms*, which tapped into an obsession with DIY, Channel 4 sensed a gap and jumped in with both feet. This trio of shows changed our viewing habits and our attitude to our homes – or rather 'property', as if a Jane Austen character had stumbled from a branch of Foxtons.

Location, Location, Location is very much a heterosexual version of *Queer Eye*, where we were told what we should aspire to: a playroom for Archie, knocking through to create a kitchen-diner, and overusing the term 'forever home'. Kirstie's catchphrase is *Just as well size isn't everything, Phil!* while Phil's is a roll of the eyes as he bumbles through a henpecked seventies sitcom husband routine for the thousandth time. The first episode is a fascinating piece of social history as they try to find a copywriter called Kate a flat in Hackney, East London, *a place where bargains can still be found, but not for long. Prices in Hackney have risen a whopping 80 per cent in the last five years*. They check out one in an old factory, Digby Works, where it costs £132,000 for a one-bed studio. When I checked in the summer of 2019, the whole of Digby Works – eighteen flats, a nursery and two warehouse units – was up for sale for which you'd get not much change out of £11 million. They see a flat in Arcadia Court near Liverpool Street – a *rather expensive* £120,000. Now it's on the market for three and a half times that. I imagine Kate made an absolute killing.

'They did a lot of research,' said architect Irena Bauman of the Blair government. 'They had task forces. They took time to understand the issues, which I thought was fantastic. I've never known another government to have done that in that way.' The urban fabric that the new government had inherited was threadbare at best. There were layers to address: crumbling Georgian and Victorian terraces and town centres, an early twentieth-century landscape of semis and suburban sprawl, the concrete remains of epic post-war reconstruction, and the piecemeal dotting about of postmodern spectaculars and cul-de-sacs from the previous Tory administration. Towns and cities across Britain outside of the south-east of England had been largely underfunded, and were blighted with high unemployment and the social problems caused by widespread poverty. Pockets of derelict former industrial land and poorly maintained homes made many of Britain's big cities feel neglected and impoverished.

New Labour looked to Richard Rogers to lead an 'Urban Task Force', with the aim of unifying the many disparate elements that made up Britain's urban fabric. He was their Kirstie and Phil, selling the opportunities of our nation back to us, to turn Britain into one great big doer-upper. I remembered reading Rogers's square, brightly coloured books from the time, *Cities for a Small Country* and *Cities for a Small Planet*, which encapsulated a sense of optimism, of grand rebuilding, and the excitement of possibility, as much a part of the New Labour cultural wallpaper of the time as D:Ream's inescapable 'Things Can Only Get Better' or Will Hutton's campaigning journalistic book *The State We're In*. They extolled the environmental value of building on brownfield sites, the worth of building more densely in urban areas, and the virtues of good design. The Task Force wanted to lure families back into cities, by addressing problems such as a lack of schools, poor air quality and limited green space. Alongside that came a focus on neighbourhood regeneration and tackling social exclusion – multiple types of deprivation in the poorest areas – that was one of New Labour's flagship policies. By 1995 there were 22.2 million homes in Britain, 10 per cent more than there had been in 1965. Households were changing, with more people living alone. And demand was still soaring – in 2000, the government predicted that 4.4 million new dwellings would be needed by 2015. Some innovative solutions were mooted: in 1998, the London Planning Advisory Committee said that 50,000 new homes could be created from converting empty office blocks.

Many of these issues were to be tackled by a new bureaucratic behemoth, the Department for the Environment, Transport and the Regions, led by the combative Deputy Prime Minister John Prescott. 'I recently visited a deprived pre-war estate in my constituency,' he told MPs in 2000. 'Most constituencies contain estates like it. There was graffiti, litter, empty houses and a general air of decay, but a very strong sense of community too. I met a woman who had lived there all her life. She said, "I love living here, but I don't want to go on living like this, John." We must not fail people like her, her family or the community.'[1] To create the sort of regeneration Rogers's Task Force had recommended, Prescott launched a host of schemes, all with the kind of ostentatiously boring names people give folders of porn on their laptops: Urban Regeneration Companies; Housing Market Renewal Pathfinders; the Sustainable Communities Plan, and so on. Many of these regeneration initiatives were funded in part by the EU.

The result of all this new policy was an almost startling change of pace as public and private sectors raced to capitalise on political support for densifying city centres. Leeds in particular came to embody both the energy of the time and how hard it was, despite all of New Labour's obsession with targets, to control these rapid developments. In just ten years, 7,000 apartments were built in the city centre, with a further 3,640 under construction in 2008 and another 7,000 with planning permission. David Ellis was a young planner who moved into one of these new blocks, Whitehall Waterfront. 'It was almost like an edge space where they couldn't quite persuade people to move in,' he recalled. Even the shop unit on the ground floor had remained unlet, becoming instead that mark of gentrification, a temporary art gallery. There had been one family with small children in the building, and another divorced dad with his regular visit from the kids, but the rest of his neighbours were those young urban professionals Sarah Beeny was always banging on about on *Property Ladder*. Whitehall Waterfront is a bulky lump, with busy panels of terracotta, cream, white and dark grey cladding betraying a sense of insecurity about its size and shape. It glitters with glass balconies, and there's a mildly upward-curving swoosh to the very top of the penthouses. Here we have the opposite of an icon, an anonymous block where a landmark might have succeeded.

'It felt like it had overreached,' said David of its isolated location in a sea of surface car parks, 'that it had gone beyond the front line, in a vanguard that was now surrounded. You got the sense that they expected all of that to be built around the same time. But for some reason that tower had been erected and there was a large buffer zone of parking. So you did feel somewhat marooned.' These days, one of those *vibrant urban quarters* we all love is finally insinuating itself between lonely Whitehall Waterfront and the city centre. Wellington Place is a mini King's Cross, all mid-rise blocks with classical proportions, artisan coffee shops and the like in the ground-floor units, very 2010s, very fixie bikes, very beards, very dungarees. David had grown up on the outskirts of Leeds and had watched these developers' towers being thrown up in the late 1990s. He remembered the indignation of his neighbours. '*Who would have wanted to live there? They're very small. Why would you want a balcony overlooking that motorway?* They were seen as quite odd and so living in them I did feel part of this new wave of city-centre residence. There was a sense that you were a little bit of a pioneer.'

Of the new apartments sold in Leeds in the decade to 2008, it was estimated that 75 to 80 per cent were sold to investors.[2] 'They were often sold off-plan to investors in the south of England,' said David, 'less so abroad then. Retired people in Surrey would buy twenty flats. I've actually got a friend who now lives in a similar one, who found out his granddad owned a flat in a 211 similar one to him. And he just bought it as an investor, he'd never actually seen it, but it was just supplementing his pension in the classic buy-to-let way.' By the late 2000s, in Leeds city centre 20 per cent of flats were empty – mostly new builds or conversions – as either people waited for them to sell or they had been mothballed by buy-to-leave landlords waiting for the prices to rise. While the top tier of luxury apartments was still selling, for most of the rest investors had overpaid for new flats and now faced making a loss, not even making the monthly mortgage repayments if they rented them out.

As all of these buy-to-let opportunities were under construction, we watched while buyers on Sarah Beeny's *Property Ladder* made a success – even if they made a pig's ear – of their investments. The most withering presence on TV since *Coronation Street*'s Ena Sharples, her series was essentially a psychopath test for new buy-to-let landlords. It was asset management, overseen by someone with a willingness to call the participants out for their bullshit decisions in the most devastatingly crushing bored drawl. How the subjects wanted Sarah to like them, to appreciate their innate gift for making the right decision to reach the *young professional market* that Sarah invoked whatever the property, whether a windmill in Ely or a basement flat in Walsall. But Sarah never did like them. She didn't approve of their tawdry taste in door handles, their thrifty purchase of a faux-granite worktop or the decision to – and this was the most unspeakable of faux pas – to add *personality*. To some extent, this was an extension of the philosophy of Ann Maurice, Channel 5's *House Doctor* from the late nineties. Maurice taught would-be sellers how to strip away every bit of personality from their home, to create a *blank canvas*, a void, a property singularity into which potential buyers would be helplessly dragged. These shows made it all feel

so easy, so obvious, so right. Buy a house to do up, get a flat to rent, sell a wreck, buy a dream. I wonder how many hours of these and other property shows I have watched over the years. And still here I am, tenant of a small private rented flat, with no desire to own, and no means of doing so if I did. They're like a comforting fantasy, as if we had the powers of a Marvel superhero or the spells of a Harry Potter character: this is how we could change the world, one doer-upper at a time.

Social researcher Chris Allen identified the groups that were driving the gentrification of Manchester's city centre in 2007: the pioneers – artists and musicians whose countercultural activities had first brought interest to neglected or impoverished parts of the city; ageing baby boomers, keen to retire with a vibrant cultural scene on their doorstep; and more transient residents, giving the urban adventure a go for a couple of years before moving on to another city or out to the suburbs.[3] Romantic notions of the city as a melting pot faced the reality of the middle-class monoculture of Docklands. And there was another group who would change districts of city centres beyond recognition – students. The New Labour government had aspirations that as many young people as possible should have the opportunity to go into higher education. As universities expanded and attracted lucrative foreign students from around the world, so the arrival of blocks of student flats in city centres everywhere from Liverpool to Plymouth, Cardiff to Wembley, would begin to change our skylines. And because student flats are built more on a budget hotel principle than on the dimensions and facilities one would have expected in an earlier age, these brashly colourful new towers house far more people than a standard block of flats. With so many policies running concurrently, so many levers being pulled, by 2007 it felt as if our cities were being driven with the choke out. 213

Following this flurry of New Labour policies came a blizzard of ambitious master plans for towns and cities across the country, most notably from artist, architect and planner Will Alsop, the era's go-to provocateur. My first experience of Alsop's work was the library built at the end of the road I lived on in Peckham in the mid-90s. I'd grown so used to the boarded-off waste ground on Sumner Road that it was a surprise to see work start on this ambitious new building. 'Its impact on Peckham was comparable to that of Owen Williams' Pioneer Health Centre seventy years earlier,' wrote critic Kenneth Powell in 2001. 'Alsop caught the mood of the local community, with its longing for change and improvement.'⁴ Another critic, Deyan Sudjic, had been less convinced. 'There is weird and wilful shape-making,' he wrote in 1996, 'the blob school of which Will Alsop is the most conspicuous British example.'⁵ The finished library was a shock. Firstly, it was a *new library*, which seemed an incredible thing at a time when chronic underfunding of these sorts of community services had been the norm for so long. Then there was its form, quite unlike any library I'd ever seen, a brightly coloured trinket box raised up over the streets.

Alsop's library was just one of many startling changes Peckham underwent around the turn of the millennium. The post-war estate at the other end of my street was also demolished, and now a mix of council, housing association and private homes in a sickly shade of Mr Kipling yellow has wodged up in its place. Popular with residents, these new homes were described by journalist Vikki Miller in *Building Design* magazine as being 'transformed from pits of urban blight into shining examples of regeneration'.⁶ With all of this investment came new middle-class residents in this once solidly working-class area. By 2010 a local multi-storey car park was playing host to Bold Tendencies, an annual art show by Hannah Barry Gallery. The concrete edifice was home to Frank's

214

Peckham Library: 'Alsop caught the mood of the local community.' © Ellen Forsyth

Cafe, whose red fabric wrap-around roof flaps merrily above the tables as if ready to drift away. Its ingenious designers, Practice Architecture, hand-built it for the princely sum of £5,000. The same year that Frank's Cafe launched, Kirstie and Phil described the already more middle-class district of Peckham Rye on *Location, Location, Location* as 'fashionable', which meant finding an affordable house for their buyers was proving tricky. Average prices for a detached house in Peckham rose from £173,200 in 1995 to £700,000 in 2020; an average flat sold for £57,123 in 1995 and £439,918 in 2020, rises of 304 and 670 per cent respectively. 'They loved Peckham Rye and now we're in Streatham,' went Kirstie's narration. 'Way to go, Phil.'

You might have expected a Labour government to have finally increased levels of council-house building, but instead the Blair renaissance relied heavily on housing associations to plug the gap 215 that had been left by that early-eighties freeze. I spoke to Shane Brownie, who had worked in the sector for decades. 'When I arrived in 93 I thought London looked disgusting!' he recalled cheerily. 'There was boarded up buildings everywhere. It was the back end of the Thatcher period. I found it quite shocking coming from New Zealand where everything's tidy.' He got a job as a research officer in Family Housing, a small housing association in Clapham. At that time the sector was full of co-operative housing schemes, where the residents had a stake in the running of their associations. But this slightly ramshackle set-up was beginning to change. 'What a lot of associations were doing was taking over a lot of these co-op buildings. Basically the council had given them to housing associations to deal with, and they were moving them onto what was called "short life"'. This meant creating short tenancies with the aim of moving as many residents out into more mainstream housing association properties.'

It felt to Shane very much like an exemplar of the age. 'I think when Blair came in – Mr Third Way – housing associations were in the right place at the right time.' They received more grants, and leveraging that against private debt meant they could do more with it. 'Having said that,' said Shane, 'Blair's record on affordable housing supply is terrible. I think the grant went up but the number of units didn't.' This would be one of New Labour's biggest failures, though none of them addressed it at the time. 'Quite often you're dealing with a lag from a problem that's caught up with you. So when Blair comes to power and Prescott's in charge, the big issue was low demand. Collapsing demand in the north, need for regeneration. And that was a crisis, people abandoning areas, house prices were collapsing. But also there was a legacy of massive underinvestment of the housing stock. Thatcher had basically just stopped funding

216   management maintenance for years in council stock. So that's

when the whole large-scale voluntary stock transfer programme came in.'

Back in July 1987, the entire municipal new town of Thamesmead in East London had been sold for £2.5 million to a non-profit company, Thamesmead Town Ltd. 'I think the sell-off is bad because they are going to put all the rents up,' said tenant Rita Davies.[7] Meanwhile, one of the new town's private house owners was more than happy: Rita Tighe said, 'I'm glad the trust is taking over because I think they'll do a better job than the council.' She even embodied the new spirit of division that had grown up between new house owners on former council estates. 'I hope they will bring the council parts up to the standard of the rest,' she said.[8] Some associations started to become big players through the sudden arrival of all this ex-council housing. Two small companies, the London Housing Trust and Quadrant Housing Association (founded by a vicar, the Reverend Nicolas Stacey), merged all the way back in 1973, forming L&Q. By 2019 they owned almost 100,000 homes in London and the south-east, and their name would appear everywhere in redeveloping areas in London like the Olympic Park or Elephant and Castle. And it wasn't just the rental market that housing associations like L&Q went after. By 2003, two and a half thousand people a year in London were part-buying a shared ownership flat through a housing association. Buyers paid roughly 20 to 30 per cent less than the market value for flats because of the grants that associations received for each unit they built. Steve Coleman, Deputy Chief Executive of Notting Hill Housing Group, said 'a rule of thumb is that poor boroughs are easier than rich ones'.[9]

A classic new housing association development in 2007 was Banstead Court, beside the Westway urban motorway in East Acton, London. It was built on a brownfield site, as 60 per cent of   217 all New Labour homes were set to be. Here, L&Q had developed a 3-acre site with architects Gardner Stewart. The problems in building in such a polluted area hung over the development. 'People in the houses on the other side of the road can't open their windows because of the diesel dust,' said the architects. 'The site is category D-listed by the World Health Organization: the worst possible and usually impossible for residential.'[10] The idea of these new flats was that the building itself would create a sound barrier, and purified air would be pumped in, rather than the car fumes from next door. 'The problem with Livingstone's quota,' complained journalist Lucy Alexander, pointing to the then London mayor's rule that 50 per cent of all new developments should be 'affordable', 'is that the developer of a luxury apartment block is obliged to fill half of it with council tenants. To the buyer who spends hundreds of thousands, it seems unfair that the bloke next door gets his free. So developers differentiate between residents.'[11] Sean Fitzsimons of L&Q pointed to developers who 'often make social tenants use separate entrances, or put them in separate blocks next to the road. Communities don't bond like that. We made sure tenants and owners signed the same good neighbour agreements. We also encourage social tenants to buy, to give them aspirations and help get rid of the stigma.'[12] Richard Rogers's urban renaissance might have been sold on ideas of creating vibrant new neighbourhoods and reviving neglected areas, but in the application of these policies private landlords, housing associations and property investors knew that it was money that drove all of this – it was the motor behind the Blair boom, and for some years it looked as if it was enabling the hopes of the Urban Task Force and changing Britain permanently. And for council tenants this seemed to mean becoming invisible.

The architects called it 'a vast weather-protected centre in the tradition of the Great Exhibition Hall of 1851'.[1] It would be built to mark a significant moment in our history, a chance for us to come together and wonder at the incredible world around us. Inside, it would be an immense activity centre with a focus on family participation. 'This themepark is based on the idea of educational fun,' stated the brochure, a sentence to make even the bravest among us shiver.[2] Visitors would progress around the attraction through a series of interactive zones, areas themed on land, air and space, communications, the body, the world, energy and the sea. It would 'help us prepare for to-morrow by making us more aware of what is happening to-day', said MP Sir John Eden.[3] And, he added, 'it will be fun.' Fun. Fun in the edutainment zones, fun beneath the roof of a vast High Tech structure, fun as we looked to the future and marvelled. A new hope, a new Britain, a new fun.

This was WonderWorld, conceived in 1982 to sit on the outskirts of Corby, a post-war industrial new town in Northamptonshire. This gigantic do-gooding covered theme park was the product of research by apartheid-era South African construction firm Group Five into the British, European and US leisure industry. The philosophy behind it sounded utopian or dystopian, depending on how full you like your glass. 'In the private sector, as in the public sector, workforces and workloads are being reduced and the need to fill the vacuum of spare time will be enormous,' went the thinking, as if straight from Aldous Huxley.[4] WonderWorld was going to distract us from all of this endless free time being lavished upon us. In 1981, Group Five brought together a team to create this new kind of attraction, to be led by Derek Walker, 219 the gifted architect/planner of Britain's largest new town, Milton Keynes. Corby was a much earlier model, and its main industry, the steelworks, had closed down the year before, resulting in 10,000 people losing their jobs and local unemployment reaching 30 per cent. The council were understandably desperate to make a go of WonderWorld. The structure was to be a large multi-level building nestled into a valley, its huge lightweight canopy suspended on trusses. Walker, it turned out, was obsessed with Disneyland. 'The external inspiration of the WonderWorld venture has developed from the manipulative marketing and management base of Disney,' he wrote, 'which has produced a new formula including an enclosure with flexibility and linked additives inspired by Paxton's Palace.'[5] It would be, he said, the antidote to 'sloppy, feckless Britain'.[6]

The zones and pavilions of WonderWorld present a version of Britain recognisable to viewers of the BBC's more sensible factual output: *Tomorrow's World*, say, or *Blue Peter*. The Land, inspired by *Wind in the Willows*, *Lord of the Rings* and TV naturalist David Bellamy. The Rhyme Zone, based on the idea of a lost village, a fantasy wonderland where nursery rhymes come to life. Here, you could visit the Jack Spratt restaurant or ride on Thomas the Tank Engine around a town square in which people practised ancient crafts: there were potters, weavers and, of course, thatchers. In the Air and Space zone there would be a Battle of Britain combat simulator (obvs), a Patrick Moore observatory (even more obvs), and Arthur C. Clarke's Mysterious Universe (which was meant to be entirely un-obvs). The Communications zone would have a Dan Dare restaurant almost two decades after the comic book hero's heyday, and a post office. There was a zone where you could learn all about health and safety – quite the draw. The Body Zone was a chance for Jonathan Miller to exhaustively overexplain how he made learning fun, while the Terry Gilliam restaurant (really) sat conveniently next to a drug store. In the Concert Hall there would be cyclical performances of Jeff Wayne's apocalyptic rock opera *The War of the Worlds* alongside a disco and rollerama. Why not hop on a monorail and hear all about nuclear power? Or visit the Jack Nicklaus golf academy, the water slides or – most thrillingly – the bank? It's hard not to see WonderWorld as a broad satire of what was actually to come.

Kirsteen McNish grew up in Corby and her father, David, worked for the council. 'Dad had said WonderWorld was seen as a serious thing initially,' she explained, 'and that lots of satellite firms were set up because of it; it had a free rates period for twelve months which in turn provided more employment.' But for Corby, it was all too good to be true. By 1990 the scheme had collapsed and there was a *Private Eye* exposé, revealing that Group Five had set up WonderWorld with just £1,000, relying on bleeding the local council for the rest. Kirsteen recalled how the local press and nearby more affluent towns and villages revelled in the collapse of the scheme and Corby's misery. 'It was portrayed as a town that was rough, hard and directionless in the media,' she said, 'which wasn't helped by this scheme falling down soon after its announcement. The reality was that the town was made up of largely decent hard-working people who had moved hundreds of miles from Scotland to live in "Little Glasgow" and it had proven good for around thirty to forty years, but then fallen on hard times.' David, Kirsteen's father, had always been suspicious of the plan, 'namely because the site had formerly opencast iron ore foundations and belonged to British Steel,' she explained, 'so they would always realistically have been on shaky ground and would have inhibited the integrity of the land.' He couldn't recall any engineers ever being involved to assess the viability of the site. As it became obvious to most   221 that WonderWorld had always been a non-starter, the McNishes found it 'particularly cruel given the desperate situation so many people had found themselves in, with no employment and hungry families to feed'. A sign announcing WonderWorld had gone up in a field on the edge of town shortly after the plan was first announced. 'Someone graffitied "Wonderwhen?" under the WonderWorld logo,' recalled Kirsteen, 'which was both comical and kind of poignant.' And even that wasn't the final indignity: 'The sign finally fell down in a strong March wind a couple of years after.' The heady dreams and cynical plans of a few blown away on the breeze.

I was born in 1970. The first twenty-nine years of my life were haunted by the impossibility of the year 2000. In the mid-seventies, even a science fiction series called *Space 1999* shied away from how futuristic that following year would be – and *they* were envisaging people living on a moonbase. Arthur C. Clarke's 1948 short story 'The Sentinel' was filmed in 1968 as *2001: A Space Odyssey* and saw humans journeying away through the stars. That's what it would be like, I thought, as the years ticked by. Instead, it was a quiet announcement in John Major's Conservative Party manifesto for the 1992 General Election that offered the prosaic reality. Alongside support for Manchester's bid to hold the Olympics in 2000 came the statement that they intended 'to help another major city [i.e. not Manchester] – chosen by competition – to hold an international trade fair to be a showcase of British innovation for the twenty-first century'.[7] There it was, our moonbase, our space odyssey, in big brown resin specs peering out from behind the wheel of a well-kept Volvo estate, probably full of brochures about kitchen worktops.

By 1995 there were sixty locations in the running. But really, cut to the chase, it was just going to end up in London, right?

When a US TV company attempted to hire the Greenwich Observatory on the prime meridian for millennium eve, it drew attention to the fact that this was probably a Good Idea, although everyone responsible vehemently denied it. The Millennium Commission dutifully whittled their list of potential sites down to four: the functional National Exhibition Centre on the outskirts of Birmingham; a deprived area of Stratford in East London beside the River Lea; Derby's Pride Park; and some dangerously polluted derelict land that had recently housed Greenwich gasworks. In the name of fair play, the four shortlisted sites immediately set about trashing each other's chances. Roger Burman, chair of the Birmingham bid, pounced on Greenwich: 'It's a contaminated gas site with toxic waste which will have huge transport problems, particularly by car,' he told the press. 'Derby and Stratford are also on old gas sites too, and so also need to be decontaminated.'[8] Meanwhile MPs from Manchester, Leeds and Sheffield fed back to the minister responsible, Virginia Bottomley, that if it wasn't going to be them then London might *just* be acceptable, but Birmingham was beyond the pale. Greenwich won the bid.

Long before a millennium celebration had been mooted, a team from Richard Rogers had been on site master-planning the regeneration of the Greenwich Peninsula and had vital on-the-ground knowledge. 'Our reason to get involved was to maximise the legacy if it came onto the site,' explained Mike Davies, partner at Rogers Stirk Harbour, who was leading the team. He was brought in to speak to the Millennium Commission in an attempt to give some sense of scale and urgency to the proceedings. The contract to operate the attractions on the Greenwich site went to Imagination, a company specialising in designing spectacular events for museums and corporate clients. They had been led since 1978 by an inspirational recluse, Gary Withers. One of 223 their most spectacular interventions had been the rebuilding of an Edwardian crescent in London's Store Street as their offices in 1990. These new spaces were designed by a survivor of modernist mavericks Archigram, Ron Herron, working with one of the pioneers of High Tech tensile structures, Ted Happold. Some of their spirit, skill and suspended fabric would make its way into the eventual millennium centrepiece. The commission had been blown away by Withers's immersive presentation, although it had been initially attached to the Birmingham bid rather than to Greenwich. Given the sheer scale of the project, Imagination realised they couldn't design the whole thing, and so yet another competition was held to design the twelve pavilions they'd proposed in their time-themed concept. One entry suggested underground pavilions beneath a grass pyramid called millennium mount; another had a 'chameleon ramp', a kind of giant Billie Jean video where the ground changed colour as you moved across it. There was a proposed 'hall of intellect, avenue of the subconscious and towers of emotion' – send help – while another centred on the obvious idea – we've all had it – of computer-controlled helium balloons moving to music.

The commission expected to raise £150 million in private finance to make the celebrations possible, but by 1996 they'd only made a quarter of that. After a desperate round of meetings with corporations including British Airways and British Gas, full-time Deputy Prime Minister and part-time millennium commissioner Michael Heseltine realised that they would never make their target. He remembered being visited by fellow commissioners Simon Jenkins and Jennie Page and having to break the bad news to them. '*I'm afraid it's over,*' he said. '*We have a deadline of a date when the money has to be spent and the private sector directors that we had appointed to carry the thing out said that they cannot* 224 *countenance spending more money that we haven't got, because* *we haven't got the money to finish the job. And they're going to resign and I'm afraid we're going to have to pull the project.* And at that moment I was all that was left of the project.' He realised, against every instinct of his party, that they would have to nationalise the scheme. There was outrage, even from people who liked nationalising things. Labour backbencher Jeremy Corbyn to Virginia Bottomley: 'Does she think it would be better if, as a nation heading into the twenty-first century, we set the real objective of ensuring that every homeless person had a roof over his head and that there was no longer a housing shortage?' These people, Corbyn asserted, were 'not excited by the idea of 2,000-feet-high office blocks, a ferris wheel or exhibition centres.'[9] The budget continued to rise, and an air of desperate incompetence began to characterise the portrayal of the nebulous exhibition in the press. Shadow culture secretary Jack Cunningham told the *Financial Times*, 'I am not signing a blank cheque on behalf of the Labour party. When they give us a full breakdown of the costs, then we will consider it.'[10] An unnamed source inside the project remarked that 'nobody in their right mind will give £10 million if there is not a firm political consensus behind the project . . . They do not want another British Library* on their hands.'[11]

Political arguments over the millennium project between Heseltine and opposition leader Tony Blair – whose Labour party was well ahead in the polls – created a pattern of unhelpful yo-yo funding. Jennie Page of the Millennium Commission

---

* Colin St John Wilson and M. J. Long's seemingly cursed British Library building beside London St Pancras station had been several decades in the making. Established in 1973 as an entity in its own right, it finally opened in 1997. It had been designed by modernist architects at the very moment of crisis in their craft, resulting in a strange hybrid building, combining the monolithic calm and functionalism of a modernist monastery with subtle hints of Japanese decoration, although the long pitched roofs, hard brick facades and nods to picturesque have become more familiar features in out-of-town malls.

recalled the resulting budget cuts had been a 'real hack-and-destroy process'.[12] Hezza had gone cap in hand to Blair to keep the project alive. 'We had big trouble persuading Tony Blair's government to continue with it,' Heseltine told me. 'I went to see Tony and I feel that was decisive.' How decisive? 'I saved the Dome.' Okay, but there were accounts from the time that record the New Labour leader cutting their meeting short because he was off to meet some business leaders. Either way, Blair was finally persuaded to take on the project, creeping budget and all, rebranding it as part of his effort to make Britain a young, forward-looking country. As Adam Nicolson, biographer of the Dome, has it, 'this was the opposition as government, government as opposition'.[13]

'We can't move the millennium,' architect Mike Davies recalls telling the commissioners in a crunch meeting, 'and they kinda got that. It's the best protection we ever had.' In December 1996 his winning design for the central structure was shown off, just three years before this as yet unstarted building had to be finished, fitted out and ready for opening. I met Davies in the Leadenhall Building (that's the Cheesegrater to you and me), where the company in which he's a partner – Rogers Stirk Harbour – are now based, and he brought along all manner of archive material. He's an unconventional figure, to say the least. On my way to the interview I glimpsed him walking through neighbouring Leadenhall Market. In all of that ornate Victorian splendour, Davies appeared as a high-tech Dumbledore, long pointed grey beard, half-moon specs perched on the tip of his nose, dressed from head to toe in bright red, as he has for decades. 'We knew Greenwich inside out,' said Davies, 'because I'd stood on the site in March that year and I remember thinking, *I don't think I've ever been so cold in my life*. I checked and there was no

land over two hundred feet between the millennium dome and

Siberia. I was thinking, my God, the biggest challenge on this site is shelter. It's midwinter. You could have an opening with minus four and hail and God knows what.'

Earlier on, Heseltine had grown impatient with the dithering of the Millennium Commission and told Mike Davies to go with Gary Withers and rethink Imagination's ideas. 'Gary had done a fantastic bit of work,' said Davies. 'There were twelve pavilions in a circle, so lots of things similar to the final project. And a central pavilion, and they all linked together with a walkway in the middle. So basically the same structure was there. And even there were twelve little spheres around the outside and those spheres would go all over the country collecting people's wishes to bring them back for the millennium.' But the pressure to deliver something in such a short time frame and on such a polluted site was weighing down on them. 'So Gary and I went back to his place and sat around with a cup of tea and said *what are we going to do?*' A return to his lightweight roots appealed to Davies. He went home and sketched out a dome to fit on the site – initially 400 metres across, and reduced to 365 metres thanks to Gary's intervention the next day, which helped with the symbolism of the whole project. This huge circular tent would nestle perfectly into the 270-degree bend in the Greenwich Peninsula. Twelve masts would hold up the tent, dividing the circle into a vast clock face. The tent's edges would be pulled into twenty-four scallops to denote the hours of the day. 'I wouldn't claim individual authorship for it,' said Davies. 'Most really good ideas come from a dialogue between people.'

Two weeks of frantic sketching and, in Mike's case, beard-stroking later, and they were back in front of the committee. They told them that they had to start immediately, that reclaiming the site was beyond urgent, and that their idea meant now that the pavilions would not have to be buildings – they 227 could be stage sets within this new structure. And then they unveiled the first drawings of the Dome. 'They were still sketches at the time,' said Davies, 'which I'd done on my circular kitchen table.' There were nervous moments as he and Withers stood in front of the group. 'They said, *lovely idea*. Heseltine said he knew where this was coming from. Bear in mind he had built a large cover for the garden festival in Liverpool. So he understood – not everybody did.' There were mutterings in the architectural press that the design was merely a version of Frei Otto's stadium for the 1972 Munich Olympics, and Ted Happold, the Dome's lead structural engineer, had worked with Otto on some of his extraordinary vast suspended tents. But Davies's inspiration went back even further: he wanted to recreate the sense of wonder he had felt when visiting the Festival of Britain, aged nine. 'You don't realise what the early influences do to you,' he told me. 'One of my favourite ten objects of all time is the Skylon, which is magnificently ingenious.' Powell and Moya's Skylon had stood on the South Bank of the Thames near where the London Eye stands now, a long spindle suspended gracefully in the air by wires, a bit of *Dan Dare* sci-fi derring-do for the Festival. 'It was the ultimate no-hands thing. I stood beside it at night and it was beautiful. . . . How the Skylon stood up was magic. My favourite buildings tend to be ones that have got a bit of magic to their structure, the Dome's no exception.' And on site they would need all the magic they could get. 'We did a survey and it turned out to be really poisonous,' said Mike Davies. 'Mercury, antimony . . .' There were pools of luminous green slime. 'The pollution history was stunning.' In the end, they removed a metre and a half of the topsoil from all over the 300-hectare site. As a final thank you to Birmingham for its bid, this toxic earth was taken to the Midlands and poured down 228 some old mine workings.

The first foundations for the Dome were laid on 23 June 1997. 'It had the most amazing number of JCBs on that site,' recalled Andrew Partridge, who was also working for Rogers. 'My son was very young, three I think, and I took him there and he was locked on to the fence, couldn't budge him for an hour. He was just mesmerised. Over fifty of them.' Mike Davies remembers the difficulty in convincing the locals of their vision and the impact it would have, not just when it was finished, but during construction too. 'There was one pub on the site and I remember at a planning meeting the man who ran the pub came up to me and he said *Are you one of the architects*? And I said *Yes I am*. And he said *Oh God, you're going to knock my building down. It's going to be a terrible problem. I've been there so many years, it's a lovely place. The Pilot Inn.* And I said, *You are going to have a problem*. He said, *Oh God, I knew you were going to say that.* I said, *The problem you're going to have is you're going to have three thousand people and you're going to be the only pub for five miles or something. And your biggest problem is getting a large enough beer pipe into your pub.*'

A month into his new job as Prime Minister and four days before those foundations were laid, Tony Blair had visited the site in the politician's away kit of hard hat, wellies and high-vis. There he issued five demands, some with more than a whiff of Corby's edutainment WonderWorld. The exhibition centre would now have to be permanent, he declared. After the cost had escalated there must be no more passed on to the taxpayer. The content of the exhibition should be *exciting*, with a focus on educational displays of British technological expertise. It must relate to the whole nation. And there was to be a new management structure to provide 'creative force'. This was an attempt to distance the Dome from the air of Majorite business expo that still hung over it. 'Are we in Britain going to give people a derelict site, 229 or the finest exhibition that the world has seen?' Blair asked the assembled media on the muddy site, most of whom were betting on the former. Now it seemed real, there was already speculation in the press about what the Dome might become after the Millennium. A Madame Tussauds theme park? A thrill-seekers' Universal Studios-type experience? Or the stadium for a possible London Olympic bid?

'There were sixty mountain climbers taken on as riggers,' recalled Mike Davies, 'who were experts at hanging off rocks. And I was comfortable because I was chairman of the sandstone climbing club of Great Britain at the time.' For the people working on site, it became a bit of a melting pot. 'We had the theatre guys,' recalled Andrew Partridge, 'and we had people in the rock business as well. There was quite a lot of swapping of technologies.' For Mike Davies, it was an inspiring experience working so closely with different disciplines. 'What was great about it was it wasn't architecture, engineering . . . You couldn't separate it. If you wanted something sorted you walked three desks and it was sorted, rather than writing a letter to the engineer and waiting a week to reply.' The Dome continued to evolve during its swift construction – principally the material used to cover it. 'What's lovely about the fabric is during the process of development it was a PVC dome,' explained Davies. He was keen to change materials to something more permanent: PTFE, a material made from glass and Teflon used on some stadiums in the US. 'It was an innovative, odd fabric,' said Davies. 'I flung a square metre of it on my gas stove at home and stood back and opened the kitchen door, expecting it to go up in flames. Nothing happened at all apart from little brown marks where the gas underneath turned it a little bit brown. It's a remarkable material.' And all these years later it's still gleaming white, and so shiny that flies have trouble landing on it. The gleaming absurdity of it adds to its almost terrifying size when spotted between buildings on the opposite bank. But it has helped it become a genuine London landmark. 'I remember when the Dome first appeared on *EastEnders*!' said Andrew Partridge, excitedly. 'It was like, *wow!*'

It might have been making its mark on the map, but what would go in it? 'We got invited to bid for two zones at the Millennium Dome,' recalled exhibition designer Peter Higgins of Land Design Studio, who, in his polo shirt and Caesar crop looked every bit a former Britpop frontman. Before he, his wife Shirley Walker and James Dibble set up Land, they had worked at Imagination, although other Zone designers came from a mix of backgrounds. 'There were so-called production companies who do trade shows and product launches. And then there were architects' – such as Zaha Hadid and Nigel Coates. Higgins bid for the Faith Zone and the Play Zone, and won the latter.

One of the designers from the process made a particularly vivid impression. 'Zaha was just brilliant,' said Peter. He recalled a meeting at the National Millennium Experience Company with all of the other prospective Zone designers, and of an encounter between Zaha Hadid and Jennie Page, the Company's Churchillian head. 'Jennie Page had been on the Millennium Commission and had rejected Zaha's bid for the opera house,' he remembered, of Zaha's cancelled scheme for Cardiff Bay. 'Jennie Page came in and was like' – he mimed exquisitely pained cheek kissing – '*heeello,* Zaha was like' – more cheek kissing – '*heeello.* And the lift started to go up and Zaha goes *fucking bitch!*' He laughed. 'She was a real hoot, you know what she was like, because she was wealthy and big and powerful and clever, she scared men shitless. And I quite liked her for that. I liked that kind of reversal of power that she took on.' On the plans for the Dome, Andrew Partridge had shown me Zaha's contribution. 'She cantilevered herself outside her zone,' he laughed. 'It does express the spirit of each architect,' added Mike Davies. 'Some people stay in their box, some people ultimately bust out of it.' Partridge explained the extraordinary fact that 'Zaha's steel was heavier than the Dome'. Davies, ever the lightweight structures guy, jumped in. 'I heard there were 1,100 tons of steel in Zaha's exhibit. *Not* more than the Dome – a *lot* more!'

There had been a relentless torment of jeering negative press around the project. But eventually Blair's love-bombing of powerful media owners such as Rupert Murdoch began to pay off. Previously critical outlets like *The Sun* were suddenly full of excitement. 'It's Domeday' ran a headline that spring, with the most begrudging of all caveats: 'Like most of our readers we believe the money could have been better spent on schools and hospitals,' ran an editorial, but now that the project had passed the point of no return 'we should all get behind it and ensure its success'.[14] They even renamed one of its reporters Mandy Millennium, their Dome Dame. New Labour's own Mandy, master of spin Peter Mandelson, had been put in charge of the project. He seemed the perfect choice, as grandson of Labour grandee Herbert Morrison, one of the driving forces behind the Festival of Britain. In a press release, Mandelson stated that 'I want the Dome to capture the spirit of modern Britain – a nation that is confident, excited, impatient for the future'.[15] He told the House of Commons that one of the main attractions in the Dome would be that familiar twenty-first-century sport 'surfball', which six months later he claimed was merely 'illustrative' – he had made it up. Expectations of what it could achieve were high. Former BBC chairman Michael Grade called the project 'a living, breathing Internet' – a reminder that only 13 per cent of the UK had used the internet by 1998, with Grade sounding firmly in the remaining 87 per cent.[16] Despite this optimism, architect Mike Davies recalled: 'I was going in taxis and people would say, *what do you do for a living*, and I would think I'm not going to tell them because I'll get all sorts of crap from the taxi drivers.'

By 1998 the costs of the project began to rise again, up a third to £758 million. Mike Davies was swift to point out that this was to do with the contents of the Dome, not the structure he'd designed. 'The cost of the interior was vastly greater than the cost of the building. The building was extremely economical. In 2000 costs, the building was £43m. That was 7 per cent of the budget. We delivered it on time, we delivered it on budget – under the budget! You can't build a supermarket for the price of that per square metre.' When it came to the insides the process wasn't proceeding too smoothly, with Stephen Bayley, former head of the Design Museum, quitting as creative director of the Millennium Experience in January 1998 after falling out with Mandelson. 'The man responsible for hijacking a project that could have been one of the great international world exhibitions, but is instead going to be a crabby and demoralising theme park, is Peter Mandelson,' wrote Bayley.[17]

That December, Robert McCrum, literary editor at the *Observer*, was persuaded by cheerleading journalist Simon Jenkins to do for the Millennium Dome what novelist Laurie Lee had for the Festival of Britain: label the exhibits. He managed to persuade McCrum to spend six months working at the Dome. There was a huge amount of co-ordination required to pull it off. For example, every town in the UK had been asked to present its story to be told in the Our Town Theatre. 'The awkward fact is the Dome has to belong to everyone if it's to justify the expenditure of money and effort,' McCrum explained.[18] Meanwhile, there were 'steel cables from Doncaster, reinforced glass 233 fibre from the Isle of Wight, masts from Bolton, the cardboard for the Living Island zone from a papermill in Halifax'.[19] Devising the names for the Dome's fourteen zones was not as easy as it sounded. 'Even the most trifling naming decision has been approved by what has sometimes seemed like hundreds of separate, competing sub-committees,' he wrote. 'Corporate sponsors such as Ford and Sky have wanted to see a return on their £12m investment and care desperately what their particular bits are called.'[20] You can see from the names of the zones that they were going for the kind of big open concepts beloved of advertising agencies. There were the touchy-feely ones in the 'Who We Are area: Body, Faith, Mind and Self Portrait. The What We Do area was either super-active or quietly contemplative: the zones were Journey, Learning, Money, Play, Rest and Talk. Where We Live was the final area, with three rather more hippyish-sounding zones: Home Planet, Living Island and Shared Ground. Sponsors included BAE Systems, Boots, British Airways, BT, Ford, Marks and Spencer, and Tesco.

Land Design Studio, at work on their Play Zone, drew on cutting-edge work from Ars Electronica, an avant-garde Austrian organisation promoting artists working in computing and the digital domain. Shirley Walker, co-designer of the zone, recalled exploring all of the new digital possibilities opened up by their contacts there, 'from interactivity to touch screens, it was mind-blowing. I just remember thinking, *Oh my God, I can't believe that you can touch a hard surface that's got a projection and you can do that and it moves*. The things that we just take for granted now, I remember thinking it was like magic!' She mentioned the ping-pong exhibit, which I loved when I played it at the Dome: a game of virtual table tennis with up to a hundred players, a mass Nintendo Wii years before its 234 time. Problems came when they were told their zone was to be sponsored by Rupert Murdoch's TV company, BSkyB, who were about to launch digital television. 'We met with Elisabeth Murdoch and we had a tour to the site with her,' recalled Peter. 'Clearly it didn't align to what we were trying to do. We came upon the idea that we would see the future of play through the digital. Which was very prescient.' It sounded audacious and visionary, just what the Dome's originators had wanted. 'But Sky weren't interested in this. They just wanted to focus on the future of digital television. And we resisted it to the point where we said to Jennie Page and Claire Sampson [Head of Production] this is not going to work, we can't work with Sky, we're out. And we literally walked out the room.' A week later he was called to a meeting with Jennie Page. 'She said to me, *look, we understand that you don't want to work with Sky for all sorts of reasons. We quite like the journey you're taking, it's looking very interesting. We are prepared to not necessarily apply a sponsor to your zone but we'll underwrite it and would that work for you?*' Peter was delighted.

Twelve days before Millennium Eve, 14,000 people were brought in as part of an enormous tech rehearsal, to test out how it would all work on the night. *Daily Telegraph* journalist Susannah Herbert visited with thirteen-year-old Jim. 'If you believe the blurb, the Dome was designed to answer three questions: Who are we? Where do we live? And what do we do?' she wrote. 'We left none the wiser. But we all wanted to go back.'[21] A lot of it was still not working and under the guise of writing a millennium message, people typed swear words into the Dome's computers. The last few days before launch were chaotic and exhausting. Twenty-four hours before showtime, the Greenwich site looked like it needed detoxifying all over again, deep as it was in piles of rubbish, as 350 cleaners and technicians worked all night to make the event happen and anxious exhibitors ran around desperately trying to get everything finished. 'It's like Dunkirk,' one told journalist Michael White, not entirely reassuringly.[22]

When the big night arrived, in an echo of other important political turning points of the twentieth century, a sealed train was to play a significant role. This one was on the London Underground Jubilee Line's new extension, terminating at Stratford. On that cold December evening, the assembled great and the good – most fatefully for the Dome, a group of powerful media owners and editors – found themselves stuck at the station by a chaotic security operation, as scanners failed and staff took to laborious frisking by hand. The do-you-know-who-I-ams must have been deafening. 'I was grabbed by the neck by the head of BAA, who was a good man,' recalled Mike Davies. 'And he grabbed me and said *You bastards. Why didn't you let us manage the fucking security.* His wife had gone home in a fury with the children at 11:45, still queueing at Stratford to get through the police security.' She was not the only one to walk away before even getting to the Dome, dreams of the millennium party, branded One Amazing Night, ending for some in a different sort of amazement altogether.

While chaos was unfolding at Stratford, Mike Davies made rather more regal progress to the Dome. He was in a boat with the Queen. 'She instructed the architect to come along with his family, which I did. There was the Duke of Edinburgh, the whole royal family was there.' He found himself nattering away to Princess Anne, a fellow yacht enthusiast. 'It was very relaxed and informal. We arrived at Queen Elizabeth II Pier, which is on the far side of the Dome, and it was named at that moment. So I had to escort her off the boat, escort her into the Dome.' I'm imagining Mike in his red suit and tie, and the Queen in tangerine, 236 walking towards the entrance and clashing awfully – visually at least. 'And then we all sat, because we got there about ten minutes past ten. And it was empty. Now all the other people should have been there. There was sixty of us sitting in the royal area making small talk! What do you say to the Queen just to pass the time of day! And she was relaxed because it was informal. Eventually people started trickling in, and they were still trickling in at five minutes to twelve. It was really last-minute stuff.'

Meanwhile, Play Zone designer Peter Higgins had his own entourage that night. He was being tracked by a BBC film crew. He and Shirley had a six-week-old baby to take care of, and it was also the first time their mothers had met. '*Right, could you do a piece live to camera to NBC in the States?*' someone asked him. 'Okay, so I go to do that. And I'm on a big tower beyond the Dome. We'd lost the satellite, we'd got the satellite, we're coming out of commercials, and action! *I'm here with Peter Higgins, designer of the Dome. – No, just a minute, I didn't design the Dome! I designed one of the Zones in the Dome* . . . And I said to him, and this is absolutely true, I said *I've got to go now because I've got to take Tony Blair round our zone at ten o'clock.*' He still looked astonished as he recalled the experience almost twenty years later. 'So I ran across the tarmac, I can really picture it, it was such an important moment in my life.' Once inside, he could see Blair, Cherie and their two kids pushing through the crowds towards the Play Zone, so he joined them in the colourful high-tech interactive zone they had created.

'He *did not* want to be in there. We have a look round and he was completely vacant, he wasn't with it. He seemed preoccupied. There was definitely something happening. Anyway, so he left. And eventually there was a big show in the middle and it was New Year's Eve, the new millennium, *da-da-da-da-da*! It was a big, big moment. So I found out the next day that just before he arrived, the IRA had issued a bomb scare. So then they go to Blair, this is my speculative thought, and they say *you know what, this is your call.* So I see him about ten minutes later! I see this petrified figure walking towards me with his children and his wife. *Sod the Queen and the rest of the parliament, all of the press barons, what about my family?* So when we walked around for that ten minutes he was obviously preoccupied and clearly went ahead and made the call that we're going to go for it. If he'd pulled the plugs and we'd have all emptied out it would just have been the biggest disaster of all time. You can imagine. This was the millennium eve, this was the new era, everybody's there, they'd already screwed up getting everybody in, can you imagine when they are all hoofed out? We were all finished. So he made the call.'

It certainly gave all of those extra precautions at Stratford some sort of context. A couple of miles away, I was one of two and a half million people who congregated along the Thames to watch the 'river of fire'. My main memory of standing by Tower Bridge that night was of trying not to drink too much because of the toilet situation. Earlier that day, Blair had opened the 'millennium wheel' – not yet known as the London Eye – although it carried no passengers because it was still undergoing safety checks. When it was finally opened, Julia Barfield and David Marks's novelty landmark became an immediate hit, attracting thirty million visitors in the first eight years, particularly remarkable considering it was only given a lifespan of five years on site, with a proviso that it would be dismantled and erected somewhere less conspicuous. Its popularity might help explain why for years it was impossible to date someone online whose profile didn't include a photo of them pouting over Westminster.

As midnight approached in the Dome, eight local school-238 children were sent by the Queen to release the huge golden curtains that surrounded the amphitheatre. When the drapes dropped, the vastness of the Dome was revealed, in a *coup de théâtre* that made even the cynical journalists in the crowd – well, the ones who had made it – gasp. Come the hour, it became clear to anyone gawping at Her Majesty that the Queen had not celebrated New Year in public before. She forgot to cross her arms to hold hands with neighbours Blair and Prince Philip, and seemed to have forgotten the words to Auld Lang Syne. None of this was important, of course, except to those editors and media owners who'd been caught at Stratford and sensed blood. 'I remember getting the Tube back,' said architect Andrew Partridge, 'and there were all sorts of strange people on the Tube. I sat down with my wife Jane, who was heavily pregnant, and there was Leon Brittan' – a former Tory minister – 'opposite. And there was a guy sitting next to him with like cans of lager smoking a cigarette and blowing it in his face.'

As the tired and emotional journalists began to file their poison pen letters, one reporter broke with the pack to share his genuine delight at being there. Charles Spencer had been sent by the *Daily Telegraph*, no doubt to maul the proceedings. Instead, he was rather overcome. For starters, his six-year-old son was 'completely gobsmacked by the Dome and all its works'. Not only that, 'the social mix was genuinely moving, a vision of the possibility of a truly classless society'. While the crowd had many establishment figures, the majority had been nominated by their communities for good works. Father and son explored the different zones on offer. Spencer rattled through all the emotions. He found the Living Island exhibit, with its Donald McGill postcard tweeness, 'positively obnoxious as it self-righteously peddles its bullying environmental message'. They loved Timekeepers, a multilevel adventure playground where you could fire foam balls at people, though for them best of all was the Body Zone, 239 providing 'moments that produce genuine awe, with amplified noises of pumping blood, and the extraordinary feeling that you have returned to the womb as sperm rush up to impregnate an egg'. But it was the communal aspects that most thrilled him, and which provided the most memorable moments. 'The Dome opening celebrations really did turn into a people's party,' he wrote, 'with the audience spontaneously taking over the stage once the performers had left it to dance in the year 2000. It's not often that one shares in a moment of communal, uncomplicated joy but this was one of them. One amazing night, in fact, just as promised.'[23] And what of Peter Higgins's forward-thinking Play Zone? 'It was pretty much perceived to be the most successful zone in the Dome,' Higgins told me, 'and there is documentation of that in exit polls.' Which he duly showed me, years of not being able to say 'but our bit was great' clearly still rankling. 'The most important thing for me was that we delivered something that was exactly entirely appropriate for the vision of the Dome. How do we see our future, and the future of play is digital, that's what we said, and we got it right pretty much.'

I visited the Dome later that year. My boss decided we'd have a brainstorming day there, and so we, the marketing depart- ment of HarperCollins publishers, mooched around the exhibit, slightly baffled by it all. The structure itself felt incredible – and quite sweaty under the gauzy whiteness of the membrane. Being beneath such a vast fabric surface was itself a memorable ex- perience, the tent-like structure maintaining a festival air, a village fete thrown in a flying saucer. We munched our sand- wiches while watching the circus theatrics of Sky Girl and Earth Boy in the Dome's slightly cringey musical interlude devised by Peter Gabriel. The zones were the main problem, a succession of themes largely illustrated in the lamest possible way. The Money Zone was typical, where a giant coin clunked through a

The central performance space in the Dome in July 2000, with the Body Zone in the background © Martin Pettitt

mock-up of the economy, someone's dullest idea brought to life (or death) with all the charm of Norman Lamont removing a corn. Along with the Play Zone, my favourite bit was the Rest Zone, designed by Richard Rogers's team, where you could lie down on a sloped surface bathed in soothing lights while listening to New Age music (look, it was 2000, we've all grown). It felt very much a family attraction, and so for a group of young cynics on a works outing it was a strange experience. We weren't quite sure what we were doing there, or what we were meant to think or feel about it. For all of the effort and expense of the attractions inside, it was the building itself that made the biggest impact, the projection of a future civilisation.

Three weeks into January 2000 and already the number of visitors was drying up. 'It's our quietest week yet,' said one worker, Julie. 'And God knows what it will be like next week. Mondays are always the worst.'[24] After a fortnight of crisis talks, £60   241 million was given to the Dome to cover its operating losses. Tony, a local from Charlton directing people through the turnstiles and ticket booths, tried to give a sense of perspective to it all. 'I am in my sixties. This may be the last job I have. It is tough when people have a go at us. We are all down. But it's January, it's cold, people are paying off their credit card bills. It will pick up when the weather gets better.'[25] Behind the scenes, as people stopped buying advance tickets a cash flow crisis grew. The government had to keep revising down the numbers of visitors expected. 'We started with 12 million,' said a government source, 'that quickly came down to 10, then seven.'[26] By September it was down to 4.5 million. By then the Dome was technically insolvent and mass redundancies were planned. After it closed, it was US sports and live events specialists AEG who completely refitted it as a huge concert venue, the O2, which opened with a suitably stadium rock concert by Bon Jovi in 2007. 'For a year Richard and I had terrible trouble,' remembered Mike Davies, 'because it was seen as *bloody architects!* Richard was getting letters saying *It's a national scandal, how can you spend £759m on a tent: Indignant from Brighton*. And of course we spent £43m on the biggest tent in the world and you can't buy one cheaper anywhere. It did the job. It's still doing the job.'

And when Storm Eunice raged across Southern England on 18 February 2022 and tore the skin of the arena, leaving a whole side of the Dome in tatters, it was stitched back together in a matter of days. Mike Davies was right. Despite it being ripped apart, first by the press and then by the elements, it's still doing the job.

I once went to a party in a *Grand Designs* house. It was owned by Tom Watkins, who'd been manager for Bros, East 17 and the Pet Shop Boys back in the day, and he'd had it built on the seafront at Pett Level in East Sussex. It was that oxymoron of *Grand Designs* style, the traditional modernist house. Flat-roofed and white-rendered, it was a throwback to the 1920s heroic modernism of the Bauhaus on an avenue of large seaside homes of a more suburban hue. He'd filled this white box with extraordinary postmodern furniture and art: uncomfortable Italian chairs in bright blues, reds and yellows; notable pieces by Philippe Starck and the Memphis Group filling the gleaming voids, their extraordinary angular forms caught like *Drag Race* contestants mid-pose.

When I talked to him about the house, he said the secret was not having to pay for anything – he'd taken his decades of experience as a ducker and diver in the music industry and used the show as a gigantic advert for the tradespeople and product designers he used in the house. Because of the coverage of *Grand Designs*, he said, he got the house built for free, though how much this is true and how much can be attributed to his perpetual desire to myth-make is hard to know. It was a lovely house, but the best thing about it was the terrace that led to the beach and the wild sea beyond. It felt like a film set, the outsides an early *Poirot*, the insides a mid-eighties Almodóvar full of furniture on the verge of a nervous breakdown. And it didn't really feel like a home, more like an eccentric small museum. Whenever I see those vast glass boxes on *Grand Designs* with their poured concrete kitchen islands and advanced curtain tech, I always wonder, *where are your things?* I know they have 243 them styled for the telly, but even so, where's your books and knitting and unwanted Christmas presents? Grand is the word. These are not scalable lifestyles for the rest of us, they are modern country houses and stately homes, for some future version of the National Trust.

You can see how the faux modernism of many *Grand Designs* projects has influenced our domestic architecture. In high-spec executive homes and conversions, you see evidence of those must-have modern finishes and worktops, expensively imported windows and tiled floors. Owners of Georgian, Victorian or interwar houses have indiscriminately built white boxes on the back of their homes, with bulky grey-framed windows and a second-hand Bauhaus aesthetic. And in the Blair years, all the big developers had a crack at faux-mo in cream and white rendered blocks with rapidly bleaching wood panels, rusting metal balconies and external accent walls of jaunty – but not too jaunty! – terracotta and Wedgwood blue. Otherwise, *Grand Designs* is at the most unrepresentative end of a property programme spectrum, away from *Location, Location, Location*'s dreams of buying the worst house on the street or the budget doer-uppers of *Property Ladder*. Most have some form of eco-credentials as an essential part of the build: Passivhaus standards, partly submerged, green-roofed, triple-glazed, solar-powered. Host Kevin McCloud, a former lighting designer, even set up his own eco-friendly housing firm, HAB (Happiness Architecture Beauty), in 2007 'to challenge the way identikit volume housing was built in the UK'.[1] While the architecture side – HAB Housing – endures, three subsidiaries used to crowdfund the purchase of development sites – HAB Land, HAB Land Finance and BAH Restructuring – went into receivership in 2019, a year after McCloud had resigned from their boards. 'The directors have reported that higher than anticipated design and project management costs, coupled with delays to the delivery of the sites, resulted in the companies experiencing significant liquidity issues,' said James Bennett, one of the liquidators.[2] To which you can sense Kevin turn and prepare for a worried piece to camera, eyebrow raised.

I visited Hackbridge, a suburb in South London, to seek out an estate that anticipated many of those *Grand Designs* ambitions and multiplied them. A ribbon of unhealthy 1930s semis cowered in the fumes beside a busy road, while across the traffic an underdressed estate of Major-era mansion blocks – plain pitched roofs, smooth basic brick, a scant gesture at timbering embarrassing the whole – looked like it had sleepwalked into the street in its pants. I'd come to see their flashy, extraordinary neighbour: Beddington Zero Energy Development, or BedZED. It's a jolt. From one angle, the terraced houses have glass walls that seem to more resemble a school, until you continue and an accumulation of balconies, built-in conservatories, gardens and the detritus of community life comes into view. The bulbous gable ends resemble the noses of particularly eco-friendly Mr Men: *Mr Green* perhaps, or *Little Miss Socially Responsible*. Their hats – chimneys in the form of tall and flamboyant funnels – are each giddy as a weathervane, keeping up a permanent kinetic street performance. Beside the terraces there's an eco village green, from whose lumpy grass sprouts a trim trail and outcrops of communal planting. It reminds me of the biodome in Douglas Trumbull's 1972 sci-fi film *Silent Running*, a combination of High Tech and hippy. What's clear about the outsides of all of these houses is that people are not hiding their lives away. It has a very un-English air of community, of sharing, of chat and involvement.

The optimistic eco-village of BedZED. © Tom Chance

BedZED was built for the Peabody Trust, the pioneering housing association, and opened in 2002. It was the world's first high-density carbon-neutral housing development. A third of the homes were for sale, a third were shared ownership, and a third were social housing. There are eighty-two houses, apartments and live-work units, as well as a cluster of business premises, to help cancel out commuting for some of the residents. It had been built on the site of a former sewage works and 80 per cent of the timber and steel used had been reclaimed, with all the materials renewable or recycled and sourced from within a 35-mile radius. Water consumption had been cut by up to 50 per cent thanks to water flow regulators and rainwater being collected for toilet flushing and irrigation of the roof gardens. You regulate the temperature of the homes by adjusting the windows and chimneys, like a sailor constantly adjusting a ship's sails and trim, with the aim that it stays a comfortable 18°C most of the time. 'The UK is like a drug addict,' said its architect, Bill Dunster. 'How do you wean it off fossil fuels? You do it so it's fun, and so you don't really notice it.'[3] 'He felt that developers 'can't do this kind of stuff. They don't believe in it. . . . They can't be innovative.'[4] He was bullish about what had been achieved in Beddington. 'If we took this on board and built at this density on brownfield sites, we wouldn't have to build the four million homes in the south-east that the government is talking about,' he insisted. 'In fact, if we took these types of eco-living concepts on board very fast, we would never have to fight an oil war ever again.'[5]

'For many residents it will mean a new way of life,' explained a feature in the *Observer* when BedZED opened, 'forsaking their car, eating local organic food, perhaps giving up the daily commute to work.'[6] 'It's a very ordinary site,' said Dunster, 'but if we were building them in Clerkenwell they'd be high-value homes, not affordable housing, which is the remit of the Peabody Trust.'[7] Geographer Andrew Tallon was rather less convinced about the social mix achieved in these affordable homes. 'Many of the residents of BedZED are middle-class professionals who live high-impact lifestyles and who like to be associated with such a "trendy" development,' he wrote.[8] Rob Starsmore, one of the initial residents interviewed in 2003, said 'I've got to be honest, it was nothing to do with being green. . . . We drove past by chance, "That looks weird", and popped into the show home. It was the high ceilings and space that grabbed us. We were living in your typical developer's home at the time, with tiny windows and boxy rooms.'[9]

While I was there, I met up with Pooran Desai, whose entre-preneurial instincts had helped set up BedZED in the first place. 'It's like a concept car,' he explained. 'You learn from it but you don't necessarily roll out a concept car.' Bioregional, the social entrepreneurs Desai had worked for, were founded in 1994. They began running projects on sustainability in forestry, 247 farming and recycling, from rented offices in Carshalton, South London. 'We were outgrowing our office space,' he recalled, 'so we asked the council, *look, have you got any land you could lease us and we could build some green offices*? They said *no, we haven't got any land we could lease you, but actually we're selling land for residential development, why don't you build an eco-village with your offices at the centre of it*? So we said, *okay!*' At about the same time he'd met the architect Bill Dunster, and was drawn to his work. Dunster had built his own house nearby, reflecting the principles of 1990s green architecture. They worked on a design based on that, got it costed and approached various partners who might help fund it, which was how they encountered Peabody.

'We were naïve I think at the time,' said Pooran, 'which helps. *We think it's a good idea so let's do it*! I was leading the project at the time, I was in my thirties, I had a lot of energy!' He laughed. 'Wouldn't take no for an answer!' This optimism was tried somewhat when it came to building it. 'The construction process was painful,' he recalled. 'Very painful. First of all the architect was terribly difficult, changing drawings at the last minute and things like that. The other thing was it was a period of cost price inflation, because it was coming up to the millennium.' Those major projects – museums, galleries, the Dome, and later Terminal 5 at Heathrow – had swallowed the available workforce. 'Peabody didn't have enough development managers to manage all the projects they had on the ground, so it was undermanaged, and the engineers and architects weren't properly managed in my view. I mean, I learned that after because I hadn't done one before.' The project went over budget, which was a huge headache for these fledgling developers. And then there were issues around getting people to understand what 248 it was they were trying to do. They had organised a car share scheme, the first in England, and had reduced the number of car parking spaces accordingly. But local planners almost canned the whole scheme because it didn't offer the standard amount of suburban parking.

The controversial car club paid back residents in a matter of months. The extra insulation paid for itself within ten years. But the green architecture? Researchers found that BedZED's solar conservatories would also pay for themselves – in 800 years. 'In a way we started to unpick at the time what were some of the sacred cows of green architecture,' said Pooran. 'Like you always point south, have conservatories on the south side and things like that.' They have long since ditched the original efforts to generate BedZED's energy on site. 'We run it on completely renewable energy now. From wood heating and buying guaranteed green electricity.' Back when it was built the autonomous house was the ideal, where you generated all your own energy and treated your own waste water, but pretty soon thinking had moved to much bigger thoughts, or decarbonising the entire national grid. 'So we started to move away from Zero Energy Development, which was ZED, which was defined in that way, and started to use the term zero carbon, which was just energy efficient buildings run on renewable energy, wherever that came from.'

Green architecture in Britain had been in slow ascent for several decades, from Edward Curtis's Solar House in the suburb of Rickmansworth in 1956 to the pioneering 'passive house' design of Wallasey School in 1961 where architect Emslie Morgan had used 'trombe wall' technology to keep a steady temperature. A very public experiment took place in 1976 when Donald Wilson from Manchester University designed an eco-dwelling as an experiment for Granada TV. The project had come about as a response to the power cuts and petrol rationing Britain had faced two years before. 'Windmills, etc., are okay, but there are   249

Your house doesn't have to look like something out of a Steven Spielberg movie to be energy efficient

An advert for Countryside Properties from the Milton Keynes
Energy World brochure, 1986. © Countryside

much more sensible things to do,' said Wilson, pragmatic words
not unlike those used by Pooran Desai about his post-BedZED
projects. 'We didn't try to avoid the use of fossil fuels, we simply
tried to reduce them,' said Wilson.[10] The secret here appeared to
be a rather blunt instrument, keeping windows to a minimum.
Those it did have were fitted with shutters, making it a rather
gloomy setting for family life. 'The fact that someone had to take
their work to the window to see didn't worry us,' said the designer. A family – the Grants – moved in to test it out on national
television, and disagreed.

These small projects were dwarfed in scale by those at Milton
Keynes, the last post-war new town, whose philosophy straddled
the fluid boundary between sixties idealism and Thatcherite zeal.
250 The first low-energy house had been constructed here in 1972,

the year before the global oil crisis hit. It had a solar collector, using sunlight to provide heat and hot water. But on 2 May 1981 something altogether bigger arrived. It was the opening day of Homeworld, an experimental housing estate at Bradwell Common built by twenty developers, all of whom had been instructed to include above-standard insulation and energy-saving innovation as part of their designs. There was a range of ambition, from the inevitable Barratt Studio Solo and numerous conventional brick houses to a timber-framed cluster block built by Super-Homes of Watford, as well as some more international entrants, including a wooden prefab by New Zealanders Lockwood Homes and a part-timber Anebyhus from Sweden. There were also further solar experiments with water heating in a pair of 'Autarkic' (self-sufficient) houses designed by Donald Forrest.

Five years later, another exhibition of fifty energy-efficient houses, Energy World, went even further. 'The Energy Park points the way to the development of low-energy housing into the 21st Century' wrote Peter Walker, the then energy secretary, in the introduction to the estate's official brochure.[11] My partner lives in one of them, designed by Newport Pagnell practice David Tuckley Associates and built somewhat improbably by Persimmon, who were desperate to be part of the housing boom in Milton Keynes. Their houses each have solar panels built into brown wooden-framed conservatories, all of which face south. The results are unusual for a developer in 1986 and positively astonishing for Persimmon: asymmetric late-modernist pads in rough pale brick with dark wood window frames, very different from the fake leaded windows and Wendy house capitulation of so many of its contemporaries around the town.

Most of the other houses in Energy World were bespoke jobs. One is mostly buried underground, like a Teletubbies version of an ancient barrow. An extravagantly roofed Swiss chalet stands at the end of a boulevard, like a 1970s easy-listening singer in flouncy skirts waiting for their close-up. Derek Walker, chief architect of the new town, designed a one-off in postmodern Rennie Mackintosh style, with elongated external wood panelling and portholes as windows. I showed an architect friend around the estate and she took one look at Walker's effort and said, not unfairly, 'well, everybody has an off day'. Around the corner at the mildly postmodern meeting point, whose shop and community hall are topped with a fancy clock, stone balls on pillars and trademark MK globe street lights and moulded steel street furniture, stands a tall steel spike hammered into the ground at 45 degrees. This giant sundial, speared like a javelin into the brick circle that makes up Solar Court, stands to remind residents out to buy some fags and a KitKat of the eternal power of the sun.

Energy World, like the experiments of Homeworld before it and Futureworld (yes, really) after, is significant, because here was a whole cluster of homes demonstrating energy efficiency, with new forms of insulation, heat recovery systems and cutting-edge 1980s technology. Okay, so as far as green credentials go, Milton Keynes has an issue. This is the town of the car, where it is more or less impossible to live without driving. Some of the homes in Energy World are almost entirely hidden behind double garages. But even so, of the most energy-efficient houses built in Britain by the mid-1990s, most of the top 1 per cent were to be found in this one new town. By 1990, the first national energy efficiency index had been introduced, copied from Milton Keynes. And, naturally, most developers of the day refused to sign up to it.

But soon the attention had shifted from producing individual eco-homes to creating sustainable communities, a dead cert for anyone playing a game of New Labour bingo. 'Sustainable communities are places where people want to live and work, now and in the future,' went the government's communities' website in 2008. 'They meet the diverse needs of existing and future residents, are sensitive to their environment, and contribute to a high quality of life. They are safe and inclusive, well planned, built and run, and offer equality of opportunity and good services for all.'[12] Of course, there is a slipperiness to the notion of 'sustainability', which can mean everything from physical and social infrastructure and environmental concerns to protecting green space and encouraging diversity, and perhaps should always include all of these factors and not just pick and choose. The government's response to this notion was the creation of – wait for it – Millennium Communities. These seven new villages around England were Greenwich Millennium Village (beside the Dome), Allerton Bywater at a former mining community near Leeds, New Islington in Manchester, South Lynn in King's Lynn, Telford Millennium Community, Oakgrove in Milton Keynes and Broomgrove in Hastings. Must-haves were *sustainability*, good transport links, energy efficiency, community involvement and local employment opportunities. Some, like New Islington and Greenwich, were quick off the mark and today have large populations of residents. Others, like Hastings and Telford, are very much works not in progress.

I asked Pooran Desai what he made of Strata Tower in Elephant and Castle, a residential block of 408 flats completed in 2010 for developers Brookfield, notable for the three dead turbines on the roof whose appearance resembles a Philishave. Its designers, Ian Bogle and Robbie Turner of BFLS, had both been instrumental members of the team at Foster + Partners, who designed the Gherkin. In 2010 its penthouse was on the market for £2.3 million, with online gossip suggesting it had been bought by John Terry, footballer and internet meme always trying to get into   253 everything. I thought Pooran might have been harsh on this feeble totem of greenwashing, but he was surprisingly sympathetic. 'At the time we didn't know that they were not going to perform on buildings,' he said, of the turbines. 'We were going to have some on One Brighton,' – their follow-up estate to BedZED. 'All the engineering models were saying they would work.' The reality was that the models didn't take into account the way air flows over a skyscraper. 'So for about five years people thought they were a good idea. That didn't seem a ridiculous idea at the time, though I'm pleased we didn't put in any at Brighton.'

Pooran's words about their dream of decarbonising the national grid rather than expecting individual homes to pick up the slack stuck with me. Britain's land and seascape has been transformed by wind turbines in the last thirty years. The first large-scale experiments began in 1984 when the Wind Energy Group – a partnership between power threesome Taylor Woodrow, British Aerospace and GEC – started building two turbines in Orkney, while another was put up by entrepreneur James Howden at Richborough at Kent. Five years later, the Central Electricity Generating Board (remember them?) announced a programme to power 5,000 homes within five years. At this point, 80 per cent of the country's energy came from coal, while most of the rest was nuclear. Yet farmer Peter Edwards and his son Martin beat the big guys when they opened Britain's first recognisably modern wind farm in Delabole in North Cornwall in 1991. Ten 80-foot turbines would power 2,000 homes. By 1996, wind turbines with their environmental benefits were being decried as a menace by Margaret Thatcher's eyebrow-heavy former spin doctor Bernard Ingham, whose Country Guardian lobbying group proudly claimed to have prevented 77 wind farms from being built. 'Environmental

campaigners that support these things are clearly aesthetically dead,' barked Ingham. 'They produce so little electricity that they hardly make any difference to the problem.'[13] In May 2019, Britain spent its first week since 1882 without using any energy from coal-fired power stations, history slowly turning like a turbine's blades.

'The average person here knows twenty of their neighbours by name, which is four times the UK average,' Pooran told me of BedZED. 'It's a great place to live, there's absolutely no doubt about that.' And the wider area in this street in Hackbridge had begun to adopt some of their standards too, to the extent that a new Passivhaus school was being built next door. Their neighbours on the other side were less keen. 'The housing estate next door, there's no community there,' he said. 'They didn't want anything to do with us. And even wanted a fence between the two.' Oh dear. There's something beguiling about BedZED. It has a sense of warmth and friendliness. Part of that is the design of the buildings, with their curves and links and the intimate relationships between them. The lack of cars. Sure, there's a middle-class Radio 4 vibe going on, but BedZED represents something positive. Zero carbon living. The thing we should all aspire to. I'd move in like a shot.

8: The Impossible Dream

Belfast, Cardiff, Edinburgh and Devolution

When protesters began to demolish sections of the Berlin Wall in November 1989, their actions helped usher in a decade of tumultuous geopolitical change. In the following years, East and West Germany were reunited, the Soviet Union was disbanded, and the former Yugoslavian alliances fell to nationalism and war. The United Kingdom was not immune to a degree of change too. One of New Labour's first acts on being elected in 1997 was to tackle the issue of devolution: a parliament for Scotland, an assembly for Wales and one for Northern Ireland, which, it was hoped, would help redress long held inequalities and appease both nationalist and loyalist feeling across the union. Here, as elsewhere, change came surprisingly fast, and with it a whole host of questions about national identity in a modern era were thrashed out by a generation of politicians who had waited for decades for such an opportunity, alongside civil servants being asked to produce elaborate new structures both figuratively and physically. The Northern Ireland Assembly first met on 1 July 1998. A new Scottish Parliament followed on 12 May 1999, and the National Assembly of Wales just over a month later, on 1 July. It was an extraordinary timetable for such complex schemes.

As devolution became a reality, each nation knew that the physicality of the devolved institutions would speak volumes about their ambitions and ideals. The Scottish Parliament in Edinburgh would end up as an ambitious, complex cluster designed by Catalan architect Enric Miralles – optimistically termed a village in the years before parliaments were routinely derided as such. The reality of these buildings would 256 be as romantic and elusive as any of the old legends of the

Scots. In Cardiff, the Welsh Assembly would meet in something rather more modest. The Senedd, designed by Richard Rogers, is – of course – a lightweight glass box, this time with crinkled canopy and central funnel to let out the 'hot air'. Here, notions of transparency would be placed at the centre of business, the lightness of the structure unintentionally mirroring the lightness of the powers devolved to Wales relative to those of Scotland. Meanwhile, Northern Ireland's assembly would place tradition over thoughts of the future, meeting at the Parliament Buildings, a vast 1930s neoclassical edifice in the Stormont Estate in Belfast. The lack of investment in a new symbolic home for the assembly was both pragmatic – given the fragility of recent peace talks – and symbolic of the uncompromising tradition-focused Ulster Unionists, who had a majority. And so across the three nations, different symbols of devolution emerge: Scotland's powerful enough to contemplate thoughts of independence; Wales's more interested in demonstrating openness to the people beyond; Northern Ireland's desire for stability overriding all. And alongside these parliament buildings came other symbols of devolution. In Belfast, a new openness following the Good Friday Agreement helped create a property boom that saw expensive new flats erected in the city centre and on the post-industrial waterfront. In Cardiff, the assembly is one of a cluster of new waterside buildings, including a concert hall and a sports stadium, and part of a whole physical remodelling of the waterfront itself. And while historic Edinburgh might have struggled to push ahead with bold new projects, such as an expensively timid tram network, its ever confident rival Glasgow created a series of spectacular new museums and regenerated districts and open spaces along the Clyde.

*

A typical day in Cardiff Bay, 2005, with cracks appearing in the bright new paving, pulses of electricity surging up from the lighting towers of Roald Dahl Plass into the clouds, and windows shattering as the earth shook. A rift in the very fabric of space and time had opened up between the Millennium Centre and Pizza Express. When BBC Cymru Wales revived *Doctor Who*, they initially set many of its stories and its spin-off series *Torchwood* in the new landscape of Cardiff Bay. 'We wondered whether Wales could be portrayed as modern and forward-looking,' said BBC Director-General Mark Thompson, 'and *Torchwood* is the answer. It's obviously Welsh and it's sexy, modern and fantastic.'[1] These shows felt of a piece with the creation of the bay itself, a tabula rasa of ambitious CGI modelling whose relationship to the ancient waterfront, the monuments of the past and the lives of the people who still live there – people hidden out of sight of the tourists and middle-class workers and residents of this new landscape – is sketchy at best. The creation of modern Cardiff Bay began in 1987 when an Urban Development Corporation was set up to regenerate the city's post-industrial waterfront. Liverpool got its art galleries and garden festival. What Cardiff got was a barrage. Not a military bombardment but an enormous hunk of maritime engineering creating an artificial harbour – turning the area from tidal mudflats to a vast freshwater lake. This extreme piece of physical remodelling was the pet project of Nicholas Edwards, Secretary of State for Wales, who rather fancied an opera house on the site of the derelict docks. None of this regeneration was for the benefit of the locals, be they the wading birds or the largely impoverished residents of Cardiff's most diverse community, Butetown. Instead, these changes would be to attract a new class of resident. The barrage was constructed in the 1990s and by the advent of devolution new Cardiff Bay had begun to grow. An expensive Docklands-style outcrop of new waterside flats and businesses began to open, leaving Butetown cut off from it all, not just physically but culturally.

Centrepiece of all this activity was set to be the opera house that Nicholas Edwards had set his heart on. Two hundred and sixty-seven practices entered a design competition in 1994 and the still relatively unknown Zaha Hadid won. The crystalline wedge of her design was swaddled in the courtyard of a larger protective building, adding an extra layer of theatricality with the opera house surrounded by the offices, bars, restaurants and public spaces required for its high-end clientele and workers. Hadid called her design 'jewels in a crystal necklace'.[2] Welsh architect Jonathan Adams, then working for Will Alsop, recalled that they had also entered the competition. 'Will's proposal was just insane!' he told me. 'It was an arrangement of strange abstract shapes, one of which was like a huge trumpet horn pointing up into the sky. You would look at it and you would think, now *where* is the opera house in that? So we didn't get through to the second round of the competition, never expected to really.' Alsop had already worked in Cardiff Bay for the development corporation, creating a couple of structures for the barrage and a long tubular visitors' centre from 1990, which Adams recalls 'more or less fell to bits'. He remembers being pleased Hadid won the competition, as a fellow graduate of the Architectural Association in London – 'we thought that it could be good news all round'. But, having declared Hadid the winner, the reality of having to sell and live with her audacious design began to give the very people who had selected it cold feet. Especially once a public exhibition of her design and those by rivals Norman Foster and Italian eco-designer Manfredi Nicoletti muddied the water, with popular opinion split across all three. Meanwhile, a media campaign ridiculing all the 259 designs and the need for an 'elitist' opera house at all claimed that the rapidly constructed Millennium Stadium sports complex next door better represented the nation.

In the end, both city and county council distanced themselves from Hadid's spectacular design, and it was left to the Millennium Commission to put it out of its majesty, and refuse to fund their part in it, fuelled by strange fears that it might attract attention and funding away from the Royal Opera House in London. The consequence of this decision would resound around the bay for years to come. 'Wales is already infamous in international architectural circles for having smugly dismissed the best opera house it never had,' said Jonathan Glancey,[3] while Alan Powers called it 'the greatest loss to British architecture over the last generation'.[4] Adams watched it with a sense that it was being sold as 'a big failure on the part of Wales or the Welsh public or it was Wales to blame. Putting aside the fact the no one else seemed to be offering Zaha any opportunities.' He also felt that a lack of communication had doomed the scheme. 'I think everyone involved was a bit naïve, from the adjudication side, people who were assessing the project for its feasibility and cost.' There were people with axes to grind and agendas to promote. 'And Zaha in hindsight was not aware of that and certainly not equipped to deal with it, and really didn't do what she needed to do in order to get it across the line through simply not realising that you had to bring people with you.'

Two projects that did get built in the bay give an idea of the ambition of newly devolved Wales. There was the Senedd – home of the Welsh Assembly – and the Millennium Centre – which took the place of the unbuilt opera house. Former Labour Prime Minister Jim Callaghan was named as chairman of the panel in 1998 to pick a design for the Welsh Assembly building, describing himself as 'not renowned for being a revolutionary in such matters'.[5] By October a team from Richard Rogers had won, with a design costed at just under £10 million. 'The concept came when we were all standing down at the bay,' said David Ardill, one of the design team. 'There is not very much there. There is water, sky and very little land; the roof is the sky and the slate the water.'[6] Wales had voted for devolution with a wafer-thin majority of 50.5 per cent. In some ways, this lack of political oomph feels like the keynote for the subdued design of the assembly building. The businesslike steel and glass of the Senedd feels more sensible Strasbourg than Celtic spirit, technocratic functionalism over grassroots passion.

This relatively modest concept was still far from plain sailing, however. Two years into construction, work was put on hold because costs had risen by 93 per cent. When Rogers's supporter Alun Michael stood down as first secretary for Wales in April 2000, he was replaced by the rather less supportive figure of Rhodri Morgan. His finance minister, Edwina Hart, sacked Rogers. 'Lord Rogers,' she said, 'is no different to any builder, any tradesman, or anybody anybody might employ that you don't think is going to do the job for you.'[7] The architects put out an uncharacteristically blunt statement saying that 'the Richard Rogers Partnership rejects being made a political scapegoat for a catastrophic failure properly to manage the project'.[8] The Assembly attempted to sue Rogers for the additional costs, but in a further show of shambolic ineptitude lost the case. New project managers from construction giant Taylor Woodrow were brought in, and Rogers's team was re-engaged eighteen months after being sacked. It was, of course, a PFI scheme, the Welsh government's home bought on credit from private contractors. The building was finally opened in 2006 by the Queen at a ceremony as slightly awkward as you'd imagine when Welsh Nationalists and royalty collide. Poet Gwyneth 261

Lewis read 'Horizon with People', a poem created for the occasion. But the contrast between this sparkling glass box and the world just beyond was clear to see. 'On Bute Street's shops, a stone's throw away, most of the shutters remain down,' reported the *Western Mail* on the opening day of the Senedd. 'There is little pomp here. Among the kind of architecture reviled by Prince Charles, figures in shell suits, hoodies and jilbaabs walk briskly through the biting wind in one of Wales' most deprived communities. The real test of what March 1, 2006, will mean for the nation's future lies both in what happens inside the Senedd, but also in what happens in such areas as Butetown.'[9]

Yet it is not the Senedd that is the centrepiece of all of this marina development. What would have been the site of Zaha's opera house became, in January 2002, the location of a rather less deconstructed form: the Millennium Centre. It's the bright highlight of Cardiff Bay. The Senedd has some nifty symbolism, but the practice's obsession with lightweight structures, which had served the Dome so well, here leaves the whole enterprise feeling rather *too* lightweight, lacking gravity. In contrast, the Millennium Centre is sturdy and startlingly present. The contrast is amplified by a second appointment for poet Gwynneth Lewis, whose words at the Senedd opening ceremony floated up and out the Richard Rogers ventilation system, but whose Millennium Centre poem remains imprinted on the very fabric of the building itself.

Its architect, Jonathan Adams, was still working in London and thinking of moving back to his Welsh homeland when a replacement to Zaha's scheme was mooted. 'The fact that devolution had just about been voted for and was going to happen was a big factor in me thinking I would move back,' he told me. 'Then the completion of the Millennium Stadium in 1999 was a big watershed moment I think, because up until then there was nothing really you could point at to say it's possible to do an extraordinary project in Wales, to get it built quickly.' It was then he saw that the old Cardiff-based practice Percy Thomas Partnership had won the commission for the Millennium Centre, though as far as Adams could see, 'they didn't have anyone who could design it. I think they had gone into administration around the same time. There was a group of eight or nine directors there who had all joined the firm in the 1950s and 60s and then were all beyond retirement age.' Keen to move back to Cardiff, he sent them a letter on spec. 'I didn't even mention the Millennium Centre specifically. As it turned out, they offered me a job there and said you can work on this.' He still had three months' notice to work, which gave him valuable thinking time. 'By the time I was ready to start I had worked out how we should design the Millennium Centre. I'd already drawn it, basically.' But it was a political problem, the new guy from London arriving and trying to take over their biggest, most prestigious job. 'It wasn't a case of stick it in front of the Percy Thomas guys as soon as I saw them, but just keep it up my sleeve and sort of tell them the story at the speed it had come to me in the first place,' said Adams. 'Initially I was just showing them pictures of bits of landscape, bits of industrial archaeology, just things. Bits of pieces of things that had some meaning to it . . . I'm just like any other person of my generation who grew up in Wales, similar things probably mean the same things to them.'

His design would be grounded in recognisably Welsh materials: steel for the roof, slate for the walls, local wood for the insides. It would be home to seven resident companies, including the Welsh National Opera. When I walked through it, the many open and hidden spaces were occupied by hundreds of schoolchildren performing different styles of music. If one of 263

The Millennium Centre, using Welsh materials: slate, wood and steel. © Gordon Plant

the criticisms of Hadid's scheme had been that it was too cool, too London, too exclusive, the success of Adams's design has been its inclusivity. No inch is wasted in this busy building. By 2004 it had already come second in a poll to find Wales's favourite building, a level of affection that no other millennium building could hope to emulate. It wasn't always an easy sell. 'I remember doing a presentation to a group of people on the assembly that included the chap who was at that time the first First Minister, Alun Michael,' recalled Adams. 'He was very amenable through the whole thing, he seemed to be happy and all on board with it right until the point when I mentioned about having the wording on the front. And at that point the smile dropped from his face and I could see him furiously scribbling notes on a piece of paper.' The Labour party in Wales might have benefited from devolution, but it was also paranoid about nationalist tendencies. Front and centre in the culture wars here was the Welsh language itself, which having been in decline for decades had seen a rise in users in the 1990s. Nowhere was the growing power of the language imprinted more forcefully than on the Millennium Centre, where the face reads in vast serif lettering Gwyneth Lewis's poem half in English – *In these stones horizons sing* – and half in Welsh – *Creu Gwir fel/ Gwydr/ o Ffwrnais/ Awen* – which you might think was a translation, but is in fact nearer *Creating truth/ Like glass/ From inspiration's furnace.* Two messages singing together, a stirring, harmonious whole.

Cultural memories were at the forefront of Adams's design, as much in the materials used as in the choice of words for the frontispiece. 'I started off with an image of a cliff on the South Wales coast,' he recalled, 'which was basically limestone cliffs as it happens, with this very strongly defined strata – a kind of architectural quality as they are.' He'd seen the amount of spoil from the slate tips in North Wales, where less than 10 per cent of the slate mined was used for roofing. What if he could replicate those cliffs with this slate? 'It was odd having this ancient material, this ancient technique for building walls, using them in a modern building. And having to deal with incredible scepticism from the builders and from the specialist masonry companies who just wouldn't believe it was possible because they hadn't encountered it before.' He remembered there being 'a lot of stories in the press about millennium projects that hadn't worked out in the way that people had suggested they would. It was the last of the big landmark projects, so people were more inclined to learn the harsh lessons than they were the positive ones. So when they were going round trying to generate interest in it there was *right, how many people do we think will come and visit this*? And they were coming up with numbers that were deliberately low – we will get 200,000 visitors a year, and people would go oh you're joking! And as it turned out we had over 265 a million. Particularly when they started showing it on *Doctor Who* if I'm honest, visitor numbers went through the roof.'

For Northern Ireland, the challenges of devolution were mighty, after almost a century of unrest, and over thirty years of the Troubles, where acts of terrorism had been normalised into everyday life, accounting for 3,532 dead and over 47,000 injured. In Belfast alone, more than 1,500 people were killed between 1969 and 2001. This was a country scarred by deep, raw and painful divisions. The Good Friday Agreement in 1998 brought with it compromises by both sides, the promise of a new police force to break with the distrusted one of the past, and new hope in self-governance for the province. A political declaration would reshape the country in remarkable ways, tearing down old walls and monuments to fighting, from barbed wire barricades to impromptu defences made permanent over time. The towns and cities of Northern Ireland stood to gain more than any other from devolution, as reminders of the conflict zone were wiped away and new symbols took their place. In Belfast, nowhere was this more dramatically illustrated than on the waterfront, where the old industrial docks were some of the last in a major British city to be gripped by Docklands fever. While the government building of Stormont remained, the signs of devolution in Northern Ireland were more the indicators of gentrification that had hit cities like Manchester and Glasgow some decades before. And there was no more blatant symbol than Obel, a squat steel and glass tower surrounded by a cluster of associated buildings overlooking the industrial remains of Lagan Weir beside Belfast's historic customs house. Plans were unveiled in February 2005, a mixture of private flats, a 144-bedroom hotel, a restaurant and offices. Donegall Quay Ltd, a consortium of three developers, won the rights to build.

Speaking for the consortium, Gayle Blackbourne uttered those timeless gentrifiers' words, 'we are confident the development will integrate into Belfast's existing skyline while providing valuable residential, commercial and retail space for the city'.[10]

Cessation of conflict unleashed unforeseen forces upon the country, one of which was a property boom. Over the border in the Republic of Ireland, the largely deregulated Celtic Tiger was roaring away, with thousands of new developments springing up in towns and cities all over the country. But by 2006 Northern Ireland had the fastest growing property prices in the UK too. People who had moved away during the Troubles were being tempted back. One such, Mike Irvine, who worked in corporate finance for KPMG, moved from Battersea to Belfast in 2002, swapping a one-bedroom flat in London for a three-bedroom town house near Stormont. 'In my close circle three or four good friends have moved back,' he told *The Times*. 'It only takes me 20 minutes to get to work, and I can be on the golf course in 5 minutes.'[11] Interestingly, it was new builds that were accounting for a quarter of sales. 'All the developments are selling off plan,' said Barry Kernahan of Halifax's new homes division. 'It has been like this for ten months.'[12] There was excitement, with a faint tone of concern, that too many new homes were under construction. Not least in the Titanic Quarter, the former Harland and Wolff shipyard where the cranes had been listed and still stand. This waterside redevelopment was due to be completed in 2021, mixing 5,000 homes into a science park along with corporate giants like Microsoft and Citigroup.

The global financial crisis crashed the Irish economy and slowed much of the frenzy north of the border too. The Aurora building was its most notable victim. At thirty-seven storeys, Mervyn McAlister's tower planned for Great Victoria Street was to be taller than the Obel and contain a whopping 291 luxury flats. It was intended to open in 2010, but after three years the project was cancelled when the Planning Service finally rejected the design as inappropriately tall for the site. McAlister wrote to the planning minister, complaining that the decision 'effectively says "Belfast is closed for business"'.[13] Environment minister Sammy Wilson was furious and said his own civil servants had acted 'abysmally'. There was a strong economic case for building the tower, he said, and they should have backed that. By February 2011, McAlister had two further large-scale Northern Irish projects cancelled and was declared bankrupt. Boom time was definitely over. In 2010, a new policy on tall buildings in Northern Ireland was published by environment minister Edwin Poots. 'We are somewhat behind the times in terms of tall buildings,' explained Poots. 'Much of the tall building development in other cities took place in the 1960s and 1970s, but obviously with the Troubles that didn't happen here. Now we are in a different period and people are looking to maximise land use.'[14] He saw the Obel as a trailblazer to be followed. 'Frankly, it gives you more of a city feel, but they need to be well-designed. If you look at New York skyscrapers which went up in the 1950s and 1960s, they are like rectangular boxes which aren't very aesthetically pleasing. You find much more appealing skyscrapers in Singapore, for example.'[15] Perhaps this is a glimpse into the sort of deregulated state that Poots hoped to see in Northern Ireland.

Obel was designed by Broadway Malyan, a vast yet slightly anonymous multinational set up in the late fifties in that hotbed of neoliberalism, Weybridge. Their work includes Trump Tower Manila and several malls in China. In Britain, if there is a large-scale private urban redevelopment project, such as Nine Elms in Battersea, there will almost inevitably be a Broadway Malyan building under construction as part of it, the kind of

Obel, an architectural SUV typical of Broadway Malyan. © William Murphy

apartment blocks that were supposed to contain a statutory percentage of affordable housing before that was quietly dropped. Their creations are the SUVs of architecture, whose blank glossy bulk clogs up city streets, their form forgettable in their ubiquity. Perhaps their most infamous building in Britain is the aerosol-can-shaped St George's Wharf Tower in Vauxhall, mainly known for the helicopter that crashed into a crane on the roof in thick fog in January 2013, killing the pilot, Pete Barnes, and Matthew Wood, a pedestrian on the street below.

When the Obel tower was completed in 2011, hopes were still high for it. Most of the 282 apartments had been sold before the financial crisis. A reporter from the *Belfast Telegraph* visited the tower a month after it had been nominated for the Carbuncle Cup, an annual award set up by *Building Design* magazine to find Britain's ugliest new building. 'It greets its main street frontage with a confused sub-barcode that meets an uncomfortable lump of clad stone, that emerges in a south-facing glazed oven,' wrote 'Neil', who nominated it. Gayle Boyce, director at Karl Properties who owned the tower, said 'honestly when we

269

saw it had been listed I think we were a bit shocked . . . I think no-one really has the right to criticise anything, whether it's a restaurant or a building, unless they have been in it or tried it.'[16] And certainly the spectacular view was its main talking point, the glass-walled apartments looking out over the city's landmarks, including the old Harland and Wolff cranes.

A lack of commercial clients came forward to fill the retail and office space, and by April 2011 only a hundred apartments were occupied. The collapse of Belfast's property market destroyed confidence in the tower as a safe investment. A studio apartment bought off plan in 2005 would have cost you £90,000. Two years later the same flat was worth £160,000, when the tower had become Belfast's most expensive piece of real estate. Yet by April 2012 a one-bedroom flat went for sale at below the original price of a studio. With losses mounting, Donegall Quay went into administration in 2012 and the Obel was taken over by the Bank of Scotland Ireland. It was kept in the news when in 2014 a South-East Asian crime gang were found to be running a massive drugs operation in the tower, supplying cannabis, cocaine, ketamine and amphetamines. The buying and selling of this fragile piece of real estate continues. Marathon Asset Management bought the entire Obel site in 2014 for around £20 million. Belfast Harbour bought the neighbouring office tower in 2018 as an investment, and so the seemingly eternal job of remarketing this strange white elephant continues.

'Be afraid, be very afraid', wrote Alexander Linklater in *The Herald* in 1997, 'when you hear Donald Dewar say that the new Scottish parliament building will . . . cost a mere £30–40m . . . This is what people say when they've never been an architect's client and haven't given public building more than a
270   passing thought.'[17] And true enough, the story of the Scottish

Parliament building can be mapped onto an episode of *Grand Designs*. It started in 1998 with a budget of £50 million. Two years later that had more than doubled, and the parliament was squatting in a souped-up version of the infamous *Grand Designs* caravan in the garden – in this instance, the Church of Scotland's General Assembly building. By 2000 the budget had climbed to £195 million, and by the end of that year both client and architect were dead. But still the project continued, and more expensively still. Within a year it was costing £260 million.[18] This is usually the point in *Grand Designs* where they have maxed out their credit cards and borrowed money from family and friends, while all dreams of being in the house for Christmas before the new baby arrives have been long forgotten. By 2003, costs had reached £375 million. And yet still in this episode of *Grand Devolves* they hadn't even got to the equivalent of the bespoke-window-units-being-delayed-for-a-month-in-Germany bit, while adding on new must-haves against the advice of old worryguts Kevin McCloud. By 2004 it had risen again to a frightening £431 million. At this point even Kevin knows that his standard *this-jewel-this-miracle-this-sceptred-bungalow* bit at the end isn't going to make it all right. In 2007, the final cost was calculated as £414.4 million, over eight times the original budget. In *Grand Designs* terms, the couple have divorced, the baby is now at university, and the caravan has been in the garden so long it is now listed.

It had all started off with another fairly straightforward-sounding design competition, focusing on three sites around Edinburgh. Scottish First Minister Donald Dewar – back in the days when Labour dominated Scottish politics – and *Newsnight* presenter Kirsty Wark were among the small jury. The shortlist contained many safe pairs of hands, and perhaps that's why a dazzling sleight of hand would stand out. There was modernist 271 star Richard Meier; New Yorkers Kohn Pedersen Fox, who'd made their mark in the UK with two of the original Canary Wharf blocks; Michael Wilford & Partners, who'd won the design for the British embassy in Berlin; old-school modernists Ahrends, Burton and Koralek, of National Gallery carbuncle fiasco; and trusted rising stars Allies and Morrison, who'd designed the British embassy in Dublin. Critic Deyan Sudjic concentrated on the more sober entries, but allowed himself a moment to imagine that even the most out-there candidate had a chance. 'What, for example, will the non-specialist see in Enric Miralles's presentation, which is spattered with fragments of poetry and Hockney-style photographic collages?' he enquired. 'There is a building lurking underneath all this, perhaps the most radical of all the proposals on offer. But teasing it out from the undergrowth demands more patience than can be expected of those unfamiliar with simple plans.'[19] There had been seventy entries to the competition, and its project manager Bill Armstrong had placed Miralles forty-fourth on the list. So when Miralles and his wife and partner Benedetta Tagliabue were announced as winners, there was general astonishment. How had this most conservative of all competitions been won by what seemed a fundamentally bonkers piece of magical thinking?

For one, most architects had complied with the brief and the suggested sites, but Miralles had gone rogue and suggested a new location, opposite the Queen's house at Holyrood, at the foot of the Royal Mile. This had once been the garden of Queensberry House, home to James Douglas, the 2nd Duke of Queensberry, who had been responsible for rolling the independent Scottish state into what would become the United Kingdom back in 1707. 'Donald Dewar was quite taken by the idea of bringing

272   back the Scottish parliament and building it in his garden,' John

Ramsay, then an architect in local firm RMJM, told me. 'As a gesture it had a certain kind of appeal about it.' Lately the house had stood derelict after years as a hostel for the homeless, its once impressive grounds the site of the old Scottish and New-castle brewery.

'The thing they really liked were Enric's ideas about bring-ing the Scottish tradition of gatherings,' explained Ramsay, 'but also the Scottish tradition of the Highland Games and that sort of thing, into the design. And he was also greatly taken by the landscape of Scotland and he was very familiar with Edinburgh from visiting it over many years.' This interest led to a fascina-tion with the history of the city, its historic fabric and the great buildings tightly packed together, and how the new parliament building might relate to that. 'Enric included in his original panels images of some fishermen's huts that were made from upturned boats,' he said. 'They were actually in Northumber-land rather than Scotland, but he had seen them on his travels and he had also seen buildings in Orkney and Shetland which are more substantial boats, that have been turned upside down to form buildings.'

There had been an initial backlash against Miralles and Tagliabue in the media because they weren't Scottish. Scottish architects reading these pieces must have found this bitterly amusing, because the country has a terrible recent record of employing and promoting its own. While many of Britain's best contemporary architectural practices have been Scots, they have often had to find work elsewhere. Perhaps the most sup-portive home-grown project to contemporary Scottish architects has been Maggie's Centres, a series of cancer drop-in centres founded by Maggie Keswick Jencks shortly before her death in 1995. Half the practices chosen for the Scottish branch-es were based there: Richard Murphy, architect of the first, in 273

Edinburgh, Page\Park for Glasgow and Inverness, and Reiach and Hall's in Airdrie. The other Scottish centres were designed by Frank Gehry (Dundee), Zaha Hadid (Kirkcaldy) and Norwegians Snøhetta (Aberdeen). Richard Murphy, architect of the first Maggie's Centre, accepted an award from the RIBA with a scathing speech, declaring that 'Scotland is one of the worst countries to be an architect', explaining that 'it doesn't matter how good you are, you cannot get a job – they favour the big commercial practices'.[20]

The Scottish Parliament was allowed to be a more romantic gesture than the value-engineered tat that a culture of PFI and its replacement, Scottish Futures Trust, would usually encourage. 'We started this project by thinking of our remembrances of Scotland,' said Miralles. 'Out of that came an image. The most clear image that we had was the idea of a university campus or monastery situation, not a big single building. It is not just what they look like. It is how they feel.'[21] Enric Miralles had been described as naughty, hugely creative, likeable and frustrating. So when he was paired with more corporate local architects RMJM, who would be looking after the day-to-day issues on site, fireworks were sure to follow. 'It was decided that Enric didn't really have the manpower to deliver the project,' John Ramsay explained to me. The brief continued to evolve, as did Miralles's design, and the partnership with RMJM had its, erm, *awkward* moments. 'I was appointed architect,' Miralles said to the Scottish architects. 'I will do everything on this job. You will take no decisions whatsoever.'[22] Ramsay explained the relationship: 'In a very crude way it was designed in Barcelona and delivered in Edinburgh.' Ramsay had joined initially as RMJM's project architect for the MSP offices, but within months had taken on looking after the cladding of the building, liaison with the security services (to become a major issue after the events of 9/11), and the relationship with what he termed 'hairy arsed builders'. But working with a practice based 1,300 miles away came with challenges of its own, not least of which was having to grapple with new technology. 'This was the early days of sending stuff over the internet,' recalled John. 'We'd get a phone call on the Wednesday and Enric's team would say, *right, we're going to send you this next batch of drawings.* And it would take overnight until lunchtime the next day to get all the drawings through and for our IT people to process them and check if they were actually openable files.' And when that wasn't an option, Joan Callis, the project director for EMBT, would fly from Barcelona to Edinburgh. 'He would come across and arrive late in the morning with a portfolio,' said John, 'and we would open the files and this would be the great moment of revelation.'

Requests for more space were made and Miralles was said to have been distracted with other projects. 'You're very good at managing, and I'm very good at drawing,' he told Brian Stewart at RMJM. 'And the problem is,' said Stewart, 'he fails to see that the drawing has to be managed.'[23] Joan O'Connor, president of the Royal Institute of Architects of Ireland and one of those who had selected Miralles, defended him. 'He was a risk, a significant risk,' she said, 'but in my judgment the end product was well worth it.' Dave Rogers of *Construction News* came to the defence of construction companies who were shouldering much of the blame for overspending. 'My personal view is that it isn't the contractors' fault,' he said. 'The problem is that too many people have a "say-so" in this project, and a lot of them are politicians. The poor old contractors have to work round every little modification that their bosses want.'[24] Alan Mack from Bovis Lend Lease, who were attempting to project manage this vast ever-changing carnival, was even more blunt about what had gone on. 'We're just very useful to be used,' he said. 'It's just a series of pissing contests going on between these various groups . . . and the project is irrelevant.'[25] 'Mack was scarred by the experience. 'They're downright liars and they make it up as they go along,' he said. 'I'm not sure I ever want to vote again.'[26] The one thing no one could get away from was that erecting a parliament building was going to be political. 'It was a political project, so everything that happened ended up in the newspapers,' John Ramsay told me. 'And certain newspapers inspired by certain political parties tried to make the most of anything that wasn't clear.' A review chaired by architect John Spencely reported that 'the design and cost have been operating on two parallel tracks: I mean, it's fundamentally stupid. Pointless. And that's really why we've lost a year, I think. That and the change in the brief.'[27] He felt that Miralles had become scapegoated: from the outside it looked like the architect's fault, but from the inside it seemed the reverse – as in the Welsh Assembly, there had been a breakdown in project management. Spencely had also observed a fashionable failing of the New Labour era: 'they're all spinning. And it just gets out of control, you know, and it actually blows back on them in the end.'[28]

Not halfway into the project, more serious issues came to bear. In April 2000 Miralles was diagnosed with a brain tumour and had to fly to the US for treatment. In a debate on 5 April, Margo MacDonald, MSP and critic of the scheme, declared 'he said he would be willing to come back and discuss with us the progress of the project. Where is he? I would certainly like to discuss the progress with him.'[29] It may have been an unintended cruelty by MacDonald, but it seemed to sum up the indignities suffered by the architect along the way. In July, Enric Miralles died. 'Enric died within a month or so of him telling us he had completed 276 the design,' recalled John Ramsay. 'It wasn't going to change

The deconstructed hamlet that forms the Scottish Parliament at Holyrood.
© Bernt Rostad

again, he was happy with the way it was and that was what the client was getting. Whether that was a decision he made because he knew he was very ill or whether it was a coincidence I don't know.' Miralles's widow and business partner, Benedetta Tagliabue, gave a heartfelt interview about the pressures on her to get the project finished after he died. Not only was she the chief architect who had to be away for days at a time to oversee work on site, she and Miralles had two children under ten. 'They knew why I could not be there,' she said. 'I had no choice. I had to go on. Never mind if I was being brave or not, I just had to go on.'[30] Within three months, the First Minister and Miralles's champion Donald Dewar was dead too, after falling from the steps of Bute House. 'So it was like two major players in the team were suddenly gone,' said John. 'And after that we were going to finish it for them.'

277

Miraculously, all eleven buildings that make up the Parliament were completed, and it opened in October 2004. For such a spectacular building, the first time I visited I almost missed it. Remarkable though it is, from the bottom of Canongate it feels perfectly normal in a city – a street – of extraordinary architectural gestures. When I did clock them, the buildings seemed like some sort of mirage, shimmering before me like a series of ghost ships washed up here on a long since vanished tide. The structures overlap, fuse together, caught out of phase with our humdrum reality and each other. Screens like bundles of hurdles bar the windows, one of many details that give a primitive and domestic sense in all of this grandeur, the remembered bustle of medieval streets. In some ways it feels like a sort of visitor attraction whose modern architecture references ancient building types.

The main auditorium is an audacious wooden ship, an inverted galleon floating above the main entrance lobby. Walking beneath it feels like you've entered a secret cave, the wooden cradle above creating a broad, low entranceway that floats upwards around the chamber. The chamber is held in the arms of oak trusses, owing its biggest debt to Barry Gasson Architects' celebrated wooden-framed building for the Burrell Collection in Glasgow, which opened back in 1983. In that earlier building, the natural materials, its remarkable use of the site, and the light and warmth of the design had helped create something quite out of time, neither postmodern nor High Tech, just engineered into the landscape. That same feeling dominates at the Parliament. The auditorium makes the most of the city's precious moments of sunlight, with skylights and windows connecting it to the incredible landscape all around. 'In visual contact with nature and geology' is how the architect put it.[31] Inside the main chamber, the sloped floor and raked seating are arranged in a v-shape to allow for what was hoped to be a gentler, more consensual politics – everyone working together rather than in constant Westminster-style combative opposition. Miralles repeatedly referred to it as 'a gathering place'.[32] 'After all,' he'd said, 'Parliament is just a way of sitting together', a remark said to have been a turning point when the judges were deciding on their winner.[33] It has a complexity that makes it, in the words of Charles Jencks, 'an anti-icon icon'.[34] It must have been a stressful job, I asked John. 'It was actually,' he said. 'We're still a very close-knit bunch, even though we don't see each other very often, I think there's a kind of *esprit de corps* that happened in that project that is unusual. We've already had a tenth anniversary reunion.' At sixty, John thinks he's unlikely to work on another significant building. 'It very certainly was the peak of my career,' he told me. 'It was the project of a lifetime for a lot of us. . . . It was a level of complexity and challenge way above anything else I've ever done in my career. But it had that kind of specialness of *this is impossible – and we did it!*'

The path of devolution has created quite different circumstances in Scotland, Wales and Northern Ireland. But there are things that bring together the dream landscape of Holyrood, the epic new waterscape of Cardiff Bay and the skyscraping visions of Belfast. First, there is the painful birth of all of these projects. Then there is the undoubted success of the debating chambers, two new and one pre-existing. And there is also a sense of the future encapsulated in each: in Holyrood, the romantic vision of Enric Miralles is an inspiring setting for a country debating independence; in Cardiff, the cultural significance of the Millennium Centre and the Millennium Stadium overpowers the political weight of the Senedd, suggesting that Welsh identity is as much tied up with sport and culture as it is politics; and 279 in Belfast there are urgent practical issues to attend to, to physically rebuild damaged and broken towns and communities. Devolution continues to be one of the most interesting political stories of our day, especially given the British parliament's ever more erratic behaviour. It may be from here that our future direction is determined.

'I said the legacy is to reposition the north-east of England as a tourist destination,' explained Paul Collard. He was recounting a meeting he'd had back in the mid-nineties while running the Year of Visual Arts, a festival across the region. Collard had taken the job because he was convinced that you could use the arts to promote economic and social regeneration. Back in 1987 he had been plucked from the Institute of Contemporary Arts to write a report for Margaret Thatcher's newly re-elected administration as part of a government focus on urban regeneration. Collard thinks he was only chosen because the ICA was the first building the civil servants came to when they left their offices in Horse Guards Parade. 'Essentially I argued that the arts could play a significant role in the regeneration of our cities only if they were built from the ground up. It wasn't a strategy that could be imposed from the top down.' Report submitted, it was immediately leaked by the opposition, and created a backlash from the very people who had commissioned it. 'The notion of working closely with local communities was anathema to Margaret Thatcher.' Her preference, noted Collard, was parachuting in undemocratic Urban Development Corporations that operated without the input of local people. 'Her view was that these places are a mess because of the people who live in them. So the last thing we want to do is work with them, you want to bring in people from the outside to try and sort them out. So unbeknownst to me she, going through her press spokesman, organised a denouncement of my report.' He watched in confusion as the press reported on Thatcher's supposed fury at his work. 'But it left me with a very strong sense that there was an amazing thing to be done with arts in terms of building and empowering communities locally. To use the arts as a means for reinventing themselves.'

Back in 1990, Glasgow became Britain's first European City of Culture, an initiative to create massive arts investment in the chosen city. While many of the spectaculars – Pavarotti, Sinatra, the Bolshoi – were flown into the city, there had also been extraordinary works by local artists, including Bill Bryden's *The Ship*, a theatre piece housed in a vast Harland and Wolff engine shed. It wasn't universally popular. Novelist James Kelman described feeling that 'the city is being run as though it were a public company . . . being made attractive to potential shareholders in line with its inevitable privatisation'.[1] 'Not everybody participated,' said academic Dr David Archibald. 'There were and still are lots of people marginalised. But it had a transformative impact on arts and art-making.'[2] And for Collard, fresh from writing his maligned report for the government, it felt like a valediction. 'They demonstrated extremely effectively that idea of community engagement through the arts being used to regenerate cities.'

The idea of cultural regeneration was pushed on by Frank Gehry's design for a Guggenheim art gallery in Bilbao, a former industrial Spanish city in decline. 'They needed the building to do for Bilbao what the Sydney Opera House had done for Australia,' explained Gehry.[3] From the moment it opened in 1997, it was a huge success. 'After it was built people started to go to Bilbao,' said Gehry, 'and that changed the economics of the city.'[4] Over a million visitors a year came to explore Gehry's strange melted metallic structure, sitting on the waterfront like a deconstructed version of Frank Lloyd Wright's streamlined original in New York. Gehry's building also saw the emergence of the architectural 'icon' as a way to describe this form of enterprising city branding. 'Icon' is a strange word here for such a complex and hard to memorise form. Rather than representing the city with a simple swoosh or easily doodled tower playing on elements of the city's heritage, the success of this building was how its complex oddness became its greatest virtue. The secret was its uniqueness. And so suddenly dozens of other cities wanted to demonstrate their own uniqueness – in exactly the same way. 'Since Bilbao I get called to do "Frank Gehry buildings",' said Gehry. 'They actually say that to me.'[5] Everyone wanted an icon to regenerate a former industrial area, to bring life back into the city. By the end of the twentieth century, Britain had more than its share of Bilbaos awaiting regeneration, thanks to deindustrialisation in Scotland, Northern Ireland, Wales and the English north, Midlands and south-west. In 1979, 30 per cent of Britain's national income came from an already declining manufacturing sector, which still employed almost seven million people. By the end of 2010 it had dropped by almost two-thirds. Particularly badly hit was the north-east of England, where the number of manufacturing jobs nearly halved between 1997 and 2011.

By the mid-1990s, Andrew Dixon, deputy for Northern Arts, was pitching for £250 million to build new arts and cultural facilities across the region, with a focus on the decaying quayside at Gateshead. 'People said *Andrew you're completely bonkers, where on earth are you going to get £250m?*' recalled Paul Collard. After all, that was more than the Arts Council total grant for the whole year. The saviour of the plan was the National Lottery. 'Nobody expected the amount of money that the lottery raised to become available,' said Paul. 'Suddenly there was this tidal wave of money available for arts capital projects. And the problem was the Arts Council, who had been battered by Margaret Thatcher for a decade, had actually run out of ideas about what to do. It was full of people with no ideas. But on the other hand there was this Andrew Dixon who had £250 million of ideas, which was the kind of scale of ideas that was necessary in order to spend all this money.' The only problem was that this funding needed to be matched. Dixon went to the European Union to see if they would part-fund it, and they said yes.

Gateshead had a history of commissioning large-scale art pieces, including a Garden Festival in 1990. This was the fourth of five festivals, starting with Liverpool in 1984 and including Stoke-on-Trent in 1986, Glasgow in 1988 and Ebbw Vale in 1992. Gateshead's had been on four sites of reclaimed industrial land, including the Dunston Staiths on the banks of the Tyne, near the MetroCentre, that early monument to out-of-town shopping. The Garden Festival had been Gateshead's first glimpse at culture-led regeneration. The following decade saw the potency of cultural branding for regeneration across the nation on an epic scale. Cool Britannia, the YBAs, Britpop, a fizzing combination of marketing and hype parcelling up art and pop as a commodity to sell Britain to the world, whether you were Damien Hirst or Oasis, Tracey Emin or Blur, Alexander McQueen or the Spice Girls. A cultural moment grew from the optimism, opportunism and boundless irony of these children of John Major. Young entrepreneurs began to experiment with what was possible in urban design too. You can see the intersection of pop, art and architecture in the work of then youthful developers such as Urban Splash and Beetham, and in a very different way, in unorthodox and challenging architectural practices such as feminist collective muf and postmodern revivalists FAT.

In Gateshead, they sought out an artistic icon to represent this hopeful new spirit. They shortlisted an Anthony (Caro) and an Antony (Gormley) and invited them up to explore their ideas. Sid Henderson, chair of Gateshead's arts committee, told their visual arts manager, Mike White, that he fancied Gormley's
chances, especially as he'd seen a maquette of an angel the artist

had produced for the ITN offices in London. *'It's only a small thing, but what I fancy is that 40 metres high on that hill over there,'* recalled Paul Collard. 'And quite rightly the arts officer said, *This isn't how you work with artists. Artists have a vision and they decide.* Sid said, *I understand that. I'd like you to take him to the top of that hill before the interview.* So Michael said, *Oh God, this is going to be so embarrassing. I'm meeting Antony Gormley here and I've got to tell him he's already made up his mind.* And he takes Antony Gormley to the top of the hill and Antony looks around and says *This is a brilliant location to do something.* And Mike says, *I should warn you, before the interview, that Sid's got this idea that you could take that angel in the ITN building and you can make it 40 metres high.* And Antony looks around and says, *Sid's right. That would work here.'*

It seems incredible to think now, but the Angel of the North could once have been rather further south. Back in 1988, Leeds City Council ran a competition for a major public art piece to be constructed in the Holbeck triangle, an area stranded between railway lines just outside the main station. 'The idea was that they would have a kind of Statue of Liberty,' recalled local artist Clifford Stead. 'In the *Evening Post* there was a competition: what would you like to see there? And the public voted.' He looked me dead in the eye. 'A Yorkshire cup of tea. *Massive* saucer with a cuppa. This is what happens when you have referendums. Stupid things win, don't they?' He shook his head. 'At number three was this man that no one had ever heard of called Antony Gormley. He said *I want to do a cast of my body. But because it's a northern gritty city it won't be in steel or marble or anything like that, I'll do it in the materials of the buildings in Leeds* – he's obviously done his research and thinks, Leeds builds everything in brick.' Oh God, I can see it now. A Leeds Look Antony Gormley. I'm laughing. The 285 council ditched the two most popular suggestions – the cup and saucer and, in second place, a giant banana. Gormley was now number one. 'So you'd think, a brick man in a brick city, *wow*! It'll sail through. No. They obviously got cold feet.' A maquette had been built and exhibited at the art gallery, but it didn't go any further. Gormley tried for a similar commission in Hull, but once again was thwarted. When Gateshead said yes and it was constructed in all its majestic glory, how those involved in those Leeds and Hull decisions must have choked on their parkin. The design caused a huge fuss, with local Conservatives and media attempting to kill it off.

Ove Arup were brought in to engineer the giant sculpture, and their immediate response was that it was, for reasons of basic physics, a crazy idea. The slightest pressure on the angel's wings would put unbearably strong forces on the sculpture's slender ankles. But they persevered with the job, designing ribs that would come from underground to strengthen the entire structure. Their solution would become much more fundamental to the overall design than anyone had expected. 'Those ribs that you see coming out of the body into the wings were going to be inside the structure,' recalled Paul Collard, 'but Antony loved the ribs so much that he changed his design so that what you're going to see is the ribs. And it's the ribs that give the power to this thing. It makes you realise what an incredibly powerful piece of engineering it is. And so that was the engineering solution that then became the design.' The steel figure was made in sections in a shipyard 31 miles away in Hartlepool. One Saturday night in February the roads were closed and the Angel was put on a low-loader to begin a slow journey north. Paul recalled how cold and snowy it was that night. 'And thousands of people came out to stand by the sides of the road and cheered. And this was really, really significant. This was an articulation of who they were, they really took ownership and believed in it. The north-east was going through a really rough stage. They knew that change was necessary. What the Angel did is say that change is possible. And also because I think it is a fantastic piece of steel and engineering, that's what the north-east was famous for. It goes back to the roots of their identity.' The press launch in 1998 brought reporters from across the globe.

Within five years of the rise of the Angel came the march of the other projects enabled by that £250 million of Lottery and EU investment. Gateshead's 1950s Rank Hovis flour mill was repurposed by Ellis Williams Architects as the Baltic Centre for Contemporary Art and opened at midnight, 13 July 2002. Five thousand people queued outside that night, and it attracted a phenomenal 300,000 visitors in just three months. Sune Nordgren, the first director of the gallery, addressed the frequent comparisons with Tate Modern. 'We both inhabit former industrial buildings, and we are both connected by a new bridge linking the traditionally prosperous north side of the river to the less prosperous south,' he explained. 'But Baltic exists to run its own press, its own digital media laboratories, and its own exchange programme. It is a facility that will attract artists from all over the world.'[6] They hadn't just copied Bilbao, they had learned from it. In Spain, local artists had felt ignored and shut out of the globalised gallery and were fighting back with work that criticised the Guggenheim. At the Baltic, local talent was very much at the heart of what they were offering. 'It has a really good legacy with a younger generation of artists,' said James Perry, who had been studying architecture at Newcastle University at the start of the decade. He had fond memories of student life in the Baltic and described it as 'probably the most popular building in the north-east of England. I know a lot of people who have worked there, it's a good place to work.'

287

The Baltic, The Sage and the Winking Eye. © Wilka Hudson

Along the waterfront, past a large car park, a starkly contrasting High Tech building by Norman Foster rose up, the Sage Centre for Music, beneath whose vast wobbly canopy could be found three of the best music venues in the country. And leading up to it would stand a glorious new pedestrian bridge for the city, designed by WilkinsonEyre. It is a spectacular design, a curved footbridge and suspension arch, which takes four and a half minutes to tilt 40 degrees to allow tall ships to pass beneath, the motion giving the bridge a nickname, the Winking Eye, almost an abbreviation of the architects'. When it won the Stirling Prize in 2002, there were a few disgruntled architects who thought it should never have been shortlisted because it was engineering rather than architecture. 'What is happening here is unique,' said Antony Gormley, spokesperson for the arts in the area since the stratospheric success of his Angel, 'with 288 a combination of cultural statements, thanks to a visionary and determined council.'[7] 'We want to change the image and perception of Gateshead,' said council leader Mick Henry, 'creating a new city centre along the Quays, while bringing art to the masses and getting over the message that you don't have to go to London to enjoy art and good music.'[8] Over all of this glowered Owen Luder's majestic brutalist Trinity Square car park, made famous in *Get Carter*, a relic from the region's last renaissance in the late 1960s.

Amid all of this cultural activity, 630 new houses and 237 new apartments were being built in the Quays, along with hotels, bars and clubs. 'One of the key arguments about art-led urban regeneration that I make,' said Paul Collard, 'is that the private sector realised that here was a huge opportunity.' There was a rush to build hotels, restaurants, apartments and an arena. EasyJet made Newcastle airport a low-cost airline hub, essential to the long-held dream of the region becoming a top tourist destination. Alan Smith was turning Newcastle's Post Office of 1872 into Red Box, a series of apartments, office spaces, a gallery and restaurant. Wimpey were converting the old Wills tobacco factory into flats. 'Geordies who have left the city are being lured back,' said Trevor Cartner of developers Helios, who had got their hands on the Georgian Exchange Buildings and were looking to benefit from a bit of that old warehouse magic.[9] And off the back of all this activity, for the first time in decades the region's population began to grow. 'Because these jobs had been created and people were coming in from outside to take them,' said Collard. 'And for me looking back, I feel we delivered the economic benefits. The place is completely reinvented. It constantly wins Britain's best short break destination. If you stood with me on the quayside in 1993 when I came to look at it, what a complete mess that place was, you wouldn't believe you could turn that into Britain's best short break destination.' But possibly not for fans of brutalist architecture, as Luder's inconveniently gritty car park and shopping centre was finally got by the council, and demolished in 2010. Don't worry, though, it was replaced by one of the biggest Tesco Extras in the country.

Regeneration and change spread out slowly from the cultural quarter at Gateshead Quays, to the now derelict Garden Festival site at Dunston Staiths, a relic of the city's industrial past. By the noughties the land was being targeted for redevelopment and sold off to housebuilders. The prevailing style of homes they could provide were those cul-de-sacs of pitched-roof red and yellow brick nonentities familiar in estates across the country. In April 2000, Wimpey's chairman, Peter Johnson, saw criticism from fashion designer Wayne Hemingway in the *Independent* of the 'Wimpey-fication' and 'Barrattisation' of Britain. Almost thirty years had elapsed since the advent of the *Essex Design Guide*, which had kicked off the housebuilders' drive for nostalgic nooks, and now perhaps it was time to refresh that approach. Thinking that Hemingway might help them evolve a more fashionable product suited to younger, more urban buyers, Johnson invited the designer to work with them on 750 homes for the old festival site. 'It's not usually a very welcoming industry, the world of architecture, to outsiders, untrained people who haven't struggled through a decade of education and torture,' Newcastle-based architect James Perry told me. 'I suppose his intervention was quite welcomed by most architects, because Barratts and Bellway and all those private limited companies, they just don't listen to architects. And so I think it's just refreshing having somebody else of that stature, a respected fashion designer, just say the obvious really.'

The estate is focused around communal courtyards and communal gardens. 'It does some very basic things,' said Perry, 'you don't have to work very hard to make good housing, but we do a very poor job of it in the UK. Fencing is dropped down quite low so you can see your neighbours. There's places to lock your bikes up. There's shared barbecues.' Hemingway had also tried to see it from a child's perspective, so there are lots of play spaces dotted about. Despite a strong dislike of the taller blocks of flats on the estate ('seven-, eight-storey linear blocks clad in all sorts of horrific colours'), Perry thinks that 'in many ways it's a lot more successful than many houses that have been built to this day really. It achieves the densities. It's got terraces, which is quite a rare thing to see, even today by a housing developer.' The resulting homes have all the hallmarks of Blair-era faux-mo, with asymmetric pitched roofs, picture windows and render in place of the supposedly contextual brick of more standard developer houses. He has friends who enjoyed living there and regularly hangs out in the local café with his partner and their daughter, where they enjoy the Staiths waterfront. 'In terms of showcase housing in the north-east, it still stands out as something that's quite successful,' he tells me. From a respected and innovative social housing architect to a fashion designer working for Wimpey, that's quite the compliment.

Yet the rise of all this development was not the only legacy of this cultural gentrification. 'We engaged the population with the notion that culture could be for them,' said Paul Collard. 'But the social change in terms of engaging that population in new employment, new opportunities didn't really happen. Because they weren't ready to take those jobs.' He recalled visiting a factory in Ashington in 2004, built with European money with the aim of generating new jobs for ex-miners. Looking out on the shop floor, 'everybody, they were all women,' he told me. 'There wasn't a single miner there. And I thought, *this is a problem*.' As new jobs arrived in the creative industries, software design and hospitality, the region's legion of ex-miners found themselves 291 entirely unskilled for them. 'And so I became aware that there was this huge disenfranchised community,' said Paul. 'They on the whole were the people who hated the Angel. Because the Angel represented change and being a different place. I think they saw the Angel as making them invisible. Of going, *but that's not me. The very fact that the Angel has become a symbol has made me redundant.*

'And of course what happened is they found their revenge because this was the community that voted absolutely solidly for Brexit,' Paul continued. 'It was how they bit back against everything.' It seems curious that a lot of areas like Gateshead that benefited from EU funds voted to leave Europe. 'We used a lot of European structural funds and we built this whole amazing cultural infrastructure, we reinvented the image of the city, we created all these new jobs, but it didn't include *them*. And I think they're left going, *what's Europe ever done for me.*' Paul sounded emotional. 'That's our failure, really. We didn't find a way of making it work for them, and that bitterness has continued to grow.' But it wasn't just the fault of the cultural community who swept into Gateshead and made those huge changes so swiftly. 'It was their fault too,' he said of the disenfranchised miners, 'because there was an opportunity there and they chose to say, *that is not for me.*'

Perhaps in the millennium redevelopment of Gateshead and others like it, the seeds of an upheaval decades ahead were sown.

It has appeared on illustrated cards and wrapping paper, aerial shots in reality TV show *The Apprentice*, Marvel's *Thor: The Dark World* and romcom *Love Actually*, as well as pretty much every advert featuring London produced in the last fifteen years, including ones for Cartier, McDonald's and London Zoo. There's even one showing it drooping to promote a treatment for erectile dysfunction. So familiar is it, it's hard to believe that the Gherkin, as designed by Foster + Partners, only got planning permission in 2000. 'It was the first tall building allowed to be built in the City of London since the NatWest Tower [opened in 1981],' said Sara Fox, who worked on it as project director.

I asked Sara if Norman Foster was very involved. 'I went to a number of client review meetings in the Fosters offices where Norman would drop by,' she said.

'He would do a quick walk round of the three walls that were inevitably covered with plans and visuals and CGIs and whatever, and he would zone in on a detail . . . he'd get out his pencil and he'd say, *you know, what I would do here is blah blah*, and you'd think, *actually, he's right*! Because it was trying to be an iconic building and because it was going to be really visible on the skyline, he was more focused on the design of this building than many projects that were going on at the same time. I'm sure you're aware that there was a big feud between Norman Foster and Ken Shuttleworth about who gets primary credit. Well, first of all, neither of them get the primary credit, and least of all Ken Shuttleworth, in *my* experience, in terms of how often *I saw him*. It was very much a team effort. The lead architect for most of the project was a guy called Robin Partington, who is not the sort of guy who blows his own horn. But if you had to say that you had to give credit to one person more than anyone else, then my vote would be for Robin.'

Partington has called it 'an analogue building', because despite its space-age geometries it had not been primarily designed on computers. 'It was more about lots of cardboard and plastic,' he explained. 'We didn't have the computer skills then to work out the design that way.'[1] But they did use computers to work out how to engineer the twisty-turny design they had settled on. The diagonal steel structure creates a rigid frame, like a stretched version of one of those geodesic domes designed by Buckminster Fuller. One of the most boggling elements to the finished building is that, smooth and circular as it is, it only contains one piece of curved glass – the dome at the top. Everything else was faceted. 'You had times when you had people looking like they were going to commit suicide because their head was about to explode,' said Fox of the design process, 'they just couldn't figure out how to resolve it. And the single most important element of this structural design was what we called the node.' These vast tubular steel tree joints resolved how the various elements fitted together from their many angles.

One of the joys of talking to Sara Fox was hearing how she cheerily dismissed the more fanciful architectural ideas of Foster's team. No sky gardens, because Sara decreed there wasn't the space or even climate to successfully grow and tend plants. She had issues with the minimalist lobby design – too small, too few doors – and made Fosters mark it out in their office car park in Battersea to show how quickly it became crowded and unmanageable. There were many engineering challenges faced by the team. As the building rises, each floor plate shifts in relation to the one below by five degrees, and so what had once been 294 an open atrium feature in an earlier version of the design, with a series of sheer drops around the edge of the building, became its familiar staggered twirl. When it was approved, the building had been a clear glass structure. In the end they decided to tint the glass that lined up with that rotating atrium, which is where the black swirl on the surface had come from. Work began on site in January 2001, and eight months later the terrorist attack on the World Trade Center in New York would hang like a shadow over the construction of this and all other tall buildings since. 'We had to get the engineers to completely recalculate how a big bomb at a certain distance would affect the cladding,' Sara told me. 'There was a huge rethink.'

The legacy of terrorist offences much closer to home also influenced the Gherkin's engineering. It had been built on the site of the Baltic Exchange, whose ruined shell was all that was left of the Edwardian edifice after being bombed by the IRA in 1992. Small and fairly inaccessible, it occupied just 1.3 acres square on a narrow one-way street. It had been expected that the exchange would be rebuilt, but owners Trafalgar House had different ideas. They engaged the services of Norman Foster, who initially designed for them what would have been the tallest building in Britain. Millennium Tower (oh yes) was to be a steel and glass slab of sky gardens, luxury flats and offices topped with what looked like two surprised rabbit ears. The City of London was quick to kill it off. Enter Swiss Re, who were looking to build a London HQ, and whose CEO Walter Kielholz had put the mockers on the company moving to Docklands, thanks to his dislike of the choppy postmodern aesthetic dominant there at the time. Instead, it was suggested they check out this troubled site in the middle of the City of London. They engaged Foster to design a completely different building for the same site, half the height of his previous one with an emphasis on sustainability. Foster's team came back with a succession of forms, the first like a loaf   295

High Tech high tide: the Gherkin overlooking the Lloyd's building. © Duncan Harris

of bread, the second an egg, until finally it resolved itself as the smooth, rounded oval tower we recognise today. According to Sara Fox, the Chief Planning Officer for the City of London, Peter Rees, 'made it clear that if it was a truly exceptional building from an architectural perspective, he was going to champion it. If it was a building like they build at Canary Wharf, he didn't want to know about it.'

The much heralded eco features of the Gherkin, which uses about half the energy of a more standard equivalent office tower, 'was totally Swiss Re,' said Fox. The Gherkin uses its circular form to aid a natural ventilation system in circulating the air, while the glass facade creates passive solar heating in winter to warm the tower. Why did they bother, in the era before Ken

Livingstone as Mayor of London began to include sustainability as a key factor in all new projects? As a global insurance company, Swiss Re saw they had a stake in the growing environmental crisis and the damage caused. Extraordinarily, they thought the features in the Gherkin were simply the right thing to do. 'No developer in their right mind would ever do it,' said Sara. 'The atrium – those light wells would never be done by a developer. Because they're just looking at the net to gross, and they're going *Christ, you've given up x per cent of every floor in light wells. Why don't you just fill them in and monetise the space*. The reason is it really adversely affects the quality of the working space on the inside of the building if you do that.'

I'm not sure quite what it is about the Gherkin that makes you happy when you see it – that's if you're lucky enough to still be able to from behind the wall of towers that has grown up around it. 'The people who work in the building say the same thing,' said Sara. 'I think there's a sense of pride. And seriously, the quality of the space inside is really exceptional . . . The daylight absolutely gets into that building.' Peter Rees, the City of London's planner, considered the finished building a huge success. 'Whoever knew anything about insurance let alone re-insurance until they built the Gherkin?' he said. 'That company generated tens of millions of pounds of free advertising off the back of that project. It all came about because they invested a little bit extra in a building with a bit of imagination.'[2] Extraordinarily, in the end not only did the planners and heritage advisers approve this skyscraper in the (then) mostly low-rise City but the Royal Fine Art Commission actually encouraged them to make it slimmer and higher, the form less bulbous and more elegant. So four floors were added. That Prince Charles disliked their eventual design 'only made us realise how good it was', said Kielholz.[3] Press reaction from the time largely focused on failing to make *erotic* 297 *gherkin* happen as a phrase. 30 St Mary Axe was chosen as its official name, which mattered not, because by that point it was known by all as the Gherkin, and lovingly so. 'That which has started as a term of abuse has ended up a term of endearment, of affection,' acknowledged a clearly baffled Norman Foster at the opening of the Gherkin. 'I've mellowed like everyone else,' he said, with all the sincerity of someone who had died and was having his mouth reanimated by Ken Shuttleworth.[4]

If you were to ask most British people around the time of the millennium to name a contemporary architect, most who could would have chosen one of two names: Richard Rogers or Norman Foster. And looking at the major projects being built in Britain at the time, of the thirty most significant, their two practices were responsible for eighteen of them. Richard Rogers, who'd been so successful at schmoozing New Labour at the River Cafe, the acclaimed restaurant run by his wife Ruth, had the Senedd in Cardiff, the Daiwa offices in London, a designer outlet mall in Ashford, Lloyd's Register of Shipping (not to be confused with his earlier Lloyd's building), and Terminal 5 at Heathrow, oh, and the Millennium Dome. Norman Foster had an even more impressive list, including London's Millennium Bridge, the British Museum's Great Court, the Gherkin, the Greater London Authority HQ beside Tower Bridge, the Jubilee Line station for Canary Wharf, the Sage Music Centre in Gateshead, the National Botanical Gardens for Wales, HSBC's Canary Wharf HQ, Wembley Stadium, Reading business park, Centre for Advanced Studies in the Social Sciences at Oxford University and the Aberdeen Business School, Robert Gordon University.* Rogers had

* The list pointed out another unfairness – all but four of these projects were based in the south-east of England.

become famous for buildings that held their guts on the outside, such as the Pompidou Centre in Paris, which looked to the playful plug-in imaginings of Archigram, those sixties pranksters who had torn up the cosy world of British modernism. Foster's, by comparison, were sleek and stealthy, everything contained within a steel and glass shell, like his Sainsbury Centre for Visual Arts at the University of East Anglia, a mid-seventies experiment in light, clean aircraft hangar-scale design.

Although their style, output and success might bear comparison, their backgrounds were vastly different. Rogers hailed from a bohemian, arty European set, bringing a kind of expansive openness and utopian sense of style with him. He's related to Ernesto Rogers, the prolific Italian modernist architect and product designer of the mid-century. By contrast, Foster was a prodigiously hard-working kid from a run-down Industrial Revolution suburb of Manchester and as such a cheeringly unlikely candidate for leading architect of his generation. They first met at a London event for Henry Fellowship and Fulbright Scholars as they were both about to travel to study in the US at Yale. Once there, they absorbed as much of the culture as possible, racing across the US whenever time permitted to catch as many of the great architectural gems of the country as they could. Not long after heading back to the UK, they formed Team 4, a kind of architectural Abba, where the personal was very much bound up with the professional. Team 4 included Richard's first wife, Su Rogers, and his ex-girlfriend Georgie Cheeseman – the only qualified architect among them – as well as her sister Wendy, who would go on to marry Norman. 'Norman and I were modernists,' recalled Richard Rogers, 'but were inspired by the amazing heritage of early industrial buildings . . . the incredible lightness and delicacy of Brunel and Paxton.'[5]

Together they designed what became the first recognisably 299

High Tech building in Britain, the single-storey Reliance Controls electronics factory near Swindon, which opened in 1967. Their old lecturer James Stirling had recommended them to the client. 'It was the first building that we built using standardised components and systems,' recalled Rogers, 'rather than the chaotic construction of traditional building techniques.'⁶ Team 4 were obsessed with building using 'light and dry' materials that clicked together on site, and so this was an early attempt to achieve that. The shed used corrugated steel for the walls, and steel cross-braces in an X on the outside, an early indication of where the architects would go in later work. Even more so than Le Corbusier's fabled 'machines for living in', High Tech buildings were designed to foreground their engineering. But it was predicated on a bit of a fib – that their modular lightweight structures were always the simplest solution for any given problem. As Colin Davies notes in his book on the subject, 'the motifs of High Tech – exposed steel structure, visible air conditioning ducts, plug-in service pods, and so on – are almost never the most economical solutions.'⁷ Often the exposed ducts, pods and concealed lighting that seem so essential to the very structure of the building are mainly the way they are for aesthetic reasons. These are the 'techno-bits' spoken of so scornfully by Terry Farrell. Despite awards for the Reliance Controls building, Team 4's work dried up. 'We thought this would lead to a flood of work,' wrote Rogers, 'but the only query we received was how the flooring was cleaned.'⁸ With time on their hands, the two young architects fell out, and went their separate ways, taking the lessons with them. 'The split of Team 4 was painful,' recalled Rogers, 'but we all remained close.'⁹

After going their separate ways, success for the two pairs was not slow in coming. Richard and Su Rogers, partnered with Renzo Piano, would go on to design the Pompidou Centre in the early 1970s. Norman and Wendy Foster designed groundbreaking schemes in East Anglia: the Willis Faber & Dumas offices in Ipswich and the Sainsbury Centre for Visual Arts in Norwich. By the start of the 1980s, it was commercial clients rather than philanthropists or governments who came calling, with one such brief from an outwardly unglamorous insurance institution leading to one of the most extraordinary modern structures in Britain: the Lloyd's building.

As at the Pompidou Centre, for Lloyd's Rogers made a play of its services being hung on the exterior, to create a vast open space in the centre for traders. Clinging to the outside are thirty-three metallic pods containing the building's toilets. Never have the loos been such a star feature. They were meant to seem as if you could plug them into the building, like capsules in the modular Nakagin tower in Tokyo. But it's a deception – once in, these pods aren't going anywhere. The internal space is held open through much gleefully expressed bracing. The towers that hold up the structures are mighty trees bursting with outgrowths, the escalators zigzagging their way up and down like vines in a jungle. The top is a great glass arch, capturing all this steely growth in its own greenhouse, with barrel-vaulted windows to mimic the Crystal Palace. Its steampunk aspirations are enhanced by the magic tricks inside. The Adam Room is perhaps the most absurd of the lot, being the second recreation of Robert Adam's neoclassical Great Room from Bowood House, Wiltshire. It had been bought at auction by Lloyd's in 1956 when Bowood was set to be demolished, and initially recreated as the committee room in Terence Heysham's 1958 Lime Street office building. Currently it exists on the eleventh floor of Richard Rogers's version, presumably killing time before relocation on a space station or, later, Mars. Meanwhile, the bell from HMS *Lutine*, a frigate sunk in 1799   301 off the coast of Holland and recovered fifty-nine years later, sits in the atrium. These archaic items nestle within the envelope, like the trinkets of a mad time-travelling thief. For elderly modernist pioneer Berthold Lubetkin, Rogers's tricks were a step too far. To him it was 'an assembly of nuts and bolts, scrap iron, celebrating a confusion of fancy props, the glorification of ironmongery and triumph of mega-technology for its own sake'.[10] I worked for a time next door in the late 1980s, in a bookshop in the ornate Victorian splendour of Leadenhall Market. I never stopped finding Metal Mickey an enthralling neighbour. My workmates were less sure.

'If you go inside Lloyd's, that's the magic moment,' said Mike Davies. 'It's not when you're outside. The magic moment is standing in there. There's nothing but traders in this space, and light. And that's what they wanted.' He recalled the underwriter who stopped him in the building in the eighties, shocked by Davies's trademark all-red attire. 'A man confronted me and said *why are you in our building in that suit?!* And I said, *well, why are you in the building in* that *suit?* He said, *what do you mean?* And I said, *well, they're identical. They're the same cut, you've got leather shoes on, I've got leather shoes on, I have a shirt and tie, we are absolutely identically dressed. Only a few angstroms in the colour spectrum separates us.'* Sartorial differences aside, the experimental architecture practice and the venerable City institution turned out to be a great fit. For one, the client was very clear about their needs. 'They said, *Mr Rogers, Mr Davies, the last thing we want is men in white coats with tool bags coming in to our market place. We make £20m a day. We don't want to be disturbed.'* In 1981 he was sent to interview the underwriters about their technology needs, and they were quite adamant they had none. '*Mr Davies. We don't need technology to run our business. All we need is my initials on the corner of a piece of paper. Good afternoon.* It was then very difficult to come back with proposals for trading boxes that incorporated techno-logical support to a bunch of guys who basically swept it off the table.' But Davies and team eventually got their way, saving the traders in the late eighties from being fried by their computers, each giving off the heat of a small electric fire. 'They eventually said *I remember you giving your statement and you were right. You foresaw our future and we couldn't see it ourselves.* This was really nice.'

Norman Foster was making his mark in the UK too. There was the minimal perfection of Stansted airport, where rather than those external ducts that Rogers liked so much, he had all the cabling for the heating and lighting equipment fed through the steel columns, out of the way. Here, his obsession for finding the most efficient envelope into which the building functions could fit reached a peak of perfection, the lightness of the terminal building contrasting so sharply with the claus-trophobic, ad hoc feeling of Heathrow and Gatwick. But not every project was a success. By the millennium, Foster faced a humiliation greater even than the negativity that met Rich-ard Rogers's Dome. In December 1996 it was announced that, together with his long-time friend the sculptor Anthony Caro, he had designed a pedestrian footbridge over the Thames to join St Paul's Cathedral with the new Tate Modern gallery at Bank-side. 'I feel great,' said Caro that day. 'It will be a tremendously beautiful addition to London.'[11] And so it is. At 320 metres long and suspended 9.5 metres above the Thames, the bridge was unlike anything London had seen before. It was a suspension bridge, but here instead of the cables rising to a mast above they were strung alongside. Its low, sleek profile was what had led the designers to call it the Blade of Light. In May 2000, the fin-ished bridge was opened by the Queen. I remember turning up the night it was opened, thinking I could stroll across and enjoy this extraordinary new feature that hovered some way below the London skyline. Like many of the crowd, I was disappointed to discover that pedestrians would not be able to pass across for another month.

It eventually opened on 10 June. This time, I thought I might wait for the hubbub to die down a bit and pop along the following week to get my stroll in. In doing so, I lost my chance to experience one of the millennium's most exciting sensations. Almost immediately, pedestrians alerted police that something was very wrong. Once people had started to cross the bridge, it began to sway and undulate. They became seasick, fell over, screamed and hung on for dear life – the full *Star Trek* 'we've been hit' routine. Rather than deterring people, the following day 50,000 were queueing to experience this accidental new attraction. Access was reduced to groups of sixty every two minutes. One of the lucky few, Mark Munro from Edinburgh, took his son. 'He thinks it is a fairground ride,' said Munro Snr.[12] There were dark mutterings of a Millennium Curse affecting bridge, Dome and London Eye, which was experiencing teething troubles with its space-age pods. Foster's bridge was closed after two days, and remained shut for two years. Dr John Parker, specialist vibration consultant at engineers Ove Arup, discovered the cause: 'If a number of people walk across the bridge, the force starts the bridge swaying,' he explained. 'Pedestrians find it more comfortable to walk in phase with the movement, feeding more lateral energy into the structure creating a vicious cycle.'[13] The modelling software used had not factored in this vital piece of information and Arups were mortified by their part in it. Tony Fitzpatrick, the company chairman, said 'I am an embarrassed man and my company is very embarrassed.' It finally reopened in February 2002 after £5 million remedial work, fitting ninety dampers along the span of the bridge to help cancel out the vibrations that had led pedestrians to march in unison in the first place. The furore robbed the structure of its *Matrix* blade-of-light seriousness, encapsulated in its popular new name: the wobbly bridge.

The work that Fosters and Rogers were doing by the time of the millennium tended to be statement architecture for blue chip clients. When I talked to Terry Farrell, no stranger to these sorts of projects, the conversation soon strayed to social housing. Farrell had designed a fair bit of council housing earlier in his career. He was less impressed by the record of his peers, such as Nicholas Grimshaw and Zaha Hadid. 'If you ask them, any of those architects, what they like doing, they will say social housing, because that's what's expected of them,' he said. 'They *actually* do opera houses and art galleries and state railway stations and so on.' Of course, Farrell himself has long been distant from such issues too, but it was an interesting illustration of what I'd long suspected. When I was researching my first book, *Concretopia*, I was most struck by how the big names of the post-war period either worked for the public sector or were busy designing council housing from their private practices. Basil Spence designed the Queen Elizabeth Square flats in Glasgow; Peter and Alison Smithson drew up Robin Hood Gardens in East London; Ernő Goldfinger fashioned two monumental towers, Balfron and Trellick; Denys Lasdun conceived cluster blocks in Bethnal Green; Neave Brown outlined his magnificent modernist street at Alexandra Road in Camden; Kate Macintosh devised the ziggurats of Dawson's Heights in East Dulwich. But when I look at the top tier – the *starchitects* – of the recent past, I'm struck by how little social housing they have produced. Instead, the projects are, as Farrell expressed, expensive and glossy galleries, museums, offices and luxury flats. The icons hide the truth. They provide lucrative work for these mega-practices and distract from the fact that they have largely given up on architecture with any social purpose beyond work and leisure.

As a philosophy, High Tech has long been viewed with suspicion. Deyan Sudjic, later director of the Design Museum, dismissed it as 'tasteful, anorexic modernity without a social cause'.[14] Postmodernist-in-chief Charles Jencks spoke of High Tech's agnosticism, its centrist dad philosophy 'avoiding social or political commitment'.[15] *Guys, guys, can we all just get on so we can continue to make huge wads of cash?* Back in 1975, Richard Rogers addressed this straight on. 'In the face of such immediate crises as starvation, rising population, homelessness, pollution, misuse of non-renewable resources, and industrial and agricultural production,' he wrote, 'we simply anaesthetise our consciences. With problems so numerous and profound, with no control except by starvation, disease and war, we respond with detachment. Today, at best, we can hope to diminish the coming catastrophe by recognition of the existing human conditions and by rational research and practice.'[16] Writing forty years later, Rogers attempted a more engaged mode. 'Architecture is inescapably social and political,' he wrote in 2017. As if to prove that, he quotes the first line of his practice's constitution: 'Architecture is inseparable from the social and economic values of the individuals who practise it and the society which sustains it.'[17] Which is, of course, different from being political; it instead suggests they are riding on a path of least resistance through the prevailing climate rather than following a moral imperative.

Meanwhile, a younger generation of architects who had worked for Rogers and Foster were beginning to make their mark on the urban design of the country and out-dazzle the old masters. Future Systems was a London practice run by Jan 306 Kaplický, Amanda Levete and David Nixon, who established

themselves with two sensational structures that lived up to
their whizzy name. Their Lord's Cricket Ground media centre
won them the Stirling Prize in 1999. Ostensibly the head of a
giant robot peering over the stands, it was such an innovative
design that it had to be constructed not on a building site but in
a shipyard. Their next blockbuster would cause even more of a
stir. Selfridges Birmingham was completed in 2003 as part of a
comprehensive remodelling of the urban centre to join up areas disconnected by epic 1960s redevelopment. Future Systems'
Selfridges department store was rumoured to be based on the
idea of a woman undulating out of a Paco Rabanne dress. It is
certainly a sensuous, glamorous entity, half Henry Moore reclin-
ing figure, half James Bond opening titles glamour model. Like
all good icons, it is architecture designed to startle. It's surely
memorable, and for those modernists who mourned the loss of

Future Systems living up to their name with the design of Selfridges Birmingham.
© Tim Parkinson

their post-war landscape, the Victorian Society who regretted the city's ambitious bulldozing in the first place, or some long-lost Medieval Society who would have those uppity Victorians in stocks, it's a powerful enough structure to deserve its place in the heart of the city, over any of the previous incarnations. Perhaps the greatest of the Fosters and Rogers alumni is David Chipperfield, whose exquisitely sober style makes him one of the few architects to appeal to both the classical and modernist factions of modern architecture. Apart from the odd Wagamama and Joseph shop in the nineties, most of his major work has been around Europe. But that all changed in a few days in 2011, when his Turner Contemporary gallery in Margate opened on 16 April, followed by the Hepworth in Wakefield on 21 May. They feel spiritual in a way that no Foster or Rogers building has ever quite managed.

The dominance of white men in almost all key positions in architecture in this period was detailed by Denise Scott Brown, co-designer of the National Gallery extension, who in the 1970s had written a brilliant piece entitled *Room at the Top? Sexism and the Star System in Architecture*, which lay unpublished until 1989. Its issues feel current still. She describes seeing her husband and partner, Robert Venturi, 'manufactured into an architectural guru before my eyes and, to some extent, on the basis of our joint work and the work of our firm'.[18] Scott Brown was one of nine architects featured in a book, but when she saw the finished product her name had been left off the dust jacket – she was told it would have spoiled the design. Venturi was invited to dinners without her, because wives were not included, and her ideas were quoted by critics and attributed to her husband. There were additional social issues that came with such a male-dominated profession too. 'Postmodernism did change the views of architects but not in the way I had hoped,' she wrote.

'Architects lost their social concern: the architect as macho evolutionary was succeeded as the architect as *dernier cri* of the art world: the cult of personality increased. This made things worse for women because, in architecture, the *dernier cri* is as male as the prima donna.'[19]

The success of the Gherkin led to a rash of other tall buildings in the City. 'For Mayor Ken Livingstone, well-sited, high-quality towers were a symbol of the dynamic social and economic life of London,' wrote critic Kenneth Powell in 2001.[20] Livingstone had been elected the first of a series of metro mayors in England the previous year and would remain in post until 2008. The Mayoralty was part of devolution, recognition that the seven million people living in London in 2000 outnumbered the population of Scotland (five million), Wales (three million) and Northern Ireland (two and a half million). New Labour prided itself on self-control and technocratic management but when Livingstone, former Labour leader of the long-disbanded Greater London Council, ran as an independent for Mayor of London, they didn't quite know what to do. He was outspoken, up for a fight and frequently in trouble. He was also popular with many Londoners, who remembered his generous-spirited reign at the GLC with fondness. Ken was generally thought of as an old Labour left-winger, but he soon showed he could make it in the new business-dominated scene post-Thatcher. He became surprisingly pally with big developers and showed he was not afraid to defy the establishment who safeguarded the skyline of the city. He waved through proposals for twenty or so towers over 300 feet in height. 'High buildings should be assessed on what they add to the skyline,' he said, 'rather than what they take away.'[21] He approved a bundle in Canary Wharf and a huddle around the Gherkin as the City attempted to beat

Docklands at their own game. These were the skyscraper wars.

The result has been a bit of a shock, even for fans of the Gherkin, which has been screened out from most of London by the resulting cluster. Sara Fox felt the rush to high-rise in the City had been a huge shame, not least because the Gherkin really only had five years where it was free from being obstructed on the London skyline. 'You can still see it from the east,' she said a little sadly. Standing apart is 20 Fenchurch Street, Rafael Viñoly's Walkie Talkie built for British Land, mothballed in the aftermath of the global crash before resurfacing in the early 2010s. Because people pay more for the view, the Walkie Talkie is wider at the top than the base, giving it a cartoonish bullying presence. 'That is the most hideous hateful horrible building,' said Fox with her trademark diplomacy. 'I revile it with every fibre of my being.' It's not an uncommon reaction. Though this is a building that fights back. In the summer of 2013, the concave south wall caught the sun and created a heat ray of such strength that it melted the bodywork of a Jag belonging to Martin Lindsay, director of a tiling company. The wing mirror, roof panels and even the Jaguar badge melted. 'When I first came to London years ago, it wasn't like this,' Viñoly told the *Guardian*. 'Now you have all these sunny days. So you should blame this thing on global warming too, right?'[22] Nice try, Rafael.

One of the skyscrapers surrounding the Gherkin these days, as if in a glass jar, is the Cheesegrater – sorry, the Leadenhall Building – designed by Graham Stirk of Rogers Stirk Harbour. It was there, where Rogers's office is now based, that I met architect and urban utopian Mike Davies. 'It's designed so you can have open-plan floors all the way through,' he explained excitedly as we sat in one corner, looking down on the Lloyd's building next door. 'And that's radically different to a typical office building. Independent of the architecture, in terms of service concept, there's nothing to touch this in London, it's a completely new idea.' The size of the open-plan floor means you can see how large the operation is here, how many sensibly dressed young people there are quietly working away on computers, and how little chat and noise.

Rogers says the technology employed in creating this tower 'makes Lloyd's look artisanal. The sophistication of computer-aided design and manufacture means that every piece of steel or glass can be specified and delivered with absolute accuracy.'[23] Its angled profile had been designed as a way of not obscuring the view of St Paul's Cathedral. But here the triumph is a High Tech goal: the banishment of an internal concrete 'core' of lifts and services. 'It's not to do with style, with postmodernism or modernism, or anything else,' insisted Davies, 'it's to do with first principles thinking.' Of course, such pronouncements about being beyond mere style is about as High Tech as it gets. Here, a steel frame encased in glass holds the building at the edges, so that each floor is uninterrupted by pillars or lift shafts. 'This is the only high-rise building in the City and at Canary Wharf which has got a room this size,' said Davies. 'The plan of all high-rise buildings here and in the States is the orthodox hierarchical plan. And they all end up structured the same way, with the bosses in the corners and chief executives next to them and then the menials and secretaries down by the lifts. This building has a different proposition, it's a social proposition, it's not just an architectural one. It says, it's an egalitarian world and Richard and I and Andrew and the junior dogsbody all sit in exactly the same space, and we're comfortable. Everybody dines with everybody, it's part of the philosophy of the practice. We're all one team.' Even the junior dogsbody. Imagine.

On my way out I couldn't deduce how to call or operate the button-less elevators, and once the office door had closed behind me there was no one to ask. 'When you look at all the lift technology, where's it all gone?' Davies asked rhetorically, in a dazzling monologue that roamed between driverless cars and how he wished the tower going up next door would leave the crane attached when it was finished, just to add a bit of drama. 'How can lifts be this open rather than in boxes?' I pondered his words as I stood suspended in this bit of infrastructure hanging over London feeling like a bit of a dick. Maybe I liked lifts in boxes. And buttons. And doors that didn't automatically lock you in blank glass lobbies. Mike is glorious and, what, twenty, thirty years older than me? But my God I felt old. On eventually reaching street level, there was a sensation of my journey into the building having been a test of my fitness for a new High Tech world – of being scanned, found wanting and spat out.

In 2009, just as the effects of the global financial crisis were beginning to bite, one of the most extraordinary manifestations of icon culture was rising. Mayfair property tycoon Irvine Sellar had commissioned Richard Rogers's old Pompidou pal Renzo Piano to design a ninety-five-storey skyscraper – the tallest in Europe – on a plot beside London Bridge station where the brick, glass and concrete of TP Bennett's 1975 Southwark Towers stood. In normal times I travel through London Bridge station every day for work, and back then it felt pretty run-down. The 1978 incarnation of the station was staggering slowly to its death, a ramshackle structure of brown corrugated fibreglass panels, dog-legged bridges and leaky tunnels between platforms. Dirty glass skylights in the form of pyramids some-how predicted the form of the skyscraper that was to be built over them. Beside it stood Richard Seifert's New London Bridge House, to be dismantled too as the station was slow-312 ly annexed by work: bridges truncated and then demolished;

access to platforms changed to boarded-up rat runs; the shops and cafés all closed and removed.

Above it all emerged a heart of glass, or rather concrete at first, 'The Shard' emblazoned on the core in an effort to prevent anyone giving it an 'affectionate' nickname. It is not an affectionate building, it's as coldly slashing as its name suggests. Which is not to say it isn't impressive. People go *oooh* when they see it for the first time from an escalator from the Underground station metres before it or from 40 miles away on the South Downs, where it can still be glimpsed. The developers called it a vertical city., If so, asked satirist Ian Martin with indignant precision, 'where's the school, the hospital, the weird newsagent's that sells tinned pies? Where's the social housing, the dodgy pub, the library?'[24] The Shard is not a vertical city, it is an exclusive enclave, a secretive gated community that wants everyone to notice it and feel small. Both the Shard and the Walkie Talkie were bailed out by Qatari investors after the crash of 2008. A Cambridge University study found that in 1980, 8 per cent of the City of London's office space had been owned by foreign investors, while by 2011 it was over half.[25]

There have been seemingly endless openings at London Bridge since work started. The Shard in 2013. The News Building, Rupert Murdoch's 'baby shard', opened the following year. London Bridge Station was declared open in 2018, but in the following years chunks were still being built, and large areas unoccupied. Even in the midst of the pandemic, shops, sports pubs and takeaways were still opening. And work in the precinct is not finished. A further louvred glass skyscraper is still being erected at what is inevitably called – in the language of Poundbury's Léon Krier – Shard Quarter. At least fifteen years of my working life have been affected by this constant work, the demolition, construction, sweeping changes and the new ideology that 313 has come to replace the old. Gone is the poky independent sandwich shop that did amazing breakfasts, the edgy rain-stained corners, the layers of history, and in their place stands a more controlled corporate environment, within which only the most financially secure chains and travellers can survive. Beside the Shard stands the concrete tower of Guy's Hospital, once a brutalist sea monster crawled from the Thames, now body-shamed and clad by architects Penoyre & Prasad to resemble a jazzy 1980s pencil case. Commenters on the website skyscrapercity. com were furious about how the hospital ruined the clean lines of the luxe offices nearby, judging it a *skysore*. For the most part they have had their way and ghosts of a more chaotic, piece-meal, historic pattern have been almost entirely erased. Yet the hospital tower remains, reminding us of life and death struggles that no amount of steel and glass perfection can hide. The new landscape at London Bridge is a tribute to the mega corporations who can afford to buy and reshape districts of cities they don't inhabit. It was a trend we would see flourish as the 2010s came to an end, and the financial crisis began to stunt the lives of all but the most financially secure.

From the off, the New Labour government had targeted social exclusion as one of the modern ills of society. A young, disruptive and ambitious expert, Louise Casey, fresh from being Deputy Director of housing charity Shelter, had been brought in to head up the government's Rough Sleepers' Unit. 'One of the things that has distressed me most is that some of the people I met nine years ago as an outreach worker are still on the streets today,' she explained in 1999. 'This cannot be right. I will feel I have personally failed if, in 2002, those same faces are still there. . . . I do believe that some of the help given to rough sleepers, however well meaning, is misplaced.'[1] Her hands-on approach was markedly different from that of the preceding Tory government: she would take her team onto the street to see where the system was failing the people concerned. The Rough Sleepers' Unit advocated tough love, encouraging people not to give money to homeless people but instead confronting individuals with questions about why they were homeless, and what they needed to escape from. This strategy, while successful, was criticised for being too confrontational for many. But it had encouraging results pretty rapidly.

Casey's PA, Amanda Synott, described the leap that the RSU was asking all of us to take. 'I'm a bit of a soft touch,' she said in 2002. 'I'm the type of person who would give beggars all the money in my purse if I could. But I don't do that now because I realize that's not helping them. . . . I remember the first time I ever took a call from a rough sleeper. I just put the phone down and just bawled my eyes out. . . . Almost every rough sleeper in London has been contacted by us. Those that are sleeping rough are choosing to do so. What I call the hardcore. Our aim at the unit is to get them off the streets, provide them with accommodation and help them get treatment for any problems or addictions they may have in the hope that they eventually become completely self-sufficient.'[2] By 2000 the number of rough sleepers had fallen by a third, 1,180 people nationwide, though the crisis was still acute in London. This also meant that many were now in emergency accommodation instead, but even in that area the strategy to tackle homelessness appeared to be working. Two years later they had reached their target of reducing the number of rough sleepers across England by 70 per cent. Such was the energy and joined-up nature of these initiatives that in 2004 the then underused Millennium Dome was repurposed to house 800 homeless people over the Christmas holidays. Organised by Crisis, the Dome wasn't just a shelter, it also housed a training fair, with courses on IT and plumbing. One of the genuine icons of New Britain colliding with the reality of a new millennium.

The Millennium Commission was wound up in 2006. Some of its projects vanished almost as soon as they appeared. The National Centre for Popular Music in Sheffield was one of the shortest-lived. Branson Coates's super-cool circular stainless-steel structures were opened on 1 March 1999 and closed by the following June. This £15 million experiment in reviving a part of the city centre fell completely flat, only receiving a quarter of the number of visitors predicted. This rather wonderful building with its eccentric rotating chimneys is now Sheffield Hallam University's students' union. Lucky them. The Earth Centre environmental theme park in Doncaster opened in 1999 and had already made staff redundant before the millennium because of low visitor numbers.

Some never even made it. Norwich's hugely ambitious and baffling virtual reality hub Technopolis became instead the city's immensely popular library. Ah yes, libraries. A flurry of new ones, rebranded as *vibrant learning spaces* – including David Adjaye's Idea Store in Whitechapel, FAT's in Thornton Heath and Will Alsop's in Peckham – seemed to be pointing the way to the balancing act that New Labour was trying to pull off: a partnership between public and private to bestow generous public facilities. Adjaye remarked that 'an Ikea looks better than most libraries. They're intimidating.'[3] His Idea Store is a wonderful building, colourful and using his trademark mixture of high- and low-tech materials, so it feels at once futuristic and slightly thrown together, favouring 'shitty materials elevated till they're beautiful'.[4] There's an abundance of junk plywood contrasting with the perfect glazed curtain wall. It feels more Apple Store than study, but goes further – where Apple's corporate chic feels a bit upmarket Argos, Adjaye's Idea Store has a more home-grown, handcrafted, eccentric hipster uncle feel about it. And the joy is, it's busy and – oh my, we're back to the Dome – fun. Actual fun. Adjaye is one of the architects best placed to take on the mantle from the generation of Norman Foster and Richard Rogers, taking British architecture to new heights. Yes, his most high-profile London project of late, a proposed UK Holocaust Memorial, has been slowed by protest and a public inquiry. Here, meditative subterranean spaces would surface dramatically as a series of bronzed fins in the garden beside the Houses of Parliament. It has been criticised for being environmentally damaging to the park, for disregarding the listed status of the location and for providing an unsatisfactory solution to the brief. How to square the demand for new building with the layers of historical, social and environmental considerations that weigh heavily on every new project? The outcome of this decision could be as contested as the National Gallery competition a generation earlier, and with equally significant consequences for a new wave of architects.

When the crash came in 2007, a chill wind blew through the 317 seemingly effortless rise of the property industry in Britain. The big housebuilders – Barratt, Taylor Wimpey and Persimmon – all stopped construction in early 2008. As well as sales of private homes, an expected 20,000–45,000 flats and houses intended for social housing would now not get built. And so the National Housing Federation, that mouthpiece of the private developers, suggested that the money from all this unbuilt social housing should be used instead to buy unsold homes from the big housebuilders. The turbulent conditions seemed to advantage the new mega housing associations, while the recession killed the dream of creating mixed communities. For the first time in twenty years, new affordable estates built by housing associations would no longer include houses for sale.

Bob Kerslake, head of the Homes and Communities Agency, said that 'people are now reluctant to build developments where there is a significant financial risk. In the past we often had a mix of 30 per cent social housing, 30 per cent private homes, and 30 per cent shared ownership. In future we will keep the same proportion of social rented and provide intermediate or subsidized rents for the rest.'[5] Meanwhile, David Orr, head of the National Housing Federation, was determined that 'we are not going to go back to the mono-tenure housing estates of the past . . . We are all aware of the dangers of building mono-estates of just social housing.'[6] Old Labour Old Danger, apparently. Developers had a legal obligation to ensure that 25 to 50 per cent of their developments were for social rent or shared equity. Post-crash, they were coming to agreements with local councils to cut the affordable housing altogether. Gordon Brown's targets – three million new homes by 2020, with 70,000 social rented homes built every year – were entirely shot. Only 22,000 social rent homes were built in 2007, and as the effects of the crash worsened that figure continued to shrink. A problem was building for the future.

Was this millennium moment, with its lottery funds and big ideals, squandered? 'There was far too much happening far too quickly and the industry wasn't learning from its mistakes,' said Peter Higgins of Land Design Studio. 'The big mistake was the iconic building and can you go and retrofit it. There's never any funding for refitting or tuning. And you might have spent £30 million. The Lowry Centre, £80 million. The Earth Centre, £100 million.* Disaster! Utter complete failure!' Higgins, it turns out, had a close shave with the Earth Centre.

'It was run by the wrong people. We were interviewed by them, it was a husband and wife team, and they were utterly the wrong people. They were kind of Greens and a little bit happy-clappy. They just didn't have a bigger picture of the business case or what constituted an attraction. It all looks good but the content was all over the place. And people just didn't go. To begin with you weren't allowed to drive, you've got to get a train and use bicycles – come on, give us a break!'

Lottery money was being spent on grandiose projects without any consistent form of oversight or strategy of how to make them succeed, and leaders were being brought in from sectors – academia or local authorities – who had no relevant experience. 'The thing you find is that the leadership or the organising principle of any project is dependent on a very well informed, clever, powerful leader,' said Higgins. 'And for so many lottery projects that person has not existed. And they're really difficult people to find.' Perhaps that is the legacy of the era, a paucity of leadership, as timidity and naivety tried to meet the challenges of a turbulent new age. Yet for all its faults, it remains a

---

* Or £55 million, according to the BBC in 2012.

period of progress and positivity, where attempts were made to reconnect urban planning to issues such as poverty, inequality and quality of life. 'Thinking back again to the nineties,' said Jonathan Adams, architect of Cardiff's Millennium Centre, 'one of the things that was so extraordinary was the feeling of everything being possible, which carried on really up until 2008. And suddenly nothing was possible.' He paused. 'That kind of optimistic sense has never come back since 2008.'

'We have very short memories,' Margate resident Dan Thompson told me on a Zoom call as he held up his laptop and showed me the view of the seafront from his high-rise flat. 'People really don't believe that the old town was derelict fifteen years ago. They're convinced that the old town must always have been this kind of chic shabby little seaside thing with quirky shops going on.' By contrast, Thompson, originally from along the coast in Worthing, recalled his first visit to the town, in 2004. 'It wasn't just a bit run-down, derelict, it was kind of burnt-out buildings and empty and boarded up,' he recalled. 'Walking around going, I don't think we'd ever save this. This is so far gone. I don't know what you would do to turn this around. It was so dramatically gone.'

Margate. Chas and Dave's 1982 single devoted to the town had originally been written as an advertising ditty for Courage Best Bitter, and dutifully ticks off all the nostalgic seaside fun of a day out in the Kentish town – jellied eels, buckets and spades, beer, cockles, winkles and sand – while telling us in no uncertain terms what you could do with yer Costa Brava. This cheerily ironic rockney song only really worked if you knew – or assumed – that Margate was one of those coastal towns that had hit hard times. As the bottom fell out of the traditional British seaside holiday in the 1970s – due to the sunnier attractions of yer Costa Bravas – places like Margate struggled to keep up. Though, as Dan Thompson reminded me, tourism was never Margate's bread and butter. 'Thanet was an industrial area, tourism was just an extra,' he explained. 'Thirty per cent of jobs here were in light industry. There were 2,000 people in this town who worked in the coal mines.' What Margate has been good at is 323 reinvention. Thompson sometimes gives history walks of the town, attempting to knit together the story of its tightly packed streets of eighteenth-century squares with its art deco amusements, brutalist high-rise and modern art galleries. 'There's always been a them-and-us thing,' he said, 'but that probably goes back to when Margate was a tiny little fishing port and these Londoners started turning up and building these outrageous modern Georgian terraces on the seafront.'

I visited during the heatwave of July 2018, one of those days where the seafront shimmered like a mirage. All around, those bygone seaside pleasures extolled by Chas and Dave – children playing on golden sand, the lights of amusement arcades, the creaking of old-school rides and roller coasters, pastel-shaded ice cream parlours, colourful boats bobbing in the harbour – had been resurrected. Like many towns, it wears its history not with any particular pride, but helplessly. On the seafront beside the railway station stands the town's burly bouncer, ready to send day trippers packing: the imposing slab of Arlington House, a crenelated concrete tower block. Across the windows of his ninth-floor flat, resident Rob Yates had posted a specially commissioned artwork spelling out BLOCKBREX.IT. At the time of the 2016 EU referendum, the Isle of Thanet, of which Margate is a part, was one of the most pro-Leave areas of the country, 64 per cent of the local vote going to exiting the EU. Two years later, Yates's statement felt almost quaint, another layer of seaside nostalgia.

Arlington House has the best views in town, and overlooks its neighbour, Dreamland, a 1930s funfair and amusement park relaunched as a middle-class pleasure palace in 2015 by fashion designer Wayne Hemingway, fresh from his Wimpey housing adventures in Gateshead. The new look Dreamland would combine spots for gigs and picture shows with a living museum of antique fairground rides. Just four years before, Margate had the highest number of boarded-up shop fronts in the country, and there was concern that the abandoned moderne hulk of Dreamland was going to be converted into a retail park or apartments by its owners, Margate Town Centre Regeneration Company. And so the council compulsorily purchased Dreamland in 2013, hoping to bring back the amusements. Thompson recalled talking to a man whose family had run stalls in Dreamland before the revival. 'And he said people get really nostalgic about Dreamland but it was shit. In the 1970s and 80s it was run-down and the rides were a bit knackered and cheap. It smelled of beer and piss, because there were no toilets, people just used to take a piss up the back of the rides.' The regeneration project was designed by Guy Hollaway Architects under Hemingway's supervision. 'You can get all the food that London or Brighton have, like properly made pizzas,' said Hemingway. 'It has got the full gamut from super-cool to rough as you like. When I am long-buried, it still won't be some rich man's playground.'[1] Not rich, perhaps, but not poor either. The revived Dreamland was not a bargain basement affair. 'We want to get the art crowd in as well as the bucket-and-spade brigade,' said Hemingway. 'It's a delicate balancing act.' It's now under new ownership once more, with plans in place to help support the business by building a hotel. 'I think there's about 400 beds in Margate,' said Thompson. 'Tiny. And that's the problem, nobody who comes here can actually stay. All the real money is going outside Margate where the hotels are.'

The prom was re-engineered in 2013. Where once a formidable sea wall cut off the beach from the town, now an arena of steps leads down to the beach – or at high tide, straight into the sea. The old stone harbour arm is topped with new colourful eateries. Inland lies the old town, with its Empire-era hotels, wrought-iron 325

A gallery situated for those Turner seascapes. © John Lord

balconies and French-style café squares, a reminder of its proximity to Europe, with Calais just 36 miles away. Beside the harbour arm sits the town's most prominent modern landmark, Turner Contemporary, a cluster of angular white sheds that form a modern art gallery. Opened in April 2011, it was designed by David Chipperfield, who manages to bring a sense of philosophical quiet to his buildings, while also having them teeming with life. It has been sold as an effort to regenerate the town, but Chipperfield has been understandably reticent to play that game. 'I'm not a great believer that projects like this should be commissioned on the basis of regeneration,' Chipperfield said at the launch. 'It's about building an institution which is important for the town, and regeneration will come, inevitably. But the purpose of the architecture of these institutions should not begin with regeneration. The building has to serve the community.'[2]

A wander round Turner Contemporary reveals gleaming white space after gleaming white space, making you feel you've

326

stumbled into the generic limbo from any number of Hollywood movies. It stands in literal contrast to another new south coast gallery, the black-skinned Jerwood – now named Hastings Contemporary after a bad-tempered split with the sponsor – whose intimate spaces make you feel close to the art rather than dazzled by it. Turner's vast foyer houses the shop, full of cat cushions, felt-tipped slogans and David Shrigley cards. From the outside, it feels pretty approachable – like one of those New Labour public libraries or a small mall. 'I saw it very much as a pavilion,' said Chipperfield, 'nearly industrial, a type of shed.'[3] I'm more of a fan of his Hepworth Wakefield gallery, whose calm, polished grey concrete has the tactile fascination of a sea-worn pebble, and whose angular gallery spaces feel somehow more exciting than the bleached-out immensity of the Turner. It was part of an initiative called Sea Change, launched in 2008 by CABE, the Commission for Architecture and Built Environment, 'to use culture to make a difference to seaside resorts, contributing to sustainable, social and economic regeneration'.[4] It joins the 'string of pearls' along the south coast including Hastings Contemporary, the Towner in Eastbourne, and the renovated modernist De La Warr in Bexhill-on-Sea. Meanwhile, the Down-from-London effect stretches much further still, from Cornwall to Kent, and around the East Anglian coast too, a creeping trail of keysafes and bunting stretching all the way from St Ives to Southwold.

Dan Thompson puts the success of Turner Contemporary partly down to the decision to spend an equal amount of money on regenerating the old town at the same time. 'The harbour arm had been done up and painted beautifully and had flags flying on it. The old town had nice shops. They even paid attention to all the big litter bins along the seafront, the big euro wheelie bins, all of those had been painted in bright, colourful colours with a slogan on them. If you got off at the station and walked it felt like everything was working together.' Funds for the gallery came from local artist Tracey Emin, Kent County Council, Thanet District Council, South East England Development Agency, Arts Council England and, of course, the European Union. Out at sea stands, inevitably, an Antony Gormley iron cast of himself, a rusty guardian staring at the waves. It joins a barnacled army of Gormleys around our coastline, from Crosby to Leigh-on-Sea. Any invading force should gird their loins in preparation for Gormley's fearsome iron dickslap.

'There's a guy I follow on Twitter who has a bit of a low-key obsession with ex-Woolworths stores,' retail planner Adam Bunn told me. 'I absolutely live for it!' he said excitedly. 'I've got the eye for it, I know in most towns I visit where the old Woolworths stores would have been.' He was speaking with the kind of fervour generally reserved for discussions of minor-league football or obscure Krautrock B-sides. For many people, myself included, mention of Woolworths still makes for a flutter of the heart. There's a general feeling that the demise of Wool-worths was inevitable, that the internet had doomed it, but that was not strictly the case. 'They got done because of a supply contract they had with Virgin Megastores,' recalled Adam, 'and then they went bust and that took Woolworths down with them.' Retail parks too had been partly responsible. They had been one of the first chains to give out-of-town stores a go with a series of scaled-up sheds in the late 1960s named Woolco, but by 1988 all of those shops had been sold to Asda. By then, all the big retail park supermarkets were beginning to muscle in on a lot of the store's most successful lines – household gadgets, kids' clothes, genre fiction, garden essentials, toys, bedding, stationery, sweets. Its record departments fell victim to the music industry's Napster meltdown in the mid-noughties. All 807 Woolworths

328

shops closed by January 2009, and 27,000 people lost their jobs. Towns up and down the country lost the anchor store on their high street, which new branches of Poundland, Wilko or Iceland springing up in their place did little to fill. 'Margate is one of only four places in the country where the old Woolworths still exists and hasn't been let to anybody,' said Adam with the kind of awe you only really see in an Indiana Jones movie when someone is describing a lost relic. 'They've still got the signage up.'*

In many ways, the stories of British seaside towns like Margate and bygone high-street chains like Woolworths feel if not intertwined then certainly heavy metaphors for each other. Both depended on the patronage of the working and lower middle classes, both increasingly offered a kind of nostalgic time capsule as the world around them changed, and both attempted constant reinventions as the tides of change grew ever more dangerous around them. And both were badly hit by the 2008 financial crash. The big difference is, of course, that Margate didn't shut. Margate is still there. And so Margate got to experience what came after. A period of austerity imposed by a new Prime Minister, David Cameron, and his Chancellor, George Osborne, who led the Conservative-Liberal coalition government of 2010. This austerity involved slashing welfare payments and cutting back funding for local authorities, who in their turn had to sacrifice services from public libraries to childcare and community support.

'That is probably one of the worst high streets I have seen in a centre, period,' said Adam, who had recently returned from a trip to Margate when we spoke in 2019. 'And I've been to a lot! And it's because of an out-of-town shopping centre that got built about ten years ago, Westwood Cross.' Designed to

---

* 'It's now an alternative art school,' Dan Thompson told me in January 2021. 'I'm not convinced that's a viable long-term use.'

serve the whole of the Thanet area – Margate, Broadstairs and Ramsgate – Westwood Cross has been remarkably successful at destroying the high streets of each. As Adam said, going full retail planner, 'it's got a cinema, loads of food and beverage to go with it, there's your day out right there.' Dan Thompson, though, had a more optimistic view of the retail park. 'If you'd have wanted a shopping centre that big in Margate, you'd have had to take a huge chunk of the town centre, and demolish it and clear it.' This would have taken, say, the 1980s shopping centre, the council offices and neighbouring Georgian relic Cecil Square. 'You would now have a thing that would be fading in the middle of the town centre.'

Margate has always been split. Two competing clock towers on the front chime the hour – one built to celebrate Queen Victoria's jubilee of 1887 (it missed that by a fashionable two years), the other constructed for the Pier and Harbour Company in 1812. Candy-floss tourism and industrial labour, waves of newcomers caught in endless flux, a reminder that towns are complex organisms of reinvention and denial. That bubble of seafront regeneration is rapidly pricked if you walk back from the sea. Just off the front I strolled up the main shopping street, as three jolly boys smashed their way into a derelict shop shouting loudly about that *cunt* who is *gonna get it*, to manic laughter. Shops open and close here with brutal rapidity, business unable to cope with the fragile local economy, its abrupt seasonal turns and the split audiences they serve. An artisanal dress shop becomes an art gallery. A cake emporium becomes a baby clothes boutique. Bunting accumulates algae, shop fronts rot in the briny air. Here, at the end of England, a feeling of instability rules, threatening to interrupt the town like a bad TV signal or a bank of sea fog. Away from the tourists flooding to and fro between gallery

and train station, Margate's straggling suburbs are poor and alienated. By 2018 Thanet had the highest child poverty rates in the south-east, with one ward being the fourth most deprived in England. 'It hasn't transformed life for local people,' said Dan of Turner Contemporary. He'd been a governor at a school on the Millmead estate on the edge of town. 'Even when Turner came into the school and did projects it didn't become a two-way relationship. That particular project was a bit kind of *we'll do art to poor people* rather than we'll work with them. So it hasn't done that. I'd argue that it doesn't have to.' Turner Contemporary's job, as Dan sees it, is to bring in the tourists and the DFLs.

The town remains split, politically, socially and economically. 'I've got a great newspaper clipping,' Dan Thompson told me. 'They interviewed some people in the bar that was on the site of Turner Contemporary to be demolished, and they're proper kind of grumpy drunk locals saying *fuck this art stuff, nobody's gonna come to Margate for that kind of thing.* And I read it and thought I bet you could have gone back to one of the little inns on the seafront 200 years ago and interviewed exactly the same people saying *Nobody's going to come here! Those Londoners aren't going to come here to go to a pleasure garden! Why would they? It's a ridiculous idea.* That's what Margate does. Nobody is local. They've all got London roots or they've come from somewhere else. You can meet people who can trace back a few generations, but that's it. It's always been about new people turning up.' And as successive generations settle here, it is easy to become divorced from the seafront and the regeneration that has happened there. 'Certainly that school on the Millmead estate that my children went to and I worked as a governor, we have children who've never been to the sea, never been to the beach at all. When you live here, it's very easy to just have no engagement with the sea.' The whole vista lost to the residents in a haze like a Turner seascape.

10: London Ruins

The Olympic Park and the Neo-Workhouse

'A local newspaper wrote an article about gentrification and they came to interview me.' I was talking to artist Martin Richman in his house, a converted factory unit in Hackney Wick, East London. 'And the quote in their subheading was something like *I've Ruined Four Areas Across London* or something like that. And it does sometimes feel that I have been a progenitor of gentrification. You turn up not really worried about if it's a bit rough and then years later you find that all your architects and your graphic designers and your other friends are all going, *Oh it's really nice here* . . .' Martin had lived in East London since the 1980s: in his current house for twenty years, on the border of what became the site of the 2012 Olympics; before that in a big town house bordering Victoria Park; and before that another warehouse space in urban Poplar. Victoria Park 'was still pretty much traditional East End at that time,' explained Martin. 'Not very arty, dodgy blokes, taxi drivers, bit racist, bit awful, some appalling greengrocers with bendy carrots and that kind of thing. It was a very unreconstructed East End when we moved there in the late eighties. And gradually over the years that's changed and now it's *charming* and *chic* and *trendy* and blah blah blah. And you can't really buy anything except a cake and a coffee.' His current haunt of Hackney Wick is a strange kind of place, half old industrial units – though that proportion is shrinking all the time – and half residential, either conversions or new builds encouraged by the mega-construction that has been going on a couple of streets away in the former Olympic Park. 'The problem with gentrification is that it never quite stops,' said Martin. 'It maybe stops temporarily for a couple of years while there's a bit of a slump on or something, but then it just sort of picks up again. It never

332

quite goes back to being hardware shops or whatever it might have been that you quite liked.'

The 2012 Olympic and Paralympic Games had been hard won for London by awkward squad Mayor Ken Livingstone working against and occasionally with his former New Labour comrades. The successful bid was announced to much astonishment in 2005. London's winning proposals included four new permanent sporting venues in Stratford: the stadium, now home to West Ham FC; the Copper Box multisport indoor arena designed by Make; Zaha Hadid's Aquatics Centre; and the Velodrome, now the Lee Valley VeloPark, by Hopkins. There would be an athletes' village too, converted into flats after the show. And new infrastructure from rail lines to cycle tracks. The Olympic Park itself would become a green space in a part of the city where there was very little. There would also be a commercial opportunity, leapt on at once by developers building a vast new shopping centre – so big it called itself Westfield Stratford City, soon the most visited mall in Europe. In the park five neighbourhoods would be built, forming a district almost big enough to call itself a town.

Then there was a quartet of towers ranging from seventeen to forty-three storeys completed just ahead of the Olympics. There, standing beside the urban motorway, as if Transformers did girl groups, were Aurora, Icona and Velocity and Halo. They were designed by architects Stock Woolstencroft, since matily rebranded as Stockwool, and are exhausting. Every trick has been thrown at every surface. These are X-Factor creations with all the synths, glitter cannons and dry ice machines going off at once. Looking at the sober brick-faced towers Stockwool now produce, it's hard not to agree with Julian Stock, one half of the outfit, who said after the fact that 'architecture has become a bit less shouty since the turn of the century'.[1] Forty per cent of Aurora's buyers were   333 based in China, so perhaps their extravagant forms were designed to appeal far beyond the confines of East London.

Westfield Stratford City got an exhaustive 114-page glossy supplement in the *Architects' Journal* in 2012. 'Westfield matters because it shows revived confidence in the Lower Lea as the crucible of London's future,' wrote Daniel Moylan, chair of the London Legacy Development Corporation, meaninglessly.[2] There was an article comparing the shopping mall to a megastructure of the sort championed and dissected by urbanist Reyner Banham in the 1970s. The shopping centre exists on another plane, up a long flight of steps from the road, so as not to contaminate itself with day-to-day street life. Stratford Underground station sits at one end of the half-mile-long curved mall, with Stratford International at the other. The stations were key to the redevelopment, with the privatisation of British Rail in the mid-1990s kick-starting a merry-go-round of land being parcelled up by one lot of millionaires and flogged off to others. My main experience of Westfield Stratford City will be familiar to many, as a place to be dashed through swearing as I realise my connection leaves from the other station. How glossy and expensive all of the products here are. Who can afford them, and in such numbers to keep this voracious machine thriving years after the Olympics have left town? And in one of London's poorest boroughs too. In Newham in 2012 almost half of the population were living below the poverty line, while 70 per cent of kids came from low-income households. Things have got harder too, thanks in part to our old friend the Right to Buy. Newham has lost 10,000 council homes through the policy since the 1980s, and while wages for the poorest haven't risen significantly, those private house prices have boomed. In 1995 the average cost of a house in Newham was £53,000. By 2001 it had almost doubled, five years later doubling again to £197,000. Prices briefly fell after the 2008 crash, but by 2015 had reached an astonishing average of £319,000, over six times that of just two decades before.[3] In the meantime, a gap had opened up between housing benefit and the cost of rent locally, and so people were being made homeless or having to move out of the capital. Urbanist Anna Minton described how Stratford has become 'a divided landscape of privately owned, disconnected, high security, gated enclaves side by side with enclaves of poverty which remain untouched by the wealth around them'.[4]

Less than 2 per cent of the Olympic budget came from the private sector. Yet despite all of that public money spent, the park has been sold off piecemeal to developers. The Olympic village was sold to the Qatari royal family, alongside their investments in Canary Wharf, the Shard and the Walkie Talkie. They join global investors such as Lendlease who owned the land on which Westfield and the athletes' village were built, and Malaysian group S P Setia, who are behind the billionaires' ghost town being built around Battersea Power Station. Being a good neighbour in nearby Hackney Wick has meant that Martin Richman was co-opted onto several organisations overseeing local development. Among these was the Cultural Interest Group, which acted as a go-between for local Hackney residents and the developers, builders and architects circling them. 'There were four or five of us who would sit around a table and the developers would bring in plans and we'd say *Not very strong, could do with having a bit more this a bit more that, could get better frontage.*' Developers would then make a few tweaks and bring the projects back. 'On a good day I felt like I was contributing and doing good things for the community that I live within,' Martin recalled. 'On bad days I thought *for God's sake why am I fucking schlepping myself out on a rainy old night to hear someone drone on about their piss poor development?*'

*

While developers were circling the district on the lookout for opportunities, the official architecture of the Olympic and Paralympic Games was being imagined into being too. At the very centre of it all was the athletics stadium, on which the mega-architectural firm Populous teamed up with Sir Robert McAlpine – the same partnership that had recently built Arsenal's Emirates Stadium. Populous have pretty much cornered the market in stadium design, producing over 200 major venues for sports from the Millennium Stadium in Cardiff to the Sydney Olympics stadium for the 2000 games. They even converted the Millennium Dome into the O2 arena in 2007. But despite their successes, it was the shadow of the troubled Wembley Stadium they had designed with Foster + Partners that would haunt them. Wembley had been a costly disaster for all involved – way over budget and delivered years late. They were also tormented by the success of the costly but spectacular Bird's Nest stadium for the Beijing Olympics in 2008, designed by Herzog & de Meuron. It had become a worldwide icon of the city and put the pressure on anyone following to try and compete. Following the crash, everyone involved in the London stadium steadfastly agreed they were not after an icon. And in the terms of High Tech it was a triumph, the lightest Olympic stadium ever, using 10,000 tonnes of steel. Populous said the design process had been a case of trying to design away as much carbon and cost as possible. The structural masts sticking out the top gave the whole thing an air of a medieval fete, jousting tournament or circus tent, but not enough for anyone to whisper the word icon within earshot.

Instead, the heavy lifting of iconicism went to Anish Kapoor, who won a competition to create the park's statement art piece beating a trademark naked Gormley and a skyscraping sculpture from Caruso St John. The Orbit would be Boris Johnson's only tangible addition to Livingstone's Olympic site and would be brought to life by Britain's richest citizen, steel tycoon Lakshmi Mittal. It was meant to be an icon, but is not. It is an unlovely and unloved monument, tangled headphone cables where there should have been music. It was expected to attract 350,000 visitors a year, but in the first twelve months brought in just a third of that. To try to rescue the costs and reputation of the tower, Kapoor agreed to a request from Boris Johnson to retrofit the Orbit with a further attraction. 'It was not always my thinking,' said Kapoor. 'The mayor foisted this on the project and there was a moment where I had to make a decision – do I go to battle with the mayor or is there a more elegant or astute way through this?'[5] He eventually agreed to another artist, Carsten Höller, retrofitting a slide into the sculpture. It was a humiliation for all involved, even Höller one suspects, who must have been keen to move on from the series of slides he'd already created for galleries around the world. It failed again but didn't fail better, with 155,000 people visiting in 2018–19.

To some extent, the rest of the Olympic Park shares that feeling of not quite producing the simple iconic image so beloved of city politicians. But two of the sports stadia, the Velodrome and the Aquatics Centre, come closest. The Pringle-shaped Velodrome designed by Hopkins was the first of the venues completed, and on budget. Its red cedar-wood cladding makes it feel more furniture than architecture, and also hides the classic Michael Hopkins tent beneath, the roof suspended on a vast net of cables. Its famous concave shape was created partly by the tension of the structure but also to echo the steep curves of the pine track. And perhaps for a country who had focused so much pressure on its championship cyclists from the breakthrough success of Chris Boardman back in 1992 to Bradley Wiggins's victory in the Tour de France just five days before the 2012 Olympics began, making this a stand-out building was entirely sensible.

Then there's the Aquatics Centre, one of only a handful of major structures in Britain designed by Zaha Hadid. One of the first had been a stage set for the Pet Shop Boys' 1999 tour. 'I was flicking through a book of Zaha's designs in the Rizzoli bookshop,' recalled singer Neil Tennant, 'and I suddenly saw all of her architectural models as stage sets – wonderful shapes to walk across while holding a microphone, wearing a ludicrous costume and having a wind machine on you maybe.'[6] Deconstruction, the style of architecture she became famous for, had been discussed by novelist and critic David Lodge back in 1988, while observing the first architectural congress on the topic in Britain. Originally, deconstruction had been a philosophical tool created by Jacques Derrida to pull apart meaning through analysis and commentary. In architecture, Lodge thought, 'it means warped planes, skewed lines, exploded corners, flying beams and what Dr Johnson, describing metaphysical verse, called "heterogeneous ideas yoked by violence together".'[7] He called Hadid's architecture 'hedonistic' and certainly if architecture is frozen music there is an air of the rave about them, extraordinary forms far from sobriety and doused in ecstasy, or at the very least, champagne.

Hadid was coming into the Olympics off the back of a hugely significant building, the Riverside Museum in Glasgow, which opened in 2011. With its S-shape and innovative multi-ridged roof, it created vast column-free open spaces for exhibits. Over the entrance is a startling asymmetric jagged roofline, like the pounding of a heartbeat on a monitor, Hadid getting our blood up as usual. If the Riverside Museum echoed its watery purpose with waves on the roof, the London Aquatics Centre was more like a great manta ray in form, the pool, diving boards and 17,500 spectators all swallowed in the belly of the beast. It was a scram-338 ble to get the building ready in time, and they blew the budget

Zaha Hadid getting our blood pumping. © Ross

three times over. The resulting structure is spectacular and has a sense of permanence that the other venues do not. Hadid had designed for the moment, with a building that became a flagship for the games, with two huge wings of temporary seating that were later removed. But she had also wanted to create something more lasting, and in the flowing form of the structure that remains, with its exposed concrete, curved wall of glass and sense of solidity, she has achieved that. Its grandeur and scale make it one of the most remarkable modern buildings in London, against the grain of the construction that would follow.

'The Olympic Park broadly thinking I think is a good thing,' said artist Martin Richman. 'On a sunny Sunday it's very social, very busy, May-June-July the wild flower meadows are all bustling and flowering and looking good, there's nice playgrounds and watery events and things.' One of the criticisms most levelled against the Olympics here was that little effort

339

was made to integrate the large population of poor and disadvantaged people in Stratford. Martin had mixed feelings on this point. 'I can't help feel that even for hard-to-reach people somehow some elements of that will permeate through,' he said. 'But that's with a very optimistic hat on. Because a lot of these people, they don't feel engaged, they don't feel that anything even half a mile from their house is for them.'

Back in 2010, the Olympic Park Legacy Company produced a book, fast-forwarding past the event itself and imagining what sort of place they wanted to leave behind. In the familiar language of inspiring-vision-thing pitch-speak, they saw Queen Elizabeth Olympic Park – as it was inevitably to be called – as 'an anchor in the social and economic regeneration of East London . . . creating places to live that are rooted in the ethos and fabric of East London's diverse and vital communities.'[8] They aimed to knit together the disparate elements of the park into 'safe and interconnected London-inspired streets, blocks and buildings'.[9] A visual render gave some idea of the ambition, the velodrome and low-rise terraced blocks in the foreground, complex paths and bridges intertwining through the park and across the River Lea in the centre, the athletics stadium a Plantagenet coronet in the middle distance. Giving away the period in which it was written, in the far distance just three simple towers rise up at Canary Wharf. By the time this plan was being realised a decade later, a bulky megopolis of nineteen (and counting) equally massive high-rise blocks had sprung up. Over twenty-five years, the park was expected to create 11,000 new homes and up to 8,000 new jobs. Three of the five new residential districts in the park would be based on terraced houses. 'Tradition and innovation, side-by-side in a landscape of great buildings, international cultural attractions and vibrant open spaces,' went the brochure.[10] They would build two primary schools and a secondary school,

340

nurseries, community centres and health centres. 'The success of the Park as a new piece of East London will depend on how well it integrates with its neighbours and on its ability to stitch together previously disconnected and isolated places.'[11] The book is full of visualisations, those architectural exercises at creating a perfect world. Here, kids ride bikes, people in wheelchairs are pushed round corners, couples lounge on seaside deckchairs, children frolic in a kinetic fountain.

The Taylor Wimpey showroom in Chobham Manor, the first new residential area to be built in Queen Elizabeth Park, is a prefabricated box standing at an angle to the regular terraces and roads all around, strangely reminiscent of a post-war block rejecting the street line among a grid of these new regular East End homes. I was here to interview Manisha Patel, architect at PRP and one of the Mayor of London's design advocates, for a radio programme made by Emma-Louise Williams about space standards. She was keen to talk about an innovation she had helped design here: the multigenerational house. 'Multigenerational living is something I've been interested in for quite a few years,' she explained. 'It all stemmed from the fact that in the nineties I was working in East London and we were designing for housing associations. And it was a very exciting time, but we were designing for families that were extended families, and I found that we were being asked to not just have three-, four-bedroomed houses, but we were getting into five, six, seven, because different generations were living together.' Her travels around the world suggested that other countries and cultures dealt with intergenerational living rather better than the British. 'We felt that there was a design of a home missing.'

A multigenerational home would allow residents to operate under one roof but to different timetables – getting up, eating, working, going out, going to bed at different times. She called   341

Stratford and the new urban area they were building at Chobham Manor 'the most inclusive area in the world . . . and that meant that we had the opportunity at competition stage to put forward a home which could challenge how we live today'. It was part of 800 homes that would form Chobham Manor, the first of five estates to be built in the post-Olympics park. These would be rows of three- and four-storey town houses and apartment blocks in regular terraces and mews, built by Taylor Wimpey and backed by housing association L&Q. The multi-generational homes sit on the corners of these urban blocks, flat-fronted dark brown brick houses, presenting a mash-up of plain seventies modernism with sober interwar neo-Georgian. 'Effectively it's a three-bedroomed house with an annexe and a shared courtyard,' she explained. 'We were pretty surprised that the first week it opened they got sold out.' Just over a quarter of the new homes would be labelled 'affordable'. L&Q and Taylor Wimpey put the first batch up for sale on a Friday in May 2014, and forty-eight homes were bought over the weekend. 'One of the developers from Taylor Wimpey bought one himself to live in,' said Manisha, 'so that was a very proud moment for us when the developer who has backed the scheme has actually bought into your idea.' The following January, people were queueing overnight in temperatures of minus four to buy one-bedroom flats in Chobham Manor worth £400,000, the buyers including a middle-aged couple from outside the city wanting an overnight pad for theatre trips and late nights in the office, and a Hong Kong resident who said, 'I'm buying this as an investment in London, a buy-to-let. It will be amazing after it's completed and I think the area around it will have developed really nicely.'[12]

After our conversation, Manisha Patel showed us around a couple of Taylor Wimpey's show flats designed by PRP, with 342 all the John Lewis fittings and Wayfair furnishings you could wish for. Both the two- and three-bedroom flats were hugely seductive, with their lack of clutter, selling a way of life that even with the tidiest of minds could never exist. Imagine being these people, with no past; furniture but no possessions, starting afresh. All the old ghosts of mistakes and mess, divorce and failure, grief and sickness packed away in a storage unit out by the ring road. But the pull of this fantasy – miles beyond my reach or that of millions of others – is potent. A chance to wish away realities and conjure a better version of yourself, with healthy food, regular exercise, a positive mental attitude. For some the dream holds, it works its charm. For the rest of us, it quickly fades, and we are left with the same habits, problems and income, in tighter, less forgiving surroundings.

Chobham Manor's postcode is E20, the same as Walford in *EastEnders*. The soap began in 1985, when another new district of East London was being built at Docklands. Chobham Manor overlooks the velodrome. Seven years after the show, the wooden wonder had that slight someone-left-a-cake-out-in-the-rain air that all of these venues share. It's surrounded by tall swaying beds of grasses softening the hard lines of the terraces of just-completed low-rise flats, in the familiar brown brick austerity style favoured by the London Mayor's design team. After saying goodbye to Manisha, I took a walk around the unfinished streets of two- and three-bedroom flats, their brick facades missing windows, doors and roofs. An uncanny rush swooped over my head, a huge crane arm swinging a speedy, almost silent arc hefting a load of planks and materials across the site and up onto the top floors. This was Abercrombie Road, named after the great mid-century planner Patrick Abercrombie, who had presided over Britain's new town boom and the rebuilding of East London and the South Bank of the Thames. Is this what he would have wished for? I wonder, I wonder. Finished homes   343 up the road were inhabited, and a steady stream of normcore millennials buzzed their way in and out, carrying laptop cases or fold-up bikes. The buildings themselves are earnestly mixed-use, with ground floors boarded up, left ready for a Costcutter or Tesco Express, a branch of Pret or Leon. 'What this place needs is people,' Manisha Patel had said as we sat in a show flat.

In some ways, E20 reminds me of the early days of Docklands – the quiet streets, the hard edge of the new builds, the erasure of history, the abrupt new beginnings so demanding and insistent. But despite similarities in the private ownership of this seemingly public land, the fate of the Olympic Park feels different. This is not primarily a business district, for one, as the stream of cheeky kids streaming down the street after school attests to. And now, in the wake of Covid, the differences seem more stark still, the green space and facilities of Queen Elizabeth Park contrasting with all that redundant office space of Canary Wharf. The kids walking through the park are the children of the old Stratfordians, mostly black, full of lairy East End energy, all seemingly heading away from the new builds towards the other side of town, the under-funded estates on the far side of Westfield. Siobhan Best moved into a social rent property in East Village in 2017 with her partner and baby. 'It was really weird how a new town had been plonked in such a run-down area with such poverty,' she said, 'something seemed very odd about the whole place.'[13]

One of the strangest things is the sober and uniform style that the new blocks in all five districts adhere to, in sharp contrast to the bristling individuality of the Olympic venues. Architect Daniel Rosbottom pointed out this new stylistic trend back in 2007 while looking at the three terraced houses designed by Stephen Taylor for Chance Street in Hackney. 'Taylor, like many of his contemporaries, has looked back past modernity to Georgian precedents for inspiration,' explained Rosbottom. This led to a design whose 'flat brick frontage, punctuated by generous windows, presents itself to the street, with metal gates against the pavement opening up to a relatively large threshold'.[14] With the arrival of this new style, he was pleased to see the back of the most ubiquitous sort of developers' houses of the last forty years: 'the codified rash of the Essex Design Guide, regarded as required reading for designers of low-density schemes, is destined for consignment to a particularly gloomy corner of our island's architectural history.'[15] But it wasn't just houses. There were urban schools, galleries and shopping arcades too. Some of the first offices in this style were 30 Finsbury Square by Eric Parry Architects in 2003, with those now familiar upright flat-fronted Georgian proportions, recessed windows and a buttoned-up sense of decorum, the facades limestone rather than brick.

You see versions of it in towns and cities all over Britain. Infill houses in Nottingham, estates in York, flats in Glasgow. Nick Walker, joint project architect for Collective, who'd designed 200 flats in Anderston for Sanctuary Scotland Housing Association, said the design had been 'from the outset informed by the surrounding context and history of the area'.[16] But that really meant the familiar fashionably pale brick or sandstone facades, recessed windows, metal-railed box balconies and steep, choppy monopitch roofs cutting into all that squareness. It's not to everyone's taste. You can imagine how Zaha Hadid hated it. 'There is one diagram that prevails across the whole town,' she said of London. 'And I deliberately drive around to look at new sites. They all have the same diagram.'[17] In Hackney Wick, on the edge of the Olympic Park, there is a whole new town of this stuff staggering its way up too. The flats are for housing association Peabody and mega developers Lendlease. They're to Georgian terraces what ghost signs are to bustling high streets – strange washed-out memories of something that once had meaning. At 345 a glance, the super-blocks that occupy sites in this former industrial area might be early Victorian warehouses with the windows blown out. The walls, faced with craggy soft brick, have a whiff of the reclamation yard about them, but for the most part these are slips – shallow brick-replicas adhered to prefabricated panels off site before construction. The result is Farrow and Ball architecture, tasteful after decades of yellow-brick Wendy houses and fibreglass, aluminium and stained-render faux modernism. More daring architects play with the formula, skewing the angles of storeys against each other, introducing acute planes that cut into the handsome oblongs, fiddling with the rooflines and bringing some of that early CZWG fuck-it coked-up hoo-ha brio to the endless sombre fauxsterity. These days, with working from home the new normal for many, the brick facades, blank windows and the tired faces peering into the glow of laptops beyond announces this style as the Neo-Workhouse.

It was kicked off by the reclamation of Giles Gilbert Scott's monumental power stations at Bankside and Battersea. The great planes of brown brick on these two magnificent post-industrial buildings, one now Tate Modern, the other centrepiece to a monstrous Nine Elms buy-to-leave yachtopia, have long adorned letterpress-printed greetings cards. Balconies on Neo-Workhouse flats echo those of the members' bar of Tate Modern, whose recessed balconies and plain metal railings have been imitated on new hipster flats across the land. In Tate Modern, converted to gallery space by Swiss architects Herzog & de Meuron in 2000, we have the ultimate in artist-led regeneration, and so it was inevitable that this workshop chic would be replicated elsewhere ad nauseam. The last four decades have seen much of the effort of architects great or small channelled into converting existing buildings – to art galleries or flats, workspaces or hotels, and most of all, endlessly extending suburban houses. Creative reuse is an essential skill for architects as we attempt to limit the effects of construction on the climate crisis. Yet now they are also expected to design new buildings that look as if they are old and have been converted. Blokey fake artisanal workshop spaces with polished raw concrete floors and exposed brickwork.

This new style of architecture has quickly become ubiquitous thanks in part to then London Mayor Boris Johnson. The London Housing Design Guide was published on his watch in August 2010, though its basis was also seen in a New Labour housing green paper from two years earlier, *Homes for the Future: More Affordable, More Sustainable*, which was pushing for higher densities, an end to suburban semis and sprawl and the return of the terrace. The government paper offered new space standards similar to those from the much missed 1962 Parker Morris report, abandoned in 1980. They pushed for housing with more entrances direct to the street rather than the single point of entry of a high-rise block, for example. It encouraged the creation of terraces and tenement blocks, and pushed an obsession with brick. The style was termed *A New London Housing Vernacular* in a pamphlet by David Birkbeck of social enterprise company Design for Homes and housing consultant Julian Hart. It was dissected by Owen Hatherley in his 2015 book *The Ministry of Nostalgia*, where he remarked that following the financial crash the parsimonious policies of the coalition government 'pushed much of the very fabric of London towards an austerity-nostalgia aesthetic' – a kind of cosy retreat from anything too confrontational.[18] Once this design guide was in place, '"the market" did the rest,' wrote Hatherley. 'Or rather "it" chose brick, terraces and clearly designed towers on clear street lines.'[19] The success of this design style stands in contrast to those other monuments of Johnson's stint as Mayor of London, the overheating new Routemaster bus and the half-baked 347 and thankfully never risen Garden Bridge. Both saw design from Thomas Heatherwick, whose steampunk kinetic torch had been a memorable centrepiece at the Olympics. These other efforts showed how attempting to capitalise on the afterglow of that Olympic moment with bold theatrical gestures wasn't as easy as it looked. Heatherwick has become the Andrew Lloyd Webber of architecture, an old-fashioned impresario employing showbiz sentimentality for blockbuster effect. The result too often suggests that any dream will do.

'I did the master plan for Hackney Wick,' architect Russell Curtis of RCKa told me. We were talking about the complex land owner-ship issues there, all those small light industrial units and clustered Victorian warehouses and factories, the old local authority estates and private dwellings. 'It's not without challenges,' he said, 'because there is something very special about Hackney Wick. And the reason that there's a lot of artists and low-cost workspace there is because it was always sort of peripheral, and now it's not. I can see how probably there more than anywhere else in London, this issue of gentrification is real because what happens is, a lot of the developers bring forward schemes and they say, *well, we can either give you affordable workspace or we can give you affordable homes. Which is it, you can't have both.* And in Hackney Wick you have to provide non-residential space because you can't put anything on the ground floor because of the flood risk.' And so the developers offer homes but not the workspaces. 'But on the other hand we need homes,' said Russell, 'and it's an area that prop-erly could do with intensification. And so again, I feel conflicted about it.' Decisions have been made, the research and mapping of Russell and his team now having a physical effect on the area. 'I think that every decision we make around this stuff has some kind of impact,' he told me. 'And I think it's very easy to look at it through polarised glasses and look and just say, well, that's gentrification, and that's displacement. And you can be very political about these things. You can take a very sort of partisan approach to it. Or perhaps we'll take a passive attitude towards it. But it's much more complicated than that.'

Martin Richman had been struck by the incredible figures being asked for these new flats intermingled among old factory units. 'Fairly prosaic two-bedroomed apartments are selling at £660,000 each,' he told me. 'And who they're selling to I don't quite get. Because your average thirty-five-year-old young couple I wouldn't have thought are in the position to do that sort of thing. I know wages have gone up since my day but even so it seems like fucking huge amounts of money.' As for the trickle-down effect of the Olympic Park on neighbouring areas such as the Carpenters Estate, with its impressive and knackered 1960s tower blocks and low-rise streets, the physical legacy for them has been rather underwhelming. 'They didn't get the bonussy things from the Olympic Park that they thought they were going to get,' said Martin. 'There's some very small little things. There's an Adidas Fitness Park just a few minutes away which came out of that, but there wasn't the employment that people were expecting. A few jobs, but very few. Rental housing has become very expensive around here. If you've got a council flat already then you're probably more or less alright. But if you haven't and you've been born around the area the chances of you getting one or being able to afford to live next to your mum and your granny is very bloody remote.' Priced out of the area, young people are having to move away from their families. And the estate itself was for a long time set for demolition, though now the local council are considering refurbishment, with new plans to densify the area with those ubiquitous flat-fronted brick blocks still up in the air at time of writing.

To Martin, standing still doesn't look like much of an option here. I thought about the landscape and habitats lost out where the Olympic Park stands today, the milk that cannot be unstirred from the tea. 'And there's definitely a part of me that loves all of that,' he said. 'But there's another big part of me that thinks you can't freeze all of that fucking stuff in jelly. You can't fix it in a moment in time. And it's lovely that nature's reclaiming the city and we enjoy all that, but a lot of it's been poisoned by industry, a lot of it's shit and it doesn't take much of a grey freezy old day to make it all look bleak as fuck frankly.' As with Russell Curtis, the conflicting, polarising voices made it hard for Martin to work out quite where he stood. 'I ended up thinking to myself cities are born to change,' he explained. 'They are intrinsic and of themselves and of necessity dynamic places. And if they're not dynamic then they're dull. And part of London for me that makes it a great and interesting city are the juxtapositions of odd communities, the different racial and socio-economic groups that pile into one another, and as we abrade against one another sometimes something great happens.' Those five new neighbourhoods, the rebuilding of Hackney Wick and Stratford, the endless restless tides of the Thames, who knew what they would produce? 'So to me the Olympic Park is now a nice park to go and if I want to go to some dodgy bar then there's about twenty that I can go to in the immediate vicinity. Do I love everything? No I don't. Do I love the standard of architecture? No I don't. It's very, very fucking prosaic. And I'm hoping it's not going to prove to be the slums of twenty years' time.' He sat there for a moment then, agitated, got up to pace around the room, unsettled like the landscape beyond.

'The last words she said to me is that the smoke was too much, she can't bear it anymore, Michelle, our daughter, is going to heaven. She said if I didn't see her again then she would be going to heaven. Then she was trying to talk but she couldn't. I could hear noise but then I couldn't hear her and the line went silent.'[1]

Mbet Udoaka was giving evidence at an inquest. He was describing how his wife Helen and their twenty-day-old baby Michelle had died in the Lakanal House fire of 3 July 2009. Their bodies were found in their neighbour's apartment, where they had gone to seek refuge from the smoke and flames of a blaze that had started some ninety minutes before. In that same room their neighbour, Dayana Francisquini, also died, along with her two children, Thais aged six and Felipe aged three. They each inhaled fumes when smoke entered the flat via the bathroom ventilation duct. Meanwhile, in Flat 79, directly above where the blaze had begun, the inquest found that fashion designer Catherine Hickman made a 999 call a minute after the fire started, 'and remained on the line receiving fire survival guidance until she became unconscious half an hour later'.[2] The advice had been to stay put, the fire service was coming to rescue them. Some residents were rescued. But not these six. Could they have escaped if not advised to stay put? 'Escape would have been daunting,' found the inquest, 'but not impossible.'[3]

Southwark Council had spent £3.5 million pounds refurbishing Lakanal House in the two years before the fire. A fourteen-storey slab block built in Camberwell, South London, in 1959, it is one of the central towers of Sceaux Gardens, an estate typical of the era. The inquest documents show both the 351 cause – a faulty TV had caught light on the ninth floor – and the appalling human consequences of the blaze. Within five minutes of the first firefighter arriving on the scene, flames had spread up to Catherine Hickman's flat through the panels beneath her bedroom window. 'The aluminium window frames were distorted by the flames from Flat 65,' recorded the inquest, 'creating gaps through which the curtains of Flat 79 caught alight.'[4] It was found that the panels used in the refurbishment were not of the required standard, and that 'this was due to a serious failure on the part of SBDS [Southwark's Building Design Service], its contractors, and its subcontractors.'[5] Renovating the building had actually made it less safe. As the report said, 'asbestos removal and replacement with composite panels had a significant impact on the fire resistance of the external wall of Lakanal House.'[6] There were no fire seals on the front door of Dayana's flat, while the material intended to stop fires spreading in internal pipework had been removed in earlier renovations, allowing the fire to spread. The inquest called it 'a serious failure of compartmentalisation'.[7] They also found that a crucial fire safety check had not been carried out.

What about possible safety features? Should such a large social housing block have been fitted with sprinklers, for example, as would have been required in a new build? Eleanor Kelly, Chief Executive of Southwark Council, wrote to the coroner to say that the Department for Communities and Local Government 'considers that decisions regarding the retrofitting or not of sprinkler systems to high rise building is for landlords to consider themselves'.[8] And so the coroner wrote to the Secretary of State for Communities Eric Pickles with a list of questions and recommendations. There was, she wrote, 'insufficient clarity about advice to be given to residents of high-rise residential buildings in case of fire within the building.' Also, she wrote, 'it is recommended that your Department encourage providers of housing in high-rise residential buildings containing multiple domestic premises to consider the retro fitting of sprinkler systems.' There were also issues around the complexity and difficulty of the documents the government had produced pertaining to 'the fire protection properties of material to be incorporated in the fabric of a building . . . with particular regard to the spread of fire over the external envelope of the building'.[9]

In response, Eric Pickles was in reassuring mode, writing that 'the guidance, published in summer 2011, takes a practical approach to ensuring that those responsible for the safety of residents and others in purpose built blocks can take a comprehensive and pragmatic approach to managing risk effectively'.[10] That word pragmatic doing a lot of heavy lifting there. As for sprinklers, 'my officials have recently written to all social housing providers about this.' There were calls to make the regulations easier to understand for the many contractors implementing them in similar refurbs and new builds, and Pickles wrote that 'we have commissioned research which will feed into a future review of this part of the Building Regulations. We expect this work to form the basis of a formal review leading to the publication of a new edition of the Approved Document in 2016/17.'[11] The year 2017 would turn out to be a key date. It was then that Lakanal House, refurbished once more after the fire, reopened. It was also when Southwark Council finally pleaded guilty to four charges concerning breaches to safety regulations leading up to the fire and were fined £270,000. And on 14 June, another newly renovated social housing block, Grenfell Tower in North Kensington, caught light in uncannily similar circumstances, this time due to a faulty fridge. In a horrific magnification of the events at Lakanal House, seventy-two people would die at Grenfell.

I spoke to Emma Dent Coad, who for a time had been on the London Fire and Emergency Planning Authority for the Greater London Authority. She had spent her days 'going through Lakanal House, lobbying various ministers over the months, sending them letters and letters and letters, about implementing the Lakanal House recommendations', she told me. 'That was even more gut-wrenching for me actually, to have been part of that and failed, and then *that*' – Grenfell – 'happened.' I went to visit Sceaux Gardens back in 2018. Tucked away behind a dazzlingly deconstructed new theatre building designed by Jestico + Whiles are the original 1960s slab blocks and low-rise units that make up the estate. It's a space dominated by the grid of white frames and green panels that form the estate's tall blocks, Lakanal and Marie Curie House, and the surrounding balcony access apartments. The towers rise out of what had until recently been a stretch of gardens between them but which when I visited was boarded off, a series of infill blocks muscling in between, of the sort being built to densify post-war estates across the city. This latest renovation of the estate had been much delayed, but here, a decade on after the fire, a sense of careful calm was the order of the day. The ground floor of Lakanal House presents a welcoming and hand-made spectacle amid all of this outsize construction work. It has been converted to a project called Art Block, run by the South London Gallery, and artwork from local kids was viewable through the huge panes of glass. Designer Morag Myerscough worked with local children to decorate the gallery space in her familiar colourful pomo patterns when it opened in 2017, and so what could have felt like quite a sad memorialised space has been creatively reused for lively community projects. But despite all of the bright colours, new builds and good intentions, the strange quiet of this inner-city estate felt a little oppressive. Buildings have long memories, as do the residents. Helen and Michelle Udoaka.

Dayana and Thais Francisquini and Felipe Francisquini Cervi. Catherine Hickman. Remember.

Some time before the fire at Grenfell, residents Mariem Elgwahry and Nadia Choucair had organised a petition and a protest outside Kensington and Chelsea Tenant Management Organisation's offices for improved fire safety, and had been reportedly threatened with legal action. Mariem and her mother Eslah perished in the blaze, as did Nadia and her husband Bassem, their three daughters Mierna, Fatima and Zainab, and their grandmother Sirria Choucair. So too did Victoria King with her daughter Alexandra Atala. Amna Mahmud Idris. Gary Maunders and Deborah Lamprell. Rania Ibrahim and her children Fethia and Hania Hassan. Young Italian architects Gloria Trevisan and Marco Gottardi. Fathia Ahmed and son Abufras Mohamed Ibrahim and daughter Isra Ibrahim. Raymond 'Moses' Bernard. Mohamed Amied Neda, who fell from the twenty-third floor. Hesham Rahman. Hashim Kidir and his wife Nura Jemal, their daughter Firdaws and sons Yahya and Yaqub Hashim. Logan Gomes was stillborn in hospital following the release of cyanide gas from the tower's burning insulation. Abdulaziz El-Wahabi and wife Faouzia died alongside their sons Yasin and Mehdi and daughter Nur Huda. Ligaya Moore. Artist Khadija Saye, known as Ya-Haddy Sisi Saye, whose work was being shown in that year's Venice Biennale, died alongside her mother Mary Mendy, who had come to visit. Jessica Urbano Ramirez. Farah Hamdan, Omar Belkadi and their daughters Malak and Leena, with their six-year-old sister Tazmin the only survivor. Mohamednur Tuccu, wife Amal Ahmedin and daughter Amaya. Mother and son Berkti and Biruk Haftom, who climbed from the eighteenth floor to the top of the tower to try to escape the flames. Sisters Sakineh and Fatemeh Afrasiabi. Isaac Paulos. 355

Khadija Khalloufi. Vincent Chiejina. Kamru Miah, Rabiya Begum, Mohammed Hamid, Mohammed Hanif and Husna Begum. Joseph Daniels. Marjorie and Ernie Vital. Sheila Smith. Hamid Kani. Steven Power. Syrian refugee Mohammad al-Haj Ali, who was the first victim to be formally identified after falling from the building. Denis Murphy. Zainab Deen and her two-year-old son Jeremiah. Abdeslam Sebbar. Ali Yawar Jafari. Anthony Disson. The last person to die from the fire was Maria del Pilar Burton, who escaped the building but died almost a year later having never left hospital. This was the biggest loss of life to fire in Britain since the Second World War. Here, the victims were an astonishing cross-section of different races, classes and nationalities, among them some of the poorest people in one of the richest boroughs in London. Amid all the grief and horror, there was a huge wave of displacement too – former residents suddenly homeless, families and friends mourning loved ones. Incredibly, a community remained.

Resident Joe Delaney recalled being there during the blaze, and over the screams and shouts he could hear 'the sort of the noise you'd hear popcorn make in a microwave. And each pop would basically result in bits of this cladding come flying off. It was literally exploding off the sides of this building. You could see it sort of land on the floor with these smoky little lumps. They look very similar to lumps of coal. There was smoke pouring off them, even as they landed.'[12] The fire had been predicted by the residents. Grenfell Action Group, of which Delaney was a member, was set up in 2010 by local residents Francis O'Connor and Ed Daffarn, and their blog reported a series of power surges in 2013 that destroyed electrical appliances in the tower, and a fire two years later at nearby Adair Tower in North Kensington, also managed by the Kensington and Chelsea Tenant Management Organisation, where numerous breaches of fire safety regulations had been found. 'They were complaining about the conditions inside,' said Dent Coad of Grenfell's residents, 'it wasn't safe and the fire doors and rubbish in the hallways and all of these things. There were things they didn't know about, they didn't know about the cladding and things like that.'

In 2016 the Grenfell Action Group reported that 'in the last twenty years and despite the terrifying power surge incident in 2013 and recent fire at Adair Tower, the residents of Grenfell Tower have received no proper fire safety instructions from the KCTMO. Residents were informed by a temporary notice stuck in the lift and one announcement in a recent regeneration newsletter that they should remain in their flats in the event of fire.'[13] The blog was widely shared after the Grenfell fire. 'It is a truly terrifying thought,' they had written, 'but the Grenfell Action Group firmly believe that only a catastrophic event will expose the ineptitude and incompetence of our landlord, the KCTMO, and bring an end to the dangerous living conditions and neglect of health and safety legislation that they inflict upon their tenants and leaseholders.'[14] In a post three months before the fire they showed that the KCTMO had at last installed fire safety notices throughout the tower, helped in part by the pressure brought about by their previous reports.

Emma Dent Coad spent her time as a local councillor in North Kensington campaigning for better housing, convinced that the council's priority was to present a superficially flawless, expensive image above all. She recalled taking students around the area and telling them 'there's an estate round here that's one of the poorest four per cent in the country. They go, *oh can we go*. I go, *yeah, it's here.*' Their reaction? '*No, no, surely not.* It's all beautiful trees growing, streets swept, the houses are not in very good repair but tolerable repair. But they sanitised it. Because I know that behind some of those doors people have next to nothing. They've got two 357

tins in the cupboard and that is it. They are hungry and malnour-
ished and their children are born undersized. There's osteoporosis
and we have rickets now. They have sanitised it and they don't
deal with it.' Not that Grenfell's residents were necessarily poor.
'There was a huge mix, it was a slice of life in Grenfell. They
weren't all poor people by any means, it was a proper slice of
North Ken life.'

And then in 2017, against the odds, Dent Coad was elected
Labour MP for the area, thanks both to her history of local campaigning and to turmoil in the local Tory party. 'From being a
rank outsider, I felt vindicated once I'd been elected,' she told
me, '*my life's work has all come together, this is great*, and then
that.' Grenfell. 'I thought *I've also been vindicated this way,
how horrible*, because I did feel vindicated actually. In a horrible way, the worst possible way. On the Friday' – when she'd
been announced as the new MP – 'vindicated for a good thing,
and then Tuesday night, Wednesday' – when the fire broke out
– 'vindicated for a horrible thing.' Architect Kate Macintosh,
whose Dawson's Heights blocks in East Dulwich were built in
the early seventies at the same time as Grenfell, remarked that
'Grenfell Tower burned 350 years after the London Rebuilding
Act of 1667, which attempted to eradicate the risks that had led
to the Great Fire of London. This legislation was scrapped in
2012 by the coalition government.'[15]

Politics and the fire were inextricably linked. The Prime
Minister, Theresa May, visited Grenfell on 22 June, eight days
after the fire, didn't meet with residents and was booed. 'I will
always regret that by not meeting them that day,' the Prime
Minister wrote a year later, 'it seemed as though I didn't care.'[16]
Then there was the dislocation between the lives of people in
former council housing like Grenfell and a new generation of
358   rich and entitled politicians who had risen to prominence in the

coalition government. 'Please don't make me sound like a prat for not knowing how many houses I've got,' pleaded May's predecessor, David Cameron, in 2009.[17] By contrast, Dent Coad, a long-term social housing resident in Kensington, bridged the worlds of personal and political. 'They were saying in the government that Grenfell could be more dangerous for the government than Brexit,' she recalled. But the abstract absurdity of that was insignificant next to the awful reality of the fire. 'I know people who died,' she said. 'I've got PTSD as most of us have, and I've had two loads of treatment, they're both fucking useless actually. I said I'd rather be angry and sad all the time actually. If I get upset I'll cry and if I get angry it'll spur me on to do something else.'

The renovation of Grenfell had taken place between 2015 and 2016 at a cost of almost £9 million. The contract was won by East Sussex company Rydon, who bid £2.5 million below their rivals, achievable by what is known as 'value engineering' the project – using cheaper alternatives to the materials and processes other bidders were offering. To re-clad the tower, they chose two products manufactured by a US-based corporation called Arconic – aluminium sheeting called Reynolux, and Reynobond PE, more aluminium sheeting, this time two panels with polyethylene sandwiched between. There was also a form of thermal insulation from a company called Celotex, owned by French firm Saint-Gobain, which sat between the building frame and the cladding, and some from their Irish rival Kingspan. The contractors also replaced the windows and heating system.

The public inquiry brought to the fore numerous shocking details about the refurbishment of the building. A product manager at Celotex told the inquiry he had been made to 'lie for commercial gain' regarding test results for the insulation used at Grenfell, which initially failed British Research Establishment 359 tests for fire resistance.[18] It only passed when additional fire-resisting boards were added, none of which was declared on the marketing for the product for high-rise buildings. One of Rydon's team at Grenfell told the inquiry that 'I felt there were several very vocal, dare I say it aggressive, residents that in my opinion regardless of what work was being carried out would still have found reason to complain'.[19] An internal memo at Arconic in 2007 suggested they should stop selling the flammable version of its aluminium composite cladding after a fire safety presentation suggested that sixty to seventy people per decade might be killed by fires caused by such a product, but they continued.[20] The same year, Kingspan changed the formula for the foam they used in their insulation. A technical manager at Kingspan told the inquiry that he'd sent an 'animated report' after the new foam boards had become a 'raging inferno' and said he was 'criticised for not being very positive about our products'.[21] While the then Chancellor Philip Hammond said at the time that the cladding used on Grenfell was illegal in the UK, a former president of the RIBA, Paul Hyett, told the inquiry that in his opinion the government guidance to architects 'endorsed in principle at least, the use of Reynobond aluminium composite panels on a project such as Grenfell Tower' and that 'most architects would have considered that such an endorsement indicated that, in principle, the panels also met the requirements of the building regulations'.[22]

'I think Grenfell really is a manifestation of a lot of systemic problems in how we go about commissioning buildings generally,' architect Russell Curtis told me. 'Not just about architecture, it's about the quality of the builder, it's about the quality of the client, it's about the whole environment about commissioning buildings.' He traced the issues back to two government reports produced during the 1990s on the relationship between architecture and construction, the Latham Report *Constructing the Team* in 1994, and the Egan Report *Rethinking Construction* from 1998. The Latham Report described the construction process as being too combative and adversarial and recommended a more collaborative approach. It was supposed to smooth out the relationship between the partners, but instead it disrupted the control of architects over the schemes they had designed. 'The builders came in and took over and promoted a new or different way of procuring buildings, which favoured *them*,' said Russell. 'I think it's fair to say that most architects are interested in social value – although we probably didn't call it that then – with their wider responsibilities to society, than they are about making loads of money. So what happened was we handed all the power over from the people that cared about *people* to people who cared principally about profit. Because contractors are there to make a profit.' Architects found themselves employed up to the point of when planning permission was given, and then dropped from the process. According to classic project management rules, there are three variables the contractors can use to affect the quality of the finished product – the cost, the scope of the work and time. 'So inevitably, what happens is that the cost becomes fixed,' said Curtis. 'And the quality reduces because the contractor's incentive is to make profit. And that's the only variable he's got to operate with. And this happens all the time.' But it wasn't just down to money. 'The main frustration is there is no longer a direct line of communication, no longer a contractual relationship between the architects and the client. And there's certainly no relationship between the architect and the people they will be building the homes for if it's a housing scheme. So, you know, we could go to site and say, *Well, I know that you've built that wall really badly, I think you should do it again*. And the client or the contractor will say, *No, fuck off, I'm not doing it*. And you've got no way of saying to the client, *look, you can't see what's happening here, but they're just not doing it properly.*'

'There's a whole sort of maze of responsibilities,' said Russell, 'and nobody's quite sure who's responsible for what. Architects won't approve drawings any more, they'll just say *don't comment on them.* Who is supposed to sign off this work? You know, the chain of responsibility is really unclear.' Without constant oversight to help knit a project together, vital decisions can be bodged. 'We had insulation manufacturers who were lying on their test results, we had architects who didn't know what they were doing, we had a contractor who tendered too low and couldn't deliver the project. Everything went wrong. But it is a tragic manifestation of a wider malaise within the construction industry.' Russell is angry that the system behind the failures at Grenfell, which grew out of those 1990s government reports, is not being examined by the public inquiry. 'You are examining the symptoms, not the underlying cause. . . I liken it a bit to the Exquisite Corpse. So you draw something, and then you draw the lines at the bottom, and you fold it over and pass it on to someone. The person receiving that information has the lines, they don't know what's drawn above. So they interpret it in the only way that they can. And that's the construction process.'

Grenfell is just one of many thousands of buildings constructed in this disjointed fashion, and certainly not the only one to use that particular form of aluminium cladding. Another is a block of ninety-five apartments in Central Croydon called Citiscape, built by Barratt in 2001 and owned by the family trust of Vincent Tchenguiz, a billionaire entrepreneur and trader. In March 2018 the leaseholders, who were already paying for their own fire wardens in the wake of the Grenfell fire, lost a tribunal to FirstPort Property Services, the building's management company, which meant 362 the residents were liable to pay £500,000 to make their building safe. It was possible that in reality it could cost well over two million. Richard Low-Foon told the tribunal that he could neither pay for the work nor sell his father's flat, and that the stress had made his father ill: 'He is in hospital because of all of this. It got too much for him.'[23] The result left the residents despairing, though local Labour MP Steve Reed continued to fight their corner, keeping the bigger picture in mind too. 'The government has consistently claimed the flammable cladding on Grenfell did not comply with the rules, but last week we saw a certificate authorising a similar material that was signed by the government's chief advisor on the fire safety of buildings,' he said. 'It is crystal clear that the government was responsible for allowing this cladding to go up so the government must accept responsibility for taking it down.'[24]

In the case of Citiscape, things moved more quickly than even Reed might have hoped. The following month, Barratt suddenly offered to cover the £2 million cost of replacing the cladding. Just days before, there had been rumours of a class action lawsuit being brought by residents and leaseholders against the companies who had installed it in the first place. In July 2021, Barratt purchased the block from its residents, making it the first to be bought back by a developer in order to fix the cladding.

By 2019, it was estimated by the government that 40,000 people in the UK were still living in high-rise towers covered with Grenfell-style cladding. But this was not the only dangerous form that was being uncovered. On 9 June 2019 there was a blaze in Barking, East London, at Samuel Garside House, a six-storey wood-clad block of flats built in 2012 by Bellway Homes. It was thought that the cladding, ThermoWood, had caught light from a barbecue on the fourth floor, and black plastic mesh used on the balconies had turned to flaming molten plastic droplets. When later tested, this combination of wood and plastic was found to be easily flammable, well below even the bottom-rated fire standard. Eight of the flats were completely destroyed, though luckily no one was physically harmed in the blaze. A government vote in 2021 left hundreds of thousands of homes such as Samuel Garside House unmortgageable by not covering the costs of making buildings under 18 metres tall safe, but instead offering the home owners loans, likely to cost them north of £40,000 each.

As far as the refurbishment at Grenfell had gone, resident Joe Delaney's view was that the bulk of the money had been spent on the exterior, just to make it prettier. 'It certainly wasn't to make the building safer for the people who lived in it, because even once that work was finished, you'd still see fire engines there on a weekly basis coming to get people out of the lifts.'[25] Emma Dent Coad agreed. 'What they were doing at Grenfell as we know, and this is all in the documents, the whole purpose of the cladding wasn't to improve the thermal performance or anything like that, it was actually to improve its appearance for the regeneration or the development that they were planning.' Back when she was a local councillor Grenfell hadn't been in her ward, but she had seen the refurbishment of a nearby high-rise in the borough at first hand – Ernő Goldfinger's much loved 1970s brutalist Trellick Tower. 'They had no idea how the building functioned,' she said of the management. 'They were fitting digital cabling into the building. I said, *Well you've got two ways of doing it. You can go up the back, there are channels up the back where there used to be gas piping and they took it all out after Ronan Point. You wouldn't even see the digital cabling going up there*. And they go, *Oh I don't know about that*. And then I said, *Also because Goldfinger knew what he was doing those beautiful balconies, where they have wooden panelling, it opens and you can put cabling up there*. He futureproofed it to a certain extent. So I said *Why don't you look behind these panels*? And they go, *Oh I don't know anything about panels.*' And so she showed them. 'But they completely ignored all of that', she recalled, 'and drilled all the way through. Concrete framed building, drill drill drill.' It ended in a huge row with them about the fire doors and reinstating the building's firebreaks. 'Trellick is different, it has two stairs,' she explained. 'They haven't stuck solid petrol on the outside and they wouldn't dare because obviously it's listed.'

A lack of expertise in the management and design of new and refurbished housing was one of the things that came up when I interviewed architect Elsie Owusu too. Owusu has designed a number of housing association blocks in London and has an inside view on the evolution of housing design and management. And she was clear that the effect of this could be plainly seen in the Grenfell fire. She pinpointed the disappearance of housing associations run by and for black and minority ethnic people as a factor, organisations swallowed up by larger, more corporate entities. 'What those housing associations did was to consult very very closely with their residents and potential future residents and begin to develop typologies which would allow communities and extended families of different generations to live together and to design their own environments, or to influence the design of their own environments.' Instead, we now have large corporate housing associations who consider themselves developers applying what she termed a 'cut-and-paste mentality' to their housing. These big housing associations were 'being given hundreds and hundreds and sometimes thousands of units and they don't have the time, they don't have the expertise, they don't have the cultural awareness to cater to the communities. So they are under the control of developers. And we can see from Grenfell what happens when the development system is allowed to take charge. And it's a really dangerous, dangerous situation, not just for thousands of people who are living in dangerous buildings, which many are, but for buildings that aren't fit for the purpose of the people who are moving into them.' What these developers are building, Owusu explains, are usually a 'large open-plan two-bedroom no storage kitchen-in-living-room type of space' designed by architects who are, as the statistics tell us, mostly young white men 'for whom that is a perfectly good typology. If you're living with a partner or you've got a roommate that may be perfectly alright for you. But if you have, as many of the Grenfell people did, an extended family, if you have multi-generational households and you have no choice it's an absolute bloody disaster.' She pointed to Peabody's £8 billion master plan for a complete rebuild of another predominantly working-class district, Thamesmead in south-east London. 'Who's in the running for an £8 billion master plan?' she asked. 'It's not going to be the small local architects, building surveyors, contractors. It's going to be stonking great conglomerates. And the system is just knackered. It really is completely knackered.'

One of the most poignant epitaphs of the pre-fire community at Lancaster West was footage of locals filmed by Constantine Gras, who in 2016 was working as Community Artist in Residence. In 2021 it was turned into the Channel 4 documentary *Grenfell: The Untold Story*. Back in 2016, Gras had invited architect Nigel Whitbread to visit the tower he had designed in the early 1970s. 'He met residents in their homes for the first time,' wrote Gras, 'and enjoyed hearing how they regarded the spacious flats (built to Parker Morris Standards) and the stunning views.'[26] Whitbread died two years after the fire. 'It is impossible to know the sadness and anger he must have felt,' wrote Gras in an obituary. Many of the tower's displaced and grieving residents are still living in temporary accommodation. And thousands of people across the UK are trapped living in homes clad in dangerous materials, be it the aluminium compound used at Grenfell or the combination of wood cladding and plastic mesh used at Samuel Garside House. There should be positive actions taken to prevent fires like this happening again. But as with Lakanal House, while the conclusions will eventually become clear, whether right will be done is not guaranteed. The decision-makers are so removed from the reality of these residents' lives that they are able to continue on, insulated from the consequences of their actions. For the people directly affected, their families and friends and wider communities, some may never recover and none will ever forget. And we should all of us remember those killed at Grenfell Tower and Lakanal House, and we should strive for much, much better in their memories, to do all in our power to stop events like these ever happening again. Yet in December 2020, fire wardens took up stations in Marie Curie House, the neighbouring tower to Lakanal House in the Sceaux Gardens estate. Southwark Council had uncovered what they called 'some issues' with the building, and posted a 24/7 fire watch on the block. After the inquiry's verdict into the fire at Lakanal House, Mbet Udoaka had said, 'We fear very much that lessons have not been learned and that it could happen again.'[27] The warnings, like memories of the lost, continue to echo

11: Hopes Under the Hammer

Housing on the Brink and Back Again

'I've always lived in old houses and established communities so it's quite different,' Janette Ray told me. 'I'm glad to do something different, you only get one life.' That morning I'd peered out of the window of Janette's spare bedroom to see half-finished homes across the way in that newly familiar flat-fronted blond-brick style, gardens marked out with wooden fences and newly laid turf. This was The Chocolate Works, an estate on the periphery of York that was being built on the site of the old Terry's factory. All around I could see the paraphernalia of construction sandwiching a few finished houses between churned mud on one side and the half-finished skeletons of houses on the other. Down to the ground-floor kitchen for a cuppa, staring blankly out of the bifold doors to the new turf and tall tan pine fencing panels. It seemed like some kind of dream, a handsome bit of new-build housing, clean and fresh and light and open. Life would surely be good in a place like this. Janette had put up bright modern art on the walls, contrasting with the cool greys of the kitchen units and flooring. She'd moved in less than a month ago, March 2018, the first resident on the street in a brownfield estate in this new outer suburb. Over the way, the grand 1926 red-brick factory building had been converted into flats a couple of years back, its clock tower still covered in scaffolding, stained glass on the time face freshly restored. An art gallery was planned for the tower, with flats below. Janette's house was part of a different phase, new-build homes designed by Hackney-based architect Richard Partington and built by David Wilson Homes, a subsidiary of Barratt. Janette combines her work as an antiquarian bookseller with her training as a landscape planner, advising on heritage issues for the likes of the National Trust, and had downsized from a Victorian town house in York town centre. Here she was, slightly giddy at the novelty of it all. 'I think they're really nice and well designed and they're very well organised for living in,' she said approvingly.

Stoked up on tea, we left for a walk around the emerging estate. She'd parked her car in the garage, surely the sign of a new build, as in my experience they're usually full of old bits of broken furniture, DIY kit and boxes of *stuff* that would otherwise clutter up the house.* Out of the five new homes that formed her terrace, only three had so far been occupied; the larger ones at either end had sold but were still awaiting their occupants. Construction crews moved surprisingly quietly behind a tall wooden barrier on the other side of the road, where more houses were going up. Through a bridge of flats suspended over the road, a more finished spectacle awaited – Bayldon Square, neatly turfed, surrounded by familiar flat-fronted brick terraces. 'I think the sense of community will be brilliant with this open space, unless they end up rowing about people noisily playing out here or whatever,' she laughed. 'Who knows? There's always something, isn't there.' The mixture of homes was cunning – town houses, flats and large family homes all integrated seamlessly into the scheme, and as we looked around it was hard to work out what was what. In an estate of 120 dwellings some were affordable, some old people's flats, some luxury pads. Only time would tell if this attempt to create a mixed community would succeed.

'It's a very urban development to have on the edge of the city,' remarked Janette as we were walking. 'It's not suburban. And the people I have met, who are lovely, they're not sort of

---

* A 2006 survey by the RAC claimed that 53 per cent of homes in the UK had a garage, but only 24 per cent of us use them to park a car. And a study in 2015 reported that almost four million garages had been converted to living space in the previous twenty years.

suburban people really.' With the green belt beyond, The Chocolate Works does feel a bit of an anomaly. Instead of the usual awkward cul-de-sac of houses blanking each other, here were dense terraces, squares, boulevards and vistas. Gordon Cullen would have been pleased, said Janette, recalling the work of the great post-war planner and illustrator, whose work on townscape – creating spaces that opened out onto each other – had clearly been an influence here to the streets of houses leading up to the grand views of the clock tower and factory in one direction, park and outskirts in the other. 'I suppose with my planning hat on,' said Janette as we stood near the boundary of the site, where some big trees had come down, 'it looks like a lot of development creep now. It's sad. I think probably they're trying to balance the books. They probably need to. Because these are very nice, it's a high spec development.' She contacted me later to tell me that the original master plan had since been torn up, and flats were being constructed on all of that edgeland green space. Infill before the original homes had even weathered. Earlier, we'd stopped by a block of red-brick flats. 'So these have been built since I moved in,' she explained, 'which is only the last four weeks. The formwork was up the day I moved in. So they go up really fast when they start building them.' A developer in a hurry.

Managing new estates like The Chocolate Works is a tricky business. Laura Wilkins told me about her time working in facilities management for a tenant management organisation on new private housing estates in the West Country. 'The biggest issues would be about bin storage,' she said. 'People would abuse it horribly.' She had to get them cleared out after they had been trashed. 'People would say, *well, we didn't do it.* I'd say, *I know! But someone's got to pay for it, or do you want to leave it like that?* The developers are there to build houses. Unless the

370

councils are really on them, bin storage is the last thing they want to think about. They put them in difficult places, they don't provide locking mechanisms . . .' Her biggest headaches were caused by salespeople omitting to mention to new buyers key issues such as the service charge levied to keep the communal areas tidy and for managing all the common spaces. She recalled a new estate in Somerset where the developer had put TV aerial sockets in the wall but hadn't provided an aerial. 'The first thing people do, apart from putting the kettle on, was plugging the TV in,' said Laura. 'But the TVs don't work. *It's got a plug, yeah, but you don't have an aerial. Why not? Well, if you look at your spec, it wasn't part of the spec . . .*' Suddenly, it's a thousand quid each to get aerials fitted. And it was hard for her to keep up with what was going on. 'Quite often the developer wouldn't tell you when the first people would occupy. So the first thing you'd know is you've got someone screaming down the phone at you that the telly's not working, it's your fault, you've got to fix it.' Much of the time was spent explaining to people that they had, to some extent, been stiffed by the developers in the small print, like in the houses in Cheltenham where the brochure showed garage doors but the finished houses didn't have them. 'There was one guy who misunderstood his freehold documents and he thought a parking bay belonged to him when it was communal,' she told me, 'and I used to get vexatious letters from him every month.' And then there was the sometimes tricky issue of managing the relationship between private and social housing residents. 'Some councils pepperpot, so they spread the social housing throughout amongst the other houses,' she explained. 'In other councils you'd get swanky developments and at the end there would be a block it was clear they hadn't spent nearly as much money on. So you're immediately creating a tension.' If anything went wrong on the estates, the home owners invariably blamed the social housing tenants. 'Conflict resolution was the key skill,' she said, 'and I'm not very good at that.'

Some of the big housebuilders are more used to conflict than others. In 2019, barrister Stephanie Barwise chaired a review into housebuilder Persimmon and discovered that there was no agreed minimum standard for their homes, increasing the risk that significant problems would be uncovered when buyers moved in. That year, their profits topped a billion for the first time. They had hugely profited from the Help to Buy scheme; at one point, Persimmon were building one in seven of the homes sold under Help to Buy and getting three times per house what they had been making before the scheme was launched. But there were issues with the quality of the company's work, with respondents to a Home Builders Federation survey into customer satisfaction for new builds placing them bottom for four years in a row. Civil engineer Darren Harris found eighty defects in his new Persimmon house in Pembrokeshire. 'The neighbours came over and asked me if I had seen the brickwork on the back of the house,' he told the local paper. The wall was shockingly wonky and uneven. 'They said to me "we have been having a bit of a laugh and a giggle".'[1] He then found he couldn't get in the front door. 'I thought there must be a problem and went back to the site office. A Persimmon agent came back with me and in the end, he had to shoulder-barge the door to get it open.' The door frame had been badly fitted, and there was guttering that didn't reach the end of the building, so water cascaded down the brickwork. Chief Executive Jeff Fairburn left the company in 2018 after an outcry that he had been given a £75 million bonus, partly funded by taxpayers because of Help to Buy. I'm sure he could face a little bit of disgrace for that sort of money. Persimmon weren't the only housebuilders to help exacerbate a wider problem, that since 2013 one in ten homes in England have been built on flood plains. Each year there are terrible stories about estates flooded and homes ruined in storms such as Eva on Boxing Day 2015, and Dennis in February 2020. But with the housing targets set by the government, there was a feeling among planners and builders that the risks of building in these areas was reasonable. 'You may have to accept the fact that there is water in the streets,' said Fiona Barbour, the flood lead for engineering consultancy Mott MacDonald. 'I think that is something that society is going to have to accept as the new norm.'[2] How comforting.

Developers aren't just mega businesses like Persimmon throwing up thousands of new homes and estates, of course. Since the Right to Buy and the buy-to-let boom of the noughties, there's a whole cohort of smaller private property speculators buying second or third homes, doing them up and selling them on. If you want a glimpse of estate agents inspecting the results, opening cupboards and looking at radiators with the detachment of alien overlords deciding whether the human race deserves to be extinguished or not based on the installation of cheap kitchens and bathrooms, there's always *Homes Under the Hammer*. A daytime stalwart on BBC1 since 2003, the presenters (for many years Martin Roberts with his gaping jackets and Lucy Alexander with her perky shouting, now grown to an ever expanding team of pun-loving smilers) meet people who have bought houses, flats and sometimes, if we're really unlucky, a plot of land at auction. The show is a record of a conquering army of small-time developers and dabblers taking possession of houses street by street throughout the land (very often Stoke-on-Trent). They nod enthusiastically along as almost identical plans are detailed – to rip out, to knock through, to *finish to a high standard throughout*. Martin, Lucy, Dion Dublin (trapped for 373 eternity into saying *there's your stairs up to your bedrooms* as if it were some crushing Sisyphean task) and the rest are desperate to get people to add bedrooms, move bathrooms upstairs and – crucially – extend, especially if they can point out that these plans are fruitless because the wide-eyed new owners haven't read the legal pack.

But the brisk, cosy formula hides a dark secret. The show never asks why – why these rapid sales and empty lots have come to pass, and why the people who once lived here have lost their homes. If you watch closely, the spectres of death and repossession haunt the presenters' gently mocking chat about garish wallpaper and swirly carpets, pink bathroom suites and lean-to outhouses. These cheery tales of tight timescales and swift sales hide the sobering truth that there have been well over a million mortgage repossessions in the UK since 1980. It belies the myth of personal security that home ownership has been sold as since the Right to Buy. The figures show northern cities like Manchester and Sunderland have come off worst, with Bolton the repossession capital of Britain in the 2010s. There they are, homes, streets and communities slowly hammered to bits. As at November 2020, they had made around 1,500 episodes of *Homes Under the Hammer*. With usually three properties in each show, that's a lot of people in Marks and Spencer suits saying *per calendar month*.

All of this private enterprise was just what successive governments have longed to see. And so for them, like out-of-control bidders on *Homes Under the Hammer*, the inconvenient truth of estates and social housing stands in the way of potential profits. In January 2016, David Cameron told Andrew Marr, 'I think sink housing estates, many built after the war, where people can feel trapped in poverty, unable to get on and build a good life for themselves, I think it is time with government money – but with massive private sector and perhaps pension sector help – to demolish the worst of these and actually rebuild houses that people feel they can have a real future in.'[3] He wanted to see what he characterised as brutalist tower blocks torn down and replaced with more housing for sale.

Nick Clegg, then Deputy Prime Minister, recalled Cameron and Chancellor George Osborne's attitude to these estates. 'One of them – I honestly can't remember whom – looked genuinely nonplussed and said, "I don't understand why you keep going on about the need for more social housing – it just creates Labour voters."'[4] But across London it wasn't Conservative local authorities but Labour ones such as Southwark, Lambeth and Tower Hamlets who were set on demolishing their postwar municipal housing and replacing them with estates of new builds. Some, such as Robin Hood Gardens near the Blackwall Tunnel and the Heygate in Elephant and Castle, have been flattened, with more expensive private flats going up in their place. Meanwhile, communities in highly regarded estates like Central Hill in Crystal Palace and Cressingham Gardens in Lambeth have been fighting council-led redevelopment of their homes for years. Aside from being relics of some of the most well-regarded architects of the twentieth century, including Ted Hollamby, Peter and Alison Smithson and Rosemary Stjernstedt, these have been home to long-established, successful and largely working-class communities. Elephant Park, the replacement for the Heygate, gives a good idea of the changes envisaged. Three thousand people originally lived in the 1970s-built council estate. Its replacement provides 2,500 homes, of which only seventy-four were built as social housing. Planning rules demanded 432 social rented homes in the redevelopment, but when developers Lendlease filed a financial assessment with the local authority it made the case that the project would not generate enough profit to be commercially viable for them, and so they were let off. A further 500 flats deemed affordable on the estate would sell for 80 per cent of the full price of neighbouring homes, far out of the reach of the former residents of the Heygate.[5] In the light of what happened in Elephant and Castle, protecting Central Hill, Cressingham Gardens and the rest against such redevelopment feels significant for the future of London's diversity in both class and architecture.

It's easy to get swept up with the lurid horror stories and angry people in local newspapers that follow the big housebuilders around, or to get depressed about the way that some local authorities have treated their housing estates and residents. But one of the most heartening developments of recent times has been the rise of a more socially conscious attitude to housebuilding. 'We won a competition against all the great and the good,' recalled architect Peter Barber, pioneer of a new wave of architects working on social housing. 'A hundred and fifty practices went in for it, it was huge, we were tiny, it was just me and another guy.' He was talking about one of his first projects, Donnybrook Quarter, a low-rise estate near Victoria Park in Hackney. The upper floors of these irregular white blocks are maisonettes with balconies, while the ground floor is given over to flats with courtyard gardens, some of which were for sale and some for social rent. 'It was a housing competition and our take was urban,' he explained. 'We said this scheme is a celebration of the public social life of the street, and it was in big letters across the middle of the competition boards.' After their unexpected win, the housing association insisted they put gates on the streets to stop people walking through. Barber was outraged and fought his corner with the help of Jane Blom-Cooper, who was on the board of the association, and won.

I asked Barber how the estate had evolved since. 'I'm a big fan of Walter Benjamin,' he said, 'and he talks about cities being nothing until they have life breathed into them by their occupancies. And the idea of a building, the architecture receding and a veneer of occupation being overlaid onto it, is something that I love. It's lovely to go back, and occasionally lovely things are happening in courtyards, people have put a shed up or a temporary gym, and turned them into gardens or extra spaces, extensions of their home. So that can be really nice, but in a way one would like that to happen more.' He recalled speaking to Neave Brown, architect of the extraordinary 1970s concrete terraces of Alexandra Road in Camden, and 'the way that the project – which is a bit like a valley in its primary form – has accrued all these lovely structures and disappeared under the landscape that different people have created in their courtyards. And me conveying my enthusiasm for that to him, and him saying *weeeell I get a little bit kind of nervous about it*. I suppose it's a high modern position and a slightly postmodern position. He felt the building had a kind of civic presence so he didn't want to see it disappear under people's crap, but I like the idea!'

Neave Brown said that what drove his generation on to design so much housing in the post-war period was that 'we hated the English class system, we hated the idea of hidden authority, we hated the idea of an elite, we hated the idea of an impoverished and uneducated poor. We wanted to create a more egalitarian society.'[6] Sentiments I'm sure Peter Barber would share. Back at Donnybrook Quarter, the notion of personalisation was followed through by the residents on their front doors. Barber designed 10-inch windows for each, 'but of course the last thing anybody wants to do is come to their front door and be seen because then you're committed to opening up . . . So what's happened down there is that every single person has put 377 a picture in their window which is personal to them. Whether it's a picture of Marilyn Monroe or a wolf . . . I suppose the point that that makes is that there isn't a causal relationship between architecture and how people behave. That you can't anticipate always what people are going to do and that when people take things into their own hands they can be rather magical.' Or not, as Laura Wilkins with her bin store woes might say.

In one of his last acts of government, Gordon Brown relaxed the rules allowing local authorities to build council housing, and additional powers were given to councils in the 2011 Localism Act. By 2014, seven local authorities had created their own private companies to build council housing for them, and just two years later ninety-eight councils were in the midst of creating them. Part of the attraction was that local authorities had seen their government grants reduced by almost half by George Osborne, assisted by Trumpian minister for local government Eric Pickles. Creating these companies would help provide vital additional income – from the homes they would rent or sell. Between 2018 and 2019 over 4,000 council homes were built in Britain, which, while still a modest number, was more than were built in the entire noughties. Karen Barke, Head of Estate Regeneration for the London Borough of Hackney, wrote: 'it's clear that local authorities must make the most of the land they own to build new housing, even on estates where properties are in good condition.'[7] Which is why many of these new developments appear as parasitic outcrops beside and between existing local authority blocks.

Television has even attempted to formulate shows that play on the emotional and ethical side of housebuilding. *DIY SOS: The Big Build* launched in 2010, just in time for the arrival of David Cameron's Big Society. Here, hundreds of volunteers entirely rebuild houses for those few deemed most in need. I have spent many a weekday evening sobbing along at the reveal of an accessible downstairs bathroom or a wheelchair lift. Of course, at a further remove there's all sorts of arguments here about those deserving and undeserving of our help, and by extension the moral choices of production teams sifting through applications and plucking a lucky unlucky few from a mass of desperate tales. In the mid-eighties, Croydon Council did all sorts of modifications to my family's council house to better accommodate my mum's wheelchair, from lowering kitchen units to building a downstairs bathroom. Now it feels like such necessary modifications would be held at the whim of some sort of *Hunger Games* production team, pitting terminal illness against disability in a bid for that sweet spot – the heartbreaking detail of stoicism or humility that will send us over the edge. *We're sorry Mrs Grindrod, you're just not going to give us the emotional wrench we need, so back to your difficult-to-use house with you.*

'The period I've been working in we feel like we're operating under the radar and it's kind of guerrilla tactics,' Peter Barber told me, 'and it's slightly despite the government position and the cultural thrust.' Yet these days there are hundreds of architecture students across the country inspired by his work and that of contemporaries such as Meredith Bowles, David Mikhail, Annalie Riches, Paul Karakusevic and Cathy Hawley. 'I suppose early on it did feel fairly lonely,' he said. 'A lot of people at that time were working on millennium projects, everyone's holy grail was to get a fantastic museum somewhere in the Midlands or a concert hall. That wasn't what I was thinking about.' Unlikely as it seems now, he worked for a time for Richard Rogers and Will Alsop, on architecture whose prime qualities were lightness and prefabrication in glass and steel. But a visit to an exhibition of Portuguese modernist Álvaro Siza's work at the Architectural Association was, as he calls it, 'quite a moment, seeing this

Peter Barber's homeless accommodation Holmes Road Studios has been a big
inspiration for a generation of students. © Sean Rafferty

architecture which was all about the city, it was about solidity
and mass and permanence as opposed to the world I was working
in, of ephemerality and lightness and off-site construction. This
was stuff built to last.' You can see Siza's influence in the irregular white blocks that make up his homes at Donnybrook Quarter.
When Rogers Stirk Harbour + Partners recently designed thirty-
six homes for Red Door, Newham's council housing company,
they were chucked off the scheme due to their insistence on modern methods of construction – meaning off-site prefabrication.
Suddenly, there's an interest in heavier materials again, a change
380   that doesn't suit those High Tech specialists.

We were chatting on the phone due to distancing rules, but I had been to his offices a couple of years before, to see the model of a project he was working on, called the Hundred Mile City. Peter Barber's office is not the gleaming white space, stripped bare-brick box or pomo luxe pad you get with so many architects. It's more like a wand shop from Harry Potter, a narrow Victorian retail unit, packed with fantastical models of built and unbuilt schemes, the architects working two to a floor on the little galleries off the rickety stairs. A model of the Hundred Mile City sat in the window, an amazing tactile object whose wonky, irregular pattern of housing was designed to fit around the edge of London. It had been dreamt up as a response to the Adam Smith Institute's report of 2015, saying 'London's green belt must be built on to curtail the housing crisis'.[8] Instead, Barber's fanciful linear city would be a hundred-mile strip on the very edge of London, four storeys high, essentially making it a giant walled city. Within the fabric he had also designed factories and schools and squares, so that this edge would be a destination (reached by monorail). It was a very charming, thoughtful and provocative project, dense but not monolithic. He imagined that once it was built, we would watch the city grow inwards once more, 'spreading like wildfire through wasteful, anti-social, car-choked suburbia'.[9] Imagine the fuss. Bring it on. Much of his work has been focused on tackling homelessness and homes for elderly people, and a social conscience emanates from every wavy brick parapet and irregular roofline.

The most famous piece of contemporary social housing was designed by David Mikhail, Annalie Riches and Cathy Hawley for Norwich City Council's regeneration company. The 105 homes of Goldsmith Street sit on the edge of the city centre, near and inspired by its famed Golden Triangle of terraced Victorian cottages. There's a mixture of flats and houses of varying sizes in these pale-brick terraces, whose cosy proximity brings to mind the Golden Triangle too. The architects successfully negotiated with the planners to reduce street width to 14 metres rather than the mandated 21, helping to give the area an intimate domestic feel rather than a car-dominated suburban one. Not that the homes are cramped. 'The ceilings are really high and there's loads of storage,' resident Alex Jenkins told the *Guardian*. 'The boys share a bedroom but it's so big it could be two bedrooms. There's so much space that honestly you don't know what to do with it.'[10] Perhaps its most celebrated aspect is that the whole social rent scheme is built to Passivhaus standards, drastically reducing energy costs and emissions. Some found the Passivhaus instructions off-puttingly complex. 'They've given us a ringbinder of instructions to understand it,' said resident Laura, 'but I'm not very good at understanding paperwork. You kind of need someone to talk you through it.'[11] One of the big issues here will be helping residents maintain the integrity of the Passivhaus technology, which means no wall-mounted TVs or floating shelves, because the screws would perforate the membrane keeping the homes airtight. 'You've got to know what you're doing or you'll break the house,' said Laura. [12] It won the RIBA Stirling Prize in 2019, a popular win seen as a game changer for this kind of development: both environmentally and socially conscious architecture, as much about community building as it is pioneering a new philosophy. In its way, it and the wave of new architecture that has come with it feels as radical and significant as the Garden City movement a century before.

Meanwhile, a recent Peter Barber project, Ordnance Road in Enfield, echoes many of the concerns of Goldsmith Street. It's one of a series of infill schemes he'd designed for the local authority, following on from pioneering work by Karakusevic Carson architects on another site in the district, Dujardin Mews. Their success

Innovative new council housing at Goldsmith Street in Norwich. © London Road

with the first piece of affordable housing built by the council for thirty years seems to have buoyed them to push on with further exciting urban schemes. Paul White, Housing Development Manager for the London Borough of Enfield, explained that 'it was important to provide an example to show other developers in the borough what could be achieved'.[13] Ordnance Road is a high street, and Barber's site sat between a four-storey post-war block and some two-storey Victorian and Edwardian shops with flats above ('As always, my sympathies were with the Edwardian and Victorian point of view,' said Barber). The first thing that strikes you about his pale-brick terraced housing here is also familiar from Goldsmith Street – it's the curves. There are rounded edges on the street corners, but here there are more extravagant touches too – grand brick arches built into the fabric of the building, straight from 1920s Vienna. 'I wanted to celebrate the street,' 383 said Barber, not for the first time. 'You'll notice there's a great deal of attention paid to how it meets the street. Both in terms of the perforated brick wall that creates the boundary, which was expensive to make and challenging for a bricklayer but which me and the project architect were really keen to hang on to . . . And then the other feature of that front facade is the arches, which again are relatively complicated – well, not that complicated but it was an expense that could have been avoided, which we thought was really worth doing. Because it's a celebration of the entrance of each person's house, because it's an encouragement and inducement to the person occupying the space on the edge of the street.' He had noted with approval that one of the residents had gone to town in that space and made a front garden by the formidably busy road.

Out the back, Barber had another urban trick up his sleeve: a mews. 'We thought it would be really nice to do a row of cottages there, so you've got the three-storey town houses facing the front but at the back you've got these little houses that are on one level and therefore ideal for older people, courtyard houses with wavy roofs and which created a very different kind of street.' Presumably the politics of doing all of this must have created some problems with the local planners? He laughed. 'You've brought back all sorts of terrible memories!' They'd been expecting a block of flats on the site with a single point of access, not eleven three-storey council houses at the front and a mews of four bungalows at the back, each home with its own front door. 'And it took us a long time to convince the planners that we could do the same number of units with houses, they weren't convinced. They couldn't understand why we were doing more houses round the back.'

Finished in 2018, the result has so much character, it's like a
big friendly shaggy dog bounding up to see you, rather than a

talk-to-the-hand piece of cool urbanism. And it's this friendliness, this care for the human, that characterises the work of all of
this new wave of architects. 'When I lived in Bounds Green up
near Alexandra Palace, we used to live in a little row of Edwardian houses,' Peter Barber told me. 'And I remember there was
a woman, an elderly woman, who used to stand at her gate all
day long and everybody knew what was going on on the street
because she was a sort of conduit.' With Ordnance Road, his aim
was to recreate some of that opportunity to chat and observe.
'The hope, faint as it may be,' he said, was 'that people might sit
out there and get to know their neighbours or passers-by.' The
opposite of those estates of new-build houses all facing away from
each other, in denial about their proximity and relationship, or
those mixed social and private estates where disassociation leads
to blame and neglect. Here is new housing encouraging a sense of
place and community. Something positive emerging from decades
of atomisation. A precious flowering of unity and hope.

Austerity: Resurrection

In the ten years before Joseph Paxton's triumph designing the Crystal Palace for the Great Exhibition of 1851, he laid out the grand vistas of Prince's Park in Toxteth, Liverpool. Princes Road, a boulevard of extravagant mansions for merchants, processed grandly by, and many of those huge Victorian villas remain today, along with their chic tree-lined central reservation. It was only as I walked towards the city centre surrounded by all of this grandeur that I glimpsed, off to my right, the mysterious edge of something smaller and more curious: Granby. This series of dinky late nineteenth-century terraces had been designed by Welshman Richard Owens, whose domestic architecture had transformed the city. As I approached it, a couple of kids were having a kickabout in what was left of Ducie Street. A triangle of waste ground formed a kind of urban meadow on one side, from where I could see the truncated raw edge of a half-demolished terrace facing it, roughly cut-off bricks reaching out into empty space where once its neighbours had stood. The remaining houses, two-storey yellow-brick jobs with arches above front doors and small bay windows, stood shut up. Weatherworn plywood, breeze blocks and metal grilles sealed these old houses from human habitation. But they had not stopped signs of life blooming across the old facades. The boards tacked to the blacked-out bays had long ago been painted with bright curtains and cosy interior scenes, while on the tinned-up houses the metal armour was decorated with more abstract designs, faded rainbows and flowers. A crumbling improvised sculpture of an elephant's head peeped from above a window frame, while higher still a line of bunting zigzagged across the street, fluttering like birds on a telephone wire, a festive touch announcing what?

That you were entering a district where the normal rules had ceased to apply? That there was something to celebrate here, even if it wasn't altogether obvious at first what? That despite appearances, Granby was alive.

Around the dilapidated shop on the corner, life and bustle revealed itself. In stark contrast to Ducie Street, the fabric of these homes had been for the most part repaired, with signs of life in the majority. A street of well-kept houses, flowers blooming through railings, fresh paint on front doors and window frames, Victorian floor and wall tiles scrubbed to a gleam. A walk in Granby Four Streets, the triangle of terraces in Toxteth near the centre of Liverpool we last visited during the riots of 1981, presents one unlikely

There are still a few derelict houses in Granby, and even those are oddly welcoming.

scene after another. The thick trunks of plane trees interrupt the narrow pavement, leaves shading the summer street of chatters, cyclists and pram-pushers. Houses painted with hippyish abandon, as if plucked from the Flower Power era, sit beside the most soberly tasteful contemporary renovations, like an abrupt form of time travel. The narrow streets were cluttered with huge planters, circular benches at which sat groups of people of differing ages and cultures deep in conversation, playing board games and chatting to passers-by. There was none of the anxiety I often feel when perambulating streets, trying to notice everything while pretending not to. Here, no one seemed bothered by me ambling about in their neighbourhood. It was the opposite experience to the one I'd had in London Docklands a few weeks before, when I posted a snap of a deserted street of 1980s houses on Instagram to receive the furious comment *there are children in there*. Reader, I deleted it, because life is too short. Here in Granby, as I stopped to take pictures of the colourful facades and planters a young woman in a headscarf asked me indignantly why I wasn't taking photos of her house, so slightly punch-drunk I dutifully obliged. You're not in Docklands now, John. Neighbours were gossiping, the sun was shining, everyone was welcome. How had this happened? How had a small network of abandoned, derelict suburban streets transformed itself into vibrant, friendly life?

Back in 1969, Shelter had interviewed Granby resident Mrs Fitzgerald about life in the semi-derelict streets. 'Many have given up the fight,' she told them, 'and, if I had been a free agent, I think I should have been one of them.'[1] By the mid-noughties, it seemed her prediction had come true, with only thirty of the 200 remaining houses of Beaconsfield Street, Cairns Street, Jermyn Street and Ducie Street still occupied. Half of one of the streets had recently been demolished as part of a New Labour scheme – the Housing Market Renewal Initiative – whose aim was to replace derelict housing with desirable new residences for middle-class families. Rubbish had been dumped in the front yards of badly boarded and 'tinned-up' Victorian terraces. Weeds grew in the roads and sprouted from the brickwork and rooflines. Graffiti and vandalism had made these already sad empty homes look even more desperate, and rubble from the dilapidated houses, collapsing corner shops and demolition sites sat in heaps, as if the area was part of a war zone where venturing onto the streets was too dangerous. On one side of Beaconsfield Street, windows had been replaced by breeze block painted black, like some sort of deadly warning. Lead had been stolen from the roofs and those windows not blocked up on the unoccupied houses had been smashed. The council stopped repairing the houses, prevented the occupied ones from being re-rented and compulsorily purchased any that came on the market. 'We were condemned,' recalled long-time resident Hazel Tilley. 'It was punishment for the riots. Bins weren't collected, streets weren't swept and a mythology built up: people came here to buy their drugs or dump their shite.'[2] The few residents remaining didn't describe their situation then as a community; they were on nodding acquaintance but not particularly friendly terms. 'We didn't really speak to one another, did we?' said Carole Foulder in a 2012 film made by housing expert Ronnie Hughes, where she and her neighbours discussed their actions. 'We just kind of all walked up and down and said hello and passed by and went to our own houses and just left it at that.'[3]

Legend has it that it was into this situation, on a sunny Sunday morning in 2006, that one Cairns Street resident began to take matters into her own hands. Eleanor Lee started by clearing away some of the broken mattresses and flotsam in the street, pickaxing concrete that had been dumped in front of the empty houses, and planting flowers in whatever cracks and receptacles 389 she could find. Her actions stirred something in her neighbours – what one of them called being guilt-tripped – and soon she found she was joined in her efforts to clean and plant up the street. 'And that was the start of this little tiny group getting together,' recalled Carole Foulder.[4] Soon, residents in Beaconsfield Street were out painting cheery curtains and letterboxes on the breeze blocks and metal grilles, a witty way of creating a friendlier neighbourhood. In time, most of the older women were out gardening and painting and clearing up the streets, in opposition to the council's solution, which was to erect a 10-foot barrier to deter fly-tippers. The work they engaged on was bloody hard. Later, they would bring tables out onto the street to create a market, which began to draw in curious urban explorers, people like Ronnie Hughes. The forgotten four streets of Granby were coming alive again.

By 2010, when he first got involved at Granby, Ronnie had long since left his job in a housing association in the city, and had become a freelance consultant working with local communities and social enterprises. He had also become a successful blogger, his site asenseofplace.com home to increasingly influential thoughts on housing, community and local history. 'My main impression was of the intelligence and determination of the people,' he told me, 'and their rage.' It was an uncomfortable first meeting. 'The rage in the room was unbelievable,' he recalled, 'and because I was the latest person to be standing in front of it, it was directed at me! I weathered that, and they said, *even between ourselves we know what we don't want, but we don't know what we do want. So, can you help*? And I said on the spot, *yeah.*' He knew there was no money in it, but it was exactly the kind of resident-generated regeneration he was keen to support. He was impressed by their bloody-mindedness and savvy. 'They were world class at stopping their houses being knocked down

. . . They had done more work thinking about the future than they thought. So we had the vision fairly quickly.' New Labour's Housing Market Renewal Initiative had attracted developers waiting in the wings to completely rebuild the area. 'But coming in, God damn them, the Conservative and Liberal coalition did the only good thing they ever did,' said Ronnie, 'which was kill off the HMRI. So there wasn't even the money for that! In the vacuum, we thought, *hello, maybe our moment has arrived.*' After decades of top-down strategies aimed at regenerating areas like Granby and generally messing them up, it was their absence in a new political world of austerity that would allow the residents the chance to take control of their destiny. Hazel Tilley recalled the council's response to their continued existence. 'I remember one local councillor turning round and saying to me: "If it wasn't for people like you, we could have this area flattened and rebuilt by now."'[5]

The next turning point was in 2011 when, with Ronnie's help, the residents made Granby a Community Land Trust. This meant that the locals now owned the land in perpetuity, with a covenant that if you sold a house there the price could only increase or decrease by whatever the median wage rise had been in Liverpool.* It was a community ownership model that stood in contrast to the private profit bubbles generated by Right to Buy, buy-to-let and even the increasingly corporate behaviour of housing associations. The mechanism had been imported from the US, and while it had existed in the UK for twenty years it only made it into law in 2008, just in time for Granby to take

---

* Some houses were sold to help finance the scheme. 'The lowest I heard of for a house a mile outside the city centre about ten years ago was £8,000,' Ronnie Hughes told me. 'We always knew we'd sell some of the houses. When we started to sell them in 2016–17 it was £100,000. So we had recreated a housing market from nothing.'

advantage. There are now almost 200 Community Land Trusts round the country. 'That was the first time that the people of Granby had owned anything,' explained Ronnie Hughes. 'They had owned individual housing but as time had shown, as for all the disappeared streets of Granby apart from those four, they could be swept out of their houses on the decision of a bureaucrat's pen.'

Owning the land was one thing, getting the money to renovate so many derelict houses was another. In 2013, Liverpool City Council launched a Homes for a Pound scheme for twenty houses in Granby and nearby Arnside Road. Applicants were vetted to make sure they lived or worked in Liverpool, had a job and were first-time buyers, and they signed an agreement that they wouldn't sell them for five years. With no electrics or plumbing, the novelty of what estate agents might describe as a 'blank canvas' would come as a shock to some, as would the amount of money needed to bring them back to a habitable standard. First in line was cab driver Jayalal Madde, whose family had been renting locally for the past nine years. Mayor Joe Anderson presented him with the keys to a four-bedroomed house on Cairns Street that had been boarded up for a decade. At some point it had been converted into flats, and Madde's first job was to turn it back into a house. The renovations cost him £40,000. 'We won't be moving now,' he told the *Liverpool Echo*. 'We are going to stay here our whole lives.'[6]

Alongside that scheme, Granby received grants from the National Lottery, the Nationwide Foundation (an independent charitable trust created by the Nationwide Building Society in 1997) and two housing associations. Soon, an architect would be needed to advise on the best way to regenerate the houses. Xanthe Hamilton of Steinbeck, a social enterprise who'd helped

fund Granby's regeneration, suggested Assemble, a collective in their mid-twenties, who she'd worked with on a previous project, a temporary theatre under a railway arch in Stratford, East London. She thought their rebellious do-it-yourself spirit might fit well with the locals of Granby. 'Just a couple of them came up at first,' recalled Ronnie. 'And really the best work that they did for us early on – because we were nowhere near needing an architect – was some graphic design. They gave us a look.' When it came time to tender for the work itself, Assemble were there. 'It was by no means certain they would get it because they weren't from Liverpool,' said Ronnie, but Assemble landed the job.

Within a year of work beginning on site, the creative young architects and Granby were up for the 2015 Turner Prize – an award not for architecture but for art. 'Assemble's project really addressed a current problem,' said Alistair Hudson, Turner judge, director of the Middlesbrough Institute of Modern Art '– the state of planning, top-down regeneration, and the way our cities are organised. This has a direct effect on society.'[7] Against all the odds, they won the prize and were awarded it by the ultimate in rebellious cool, Sonic Youth's Kim Gordon. 'I got sick of dealing with the *yes, but are you art*? question,' said Ronnie. 'As if any of us cared about that.' He laughed as he recalled all the press attention they received. '*If I do* China Daily *this morning, can you do the* New York Times *this afternoon*? . . . It was just lovely. We were flying by the seat of all of our pants. It was really exhausting. And it was like a story. I mean, *I* found the story empowering, and I was in it!'

One of the things Assemble brought to the project was the Granby Workshop, a studio installed in one of four crumbling old corner shops to help formalise the creative work of the residents. These days, they make and sell tiles and tableware, including a range called Granbyware, formed from recycled ceramic. They also had a vision for two of the most derelict houses in Granby,   393 to create a Winter Garden – 'the cream on the cake, the cherry on the fountain', according to Ronnie. Too far gone to renovate, Assemble helped the locals reimagine them as a glasshouse. And it was here that the Turner Prize win helped, because, as Ronnie says, 'we became art' – and art money is bigger than housing money. He had been booked to speak at an Arts Council conference, and used it to test how far they could push the art angle. 'I told the Granby story up till then and at the end of it, *can you give us some money for this idea?* They did! Except that the money we asked for wasn't as much as their smallest possible grant.'

Granby Four Streets has led to a wider revival of the area. As I walked through the renovations, the next street I came to had a far more uniform look than the contrasts of that bubbling social enterprise. Here, the Victorian terraces had all been spruced up with identical grey window frames, dark brown doors, grey slate roofs and black railings. A monument to *Wallpaper** magazine and sandblasting. It was Granby through the dishwasher, with all signs of history dissolved away. Outside the small houses stood big cars, 4x4s, Audis, modern Mini Coopers twice the size of their forebears. This was the result of developers seeing an opportunity created by Granby Four Streets and trying to replicate it. They might not have had the same tenant input or feel for local history, but they were still better than dereliction, better than the reputational blight that has hung over Liverpool 8 since the riots. It's a shame Granby Four Streets hasn't led to more renovation on a similar community-led basis here, but it's also extraordinary how the residents have acted as a catalyst of change far beyond their own streets.

Granby is a story of transformations within transformations, a kind of fractal process from micro to macro and back again.

Inside the magical transformation of Granby Winter Garden.

Winning the Turner Prize allowed the world to see what was being done in Granby as not just bricks and mortar, not even just a story of improved living conditions or social justice. Suddenly, Granby stood for the ineffable qualities of the soul, of beauty, of philosophy. And so just as worlds were being bridged, the two empty shells were knocked together – 'like the Beatles in *Help!*' as Ronnie had it. In that shell Granby now has a community garden, a space for art and gatherings and tourists like me. It sits quite demurely in the middle of Cairns Street, and you might not notice it at first, with its original brickwork and facia. But the roof is glass, and while the beams of the upper floor remain, the floorboards have gone, opening up the structure to light. Large trees have been planted on the ground floor and weave their way through the structure. There are remnants of some of the old rooms, now repurposed as spaces for planting and – appropriately for a glasshouse – reflection. 'The miracle of it was to have something that the people there didn't *need*, they only wanted,' said Ronnie. 'Everything else there was about rage, human rights and need.' The arrival of Granby's Winter Garden would demonstrate the maturity of its regeneration to the world. It opened its blue doors to hundreds of visitors on the first day of spring 2019, just as the trees inside were coming into bud. For Ronnie, as well as the residents, its success was the joyful expression of life it gave them. 'As the day turned into the evening, I was really conscious that there were children running in and out of the houses – and it was the children of *here*. And it was that hair-on-the-back-of-your-neck moment.' Ronnie was welling up. 'If this isn't a utopia then I don't know what is. A little utopia made by the people who lived there.'

Croydon was a mess and so was I. Back when the twentieth century was going to sleep, I had taken a walk with my Polaroid camera around the town's decaying concrete monoliths. Lunar House. The Threepenny Bit. The Nestlé building. Taberner House. Towers with no great national recognition but local landmarks all the same. Despite its monolithic concrete posturing, I'd woken with a feeling that this post-war landscape was suddenly a fragile and fleeting thing. The tail end of a 1950s and 60s redevelopment known as 'New Croydon', it would surely not last long into the coming millennium. Looking back, my feelings were clearly inspired by more urgent personal events: the recent death of my mum, and my dad's terminal cancer. As I trudged round in the cold December drizzle, I was inevitably projecting a sense of loss on this landscape, not that the darkened windows of the towers and the litter blowing around the underpasses needed much help on that front. The Polaroids turned out a grey, bleak and slightly blurry record of a really bad time in my life. I was grimly delighted.

This was a landscape that had reflected my experiences and moods over the decades: coldly impersonal one day, friendly and intimate the next, thrillingly anonymous sometimes, mostly a bit lost and casting around for inspiration. I don't drive, so it's a town I have explored over and again on foot. If every one of my journeys could be repeated simultaneously, how crowded the pavements would be with mes of all ages, plugged into Walkmans, Discmans, MiniDiscs and iPods, with all the attendant bad hair and cheap trainers, dodging around my former and future selves like some kind of supernatural silent disco. Strangest of all, a surprising number of these walks would be as 397 part of tours of the centre, with residents, international students, town planners, architects, residents, even the National Trust. That grim day in December 1999, I took shots of wet concrete, subway graffiti, empty office blocks, grubby tiling – the full Croydon. Afterwards, with no explanation, I mailed the Polaroids out to thirty friends, in letters postmarked 1999 to arrive in early 2000 like little glimpses of the past. No one mentioned receiving my latest effort in attention-seeking melancholia, which was a relief. The evidence of my trip would be consigned to what? – drawers or the bin – records in most cases discarded long before the landscape I'd imagined they would outlast. I'd all but forgotten about them until one old pal contacted me on Facebook nineteen years later and showed me evidence that one still existed. His was a wall of graffiti in an underpass I could now no longer quite place, riotous in a way that the carefully curated street art invasion of my home town since is anything but. Now many of those underpasses have gone, and carefully controlled expressions of council-sanctioned art appear instead on the sides of concrete office blocks and brick gable ends, an aesthetic borrowed from New York, Belfast, Berlin, robbed of all politicisation other than that of gentrification.

Fast-forward twenty years from that exercise in miserabalism and in mid-February 2020, a month before the country entered lockdown, I self-consciously retraced those already painfully self-conscious steps, leading a group of people on a tour of the town centre's post-war relics. I'd named it Polaroids of Croydon. I'd been asked to run it by architect Charles Holland, who was master-planning a piece of what is called 'public realm' – in this instance, a windswept plaza beside the town's problematic urban motorway. On the walk, we would reimagine the town's vanished modernist towers and gawk at the curious survivors, and I could evaluate how accurate those feelings had been all those years ago.

Croydon has indeed changed, but not in ways I could have predicted. Back then, the town existed in a kind of bubble of anonymity, its main image one of boredom from another era. That held true until the riots of 2011, a sudden outburst in a place gripped so long by inertia. It was a reminder of the inequalities of the borough, pockets of poverty surrounded by middle-class wealth and aspiration. Since then, the transformation has been rapid and sometimes shocking. Some of the town's most recognisable towers – the sleek local authority offices Taberner House and the ribbed slab headquarters for Nestlé – have disappeared. The retail heart of the town, the Whitgift shopping centre, has long been under threat from a new scheme from Westfield and developer Hammerson. Plots of land by the station that had lain empty my whole life have been hastily filled with towering apartment blocks, as if thrown up in a flustered *what open space?* The weirdest thing for me hasn't been the amount of rebuilding – Croydon has always loved a bit of that. It's that Croydon became for a time – and it still seems absurd as I type it – *hip*. A temporary mall made from shipping containers popped up. Huge new residential towers with glossy surfaces now stand effortlessly above those old New Croydon landmarks. Ageing office blocks have either been occupied by the sort of new tech companies who had been priced out of Shoreditch and Old Street's 'Silicon Roundabout' or have been converted into planning-free microflats smaller than a budget hotel room. Yet eight months after the Polaroids of Croydon walk, that bubble burst. The council was on the verge of bankruptcy and the government was sending in inspectors to investigate what had gone wrong in the town's latest improbable rise and fall.

Improbability was New New Croydon's watchword. In 2016 the National Trust ran a series of tours titled 'Edge City: Croydon', as an example of an intact post-war landscape of 399 the sort that had suddenly become hugely fashionable. 'The project's aim,' they explained, 'was to change the perception of heritage from simply country houses and coastlines.'[1] Good luck there, kids. Their headstrong London branch had been trying to attract a younger audience to the organisation by championing some counter-intuitive – for the National Trust at any rate – modernist developments, from Ernő Goldfinger's Balfron Tower in East London to the concrete landscape of the Southbank Centre. As a proud defender of Croydon's post-war architecture, I'd been asked to speak at the launch, held on the roof of a multi-storey car park, also the venue of a popular pop-up cinema, and since demolished. I was surprised that whenever some of the buildings we were meant to be celebrating were mentioned in the speeches, a senior member of the council could be heard yelling gleefully *they're coming down!* Making strange self-hating yelps like this has long been the role of politicians in the town – vice-signalling, perhaps. Tear them down and put up the latest version in their place. Croydon would erect an *iconic* building every few weeks if they had the money. Everything would be gratuitously *iconic*. Blocks of flats, offices, shopping centres, traffic islands, bollards, bins. *Iconic* up to the eyeballs. And it would tear down last year's version of the same in a race to build the new. Not because Croydon has tacky urban designers, but because sometimes it seems as if the politicians in charge have absolutely no sense of history. Caught forever in some form of midlife crisis, things are *amazing* and *just what's needed* until they are thrown in the bin in favour of something newer. As the whim takes it, Croydon is swept along with the latest enthusiasm. I am being grossly unfair, of course. But then anyone in power yelling *they're coming down!* about buildings they are supposed to be *for one fucking evening* celebrating can take a bit of gross unfairness. Gross unfairness is only fair.

The photograph showed eight young men and women posing moodily on the roof of the Whitgift Centre car park, a better-scrubbed Arcade Fire with the concrete towers of town arranged behind them like giant amps. This was a new generation of architects and planners snapped for 'Croydon: the Future', a 2009 article by Rory Olcayto in the *Architects' Journal*.[2] 'Croydon is a place which imprints on your brain,' said one of their number, Zineb Seghrouchni, an urban designer at Dutch architects OKRA, who were working with the council. 'It has presence. I'm fascinated by the typologies in a relatively small area. It makes for an animated walk-through.'[3] Architects say 'typology' a lot – not a portmanteau of typing and apology, though it should be. Olcayto followed them to one of a series of Croydon Metropolitan Centre Summits in the Fairfield Halls arts centre, where teams from different organisations and projects could get to meet one another. By way of an introduction, Mike Kiely, Croydon Council's head of planning, informed them that 'Croydon is broken'.[4]

What seemed so amazing, after years of huge corporate practices hoovering up all the talented people straight out of university, was that so many young designers were excited to be working for and with a local authority, in a way not seen since the 1970s. One of them, Finn Williams, later reflected that 'when I moved from private practice to Croydon Council, it was fairly unusual amongst my peers. If I'd stayed in the private sector, I would probably have ended up setting up my own practice and designing residential extensions for friends of my parents. But working in Croydon's placemaking team was a bit like having our own small office, with a guaranteed flow of work, the freedom to make decisions for the public good rather than private profit, and the luxury of really getting to know a place and its people – rather than being parachuted in and out of places on a contract.'[5]

Vincent Lacovara, then Senior Urban Designer at Croydon Council, had grown up in the town and was enjoying the opportunity to correct some of its peculiarities, and to celebrate others. 'Some projects will start next year, and make things better,' he told Olcayto, 'some will happen in twenty years.'[6] Round about the same time this article was written, I had gone on a walking tour of the town's 'seven hills' – its seven multi-storey car parks – led by Lacovara, where I was amazed to find other people as interested in the town's recent history as I was. Perhaps his greatest feat has been not the planning itself, but a sense that it is a worthwhile endeavour to consider the town's various bits of history – from medieval streets to thundering urban motorway – as equal. When the teams met, it was classic topsy-turvy Croydon as architects Studio Egret West tackled East Croydon, while a company called East master-planned – of course – the west. They might all have different focuses around the town, but were joined in an effort to make this landscape of underpasses and flyovers, buildings on legs and subterranean car parks work for people at pavement level. It seems a pretty basic ask, but it was resolutely something that Allan Holt, the town's post-war borough engineer, had failed to do.

This young team had inherited a plan drawn up by that king of back-of-an-envelope architecture, Will Alsop, who had briefly lived in Croydon in the 1970s and called its post-war landscape 'the English version of Manhattan'.[7] His brief in the mid-noughties was to make Croydon the third city in London after Westminster and the Square Mile – the town's longed-for dream. He suggested bulldozing the town's sprawling 1970s shopping centre, the Whitgift, to replace it with shops at ground level and towers of flats above. There was also a plan to bridge East Croydon with a 'vertical Kew Gardens' while developers Lendlease were going to build Park Place, a new shopping centre in the shell of the town's enormous Allders department store. Make, the company created by Ken Shuttleworth, were also doing their relentless icon thing with four faceted crystalline towers in a row beside East Croydon station. The young urban designers were not impressed. 'Will's vision was the kind of last hurrah of a previous regime that had an idea of a kind of futuristic pride,' Finn Williams told me. 'And that was almost a bit quixotic, always a bit bizarre to me.' He recalled that the council's outgoing executive director at the time he joined in 2009 'really wanted to see cranes over Croydon. And he didn't really mind what they were building, as long as cranes came. And the attitude was the bigger and bolder and brasher the better. It was almost like development at all costs, you know, just make something happen.' The new placemaking team, led by Lacovara, inherited a lot of schemes from this period. 'There was lots of great ideas and energy in that Will Alsop plan,' said Finn. 'But it also spurred, or allowed, a lot of speculation. It was perhaps slightly unrealistic. And some of those schemes that happened on the back of that last regime became zombies – we called them zombie planning applications, schemes that lived on throughout our time but we had very little control over because they were living dead from a different attitude to planning. So some of the towers that I wasn't really involved in, I've been really distraught to see being built, were zombies that lived on from that previous regime.'

Interestingly, in the period that followed, grand strategies like Alsop's for Croydon arising from Richard Rogers's New Labour urban renaissance began to fall from favour. 'There's a bit of a discussion going now about strategies,' architect-planner Irena Bauman told me in 2018. 'Has the time passed now for strategies? Because they take so much time to produce. And by the time they are completed they are usually out of date. Even on the   403 day of completion they are out of date. There's a lot of discussion about abandoning strategising. Scary!' But liberating too for towns like Croydon, who could commission grand strategies like Alsop's as a rebranding project, get tons of media coverage for it, and then quietly abandon it, half finished, a decade later. After all, strategies are so passé. Finn Williams described to me New New Croydon's team approach as being 'radically pragmatic', by which he meant 'this wasn't about making more big promises. It was about working with what we've got. . . . We wanted to kind of accept what was already there and enjoy the contradictions of it, and then just fit into that.'

The first thing Finn was tasked with was a master plan for East Croydon, around the town's main railway station. 'I've come from a background doing master plans,' he explained. 'I'm working as a consultant. So when we were given this master plan area to work on I rolled up my sleeves and thought, right, I know how to solve this. And drew it up, made a model, came up with a solution within a couple of weeks, presented it to our bosses in Croydon, and they just looked completely shocked. *You can't just come up in isolation, in a vacuum, with the solution to this master plan. You've got to bring everyone on board.*' Finn took a deep breath and looked back at the zombie schemes lumbering over his patch: Foster + Partners' High Tech Croydon Gateway, Make's 'pretty horrific' four finger towers, 'both of them turning their back on the station, and none of them addressing or supporting the role that the station should play in the city.' He worried about the capacity of the station being so limited, and its orientation, the entrance as far away from the centre of town as possible on that site. 'Instead of tabling our perfect solution, we worked in a much more open way to take those existing schemes as a starting point. And then over a period of time, working very closely with all the 404 different parties and bodies in the area, soften those schemes, loosen them up, make them more malleable and get them to a point where they realised that actually they needed to address the station link into that new bridge and create a piece of public realm, help the interchange, create meaningful public space.' It was an ingenious piece of political manoeuvring from the new team. 'The master plan we ended up with was very similar to the model that we made in two weeks. But really, the value of it was that everyone was properly bought into that and that they owned those schemes, and they ended up delivering them bit by bit.'

The new public space and blocks of flats around the station still disconcert me, but I can see how clever it all is, and how much better than the usual single-use plonked-on bit of planning you might expect from the old days of Croydon. The part that makes it all worthwhile is the new pedestrian bridge for the railway station, which created a new entrance facing the town centre for the first time. Finn says the design 'tries to reference and celebrate both the 50p building and the faceted white space frames of Lunar House and Apollo House', three of the town's most well-known post-war towers. He talked about persuading architects and developers to respond positively to the existing architecture of the place, rather than, as was more typical, '*we're just going to have to come up with some crazy crystalline forms that have nothing to do with Croydon because it's really uncool*'.

So much of the urban designers' work here was about changing perceptions of Croydon, to the outside world, and to the council itself. 'I remember early on,' recalled Finn, 'when Vincent and I started there, a developer came to a meeting, and Vinny was trying to persuade him to get a really good design team on board. And the developer said, *Look, it's only Croydon. We don't use our best teams for Croydon. That's what we do in central London, you're Croydon, you get our C team or D team.* And there was that kind of acceptance across the council, 405 particularly in development management early on that we're lucky if we got anything – that cranes over Croydon attitude, that *let's just get something and hope it's all right*. And developers knew that existed. So they were able to quite easily drive wedges between our positions as a local authority, because I would be pushing really hard for something and a colleague wouldn't. So they just go with the path of least resistance.' He described their approach as an offside trap, the whole team working together to ensure they got the best out of the architects and developers who were trying to build there. 'And that's quite a fun process to be part of, I mean, I still miss it, you know, negotiating hard and pushing and trying to outwit the big teams of consultants.' I'd totally watch the box set.

Brick By Brick, Croydon's housing company, was founded in 2015, charged with creating new homes for sale and rent across the borough to make a profit for the council. They had their own in-house architects too, a group called Common Ground, yet another collection of eager young things with big ideas and a social conscience, aiming to change the world one placemaking scheme at a time. Sites for Brick By Brick were scattered all over the borough, from large town-centre brownfields to awkward suburban infill. There was even talk of building on a nature reserve, part of the green belt opposite the house where I grew up in New Addington, which seems wilfully destructive. The model would allow the council to make money from sales or rent from homes they built themselves on land they owned, rather than selling the land to a private developer. 'Local authority budgets are biting more and more,' said Colm Lacey, Croydon Council's director of development in 2017. 'For example, in Croydon we've lost more than half of our central government budget since 2010. . . . [a lot of authorities] have cottoned on to the fact that they need to be more commercial and make more money as one way of addressing that gap.'[8] Jo Negrini, the council's then Chief Executive, brought the idea of a council-owned construction company from Newham, where she had been Director of Strategic Regeneration, Planning and Olympic Legacy. 'We're trying something new,' goes Brick By Brick's uplifting sales pitch. 'We want to provide properly designed, affordable homes for local people. We want to add value to existing neighbourhoods, and deliver a return to our main shareholder, Croydon Council. Brick By Brick is a property developer that believes in doing things differently.'

And Brick By Brick weren't the only developers in the town hoping to tackle housing in innovative ways. Two tall concrete cores sticking rudely up from beside a small modernist church were signs that something big was happening. This was a modular tower being built by Covent-Garden-based developers Pocket Living. 'We create cleverly designed homes for local people so that they can stay in their communities and continue to make London great' is how they describe it. A cover image on their website of a twentysomething bearded cyclist leaves no ambiguity about their target demographic: single young urban professionals who want the advantages of city life on their doorstep – what they call 'young, middle-earning Londoners who can contribute to the city in so many ways but can't afford to buy their first home'. The flats are sold to local first-time buyers, these days aimed squarely at those taking advantage of the government's Help to Buy scheme.

Marc Vlessing, founder of Pocket Living, told me he set the company up 'to create the most affordable starter home for people on modest salaries'. The mass-produced model he most wanted to emulate was the Volkswagen Beetle, whose lightweight frame and bodywork proved so appealing and 407 adaptable over decades of manufacture. Croydon is only one of twenty-five developments across London, from Haringey to Hounslow, Barking to Kingston. Their unique selling point was that all Pocket Living's flats are an identical 38 metres square, with a bedroom big enough for a super king-size bed, a desk and a built-in wardrobe, enough space in the living room for a five-seater Ikea sofa and a dining room table that, when expanded, could seat eight people for Christmas dinner. The interior of the flats going up in Croydon don't feel fundamentally different from their first block in Weedington Road, Camden, back in 2008, although that small low-rise project and Croydon's two towers feel vastly different in terms of their scale and impact, and these new flats have adopted fashionable prefabrication techniques. Their single-minded business model has helped them navigate the complexities of Britain's planning regulations. While other smaller developers have struggled with endless bespoke projects against corporate giants, with such a simple product the planners immediately know what a Pocket Living development would mean.

'We think like boat builders,' explained Vlessing. Having poked my nose around a Pocket block in Lambeth North, built on the site of some garages from the neighbouring post-war estate, I think I'm more of a cargo ferry kinda guy. It was easy to imagine how quickly under my hands it would go from serene mid-mod furnished show home to resembling Del Trotter's cluttered Peckham high-rise flat in *Only Fools and Horses*. But then I am not the target market: too old and too analogue. 'An awful lot of these people are going to remain single and are probably not going to get married,' said Vlessing of what he called the Pocketeers. 'They're never much younger than twenty-eight, they're never much older than thirty-eight, they never earn much less than 29,000, they never earn much more than 45,000, 90 per cent of them are single.' Almost two-thirds of their buyers are single women, who, he says, appreciate the safety such an environment affords. Pocket Living may have found a niche in the market in the midst of a housing crisis, and have been surprised how long their buyers were staying, on average eight or nine years. What will these developments be like in thirty years, I wonder. Will they continue to cycle through new tenants, or become cluttered flats full of elderly singles – Pocket Assisted Living perhaps?

Other developers have targeted the millennial market with what is termed hotel-style living: even smaller halls of residence-style apartments bolstered by communal lounge-bar entertainment spaces in place of privacy. This, they say, is to foster community. 'We have things like Quintain,' Manisha Patel, urban designer and London mayoral Design Advocate, told me, 'thousands of homes which are built to rent at Wembley, we also have a number of other developers who are developing all over London and it very much is a hotel lifestyle. We're looking at spaces where people come and congregate, they have a social life, they're there, they want to be drinking and having coffee and social media plays a big part in this, we're looking at home-working, we're looking at different functions happening within a building.' Millennials love to live together, we are told, and their addiction to social media means that they seek out high-end Instagrammable locations. It's the sort of fantasy the pandemic has, I hope, cured us of.

It was the start of 2020 when architect Charles Holland asked me to run a couple of tours around the centre of the town, something I'd grown surprisingly used to over the years. Polaroids of Croydon was part of the public consultation for his project to design a new public space beside the Fairfield Halls, a Festival of Britain-inspired arts centre overlooking Croydon's cherished   409 urban motorway. When we reached the end of the tours, cold and tired, we sought out the work of Charles and fellow designers MICA and Adam Nathaniel Furman, displayed in the refurbished arts centre. Charles talked gently about the scheme to the hardy souls who'd clung on to the end, of his fascination with the old Fair Field now submerged beneath a 1960s suspended deck, and how his newly designed version would be a field that actually sat above a subterranean car park. The vision was playful and worked on levels like an old computer game. Trees planted on the lower level would poke up through voids cut in the deck above. Kiosks would be built in the form of some of Croydon's most famous post-war skyscrapers: a dinky Threepenny Bit, Richard Seifert's East Croydon landmark; a resurrection of former council offices Taberner House in miniature, in all their glamorous bevelled glass glory. There would be fountains and pools and reeds and places for the increasing number of residents in central Croydon to come and sit. 'It's an amazing site,' enthused Charles to me, 'where you've got what was a railway cutting and before that was a field where they had medieval fairs and stuff like that, and then it becomes a car park with a podium over the top, and then it becomes part of that post-war urbanism of Croydon of elevated things and subways, a very modernist urban space. And I think for us we're not trying to get rid of one to get back to the other . . . we think some of those quite bucolic origins are quite interesting to work with but in conjunction with the incredible modernist history that's around as well.'

For decades, this area – formerly known as College Green – had been in a terrible state, paving stones loose and frequently missing, benches rotten or smashed, planting long since neglected and scratty. It seemed strange the council had been happy for this ruin to sit at the heart of the town for so long, a symbol of abandonment and decay. 'There's an enormous amount of new housing, apartments and stuff going in there,' said Charles, 'so a really nice piece of public space is really vital.' What was notable on the walks was the optimistic spirit of the residents who'd come along. Rather than the usual Croydon-bashing or fear of the future, these were people curious about the recent history of their town and where it was going next.

It was only two years since London Mayor Sadiq Khan had approved a £1.4 billion plan, designed by giant architectural practice Allies and Morrison, to redevelop the Whitgift shopping centre. This Westfield development would crash out of the old 1960s centre, across North End – the town's main shopping street – and into the town's other mall, Centrale. It would turn much of the town centre into a single indoor retail behemoth, adding further tens of thousands of feet of shops at the very moment that some of the biggest names of high-street retail were closing for good. It would also create a thousand new homes, some through the London Living Rent scheme. But by 2021, after years of announcements, Hammerson, who were co-funding the scheme, pulled the plug, following hints that it might happen in increments rather than in one go, and that there could be fewer shops and more hotels and restaurants. It felt like an intervention from a different age. I am reminded of the redevelopment of Birmingham New Street station, a seven-year engineering project that turned the tangled 1960s edifice into a vast gleaming white shopping centre, Grand Central. It's the latest manifestation of those railway station air rights developments pioneered by Terry Farrell in the 1980s. Grand Central is co-owned by Hammerson and opened in 2015 with sixty shops, including a massive John Lewis as the anchor store. By July 2020, John Lewis confirmed they would not be reopening their £35 million shop post-lockdown, describing it as 'financially challenged before the pandemic and we have not been able to find a way that would allow us to turn that around'.[9] Meanwhile, in Croydon the effect of all of this wishful thinking was that the existing fabric of the town centre looks increasingly tatty, neglected and deserted.

Back in October 2020, another chill wind had blown through the town. News emerged that there was a gigantic hole in the borough council's finances, throwing their ability to deliver even the most urgent and basic services into doubt. Residents relying on anything from social care to school provision faced the frightening possibility of extreme budget cuts. Effectively declared insolvent in November, the council announced it would fund only a bare legal minimum of services for the foreseeable future – such as social care for the most vulnerable – which could be fatal for the borough's thirteen libraries, nine children's centres and its waste recycling scheme. Much of this financial crisis had been brought about by the delayed effects of austerity, which had cut local authority funding by almost half. Many councils around the country were now finding themselves in dire straits, following the bankruptcy of Northamptonshire in February 2018. But it had been exacerbated in Croydon by the entrepreneurial spirit of the ambitious council, sadly unmatched by its business acumen.

One of the most contested issues was Brick By Brick, set up in an attempt to mitigate some of the government's cuts, once encouraged by Boris Johnson as Mayor of London and now demonised as risky and reckless. Brick By Brick's annual report shows them making a loss of a quarter of a million in 2017 and three times that in 2019. The losses were due, they said, to hiring more staff and not having enough finished properties for sale. But that wasn't the whole story. In July 2020 the council, already struggling with costs from the Covid pandemic and government austerity cuts from the previous decade, had been forced to borrow £30 million to buy 185 unsold flats from Brick By Brick. This followed spending £6 million six months before buying twenty-four newly built flats in Longheath Gardens near the town centre in Addiscombe, which had been originally built as shared ownership homes. Why, in the midst of a housing crisis, had they not sold? Well, it was only when buyers began to apply for mortgages that it emerged Brick By Brick hadn't registered themselves with the Greater London Authority and Homes England as an approved shared ownership supplier, and so were not legally allowed to sell them. Local reporter Steven Downes broke the story on his website Inside Croydon, and a couple who had their mortgage turned down because of it told him, 'we're just annoyed because they are still advertising while potential buyers now are left in limbo having paid reservation and mortgage fees and such like. Now we're being told that the wait could be 12 months.'[10] PricewaterhouseCoopers were called in to provide a quick audit into Brick By Brick's affairs. It criticised the lack of financial management and absence of a finance director to monitor or forecast their performance. They observed that the company's 'ambitious strategy of developing large numbers of small, complex and more risky sites has led to significant delays . . . The severity of this situation has not been exposed until late in 2020, as the formal controls that should have been in place were absent.'[11] The report recommended Brick By Brick continued to trade, finishing building and selling off their existing schemes and the council writing off the debt.

At the start of 2020, I'd taken a look at some Brick by Brick houses being built near where I'd grown up in New Addington. They were a curious bunch, tacked onto the back wall of a massive new Leisure and Community Centre. Out front, the bulky buff brick structure contained a café, gym, pool and community hall, with a sports hall on the top floor housed in a huge light box overhanging the plaza out front, like an invading spaceship from *Independence Day*. Oh my goodness, I realised as I stood there on that misty winter morning, the glowing box looming out of the grey above me – New Addington has only gone and got itself an icon. Not a real icon, obviously, it is not the V&A Dundee and no one would be able to pick it out of a line-up as a signifier of an actual place. But it's a wannabe, a *Big Brother* house, gleaming and massive, lording it over the shops and flats and semi-detached houses around, a box of bling promising transformation and glamour. Inside, the pools are beautifully finished, the gym and sports hall huge, the café the perfect place for a spot of gossip and a flapjack. It's the enormous windowless community hall that residents I spoke to were up in arms about – £100 an hour to hire, closing at 10 p.m., no alcohol licence, two security people needed to be hired for every event. Hopeless for birthdays and weddings. Quite a change from the tiddly toddler- friendly 1950s hall next door that it has replaced, with its air of poster paint, lametta and sausage rolls. As a result, people were taking their parties elsewhere, to the local rugby club and beyond – or at least they were before lockdown hit.

The centre is the work of sport and leisure specialist architects GT3, who have offices in Newcastle and Nottingham, and have designed many similar facilities for Oldham, Hornchurch, Redcar, Morden and Dover, among others. Construction giant Willmott Dixon built and landscaped the centre. Their hoarding facing the estate's parade of shops read 'Building Lives Less Ordinary' – a strange out-of-touch throwback to the title of a little-loved Britpop-era road movie starring Ewan McGregor. But the least ordinary touch is out the back of the building, where, clinging to the brick facade, those eight single-aspect flat-fronted brick town houses were going up, roof terraces cowering beneath 414 a vast wall of air vents from the pool and gym. This is the kind

Houses built onto the back of New Addington's new Leisure and Community Centre.

of hybrid multi-use development being encouraged by cash-strapped councils the country over. Assets are being monetised, and as quickly as possible. Here, the houses don't feel like part of the original design, but an attempt to make some quick bucks back to help offset the cost of this enormous new facility. The many years I lived in New Addington, there were three main problems: it was – and remains – impoverished, transport was hopeless – which the arrival of Tramlink has helped fix – and there wasn't much to do. The new leisure centre is in many ways a great thing for an estate that has struggled since it was created with a lack of distractions.

But, ultimately, is the leisure centre in New Addington a distraction in itself, much as the creation of bolder and more famous icons have largely been across the UK? Is it a sleight of hand, hiding the real issues behind a veil of pomp and 415 sparkle? Usually, those icons are detached from the realities of housing and our normal lives. The Shard doesn't care if people are homeless as long as they are not sleeping around its base; Beetham Tower's flats are deliberately the very opposite of council housing of a previous generation of high-rise. But at New Addington Leisure Centre, an icon on a budget, it is trying to do everything at once. It wants to be a bit of magic and dazzle. It wants to be civic and responsible. It wants to be friendly and approachable. And it also wants to sneak in some council-built housing literally round the back. Which, in a housing crisis, and with such pressure on local authorities to make money, is perfectly understandable. Certainly, the pressure for councils is to urbanise. Yet the basic drift of the last ten years would lead anyone to the conclusion that good things are generally not happening to people in poor areas like New Addington. So what is the new leisure centre all about? It seems clear – it is to free up the land round about to build on. Farewell ex-swimming pool, gym and community centre, hello large brownfield site to redevelop as tightly packed urban housing. Relics of post-war civic investment like libraries and pools are all vulnerable to this spirit of monetisation, and the people who have made this happen – the developers and politicians who see all of this in terms of profit – want the rest of us to see it like that too. To resent the generosity of the post-war settlement, to see every relic of civic largesse as a *Grand Designs* project waiting to happen. One of the grim ironies is that as the council slides into bankruptcy, one of the areas they'll find harder to fund is leisure centres. Here is an echo of Birmingham, who demolished their beautiful brutalist central library, replaced it with a fancy new one by Mecanoo, just as austerity hit, and ran out of money to fund it full time. Croydon and Birmingham, odd cousins continuing their mirrored existence.

Back when I spoke to Finn Williams about his time working for Croydon in the early noughties, he had an interesting thought about whether trying to change the town's boom and bust ways was not so much a lost cause as even desirable. 'It's always had this kind of slightly schizophrenic approach to how ambitious it's going to be or how conservative it's going to be,' he said. 'That is what makes it such a fascinating place, because it's full of those contradictions. It's not like it's ever had a coherent plan carried out here. And maybe that's part of the character of Croydon, that the unfinished and probably the overambitious is part of what makes Croydon really special. And our job as urban designers is not to try and change that because it's baked into its position in the world, but is to celebrate and make the most of it and make it work.' His role then had been at the bottom of the heap, so these dramatic political cycles happened way above him, but he'd seen enough to know how the town has operated for the last two centuries. 'I wouldn't be surprised if Croydon continues to get caught up and repeat its own cycle of mistakes. And that builds more layers in the future. I don't think it's possible for it to keep up that momentum that it's had over the last ten years for another ten years.' Yet as Covid changes the demographics of the city and people move out of central London, Croydon will end up playing an important role regardless. 'There will still be interest and pressure on Croydon,' said Finn. 'And it's just whether politically they can sustain that kind of ambition over such a long period of time.'

I'd love the leisure centre to be a success, and for it to have a hugely positive impact on the community in New Addington; and a reimagined Brick By Brick to be a winner too, building ethically and effectively, making great homes for the people of Croydon and money for the cash-strapped council; the centre of Croydon to recover from the Covid crisis and celebrate its resilience, and 417 not always seek to sweep its past away; Charles Holland's public square to get built, with its crazy kiosks, public art and trees sprouting from a hidden lower storey; more reuse and less demolition, as we attempt to tackle the climate emergency; the solution for Croydon's future to come from smaller projects rather than a constant desire for sweeping change; for the smokescreen of austerity to be a thing of the past; and to think that these things will not always be met with cynicism and dismissiveness; to walk through Croydon and feel hope and excitement rather than worry and regret. As I write, vaccines are making incredible inroads against the Covid pandemic, and there is a sense of hope that a new sort of life will be possible beyond all the lockdowns and social distancing. We need to make sure it will be better than the one we have left.

'It was a party day,' recalled architect Elsie Owusu. Number 60 Aden Grove, the low-energy house she'd designed with the artist Peter Blake and pioneering Passivhaus maker Martin Peat, was being delivered on site in Hackney on a low-loader in prefabricated chunks. 'Everybody was out in the road saying *told you it'd be a nuisance*,' she said. It took just three days to erect the house. 'And when it was finished they were all like *why didn't you tell us it was going to be nice?* And I think this is a lesson in architects not being able to speak human.' She had fond words about Martin Peat, whose Passivhaus engineering made the house possible. 'When the Bedford car businesses closed down,' said Owusu, 'what he did was took people from the car plant into his factory and designed a system that was more like making cars than it was making houses. He built the house in the factory, he did a full-scale prototype so the clients could come and look at it and walk around it.' The neighbours, so wary at first, ended up approving of their work. 'We had them over for a glass of champagne once it was finished,' recalls Owusu, 'and they were all like *oh, we want to live in a house like this*. And we were like *of course you do, darling!*'

Owusu is one of the signatories of UK Architects Declare Climate and Biodiversity Emergency, a public and concerted declaration of intent written in 2019. When I last checked, it had been signed by 1,255 companies, including giants like Populous and Arup, mid-sized companies like Page\Park and Alison Brooks Architects and small practices such as Living Space in Exeter and Freehaus in London. Many were experimenting with low-carbon development, a move on from those nods to sustainability of the nineties. Architects Declare was founded by Steve   419

Tompkins of Haworth Tompkins, alongside Michael Pawlyn, one of the original designers of the Eden Project, and their website lays bare the issues at stake: 'Buildings and construction [account] for nearly 40 per cent of energy-related carbon dioxide (CO_2) emissions whilst also having a significant impact on our natural habitats.'[1] Back in 2010 it was estimated that London's ecological footprint was 125 times its surface area, and if everyone on Earth all used the same resources as residents and businesses in Bristol we would require an extra couple of Earths to sustain us.[2] But what has the declaration meant? Some of the signatories, including Foster + Partners, Zaha Hadid Architects and Grimshaw, have since designed new airports and ZHA had also designed the kind of mega-office complex in Shanghai that was being criticised by Architects Declare. Fig leaves of greenwashing – green roofs on luxury housing towers, green strips on pedestrian bridges, green walls on office blocks – are still slathered over plans requiring massive amounts of steel, glass and concrete. Meanwhile, the consequences of sudden environmental change are having both direct and indirect effects on our homes – from flooded towns to moorland fires, overwhelmed sea defences and fast-changing coastline. We all need to change our ways – but clearly some more than others. In the face of environmental catastrophe, what can architects, builders and planners do that doesn't simply present superficial solutions to problems that affect us all on the most profound level? Perhaps, we shrug, the impact of being alive is simply to make matters worse.

The 2010s may not have been a glorious decade for Britain. Austerity in all its guises has robbed much of the generosity and joy from our towns. Tax-shy online businesses have hollowed out our high streets. While the Olympics produced a moment of spectacle, the tragedy at Grenfell has cast a much longer shadow over our public life. A shortage in housing has had profound effects on a younger generation and the poorer residents of rich cities. Meanwhile, a rise in cheap divisive politics has made us a more turbulent place. Talk of a Northern Powerhouse and 'levelling up' society needs to turn to deeds. Yet despite all this, there have been glimmers of hope. The return of socially conscious architecture, encapsulated in the work of Peter Barber, Mikhail Riches, Cathy Hawley and Karakusevic Carson, has given reason for optimism. After decades of shame being heaped on the notion of council-house building and social housing more generally, these and other like-minded architects have begun to change those lazy preconceptions. This is now the most exciting sector in architecture, attracting the most creative and thoughtful young practitioners against the grain of a national narrative of turbo-charged Thatcherism we are sold today. With that come guerrilla tactics dismantling some of the props of our planning system, from reducing car parking to narrowing roads and increasing density, all of which foreshadow the changes we need to make as a society. Councils building their own housing is also something to cheer, despite the complex and problematic politics and finances of them. Here's hoping the next wave can learn from the mistakes of Croydon and start to make really positive strides towards tackling our housing crisis. Councils can bring unity and scale to these projects if they can learn to use their powers effectively. Architects Declare, while not yet the most powerful organisation, will hopefully lead us somewhere better, provoking a rise in environmental standards across architecture and construction and bringing about a philosophical change in our attitude to new builds versus the creative reuse of old buildings. Then there's the improvisational chutzpah of collectives like Assemble, with their modern reinvention of arts and crafts ideals, working across disciplines with a social mission far beyond the confines of the briefs they are given. What was achieved at

Granby is a tribute not just to them, but to the ingenuity, vision and bloody-mindedness of the residents. If one thing could be taken from this period as inspiration for the next, the rebirth of Granby stands as a moving symbol of the power of communities working together, and the reminder that the solutions to our problems do not always have to come from the top. Not that this is a way of letting those with money or power off the hook. We need to remember that the success of the things we build lies not just in the financial profit generated but in the ongoing social success of them too, as well as in the environmental impact of their construction and life. For many, the 2010s have been a lost decade. But for some its instability has created opportunities to reset, experiment, and imagine a better way of life.

The robots came to Milton Keynes in April 2018. Small white buggies about the size of a Labrador, I'd encounter them trundling around the town's pedestrian Redway path network or nipping in and out of alleyways and over footbridges, illuminated orange pennant waggling atop their aerials. Get too near and they stop abruptly, sensors set to avoid damage or lawsuits. I'd seen one plunge into a lake, which made me worry about driverless cars, also due for trials in the town. By 2020, Milton Keynes had a couple of hundred of these plastic buggies, the largest fleet of autonomous robots in the world, delivering prescriptions and food during the pandemic. Starship Technologies, the suitably other-worldly named San Francisco tech firm, had chosen Milton Keynes for their UK pilot because its planned grid of roads and paths made navigation simpler for the small autonomous trucks.

The robots feel charming or sinister, depending upon your state of mind when happening upon them. Usually I find them a cheery sight, their purposeful plastic trundle as fixedly resolute as a Lego minifig's grin. But in the modern plaza and underpasses of Milton Keynes Station Square, their presence feels rather more disturbing. For a time, a small homeless encampment had grown up in what was called Tent City. By 2018 the town had the worst youth homelessness rate in the country, despite having the fourth highest average earnings of any place in Britain. It also had the highest proportion of homes bought under Right to Buy of any British town – an astonishing 71 per cent compared to a national average of 40 – and with all those buy-to-let landlords, accommodation is notoriously unaffordable for those on low incomes or benefits. The resulting landscape was one of personal and social heartbreak, commuters hurrying past the tents and sleeping bags of those forced to sleep rough, suddenly joined by robots, weaving around people and possessions like an experiment in techno-medievalism. These were glimpses of a future where smart cities meet our messy and imperfect lives. Robots, drones, driverless cars and deliveries by zero-hour employees all threaten to replace age-old patterns of human interaction and employment in ways that would have seemed laughably fantastical a few years before.

The Covid-19 pandemic has further changed our relationship with the world we have built. For those lucky enough to have a home to be locked down in, be it bloated overextended suburban zeppelin or tiny micro-flat, it has forced us to become more intimate with our surroundings than we might have ever expected. We've all read thousands of words clumsily comparing the crisis to the Second World War, but some aspects do bear a likeness. And they are our inequalities, and how we hope to address them. In 1945, with a desire to build a better world, there was a drive for council housing for all; for the construction of new towns and demolition of slums; a welfare state to keep us safe in moments of hardship; and a National Health Service. It has struck me more than once over the course of researching and writing this book that in some ways the period 1980–2020 represents the mirror image of the post-war era. The pattern may be as symmetrical as butterfly wings, but the consequences are not pretty. In the last four decades, that high tide has receded and we have crept back towards the conditions and mentality of the 1930s, that faded hangover of Victorian patronage with notions of the deserving and undeserving poor; a lack of safety net for people in times of trouble; a period of racial and social divisiveness. Not the gleaming streamlined moderne of cruise ships and railway posters, but the seedy claustrophobia and shabbiness of boarding houses in Patrick Hamilton novels or the crumbling working-class housing depicted in the paintings of the East London Group.

For much of the period since 1980, we have striven for an idea of perfection. For the Thatcherites it was something the market would deliver, for New Labour the renaissance would arrive through targets and checklists, for the austerity governments of the 2010s deregulation and nudges were to show the way. But ultimately, all of these notions have been folly. The market let developers take over the role that local authorities once had in creating mass housing, and they failed to fill that gap. New Labour targets attempted to game the system through culture-led regeneration, telling us that if it looked okay then it was okay. And the retreat from government responsibility and funding in the austerity years has left a Wild West of corruption, temporary patches and devastating personal burdens. The most successful aspects of these times have been those that have either had a community focus – be it Granby's Turner-winning ambition, BedZED's eco credentials or Peter Barber's socialist values in brick – or dazzling ambition – from the Gherkin's revolutionary design, the Dome's lightweight structure or the exuberant riot of postmodern design. The least successful – Poundbury's tepid nostalgia, Persimmon's penny-pinching estates, the dead plazas of Docklands – attempt to evoke an idea of history that is bogus and a future that is denied.

The first symbol to make a splash in the midst of the pandemic would be found at the heart of the Nine Elms development at Battersea Power Station, a super-rich enclave that had been growing throughout the previous decade. Here there was a new US Embassy designed by KieranTimberlake, and blocks drawn up by big names including Rogers Stirk Harbour, Frank Gehry and Make, with some of the master-planning undertaken by 425

Terry Farrell. So irrelevant to the lives of most people was this huge development that it had largely passed unremarked – until, that is, the arrival of the sky pool. The clear acrylic infinity pool at Embassy Gardens bridges two expensive new blocks. Images of those affluent few experiencing this hyped-up elevated aqueduct filled the media in June 2021, the ultimate in isolation chic. I hope it has a transparent verruca bath too, for passers-below to enjoy. A month beforehand, its developers, Ballymore, had been in the news when another of their towers, New Providence Wharf in Poplar, suffered a major fire. It was a reminder that dreams of a luxurious future will not be enough to free us from the responsibilities of the present. In the meantime, hoardings at Embassy Gardens on a development calling itself Everything Nine Elms display uplifting mottos, including the slogan *Food, drink, fitness, art and chance encounters on a par with the best of everywhere*. Just savour that for a moment.

The transformations of the next few decades will be carried out by a younger generation of architects and planners, those coming through the education system now. I've been lucky enough to see the work of architects studying on Alison Davies's remarkable course at the University of Nottingham. Alison brings in ideas and lessons from council housing, new towns and post-war developments, be it Park Hill in Sheffield or the eco-homes of Milton Keynes, and introduces students to these often quite distant and alien concepts and the philosophies that lay behind them. The students are encouraged to apply strong social and ethical thinking to their work, and the designs they propose are remarkably powerful. Zero sky pools are a given. This is a spirit reflected in architectural courses across the country. If some of that energy and thoughtfulness filters through to our future homes and towns, we will be very lucky. Although 426 what we really need are courses to encourage ethical investment and development, because without that all the best intentions of architects are meaningless.

Travelling around Britain exploring the extraordinary – and sometimes all too ordinary – places we've created since 1980 has been a privilege, and one that lockdowns and Covid restrictions have reminded me not to take lightly. In the architecture of devolution – the Senedd, the Scottish Parliament – I saw an ambitious version of Britain that encapsulated a desire for positive change. In Liverpool I saw the resurrection of derelict streets by its most tenacious inhabitants. In suburbs and urban centres around Britain I saw the evolution of the developer's house, from the vernacular details of the *Essex Design Guide* to an explosion of faux-modern flats and flat-fronted brick. In my home town of Croydon I saw the efforts of an overambitious local authority to embrace change, from hipster pop-ups to tech start-ups and new attempts to build council housing. At Grenfell and Lakanal House I saw communities torn apart by the neglect of the people and structures meant to keep them safe. I saw out-of-town malls and business parks, and the strange secretive landscape of infrastructure that they represent. I saw extraordinary postmodern edifices, from the *Metropolis* excesses of MI6 to the shy bulk of the Leeds Look. In Manchester, a sense of cultural restlessness reinvented the city centre, from ghost town to bustling cool. And in old ex-local authority houses I saw how the municipal dreams of their builders had been converted into the private profits of buy-to-let landlords. And in all of those icons – some would-be, some legit – I encountered the dreams of the age writ large, for good or ill.

For me, it has been a journey filled with revelatory moments and unexpected discoveries brought to life by the generosity of the people who spoke to me about their lives and work. It is a reminder that all around us, in every street and home, no matter 427 how unpromising, there lie remarkable tales of ingenuity, and often absurdity. Lockdown gave us a moment to consider the riches – and poverty – on our doorsteps, to notice the strange ways our neighbourhoods have grown up, and the peculiar things we have done to them over time. It's a reminder that these things might start with politicians and planners and architects, but they end with us, the residents and workers, the managers and maintenance crews attempting to adapt to these new environments. None of these landscapes exists in the abstract, and none is a success or failure without our lived experience to prove them. Everything – be it Barratt starter home, waterside flat, flashy museum or retail park – has a story. And as soon as you notice it, you become part of that story too.

Acknowledgements

A book like this is very much a collaborative effort, and I would first and foremost like to thank all of the interviewees who gave up their time to help me make some kind of sense of where I was going and what I was looking at. I'd like to dedicate it in particular to Gaby Charing, who died in 2020, leaving behind her partner, Liz Day. I'd like to express my gratitude to Jonathan Adams, Helen Angel, Peter Barber, Irena Bauman, Leigh Bird, Shane Brownie, Adam Bunn, Emma Dent Coad, Paul Collard, Linda Cress, Andrew Cross, Russell Curtis, Mike Davies, Pooran Desai, Peter Elliott, David Ellis, Terry Farrell, Catherine Flinn, Sara Fox, Jack Hale, Michael Heseltine, Peter Higgins, Charles Holland, Ronnie Hughes, Simon Lee, David Lock, Peter and Peggy Logan, David McNish, Kirsteen McNish, Matt Morris, Katrina Navickas, Elsie Owusu, Andrew Partridge, Manisha Patel, James Perry, Carla Picardi, John Ramsay, Janette Ray, Eddy Rhead, Janice Richardson, Martin Richman, Deborah Sugg Ryan, Clifford Stead, Lynne Strutt, Dan Thompson, Marc Vlessing, Shirley Walker, Laura Wilkins and Finn Williams. I'd also like to thank all of the photographers who kindly let me use their excellent work. As far as I am aware, the information was correct at the time of writing, but I am sure that the news will outpace me by the time the book is in the wild. The pandemic reduced my capacity to travel, meet with interviewees and explore archives to some extent, but I hope the resulting book still holds up.

A number of brilliant organisations exist to support the built environment and communities. If you have time, I would recommend looking up the Twentieth Century Society, the manchester modernist society, Something Concrete + Modern and Docomomo.   429

There are also incredible campaigning groups, such as Save Cressingham Gardens, Save Central Hill and the Architects Climate Action Network, and in Granby there is the successful community-run market and workshop. The work on housing and homelessness carried out by Shelter, Crisis, Centrepoint and The Big Issue, along with many other local organisations, has been a vital source of hope for many in difficult circumstances, and all deserve our respect and continued support. I would also urge you to support the work and cause of the Grenfell survivors, through Justice4Grenfell and Grenfell United.

Lots of people have helped hugely with the research for this book, in particular Mike Althorpe, James Bainbridge, John Boughton, Susannah Charlton, Catherine Croft, Alison Davies, Laura Davies, Richard de Pesando, Steven Downes, Tim Dunn, Tom Dyckhoff, Hannah Griffiths, Lynsey Hanley, Colin Harvey, Molly Ker Hawn, Jason Hazeley, Alison Inman, Susan Le Baigue, Alex Linsdell, Peter Matthews, Andy Miller, Ana Moldavsky, Richard Pulford, Lorna Rees, Deirdre Rustling, Amy Ryall, Hayley Sothinathan, James Ward, Tom Watkins, Joseph Watson, Sarah Wickens, Emma-Louise Williams, Richard Woods, Alexandra Young and Zoe at the Archie Parker. I would also like to pay respect to Dawn Foster, whose campaigning journalism continues to be an inspiration.

Love to all those at Faber for making this happen, especially my exceptionally kind and skilful editor Fred Baty, and Lee Brackstone, who took a punt on the book in the first place. There's the beautiful cover design by Donna Payne and page layouts by Kate Ward, along with Jenni Davis's heroic copy-editing, Sarah Barlow's proofreading, Mark Bolland's indexing, Pedro Nelson's production work, Hannah Marshall's marketing and Lauren Nicoll's publicity, which have all been brilliant.

430 Special thanks too to Rachel Alexander, Andrew Benbow,

Niriksha Bharadia, Sam Brown and team, Mary Cannam, Benedetta Costantini, Catherine Daly, Rachel Darling, Ella Griffiths, Katie Hall, Laura Hassan, Jess Kim, Sarah Lough, Kim Lund, Kelly Martin and team, Stephen Page, Sian Rokita-Evans, Sara Talbot, Phoebe Williams, Dave Woodhouse and to everyone at Faber who has worked on the book, I really appreciate it. I'd also like to thank the bookshops, libraries, archives, festivals and arts organisations who have supported my books, had me to talk, and allowed me to make a nuisance of myself.

Lastly, I'd like to thank my partner, Adam Nightingale, for all of the support and help throughout the writing of this book during the pandemic, and to his mother, Ann, and sister, Jane. Love and thanks too for my brothers Ian and Paul, sister-in-law Fern, nieces Lily and Daisy, nephew Ant and godson Dylan, inspirations all. And to Nicola Barr, friend and agent, for making any of this happen at all.

Most of all, thank you for reading.

References

Introduction

1 *Guardian*, 17 June 1980, p. 4.

PART 1: PENTHOUSE AND PAVEMENT

Docklands: Before

1 PLA report in *The Times*, 15 June 1978, p. 16.
2 Tom Dyckhoff, *The Age of Spectacle* (Random House Books, 2017), p. 52.
3 Ted Johns, *East London Advertiser*, 29 January 1971.
4 Janet Foster, *Docklands: Cultures in Conflict, Worlds in Collision* (UCL, 1999), p. 260.

1: New Blue Dreams

1 conservativehome.com/thetorydiary/ 2014/how-thatcher-sold-council-houses-and-created-a-new-generation-of-property-owners.
2 *Daily Telegraph*, 6 December 1978, p. 12.
3 Pablo Bronstein, *Pseudo-Georgian London* (Koenig Books, 2017), p. 34.
4 *Daily Telegraph*, 23 February 1981, p. 10.
5 *Another Chance for Cities: Shelter Neighbourhood Action Project*, Shelter, 1972, p. 53.
6 Shelter, p. 9.
7 Shelter, p. 212.
8 Shelter, p. 213.
9 Andy Beckett, *Promised You a Miracle* (Penguin, 2016), p. 68.
10 Beckett, p. 70.
11 'Thatcher Urged "Let Liverpool Decline" after 1981 Riots,' bbc.co.uk, 30 December 2011.

12 *Guardian*, 3 May 1984, p. 26.
13 *Guardian*, 9 March 1985, p. 1.
14 *Observer*, 23 May 1982, p. 17.
15 *Daily Telegraph*, 17 July 1987, p. 13.
16 Alice Coleman in *Utopia London* (film, dir: Tom Cordell), 2010.
17 Elizabeth Wilson, *The Sphinx in the City*, Virago, 1991, p. 153.
18 Chris Moores, 'Thatcher's troops? Neighbourhood Watch schemes and the search for "ordinary" Thatcherism in 1980s Britain', in *Contemporary British History*, Volume 31, 2017 – Issue 2: New Times revisited: Britain in the 1980s, pp. 230–55.
19 Moores, pp. 230–55.
20 Moores, pp. 230–55.
21 *Observer*, 20 July 1980, p. 33.
22 *Independent*, 21 October 1989, p. 40.

Docklands: Romance

1 *The Times*, 27 October 1987, p. 12.
2 'CZWG Has Another Postmodern Landmark Listed,' *Architects' Journal*, 18 April 2018.
3 Reg Ward in Janet Foster, *Docklands: Cultures in Conflict, Worlds in Collision* (UCL, 1999), p. 57.
4 Ward, p. 63.

2: Fruiting Up a Whole Concoction

1 Charles Jencks, *AD News Supplement*, July 1981, p. 4.
2 Kenneth Frampton, *AD News Supplement*, July 1981, p. 2.
3 *AD News Supplement*, July 1981, p. 13.
4 Alice Coleman, *AD* 10–11, 1986, p. 70.
5 'Whitehall leads the exodus from London,' *The Times*, 12 October 1992.
6 *Daily Mail*, 5 August 1993, p. 7.

7 *Independent*, 13 August 1993, p. 17.

Docklands: Rent

1 *Observer*, 2 August 1981, p. 2.
2 *Observer*, 2 August 1981, p. 2.
3 *Guardian*, 20 August 1981, p. 22.
4 *The Times*, 27 February 1982, p. 2.
5 *Independent*, 7 December 1987, p. 3.
6 'Facelift that's worth a fortune,' John Brennan, *Financial Times*, 13 December 1986.

3: The Chatsworth, the Queensborough, the York

1 Barratt 1958–2018 commemorative brochure, 2018, p. 42.
2 *Observer*, 27 January 1980, p. 22.
3 Fred Wellings, *British Housebuilders* (Blackwell, 2006), p. 155.
4 Wellings, p. 86.
5 Ideal Homes Goldsworth Park brochure, 1982, p. 8.
6 *Observer*, 28 September 1997, p. 37.
7 *Daily Telegraph*, 23 November 1988, p. 39.
8 *A Design Guide for Residential Areas*, County Council of Essex, 1973, p. 19.
9 County Council of Essex, p. 15.
10 County Council of Essex, p. 15.
11 County Council of Essex, p. 89.
12 County Council of Essex, p. 61.
13 County Council of Essex, p. 62.
14 County Council of Essex, p. 69.
15 County Council of Essex, p. 90.
16 County Council of Essex, p. 132.
17 *Independent*, 17 February 1990, p. 40.
18 *Independent*, 17 February 1990, p. 40.
19 *Independent*, 17 February 1990, p. 40.
20 *Daily Telegraph*, 6 December 1989, p. 32.
21 *The Times*, 25 May 1998, p. 9.
22 Barratt 1958–2018 commemorative brochure, 2018, p. 46.
23 *Guardian*, 13 March 1982, p. 24.

24 *The Times*, 6 May 1985, p. 2.
25 Pablo Bronstein, *Pseudo-Georgian London*, Koenig Books, 2017, p. 13.
26 Bronstein, p. 30.
27 Danny Dorling, *All That is Solid: How the Great Housing Disaster Defines Our Times, and What We Can Do About It*, Allen Lane, 2014, p. 35.
28 *Guardian*, 14 March 1980, p. 17.
29 *Guardian*, 6 August 1985, p. 1.

Docklands: Canaries

1 *Guardian*, 3 July 1981, p. 15.
2 *Guardian*, 26 November 1985, p. 24.
3 *Guardian*, 26 November 1985, p. 24.
4 Stephen Gardiner, *Observer*, 13 October 1985, p. 25.
5 *AD* Vol 58 11–12, 1988, p. 10.
6 *Guardian*, 7 October 1985, p. 19.
7 *Guardian*, 7 October 1985, p. 19.
8 Peter Wade in Janet Foster, *Docklands: Cultures in Conflict, Worlds in Collision* (UCL, 1999), p. 149.
9 Wade, p. 150.
10 Reg Ward in Janet Foster, *Docklands: Cultures in Conflict, Worlds in Collision* (UCL, 1999), p. 150.
11 *Architects' Journal*, 19 October 1988, p. 60.

4: The Prince and the Paupers

1 HRH The Prince of Wales, *A Vision of Britain* (Doubleday, 1989), p. 153.
2 *Daily Telegraph*, 31 May 1984, p. 3.
3 *Daily Telegraph*, 31 May 1984, p. 3.
4 *Daily Telegraph*, 1 June 1984, p. 21.
5 HRH The Prince of Wales, p. 9.
6 *Daily Telegraph*, 1 June 1984, p. 21.
7 HRH The Prince of Wales, p. 7.
8 HRH The Prince of Wales, p. 7.
9 HRH The Prince of Wales, p. 7.
10 *Daily Telegraph*, 31 May 1984, p. 3.
11 Marco Iuliano, *One Poultry Speaks* (Liverpool University Press, 2017), p. 20.

12 *Daily Telegraph*, 21 September 1984, p. 19.

13 Mark Girouard, *Big Jim* (Chatto and Windus, 1998), p. 260.

14 *Daily Telegraph*, 12 March 1986, p. 13.

15 *Daily Telegraph*, 12 March 1986, p. 13.

16 *A Vision of Britain*: scripts from the series in AD Vol 58 11–12, 1988, p. 8.

17 HRH The Prince of Wales, p. 73.

18 HRH The Prince of Wales, p. 155.

19 Speech to the Institute of SocioEconomic Studies, 15 September 1975.

20 *Guardian*, 4 April 1988, p. 3.

21 Homelessness: Report by the Comptroller and Auditor General, HMSO, 1990.

22 Michelle Beauchamp, *On the Streets* (Harrap, 1989).

23 *Guardian*, 23 November 1988, p. 25.

24 *Guardian*, 23 November 1988, p. 25.

25 Beauchamp, p. 38.

26 Beauchamp, p. 45.

27 *The Times*, 13 April 1989, p. 12.

28 *The Times*, 31 December 1988, p. 3.

29 *Observer*, 8 January 1989, p. B5.

30 *The Times*, 29 October 1990, p. 4.

31 HRH The Prince of Wales, p. 139.

32 Deyan Sudjic, *Foster Rogers Stirling* (Thames and Hudson, 1986), p. 112.

33 *AD*, Vol 59 5–6, 1989, p. 7.

34 *Daily Telegraph*, 2 September 1999, p. 1.

35 'My Own Private Metropolis,' *Financial Times*, 9 August 2008.

36 *Daily Telegraph*, 11 July 1998, p. 18.

37 Beauchamp, p. 17.

38 HRH The Prince of Wales, p. 107.

Docklands: Towers

1 *AD* Vol 58 11–12, 1988, p. 43.

2 *AD* Vol 58 11–12, 1988, p. 41.

3 *AD* Vol 58 11–12, 1988, p. 41.

4 Kenneth Powell, *New London Architecture* (Merrell, 2001), p. 15.

5: Out-of-towners

1 *Guardian*, 7 August 1989.

2 *Guardian*, 7 August 1989.

3 *Western Daily Press*, 15 December 1989, p. 9.

4 *Western Daily Press*, 15 December 1989, p. 9.

5 *The Times*, 13 January 1987, p. 10.

6 *The Times*, 13 January 1987, p. 10.

7 *The Times*, 22 September 1984, p. 21.

8 *The Times*, 23 April 1987, p. 21.

Docklands: Ghosts

1 *Independent*, 7 December 1987, p. 3.

PART 2: FOR TOMORROW

Millennium: Transformations

1 'Art at the Seaside,' *Independent*, 6 June 1997.

2 *Guardian*, 27 December 1999, p. B10.

6: Unfinished City

1 *Guardian*, 9 December 1987, p. 25.

2 Ray King, *Detonation: Rebirth of a City* (Clear Publications, 2006), p. 114.

3 King, p. 114.

4 *Observer*, 16 June 1996, p. 1.

5 King, p. 31.

6 King, p. 140.

7 King, p. 61.

8 *Guardian*, 22 November 1999, p. 8.

9 *Guardian*, 22 November 1999, p. 8.

10 *Observer*, 21 September 2003, p. 39.

11 *Observer*, 21 September 2003, p. 39.

12 *Observer*, 1 December 2002, p. B19.

13 Emile Raphael, In Residence: Ian Simpson, YouTube, 2016

14 King, p. 218.

15 'The Estate We're In,' *Guardian*, 24 February 2007.

16 *Guardian*, 15 February 1999, p. 16.

17 *Observer*, 29 September 2002, p. 3.

18 'Dream Homes Now a Nightmare,'

Manchester Evening News, 18 April 2010.

19 'The Estate We're In,' *Guardian*, 24 February 2007.

20 *The Times*, 27 March 2009, p. 8.[S1]

Millennium: Renaissance

1 Hansard, 16 November 2000, vol 356 cc1089–104.

2 'Trouble Up North As Apartment Prices Slump,' Alexander Garrett, *Observer*, 9 March 2008.

3 Andrew Tallon, *Urban Regeneration in the UK* (Routledge, 2010), p. 208.

4 Powell, p. 22.

5 *Observer*, 29 December 1996, p. 11.

6 John Boughton, *Municipal Dreams* (Verso, 2018), p. 203.

7 *Daily Telegraph*, 15 July 1987, p. 13.

8 *Daily Telegraph*, 15 July 1987, p. 13.

9 *The Times*, 31 January 2003, p. 6.[S1]

10 *The Times*, 30 November 2007, p. 6.[S1]

11 *The Times*, 30 November 2007, p. 6.[S1]

12 *The Times*, 30 November 2007, p. 6.[S1]

7: One Amazing Night

1 *AD*, Wonderworld Supplement, 9 / 10 1982, p. 2.

2 *AD*, Wonderworld Supplement, 9 / 10 1982, p. 48.

3 *AD*, Wonderworld Supplement, 9 / 10 1982, p. 38.

4 *AD*, Wonderworld Supplement, 9 / 10 1982, p. 3.

5 *AD*, Wonderworld Supplement, 9 / 10 1982, p. 11.

6 *AD*, Wonderworld Supplement, 9 / 10 1982, p. 10.

7 Adam Nicolson, *Regeneration* (HarperCollins, 1999), p. 9.

8 *Observer*, 3 December 1995, p. 19.

9 Nicolson, p. 28.

10 *Guardian*, 12 December 1996, p. A2.

11 *Guardian*, 12 December 1996, p. A3.

12 *Observer*, 28 May 2000, p. 18.

13 Nicolson, p. 110.

14 *Guardian*, 28 February 1998, p. B6.

15 *Guardian*, 28 February 1998, p. B6.

16 *Guardian*, 28 February 1998, p. B6.

17 'A Battle Against Philistinism,' *Independent*, 29 September 1998.

18 *Observer*, 13 June 1999, p. D3.

19 *Observer*, 13 June 1999, p. D3.

20 *Observer*, 13 June 1999, p. D3.

21 *Daily Telegraph*, 20 December 1999, p. 3.

22 *Guardian*, 1 January 2000, p. 3.

23 *Daily Telegraph*, 3 December 2000, p. 21.

24 *Observer*, 30 January 2000, p. 12.

25 *Observer*, 30 January 2000, p. 12.

26 *Observer*, 10 September 2000, p. 17.

Millennium: Ecologies

1 *building.co.uk*, 22 October 2019.

2 *bbc.co.uk/news* 17 October 2019.

3 *Guardian*, 25 January 2003, p. C67.

4 *Guardian*, 25 January 2003, p. C67.

5 *Observer*, 19 January 2003, p. G52.

6 *Observer*, 4 August 2002, p. 46.

7 *Observer*, 4 August 2002, p. 47.

8 Tallon, p. 168.

9 *Guardian*, 25 January 2003, p. C68.

10 *Observer*, 27 February 1977, p. 23.

11 *Energy World Official Guide*, Milton Keynes Development Corporation, 1986, p. 4.

12 Tallon, p. 157.

13 *Guardian*, 24 September 1996, p. 7.

8: The Impossible Dream

1 Mark Thompson in Hugh Mackay (ed.), *Understanding Contemporary Wales*, Open University and University of Wales Publishing, 2010, p. 292.

2 Albena Yaneva, *Mapping*

Controversies in Architecture (Routledge), p. xii.

3 *Guardian*, 13 December 2001, p. 10.

4 Alan Powers, *Britain*, Reaktion, 2007, p. 224.

5 'Rogers Wins in Cardiff With Low-Cost Scheme,', *Architects' Journal*, 22 October 1998.

6 David Ardill, *The Herald* (Glasgow), 26 October 1998, p. 17.

7 *Guardian*, 1 February 2003, p. 12.

8 *South Wales Evening Post*, 18 July 2001, p. 3.

9 *Western Mail*, 2 March 2006, p. 2.

10 'Supertower Lifts Belfast Skyline to New Heights,' *Belfast Telegraph*, 22 February 2005.

11 *The Times*, 7 July 2006, p. 6.[S1]

12 *The Times*, 7 July 2006, p. 6.[S1]

13 'Belfast Tower Rejection Sparks Row,' *Architects' Journal*, 14 January 2009.

14 *Belfast Telegraph*, 2 January 2010, p. 12.

15 *Belfast Telegraph*, 2 January 2010, p. 12.

16 'View From Penthouse of Ireland's Tallest Building,' *Belfast Telegraph*, 29 July 2010.

17 Susan Bain, *Holyrood: The Inside Story*, Edinburgh University Press, 2005, p. 34.

18 Douglas Fraser, *The Herald* (Glasgow), 22 February 2007, p. 15.

19 *The Herald* (Glasgow), 8 June 1998, p. 11.

20 'The Slow Ruin of Edinburgh,' *Prospect*, 16 March 2017.

21 *The Herald* (Glasgow), 7 July 1998, p. 8.

22 Bain, p. 58.

23 Bain, p. 62.

24 *The Herald* (Glasgow), 5 October 2002, p. 6.

25 Bain, p. 94.

26 Bain, p. 108.

27 Bain, p. 92.

28 Bain, p. 92.

29 Bain, p. 102.

30 *The Herald* (Glasgow), 28 August 2004, p. 26.

31 Charles Jencks, *The Iconic Building: The Power of Enigma* (Frances Lincoln, 2005), p. 119.

32 Miralles in Jencks, p. 119.

33 *The Herald* (Glasgow), 7 July 1998, p. 8.

34 Jencks, p. 127.

Millennium: Angel

1 'Glasgow – City of Culture 25 Years On,' *The Scotsman*, 27 September 2015.

2 'Glasgow – City of Culture 25 Years On,' *The Scotsman*, 27 September 2015.

3 Frank Gehry in Jencks, *The Iconic Building: The Power of Enigma*, p. 12.

4 Gehry in Jencks, p. 12.

5 Gehry in Jencks, p. 9.

6 *Guardian*, 24 June 2002, pp. B12–14.

7 *Guardian*, 12 July 2002, p. 5.

8 *Guardian*, 12 July 2002, p. 5.

9 *Guardian*, 24 May 2000, p. C4.

9: Icons Assemble!

1 Kenneth Powell, *30 St Mary Axe: A Tower for London* (Merrell, 2006), p. 63.

2 *Architects' Journal*, 20 January 2011, p. 25.

3 Powell, p. 37.

4 *Building the Gherkin*, Condor Films/icanfilms, 2006.

5 Richard Rogers with Richard Brown, *A Place for All People* (Canongate, 2017), p. 81.

6 Rogers with Brown, p. 85.

7 Colin Davies, *High Tech Architecture* (Thames and Hudson, 1988), p. 6.

8 Rogers with Brown, p. 87.

9 Rogers with Brown, p. 87.

10 Alan Powers, *Britain*, Reaktion, 2007, p. 213.

11 *Guardian*, 11 December 1996, p. 2.

12 *Guardian*, 12 June 2000, p. 7.

13 Guardian, 30 June 2000, p. C5.

14 *Observer*, 29 December 1996, p. 11.

15 Jencks, p. 43.

16 Richard Rogers and Renzo Piano, 'Architecture', *AD*, May 1975, pp. 276–77.

17 Rogers with Brown, p. 8.

18 Denise Scott Brown, 'Room at the Top? Sexism and the Star System in Architecture,' *AD* Vol 60 1–2, 1990, p. ix.

19 Denise Scott Brown, 'Room at the Top? Sexism and the Star System in Architecture,' *AD* Vol 60 1–2, 1990, p. x.

20 Powell, p. 23.

21 *Architects' Journal*, 20 January 2011, p. 33.

22 'Walkie Talkie architect "didn't realise it was going to be so hot"', *Guardian*, 6 September 2013.

23 Rogers with Brown, p. 169.

24 Ian Martin, 'The city that privatised itself to death: "London is now a set of improbable sex toys poking gormlessly into the air"', *Guardian*, 24 February 2015.

25 Tom Dyckhoff, *The Age of Spectacle* (Random House Books, 2017), p. 37.

Millennium: Legacy

1 *Guardian*, 18 November 1999, p. 24.

2 *Guardian*, 25 February 2002, p. D5.

3 Dyckhoff, p. 202.

4 Dyckhoff, p. 203.

5 *The Times*, 12 December 2008, p. 6.

6 *The Times*, 12 December 2008, p. 6.

PART 3: LITTLE DARK AGE

Austerity: Class

1 *Architects' Journal*, 9 August 2018, p. 10.

2 *Architects' Journal*, 7 April 2011, p. 21.

3 *Architects' Journal*, 28 April 2011, p. 25.

4 www.networkforeurope.eu/sea-change

10: London Ruins

1 Oliver Wainwright in Hilary Powell and Isaac Marrero-Guillamon (eds), *The Art of Dissent* (Marshgate Press, 2012), p. 275.

2 'Eastside Story: Westfield', *Architects' Journal*, September 2012, p. 9.

3 'Average house price in Newham slides again after record February,' *Newham Recorder*, 17 June 2021.

4 Anna Minton, *Ground Control* (Penguin, 2012 edition), p. xii.

5 'Anish Kapoor says addition to artwork was "foisted" on him by Boris Johnson,' *Guardian*, 26 April 2016.

6 *Guardian*, 9 July 1999, p. B2.

7 David Lodge, *Guardian*, 8 April 1988, p. 25.

8 *A Walk Around Queen Elizabeth Olympic Park*, Olympic Park Legacy Company, 2010, p. 6.

9 Olympic Park Legacy Company, p. 6.

10 Olympic Park Legacy Company, p. 10.

11 Olympic Park Legacy Company, p. 18.

12 'Londoners queue overnight in sub-zero temperatures to buy one bedroom flat for £400k', *Independent*, 23 January 2015.

13 Tim Burrows, 'Legacy, what legacy? Five years on the London Olympic

park battle still rages', *Guardian*, 27 July 2017.

14 *Architects' Journal*, 18 October 2007, p. 26.

15 *Architects' Journal*, 18 October 2007, p. 26.

16 *Architects' Journal*, 8 November 2018, p. 45.

17 *Architects' Journal*, 25 September 2015, p. 11.

18 Owen Hatherley, *The Ministry of Nostalgia* (Verso, 2016), p. 185.

19 Hatherley, p. 184.

Austerity: Fire

1 Mbet Udoaka, Lakanal Inquest Transcript Day 2, 15 January 2013.

2 Inquisition and Narrative Verdict for Catherine Hickman, 28 March 2013.

3 Inquisition and Narrative Verdict for Catherine Hickman, 28 March 2013.

4 Inquisition and Narrative Verdict for Catherine Hickman, 28 March 2013.

5 Inquisition and Narrative Verdict for Catherine Hickman, 28 March 2013.

6 Inquisition and Narrative Verdict for Catherine Hickman, 28 March 2013.

7 Inquisition and Narrative Verdict for Felipe Francisquini Cervi, 28 March 2013.

8 Eleanor Kelly letter to Frances Kirkham, 23 May 2013.

9 Frances Kirkham letter to Eric Pickles, 28 March 2013.

10 Eric Pickles letter to Frances Kirkham, 20 May 2013.

11 Eric Pickles letter to Frances Kirkham, 20 May 2013.

12 Joe Delaney in 'Grenfell Tower and Social Murder' (video), Introduction to Criminology (Open University, 2019).

13 grenfellactiongroup.wordpress.com/2016/11/20/kctmo-playing-with-fire/

14 grenfellactiongroup.wordpress.com/2016/11/20/kctmo-playing-with-fire/

15 Kate Macintosh in *Project Interrupted: Lectures by British Housing Architects* (Architecture Foundation, 2018), p. 188.

16 'Grenfell Tower: I "regret" my reaction, says Theresa May', bbc.co.uk, 11 June 2018.

17 David Cameron in Danny Dorling, *All That is Solid: How the Great Housing Disaster Defines Our Times, and What We Can Do About It* (Allen Lane, 2014), p. 45.

18 'Celotex manager told to "lie for commercial gain" over safety test of insulation sold for use on Grenfell,' insidehousing.co.uk, 16 November 2020.

19 'The contracts manager for Rydon during the Grenfell Tower refurbishment described residents who raised complaints about fire safety and cladding as "vocal and aggressive" at the inquiry today,' insidehousing.co.uk, 22 July 2020.

20 'Grenfell Tower inquiry: Fire predicted a decade before, memo shows,' bbc.co.uk/news, 10 March 2021.

21 Robert Booth, '"A raging inferno": testimony reveals how deadly cladding ended up on Grenfell Tower,' *Guardian*, 16 December 2020.

22 'Government guidance "endorsed" use of deadly ACM cladding panels before Grenfell, expert says,' insidehousing.co.uk, 2 November 2020.

23 'Tower Residents told to pay £500,000 to replace Grenfell-style cladding,' *Guardian*, 13 March 2018.

24 'Tower Residents told to pay £500,000 to replace Grenfell-style cladding,' *Guardian*, 13 March 2018.

25 Joe Delaney in 'Grenfell Tower and

Social Murder' (video), Introduction to Criminology.

26 'Nigel Whitbread 1938–2019' in *RIBA Journal*, 31 October 2019.

27 'The Lakanal Fire – 10 Years On,' *Southwark News*, 28 June 2019.

11: Hopes Under the Hammer

1 'Persimmon Homes is building fewer houses after complaints it put "quantity over quality"', walesonline. co.uk, 15 January 2020.

2 'Flooding risk in the UK: Building thousands of homes on flood plains "gambles with lives"', inews.co.uk, 19 February 2020.

3 'Housing estate "turnaround" pledged by David Cameron,' bbc. co.uk/news, 10 January 2016.

4 'Tories refused to build social housing because it would "create Labour voters", Nick Clegg says,' *Independent*, 3 September 2014.

5 Oliver Wainright, *Guardian*, 25 June 2015.

6 Neave Brown in *Project Interrupted: Lectures by British Housing Architects* (Architecture Foundation, 2018), p. 14.

7 Karen Barke in Paul Karakusevic and Abigail Batchelor (eds) *Social Housing: Definitions and Design Examplars* (RIBA Publishing, 2017), p. 24.

8 Peter Barber in *Project Interrupted: Lectures by British Housing Architects*, Architecture Foundation, 2018, p. 72.

9 Barber in *Project Interrupted: Lectures by British Housing Architect*, p. 72.

10 'Spacious and green: inside Norwich's award-winning new council houses,' *Guardian*, 11 October 2019.

11 'Spacious and green: inside Norwich's award-winning new council houses,' *Guardian*, 11 October 2019.

12 'Spacious and green: inside Norwich's award-winning new council houses,' *Guardian*, 11 October 2019.

13 *Architects' Journal*, 8 November 2018, p. 67.

Austerity: Resurrection

1 *Another Chance for Cities: Shelter Neighbourhood Action Project*, Shelter, 1972, p. 9.

2 Oliver Wainwright, 'The Liverpool locals who took control of their long-neglected streets,' *Guardian*, 27 November 2014.

3 Ronnie Hughes, 'Talking Granby 4 Streets,' YouTube, 2012.

4 Ronnie Hughes, 'Talking Granby 4 Streets,' YouTube, 2012.

5 Hazel Tilley in Paul Karakusevic and Abigail Batchelor (eds), *Social Housing: Definitions and Design Exemplars* (RIBA Publishing, 2017), p. 73.

6 'Liverpool £1 house owner explains how he transformed derelict shell into dream family home,' liverpool-echo.co.uk, 24 December 2014.

7 'Assemble Wins 2015 Turner Prize,' *Architects' Journal*, 8 December 2015.

12: The Rise and Fall of Hip Suburbia

1 www.nationaltrust.org.uk/features/edge-city-croydon

2 Rory Olcayto, 'Croydon and the Future of British Town Planning,' *Architects' Journal*, 3 December 2009, p. 26.

3 Olcayto, p. 29.

4 Olcayto, p. 30.

5 Finn Williams in Paul Karakusevic and Abigail Batchelor (eds) *Social Housing: Definitions and Design Examplars*, RIBA Publishing, 2017, p. 13.

6 *Architects' Journal*, 3 December 2009, p. 31.

7 *Architects' Journal*, 15 November 2007, p. 8.

8 *Architects' Journal*, 9 February 2017, p. 18.

9 'John Lewis Grand Central closure – store reveal why they are shutting in new statement,' birminghammail. co.uk, 14 August 2020.

10 'Brick by Brick forced to suspend sales of dozens of new homes,' insidecroydon.com, 11 January 2020.

11 *London Borough of Croydon: Independent strategic review of Brick by Brick Croydon Ltd, Growth Zone, Croydon Affordable Homes LLP, the Revolving Investment Fund and the Asset Investment Fund*, Price Waterhouse Coopers, 13 November 2020, p. 8.

Austerity: Legacy

1 www.architectsdeclare.com

2 Tallon, p. 161.

Index

Index

Index

Index